KT-448-734

Theory and Practice
of Education
An Introduction

Theory and Practice of Education
An Introduction
Second Edition

Meriel Downey and A. V. Kelly

Harper & Row, Publishers

London New York Hagerstown San Francisco

Copyright © 1979 M. E. Downey and A. V. Kelly
All rights reserved

First published 1979
Harper & Row Ltd
28 Tavistock Street
London WC2E 7PN

No part of this book may be used or reproduced in any
manner whatsoever without written permission except
in the case of brief quotations embodied in critical
articles and reviews.

British Library Cataloguing in Publication Data
Downey, Meriel Elaine
    Theory and practice of education. – 2nd ed.
    1. Education
    I. Title   II. Kelly, Albert Victor
    370.1   LB1025.2

ISBN 0-06-318113-4 cased
ISBN 0-06-318114-2 Pbk

Typeset by Input Typesetting Ltd
Printed and bound by A. Wheaton & Co. Ltd., Exeter

Contents

Foreword

The publication in 1975 of the first edition of this book was prompted by the conviction that an integrated and practically relevant approach to the study of educational questions was needed and the belief that little of the current literature in the field of education theory was able to meet that need. The response to that book from practitioners of education, both serving teachers and students in training, has been such as to suggest both that we had been right to identify this need and that we had perhaps begun the process of meeting it. It is this that has encouraged and emboldened us to attempt a second, revised and extended, edition.

Among the revisions that we have made are several that have been suggested by our own criticisms of the earlier edition and those of many interested colleagues and students. For the most part, however, they reflect the continuously developing nature of educational theory and practice. For, even in the relatively short period of four years, major changes have taken place that render adjustments both of emphasis and of content necessary. Developments in curriculum theory in particular, such as the advances that have been made in the study of curriculum evaluation and the impact of recent demands, both popular and political, for greater public control of the curriculum and the increased accountability of teachers, have made it essential to revise quite considerably the chapter on 'The Curriculum'.

The additional chapters are the result of this same kind of development. New issues are constantly coming to the fore in both the theory and the practice of education, and several of these seem to us to have reached such a degree of importance as to warrant additional chapters devoted to a discussion of them. Moral education has always been a central concern of educators, but its importance in direct practical terms to the individual teacher has grown very rapidly in recent years and we felt that scant justice had been done to this topic by the small section we allocated to it in the first edition. Recent studies of classroom interaction, too, have highlighted the importance of an understanding of this aspect of his work to the teacher, so much so that we have decided to open the new edition with a discussion of this. And finally, the rapidly developing notion of the 'open school' seems now a more appropriate note on which to end the book and attempt to draw its many strands together. This is a notion which more than any other seems to symbolize and illustrate the direction in which educational theory and practice is moving. Not only does it involve the idea of equality with which we concluded the first edition, it also brings in the equally important consideration of human and individual freedom. And it seems to us that the reconciliation of these two, sometimes conflicting, ideals is crucial for the continuing evolution not only of educational theory and practice but also, perhaps, of the theory and practice of all forms of social living.

We hope that those who received the first edition of this book so generously, and thus supported us in what we were trying to do through it, will accept our reasoning and the additions and revisions consequent on it and welcome this second edition with equal generosity.

Meriel Downey
Vic Kelly

January 1979

Introduction

Although the picture is a good deal more cheering than it was, the theoretical basis of the practice of education is still far from satisfactory. The gulf between theory and practice continues to yawn so that discussions of educational issues can still be divided into those that are academic to the point of almost total irrelevance and those that, in their determination to be practical, lose sight of the need for a proper rigour and the right kind of academic basis. The academicism of the former has been rejected by many practising teachers so that, since there can be no practice in any sphere without principles of some kind, they have come to rely on little that is more substantial than folk-lore, intuition or even passing whims and fancies. On the other hand, the absence of any kind of intellectual base for the other kind of debate has prevented the emergence of a satisfactory form of educational theory and has led to an undue reliance on other more clearly established bodies of knowledge – in particular those of philosophy, psychology and sociology.

Decisions of educational policy, therefore, some of them of a far-reaching kind, have been made either under the urgings of some ideological view promulgated by whatever political faction happens to be in power, as has been the case with the comprehensivization of secondary education, or on the basis of evidence culled from some other field of knowledge which can have only a partial contribution to make to any educational issue, as was the case with the establishment of selective forms of secondary education. At the same time, the decisions made by the individual teacher in relation to the education of his own pupils are still too often made on the basis of a less than adequate appreciation of their significance and implications or of alternative approaches that might be more productive.

The fundamental problem is that no one has ever been quite clear what education theory is and, until recently, no one has been sufficiently convinced of its importance to endeavour to find out.

The term 'theory' seems to have at least three different meanings. In the first place, it is most commonly used to refer to an explanation of a group of related scientific phenomena, as when we speak of the theory of radiation. In this kind of context, it denotes a set of interconnected hypotheses that have been framed in order to describe and explain a particular series of natural phenomena. The word 'theory' is also used, however, to refer to a body of doctrines, a collection not of descriptions but of prescriptions, intended not to explain but to guide action. It is in this sense that the word is used when we speak of such things as Marxist theory, where the concern is to offer a coherent body of opinion, a 'philosophy'. Finally, we find the term used in an intermediate sense, in which it does no more than pick out a related body of problems, as when we speak of the theory of knowledge. Here we are neither referring to an explanatory system nor to any particular set of views; we are merely indicating the relatedness of certain kinds of problem.

Much of the difficulty that has surrounded education theory arises from the fact that no one has been clear into which of these categories to put it, or, indeed, whether it fits into any of them. Some have seen it as being a kind of scientific theory, an attempt to frame hypotheses to explain certain phenomena. They have been attracted, therefore, as we have seen, to the scientific theories of psychology or sociology and the result of this has been that their view of educational problems has been one-sided and inadequate and their practice consequently misguided. A scientific theory is concerned, as we saw, to describe and explain; it may even be used as a basis for prediction, although in the case of the human sciences this is fraught with particular difficulties; but alone it can never provide guides for action; practical decisions must be made also in the light of other considerations. Any view of education, therefore, that excludes such considerations because it is taken from the standpoint of any of these disciplines will be a warped and dangerous view, as the history of the development of the educational system in Britain can reveal.

Others have, therefore, taken the view that education theory involves the generation of bodies of doctrine, collections of more or less coherent prescriptions as to what teachers and schools ought to be doing. This approach has led to the production of a great deal of what has rightly been castigated as 'mush' or 'beautiful thoughts' and has done more than anything else to bring educational theory into disrepute. As a result, it has in recent years been rejected entirely in favour of a more rigorous and differentiated study of the 'foundation' or 'contributory' disciplines of education, in particular philosophy, psychology, and sociology. Unfortunately, this seems to have been an over-reaction, a rejection of the baby with the bath water. For the merit that the prescriptive approach did have was that it injected into discussions of education a sense of purpose, an awareness that education is a practical activity, essentially concerned with issues of value, and some ideas about what teachers and schools ought to be doing, of a kind that can never come from the sciences of psychology or sociology or from the analytical processes of the philosopher. This element is vital if education theory is to have full relevance for educational practice.

In fact, it seems that education theory has elements in it of all the three kinds of theory that we delineated. It denotes a range of problems, those practical problems that teachers and others concerned with the practice of education need to give thought to and to make decisions about; it needs to offer some set or sets of views that may help us to decide on the directions in which these decisions are to take us; and it must also contain a proper and rigorous scientific basis to ensure that these decisions are theoretically sound and consistent with whatever evidence is available.

If this is what education theory is or ought to be, two things seem to be required to ensure that it offers the teacher the support he needs. In the first place, it must start and end with the problems that the practice of education throws up; it must be firmly rooted in the school and the classroom and must have a direct practical relevance to all aspects of the teacher's work. Without this, it is the study of something else and not of education, which is after all a practical activity. Secondly, if it is to deal adequately with issues of this kind, its approach must not lean too heavily on other disciplines or bodies of theory devised for other purposes. We have already commented on the disastrous consequences of basing educational decisions only on psychological or sociological considerations. We must add our conviction that it is not enough that the study of education should draw on all relevant disciplines separately. A much more concerted approach than that is needed. It is not what each individual discipline or subject has to contribute to any particular issue that is interesting, important, and useful; it is the combined effect of them that is needed, along with something more, a full account of and allowance for the aims and purposes of our activities.

Lastly, both of these objectives must be achieved without loss of rigour. We must not return to the days of 'mush' or 'beautiful thoughts' unless it be to sort out the mush and find a sound basis for the beautiful thoughts. We should now be entering a further stage in the development of educational theory when it can stand in its own right as a rigorous body of theoretical knowledge that all teachers can respect and profit from in the practice of their profession.

It is towards that end that this book has been written. We hope that it will link theory to practice and bring a coherence to the theory itself in a way that will not only help students of education to pass their examinations but will also improve their professionalism as teachers. We hope too that it will prove of value to practising teachers and will lead to a better understanding of some of the highly complex professional tasks they must undertake.

We have tried to focus, therefore, on those aspects of education theory that are directly relevant to the practice of the teacher in the classroom. All areas of education theory should have such relevance for the work of the schools but, since some selection had to be made, we felt it appropriate here to concentrate on those areas which are of immediate import for the individual teacher.

We have begun with an examination of that interchange that occurs in every classroom between the teacher and the pupils and among the pupils themselves, since the teacher's understanding of the educational process must begin with an appreciation of that interaction that is its base. We have then considered, as a particularly important aspect of this interaction, how the judgements that teachers make of their pupils and the attitudes they have towards them can determine the progress those pupils will make in their education. We go on to discuss in more detail some of the most significant of these judgements and attitudes – the views the teacher holds about the nature of intelligence and the kinds of ability he values, his approach to the problem of motivating his pupils, the multiple impact of language differences, the methods of control that he favours, and his attitudes to questions of freedom and authority and relationships generally, examining in particular the implications of these for the moral and social education of children. We have then looked at some of the questions that need to be asked about the curriculum, since the current trend towards an increased individualization of educational provision places responsibility for many decisions in this area on the individual teacher. Many of such decisions were hitherto taken for teachers by those who drew up syllabuses of various kinds and this has recently, as a consequence, become the focus of much public and political debate. A discussion of the notion of equality of educational opportunity follows and an appraisal of some of the practical measures that have been introduced in an attempt to attain in our educational provision the ideals that that notion encapsulates. Finally, we have taken a critical look at the concept of the 'open school' since, as we said in our Foreword, this seems to us to be an ideal that not only brings together all of the other issues we have explored, but also one that, in attempting to reconcile the sometimes conflicting ideals of human equality and human freedom, offers a focus for the continuing evolution not only of the theory and practice of education but perhaps also of all aspects of social living.

If we have failed to attain our objectives, we hope that this will be attributed to our own inadequacies rather than to any fundamental weakness in the view of education theory from which we start, since it remains our conviction that unless something is done to establish the study of education along the lines we have indicated, both the theory and the practice of education will continue to be held back from their proper development.

1 Classroom Interaction

Education, as most teachers, parents, and pupils will agree, is essentially a social process. When children come to school, they do not simply learn a given body of knowledge which they carry away in neat packages as though they had been shopping. Rather they learn from other people, both teachers and peers, by sharing their knowledge and experience, by seeing the world through their eyes and by developing an understanding of what others consider important and worthwhile. Their learning is not only cognitive but also social, emotional and moral. In other words, children are not only developing their intellectual abilities by mastering concepts and retaining facts relating to various curriculum areas, but are at the same time learning to communicate with others, to form judgements of them and eventually to develop autonomy both intellectually and morally. Almost all learning situations provided in school are then essentially social in nature, apart from the occasions when pupils, usually older ones, withdraw on their own to the library for private study to consolidate what they have learned in the company of others. The ways in which teachers and pupils interact and the factors which influence this interaction will be of prime importance if we are to try to understand the social context of education.

This chapter sets out first of all to describe the origins and the development of techniques of interaction studies. We shall then go on to analyse some of the factors affecting teacher-pupil interaction and to consider the effect of teaching style on pupil behaviour. Studies of pupil interaction, the use of language by pupils and teachers, and the implications of curriculum development for classroom interaction will be discussed. Many of these issues will be developed in greater detail in later chapters in the book.

Methods of studying classroom interaction

Interaction studies have their roots in social psychology and were first developed by American researchers. Lewin, Lippitt, and White (1939) first drew attention to the importance of group dynamics and leadership patterns for the way in which children work together and behave, depending on whether the group leader adopted an authoritarian, democratic, or laissez-faire style. Their studies however were essentially laboratory-type observations, where adult leaders were trained to exercise particular leadership styles with groups of children working in an extra-curricular setting. Anderson and Brewer (1945) used a similar typology, which they attempted to relate to styles adopted by teachers they observed working in school with young children. Observation showed that with a democratic or socially integrative teacher, children were relaxed and friendly, worked well together, and showed an interest in what they were doing. Children working with an authoritarian or dominative teacher were likely to be over-submissive, yet aggressive and uncooperative when left on their own. Studies of this nature abounded in American research during the 1950s and early 1960s, while at the same time, in this country and in the U.S.A., psychologists were developing sociometric techniques, based on the work of Moreno (1934), in order to map patterns of interaction between pupils. The procedure is in fact so straightforward that it has been used by many class teachers to help them group children at the beginning of the year in a way that the pupils themselves find acceptable. All that is needed is for the teacher to ask his pupils relatively simple questions, for example, to say whom they would like to sit next to, work with on a group basis, or choose as a partner for P.E. From this information, friendship patterns within the class emerge; isolates who are not chosen by anybody are identified; highly popular children and closely knit cliques are recognized.

However, interaction studies of a more systematic kind were not developed until Flanders (1970) introduced his Interaction Analysis Categories (FI.C), designed primarily for examining teacher-pupil interaction by coding and classifying classroom talk. Since then interaction analysis of this kind has become very widespread, not only in the

U.S.A. and Britain but also in Australia and New Zealand. Flanders devised a series of ten categories into which public classroom talk could be classified: seven categories for teachers, two for pupils, and one residual. An independent observer listening to classroom talk then records and codes what is being said over a given period of time, say, forty minutes. Eventually the score for any one teacher can be worked out arithmetically and compared with scores gained by other teachers, as a measure of what proportion of their teaching time is spent talking. Such studies soon revealed that what is now known as the law of two-thirds operates in most classrooms where class teaching is the principal method used. Two-thirds of classroom time in typical American schools is usually spent talking, and two-thirds of this talk is done by teachers. Wragg (1973), using a similar technique, found that the same held good for British classrooms. And although it might be expected that the proportion of talk would be reduced in less formal, more open classrooms, where pupils are encouraged to talk more among themselves, Walker and Adelman (1975) found that teacher talk still dominates to a similar degree, although it is of a less public nature.

The sort of systematic observation schedule, introduced and developed by Flanders, has clear advantages over earlier methods of studying teacher style. Firstly, it was planned specifically for classroom analysis, unlike the earlier studies which were based upon techniques drawn from social psychology and developed within a laboratory setting. Secondly, it pioneered the way for studies of different teaching styles such as those carried out by Ashton (1975) and Bennett (1976) and also gave impetus to studies of language in the classroom, of which there were very few before the 1970s. Nevertheless, although this kind of analysis can provide systematic data on certain aspects of classroom interaction, for instance by showing the overall differences between ways of teaching, it has its limitations. It does not show enough detail about teacher-pupil interaction to explain why teachers differ from one another or why their behaviour varies according to the particular group of children they are teaching.

To try to answer such questions, research techniques have been developed which do not rely on prespecified schedules, but which allow categories and concepts to emerge over a period of time during the research. Techniques of participant observation, hitherto not used in the classroom, have during the past decade become recognized as far more productive and accurate, while at the same time imposing fewer restrictions on the observer. More flexible teaching methods and open classrooms have made such a development possible in that both teacher and pupils feel less inhibited by a researcher, when they are already used to working informally and very often welcome visiting speakers to contribute to their work. And many researchers, like Lacey (1970), who taught in the school in which he gathered the material for his study of Hightown Grammar, have some teaching built into their research programme. After a two-month period of finding his way around, getting to know the teachers and the structure of the school, Lacey spent a further sixteen months in the school, during which he taught twelve periods per week and observed for a further twelve. Similarly, Hargreaves (1967) spent a whole year at Lumley secondary school, teaching all the fourth-year boys, on whom the study was focussed, at some stage, as well as observing the same boys being taught by other teachers. Both took part extensively in extra-curricular activities. Woods (1976) spent a year in a mixed rural secondary school, as participant observer, in order to collect data for his study of survival strategies used by teachers. Such methods avoid the use of prepared observation schedules since these fail to allow for the unexpected. On the contrary, observers are free to record any unit of teacher or pupil behaviour that they find relevant to their investigation, but unless the observer is intimately acquainted with the particular teachers and pupils he is studying, much of the significance of their behaviour is likely to be misunderstood or to prove completely baffling. Walker and Adelman (1976) show how classroom talk (or indeed conversation of any kind) is full of hidden meanings, and jokes are shared only by those among whom they have arisen. A stranger walking into a classroom and hearing the following snippet of conversation would surely wonder what was going on:

Teacher: Wilson, we'll have to put you away if you don't change your
         ways and do your homework. Is that all you've done?
Wilson: Strawberries, strawberries. (Laughter from class)

Apparently the teacher had once commented that some boys' work was like strawberries, 'good as far as it goes, but it doesn't last nearly long enough'. This remark had in time become part of the culture of that particular classroom. Such personal meanings are not readily accessible to those outside the immediate experience of the group. To understand the richness of such associations, the researcher has himself to become, at least for a time, a member of that group. No amount of analysis in the Flanders style would uncover such hidden meanings.

Most researchers concerned with classroom interaction studies insist now on the importance of long-term participant observation studies. Furlong (1976), in a case study of how pupils judge their teachers, acted as participant observer in a class of fifteen-year-olds for two terms in a school where he had taught for three years. It was this context that prompted him to develop the concept of an 'interaction set', a more flexible tool than 'friendship group' that can be used to explain how and when pupils interact to control classroom activity. Short-term observations would not have allowed time for the nature of this particular kind of group perspective to become apparent.

Walker and Adelman (1976), as we have already seen, use long-term observation and have developed valuable techniques of recording data, using both film and audio recordings as well as taking extensive notes as they watch whatever is going on in classrooms. In 1973 they initiated the Ford Teaching Project, designed to monitor the practices of forty teachers in fourteen East Anglian schools who were attempting to use enquiry/ discovery methods. Similar techniques are being employed in their SAFARI project, which sets out to examine the effects of four major curriculum innovations: Nuffield Secondary Science; the Humanities Curriculum Project; Geography for the Young School Leaver; and Project Technology. Because Walker and Adelman are interested not only in teacher-pupil interaction, but also in teachers' interaction with heads of departments, heads, advisers, and so on, they are extending their methods to include case histories and life histories of individual teachers. Classroom interaction, they claim, is affected not only by what goes on inside the four walls, but also by outside influences impinging upon the teachers' interpretation of what is significant and upon his relationships with others who less often enter his teaching arena.

Methods of studying classroom interaction have thus developed with changes in teachers' and educators' interpretations of what is significant in a teaching/learning context. The concept of education embraced by most teachers today sees teaching and learning as a two-way or multi-channel communication process rather than a predominantly one-way input/output model.

Teacher-pupil interaction

Interaction between teachers and pupils depends not only on a deliberate policy adopted by the teacher to encourage pupils to communicate with them and with their peers, but also upon factors implicit in the situation which impinge upon social behaviour. Some of the most important forces influencing the nature of interaction are the physical setting; rules, rituals and routine of the classroom; interpersonal judgements and mode of communication, both verbal and nonverbal. We shall therefore consider here ways in which some of these factors can affect classroom interaction, leaving a discussion of language until later, since it is important enough to warrant a separate section.

Until fairly recently, studies of interaction had curiously ignored the nature of the physical setting in which interaction takes place. However, if we examine the spatial context more closely, we shall appreciate how the use of space within the school and the classroom affects social behaviour. The location of the school itself can have a significant impact on the formation of friendship groups and cliques. The vexed problem of split-site buildings affects not only the way in which pupils interact as they have to make a rushed change from one building to another, but also the way in which teachers have contact with one another. It is not unusual for some teachers to be quite unacquainted with colleagues working mainly in another building. One administrative solution to the problem of time-wasting movement brought about by constant switches from one building to another has been to allocate teachers and pupils mainly to one site. But this often results in an unhappy rift between younger and older pupils, not to mention apparent stratification of teachers into upper and lower school staff. However, individual teachers seldom have any control over such major physical considerations; it is the physical layout of their own class-room that they can plan themselves up to a point.

Traditional classrooms provided for chalk and talk teaching methods, with a class of children sitting in straight rows facing the teacher and a blackboard. The teacher's authority was symbolized by his or her position behind a desk, often raised onto a dais. In this way the teacher was not only physically separated from his pupils, often indeed regarding his desk as a protective barrier, but was psychologically remote from them. Such a physical context was highly appropriate for didactic teaching methods where the teacher talked most of the time, on average two-thirds of it, as Flanders showed. Adams and Biddle (1970), using videotape recordings from a large number of classrooms, showed that teachers interact most of all in this kind of setting with pupils sitting in a V-shaped wedge down the middle of the room, paying less attention to those at the sides and at the back. Pupils are clearly aware of this, as most teachers know who have witnessed the rush for places in the back row by those who wish to escape notice. Most infant and junior schools have long since dispensed with the formally arranged classroom in favour of one where furniture is easily moved about and can be arranged to meet the needs of particular activities, which in turn encourage different kinds of interaction among children. Experiments with open-plan classrooms and school buildings allow added flexibility, though it has been noted that most children feel more secure when they have a home base and a specific place in which to keep their belongings. Human beings, incidentally, seem to have a similar sense of territory to animals. This is apparent when we observe how many students sit in the same place in seminar week after week or how teachers occupy the same chair in the staff-room year after year. Secondary schools have been rather tardy in breaking away from formally arranged seating, but many curriculum innovations in operation nowadays require a far greater degree of flexibility and hence a greater proportion of pupil interaction than class teaching. The Humanities Curriculum Project, designed to develop in pupils of fourteen to sixteen the ability to think critically about controversial issues, uses discussion as its main learning technique. Clearly pupils cannot discuss seriously unless the physical setting allows them to watch other members of the group as they are talking. Seating arrangements must allow for this and not inhibit the give-and-take of argument between pupils by a setting where remarks can only be addressed to the teacher. Indeed, the teacher, as neutral chairman, cannot be in a position which suggests to group members that he knows the answer to problems under discussion. Similarly Wilson (1973), in his work on moral education, stresses the importance of making the social context of learning fit the content and methods being advocated. For example, open discussion groups need the sort of seating layout where multi-channel communication can go on and face-to-face interaction is facilitated.

However, we know from the work of Argyle (1969) the importance of the function of nonverbal communication in interaction. Gestures, facial expression, bodily posture, eye-contact all play an important part in conveying meanings implicitly to others. A teacher who sits behind a table or a desk so that children who want to speak to him have to form a queue, is implying by his very position a different sort of interaction with his class from one who walks around and sits down with an individual or a group to discuss their work. Tone of voice too can suggest enthusiasm and general interest or, on the other hand, impatience and exasperation, without any change in the actual words used.

To some extent we all, teachers or not, use nonverbal means of projecting a particular self-image to others, or, as Goffman (1959) puts it, we present a personal front to others. Teachers, sometimes deliberately, but occasionally without being aware of it, play upon external features to convey to their pupils the sort of personality they would like pupils to think they have. Dress, hairstyle, mode of speech, and posture can all help to project a particular self-image which can encourage or inhibit interaction with pupils. Delamont (1976) showed how pupils' judgements about their teachers can be affected by the personal front they project. Of two teachers she observed in the same school, one dressed severely in tweed suits, seldom sat down in class unless she was marking books, and hardly ever indulged in casual conversation with her pupils. The other teacher dressed fashionably in styles the girls themselves might have chosen, carried her books in a shopping basket rather than a brief case, sat in a relaxed fashion on pupils' desks, and chatted informally with them. Most pupils felt more at ease with the second teacher but all agreed that the other was very efficient and made them work hard and behave properly. It is interesting however that pupils do not always appreciate teachers who try to adopt a casual image. Many of them prefer to maintain a minimum of social distance and regard it as an encroachment on their privacy if teachers dress or speak in their style.

Interpersonal judgement, as we shall see in the next chapter, is one form of social interaction and as such is an integral part of classroom dynamics. The process of forming judgements of others is essentially interactive rather than reactive in nature. When we perceive others and judge their behaviour, the judgement we make in turn affects the way they behave towards us. Thus, as we know from the ample evidence drawn from research on self-fulfilling prophecies, unfavourable judgements made by teachers of pupils are coupled with low expectations of attainment. In response to this, pupils often do achieve little, partly because their motivation is depressed and partly because the teacher offers little to stretch their abilities (Downey, 1977).

Judgements made of an individual by others of significance to him play an important part in the development of the self. G. H. Mead (1934) sees the self as a social product arising from the experience of a child interacting with significant others, as he terms them, namely parents, peers, teachers, and so on. The self, in his view, develops as a result of the interpretations a child makes of how others perceive, judge, and evaluate him. Thus the self or self-concept is influenced initially by the child's parents, but since its development is continuous, it is affected too by his teachers and peers when he comes to school. Teachers can either reinforce the view a child has of himself, be it a positive or negative one, or help to reverse a child's negative self-concept or boost his self-esteem by creating in him a more positive view of himself and his abilities.

Concern about the negative effects of teacher expectations upon pupil performance, motivation, behaviour in class has been widespread over the past decade, particularly since the publication of the rather dubious findings of Rosenthal and Jacobson (1968). However, later evidence has substantiated the claims they made (Downey, 1977) and most teachers are at least aware of the influence they can have over their pupils in this respect. But as we mentioned earlier, since interpersonal judgement is a two-way and therefore essentially an interaction process, we should expect to find that pupils' judgements of their teachers affect them in some degree. So far there is little systematic evidence to show the nature of this influence clearly, but what little there is suggests that most pupils have similar expectations of their teachers. In Taylor's study (1962), pupils were required to indicate their notion of a good teacher by rating him on control, personal qualities, and teaching skills. Nash (1974) used Kelly's personal construct theory to investigate pupils' attitudes towards their teachers, in order to discover primary school children's concept of an ideal teacher. More recently Furlong (1976), using participant observation techniques and talking casually to a class of fifteen-year-olds, investigated their expectations of a good teacher. All these studies, despite their vary-ing methodology and the different age groups under scrutiny, suggested that most pupils have a similar, fairly stereotyped concept of the ideal teacher. He is one who can keep a class in order, make them work hard, explains clearly, provides a clear structure for them, and who is fair in dealing with them. It seems strange at a time when students and pupils are demanding more responsibility that the concept of an ideal teacher that emerges from these studies is of one who allows little freedom of choice. Pupils seem to want guidance and to be made to behave well and to work hard. It is when a teacher does not live up to these expectations that pupils tend to misbehave, as Furlong's study showed. But some degree of negotiation inevitably goes on in a classroom. Although pupils like teachers to be strict, there has to be mutual agreement about what counts as being strict as Werthman (1963) showed in the study of delin-quent adolescents in school. Through this process of negotiation, to which we shall return later on, acceptable norms of behaviour are worked out between the teacher and his class, though clearly, since they are arrived at by mutual consent, the norms will vary according to the particular class and the particular teacher.

Interaction in most classrooms is supported by some kind of routine or ritual which provides a structure or framework for the pupils and gives support to teachers. In fact, Woods (1976) regards ritual and routine as part of a teacher's survival kit. However, the regularity of routine imposes a structure on school life which both pupils and teachers come to accept. Among the most common routines are of course school assemblies, registration, handing in homework, and queuing up for lunch. Teachers who regularly begin their lessons with some sort of formal greeting can usually be sure of a response even though behaviour may deteriorate later. School rules too provide a structure for teachers and pupils and, provided they are rationally based, most pupils will accept them without undue infringement. Rules within any one classroom are negotiable but, once they have been agreed upon, become an essential part of classroom interaction, so that children who see others breaking them are often duly indignant. Rules of this kind must hold for teachers and pupils alike. For instance, if children are not permitted to wear outdoor coats in class, they can see no good reason why teachers should have the privilege of doing so. Rules and classroom ritual are essentially unwritten. They are apparent only to those who participate and as such are a part of classroom interaction accessible only to an observer who spends a long period of time as a participant.

Teaching styles and pupil behaviour

Our discussion of aspects of classroom interaction, such as the physical layout adopted by the teacher, his personal image, interpersonal judgements made by teachers and pupils of one another, suggests that there is a wide discretionary area where teachers are free to adopt their own style, regardless of the type of school in which they teach or the age group of children with whom they are concerned. As we have already seen, early studies of variation in teaching styles were rooted in leadership studies carried out by social psychologists. However, since the mid 1960s those concerned with the theory of education, as well as practising teachers, have tended to use pairs of terms to distinguish pedogogical styles such as 'progressive/traditional', 'child-centred/teacher-centred', 'formal/informal', 'discovery-learning/instruction'. Teachers consider themselves progressive if they work in an unstreamed situation, use discovery methods rather than instruction, encourage collaborative or individualized learning rather than relying mainly on class teaching. Interest and even controversy have centred around the relative advantages and disadvantages of different teaching styles for pupils' progress and behaviour in class. Teachers employing informal methods have claimed that their pupils are more cooperative, more interested in their work, are better behaved, and even make greater progress. Some early research comparing streamed with unstreamed classes at the primary level indicated an improvement in the social adjustment of pupils even though there was no significant difference in scholastic performance (Kelly, 1978).

Flanders (1970) was one of the first to attempt a systematic analysis of factors which affect classroom interaction by examining the degree and nature of verbal exchange in American classrooms. Flanders initiated an eight-year research programme involving the development of interaction analysis as a tool for quantifying patterns of teacher influence upon pupils. One-hundred and forty-seven teachers representing all age levels took part in the study. Overall findings, as we saw earlier, produced the rule of two-thirds: about two-thirds of the time spent in the average classroom is taken up by somebody talking. Although these are findings for the average classroom studied, Flanders' hypothesis that the more indirect the teacher's influence the more favourable were pupils' attitudes towards school, was supported by a comparison of differences in interaction scores. Teachers who spoke for only about 50% of the time and who were less directive when they were speaking produced in their pupils more constructive attitudes towards classroom activities, hence their interaction was of a more positive nature. In this country Wragg's study (1973) of classroom talk suggests that positive interaction, indicated by the proportion of pupil talk, tends to diminish as children progress throughout secondary school. The amount of pupil talk in the classes he studied fell from 32% in the first year to 23% in the fifth year. Unexpectedly, pupils also talked less in the sixth form than in their earlier school careers. A greater degree of pupil participation might have been expected since most sixth-form pupils are taught in smaller groups.

Notions of freedom and control are central to problems of teaching style, and findings suggest that a teacher's personal style is revealed by the proportion of time he spends talking and the nature of the language he uses. Before we look more closely at teachers' use of language in the classroom, let us explore a little more some of the studies of teaching style.

Ashton and others (1975) in a national survey of 1513 primary school-teachers found that, although they readily saw themselves as either progressive or traditional, there was a great deal of consensus between them over basic issues. They all gave high priority to the basic skills of literacy, numeracy and oracy, and agreed that children should be brought up as acceptable members of their community and to conform to its conventions. It seems then as though their overall aims were the same although they claimed to exercise different methods of achieving these aims.

Drawing on a sample of 871 primary schools in Lancashire and Cumbria, Bennett (1976) analysed different teaching styles and attempted to assess the effects of these on pupils' progress. The two major questions he set out to explore were, firstly, whether different teaching styles resulted in disparate pupil progress and secondly, whether different types of pupil performed'better under certain styles of teaching. From responses given to questionnaires by all third- and fourth-year teachers in the schools studied, twelve teacher styles or types were distinguished by a process of cluster analysis. These ranged from the very informal to the highly formal with, of course, mixed styles in between. Two further measures were taken to confirm the validity of this categorization. Firstly, research staff spent two days with a selected sample of teachers, observing and recording their techniques, without prior knowledge of the categories into which they had been placed. Secondly, local authority advisers who were well acquainted with their teachers were asked to make their own independent judgements of them in terms of the research clusters. Of particular interest to a study of classroom interaction are teachers' attitudes to the methods used by others and their reasons for using the ones they do. Informal teachers were those who favoured integration of subject content and allowed pupils choice and responsibility for pursuing their own tasks. They allowed children to sit where they wanted, to move about the classroom, and to talk to one another while they were working. Formal teachers preferred to teach subjects separately and chose class teaching as their main approach. They did not allow pupils to choose their own seats, nor were talking or walking about the classroom permitted. These examples are of course extreme types; mixed styles, as a closer analysis of Bennett's findings reveals, vary in the extent to which they approach a high degree of formality or informality. Although the overall findings suggest that pupil progress in the basic skills is promoted more by formal and mixed styles of teaching than by very informal ones, informal teachers were on the whole antipathetic to formal methods. They claimed that formal teaching styles failed to encourage responsibility and self-discipline, that they do not allow pupils to think for themselves or develop to their full potential. Moreover, such methods, in their view, do not make sufficient demands on teachers. These views seem to suggest that the sort of classroom interaction they favour is one where children can enjoy what they are doing, feel socially at ease, and can exercise their imagination and initiative. However, informal and unstructured classroom environments where direct teacher control is less evident do not appear to suit all children. Anxious and nervous children seem to be unable to cope with the responsibility of self-directed activity and waste a good deal of time in aimless wandering about, gossiping, fidgeting, and gazing out of the window, and they furthermore spend less time interacting with their peers, unless in a contentious manner.

Bennett's findings provide little evidence of a general movement towards informality in the primary school, at any rate at the upper age level. Only about 17% of the teachers in the overall sample were in fact teaching in the informal manner described by Plowden, while the majority used mixed styles. The more recent government survey (1978) of 542 primary schools visited by HMIs between 1975 and 1977 shows a trend towards greater formality with about 75% of teachers in the sample using mainly didactic methods, compared with only 5% teaching by discovery techniques.

Bound up with issues of teaching style and classroom interaction are also a teacher's view of education, his aims and objectives, and his concept of an ideal pupil. In fact all these factors are interdependent and must be considered as mutually influential. As early as 1952, Becker introduced the concept of an ideal pupil, showing how teachers classify children according to their notion of what constitutes such a model. Becker's data, drawn from interviews with 60 teachers in Chicago schools, showed that, for most of them, the ideal pupil was one who was cooperative and obedient, enabling them to do their jobs effectively with the minimum of conflict or stress. Such pupils behave well in class, do their homework assiduously, and arrive punctually. However this ideal exists only with teachers whose aims are primarily cognitive and who employ mainly didactic methods. Pupils who try to be independent, to initiate and direct their own learning, and who attempt to collaborate with their peers are likely to fall short of the ideal held by a traditional teacher. They disrupt the smooth running of the class by wanting to assume independence and by asking awkward questions for which the teacher's well-planned lesson content is not prepared.

Self-styled progressive teachers, as we have seen, have different overall objectives and hence are likely to hold a different ideal pupil concept. They emphasize the importance of social and emotional development and stress the value of self-expression, creativity, and the enjoyment of school. Docile pupils who sit waiting to be told what to do will hardly meet their ideal. Similarly, teachers in community schools, where the curriculum is geared largely towards social education, will have yet a different concept of an ideal pupil. Pupils in schools involved in the Midwinter Community Project (1972), for example, were taught to develop social skills and competence in the hope that later they would be able to take action against the kind of deprivation that they and members of their community had to endure. Interaction in classrooms where such aims are fostered is clearly of a different order from that usually encountered in schools whose aims are purely intellectual.

So far we have discussed the effects of teaching style upon pupil behaviour, but since we are concerned with interaction processes, it would seem surely that there must be some indication of the effect of pupil styles upon teacher behaviour. Klein (1971) showed experimentally that student behaviour can affect teaching style, by training a student audience to alter its behaviour towards a lecturer, according to a prearranged plan. When students were highly attentive, the lecturer was lively and relaxed, but when they became bored and restless, the lecturer showed signs of impatience and exasperation. This experience is one not unfamiliar to practising teachers who will naturally feel that they do not need experimental evidence to point out the obvious. However, the study does indicate the possible strength of group power among pupils and its effects upon teachers. Lacey (1970) and Hargreaves (1967) both showed the force of friendship groups among secondary school pupils in establishing and maintaining classroom norms. A troublesome pupil in an A stream is regarded as a deviant not only by teachers but also by pupils. Thus group behaviour of this kind supports the teachers' standards, aims, and teaching style. But when a whole group of pupils adopts what the teacher regards as deviant behaviour, as Hargreaves showed among his lower stream pupils, the teacher is forced to change his tactics and negotiate with them, in order to survive.

Furlong (1976) introduces the notion of an 'interaction set' to show how a set of pupils, whether they normally belong to the same friendship group or not, can band together to act against the teacher and force him to relax his routine or refrain from punitive measures, if they all perceive and interpret the situation in the same way. Members of an interaction set can, for instance, interpret a teacher's behaviour as unfair and, by obstinate refusal to attend to his wishes, press him to act differently. As we saw earlier, Furlong's study of fifteen-year-old girls showed that, provided teachers lived up to *their* ideal concept of an efficient teacher, they caused few behavioural problems. It is only when the teachers deviate, by not being strict or directive enough, that trouble arises. Teachers using the Humanities Curriculum Project and attempting to take on the role of neutral chairman have often encountered difficulty because by the nature of their role they have to remain silent when pupils expect them to take the lead.

Pupil-pupil interaction

It would be impossible to discuss any aspects of classroom interaction without some mention of how pupils interact among themselves; thus our discussion so far has inevitably touched on pupils' classroom behaviour, even though this was not the focal point of the discussion. But let us now look at some specific studies of pupils in class. If teachers accept that group work is an important educational device, as most if not all those concerned with younger children do, as well as a good many of their secondary school colleagues, they need to look carefully at methods of grouping within their classes (Kelly, 1978). The methods and rationale behind them will naturally influence the kind of classroom interaction that ensues.

There seem to be three main approaches in schools: grouping by ability, by friendship, and by interest. Although grouping by ability within the class negates the principle of nonstreaming within the school, there are still those teachers, as Barker-Lunn (1970) and Ferri (1972) showed, who do attempt to create relatively homogeneous groups within an unstreamed class. They claim that children progress better when they work with peers of roughly the same ability and that, at any time, pupils can be moved to another group fairly easily. However, as we are well aware, groups of pupils soon become labelled as bright or dull and the danger is that friendship patterns will be established only within those groups and not between them. In addition, those in the 'top' group will regard themselves as superior to the 'duds'. Lacey (1970) showed that friendship made in the first year when boys were unstreamed tended to be broken in the second year as a result of streaming.

The second approach adopted by many teachers is that of friendship grouping. As we saw earlier, there is a simple sociometric device adapted from Moreno's techniques that enables teachers to discover from their pupils whom they regard as their friends and to allow them to work together. Friendship clearly is an important factor in school, especially in its bearing on children's behaviour. But as most teachers realize, friendship patterns among younger children are not very stable, and a group working together amicably one week will be at odds the next because of some apparently trivial disagreement that looms large in the children's minds. Probably the best known studies of friendship groups among older pupils are those by Hargreaves (1967) and Lacey (1970). Both studies took place in streamed boys' schools and revealed how far academic segregation can lead to polarized subcultures within the school. Cliques of 'goodies' adopting pro-school norms were to be found in A streams, while those adopting anti-school attitudes collected in the lower streams. Antagonism between these cliques soon built up and, even in physical activities, when year groups of boys were not segregated, the barriers between the groups were not broken down.

There are however some children who do not find it easy to make friends and seem isolated in class. These are usually individuals who are extremely shy and withdrawn and very often display some deep-seated anxiety problem. Children with low self-esteem are often those who find it difficult to make friends, as Coopersmith (1967) showed. They do not feel confident that others will accept them, are doubtful about their own opinions and judgements, and are unlikely to take much part in discussion or to engage in activities with others. They prefer to remain listeners or onlookers. On the other hand there are some insecure children who try to buy friendship by some kind of bribery, such as offering sweets or the use of expensive equipment or even acting the fool in class, as Lacey showed in his example of the unfortunate Priestley.

Interaction that is understood only in terms of friendship groups leaves some interesting features unexplained. It assumes that membership of a friendship group is constant and that nonmembers never participate in group activities. It assumes too that, in order to remain a member, an individual must succumb to group pressure and abide by the norms set out by majority consensus. However, there are occasions when an individual feels morally obliged to disagree with his friends and to act independently. This is after all what moral autonomy implies and what we hope all pupils will eventually learn to achieve. On the other hand, there are also occasions when pupils who are otherwise regarded as outsiders decide to go along with a group adopting its behaviour patterns. Long-term observation of what actually happens in classrooms shows that pupil interaction does not necessarily involve all friends of any one group and may include some who are not usually friendly. In other words, who interacts with whom depends very much upon prevailing circumstances. Furlong's notion of an interaction set (1976) is a useful explanatory tool here. Individuals are not forced by group pressures to act with others but can give tacit support, if they so choose, by their mere demeanour, for instance by smiling, nodding approval, and so on. Furlong cites occasions where the same rather troublesome pupil is at one time supported by her friends when she has defied the teacher but later is ignored by them when they choose to work alongside normally hard-working pupils. The interaction set has thus changed according to the way in which pupils interpret the situation and decide to act.

To resume our discussion of methods of grouping practised by teachers, the third main approach is to group pupils by interest. This presupposes that some sort of interest-based or enquiry-based teaching is going on and in this context it clearly makes sense for pupils who share common interests to work together. It follows that working groups of this kind will be flexible. A set of children working together for drama, for example, will not necessarily share the same interests in an environmental studies project. And if we consider one of the important social aims of grouping pupils within a class we should surely hope that they would not always work with the same people but should have the opportunity to cooperate and collaborate with others of different talents, personality, temperament, and background. Social experience is thus broadened and the flexibility ensured by changing groups should help to prevent rigid prejudices being built up within an insulated in-group.

Several recent curriculum projects, designed for use by secondary school pupils, rely on group discussion and group activities – the Humanities Curriculum Project, McPhail's Lifeline Moral Education project, the Schools' Council Social Education project, to mention but a few. And, for these to have real educative value, it is essential that pupils do learn with one another, above all to develop the skills of conversation and discussion so that they address their remarks to one another rather than to the teacher as an authority figure.

Language and classroom interaction

Most people in a society such as ours share certain cultural assumptions about the relationship between teaching, learning, and talking. We not only expect teachers to talk to pupils much of the time but also assume that pupils show what they have learned by answering teachers' questions. Pupils themselves expect teachers to talk and such expectations are difficult to shed. One of the most disconcerting aspects of the changing role of the teacher required by some of the moral education projects, for example, is that the onus is on the pupils to initiate and maintain discussion. A teacher who sits silently waiting for pupils to begin is regarded with great suspicion by them. As we saw earlier, about two-thirds of average classroom time is spent in talk. A closer analysis of teacher talk reveals that about 50% is taken up with lesson content, while 25% is spent in control of some kind. Perhaps this tradition is related to the tendency in our culture for people to talk most of the time when they are together. Silences are often felt as embarrassing and balance is restored by remarks which are frequently trivial, hence the prevalence of small talk when comparative strangers meet on a social occasion. This is comically illustrated by a recent Andy Capp cartoon which showed a neighbour remarking to Florrie Capp, 'Your old man's a strange one isn't he, he only talks when he's got something to say.'

However, typical classroom talk that most participants expect is not the sort that would generally be accepted in most situations outside school. Cross-questioning, interrogation, and correction which would cause consternation, bewilderment, or indignation in everyday life are the general order of life in the classroom. Much school discourse is characterized by its three-fold structure: the teacher asks a question, the pupil replies, then the teacher evaluates his answer. Since the questions are not genuine ones, asked by somebody seeking information, this model indicates one kind of teacher control. Verbal exchange takes the form of a pseudo-dialogue, as Stubbs (1975) terms it, where pupils are kept in their place by the sort of talk that is expected of them. Indeed, intending teachers are usually encouraged by their supervisors to get pupils to talk more, and often a high proportion of class participation is taken as a criterion of successful teaching for those on practice during their professional training. However, since the assumption that teaching and learning necessarily involve talking is very culture-specific, teachers are likely to encounter difficulties when working with children from different cultural backgrounds. Dumont and Wax (1972), for example, showed that European teachers working with Cherokee Indians found themselves entirely at a loss, since learning for these children was not equated with talking in class. In their culture, speech is minimal in the learning process which relies far more on observation and participation. Even young children regard it as rather odd to be asked questions to which they know the teacher already has the answer.

Analysis and observation show that the kind of language used in any social exchange is situation-specific. Only in certain social situations is the monitoring of speech such as we have described permissible. This suggests a context where specific role relations hold between speakers. A policeman can cross-question a motorist for example; a judge can interrogate the defendant in court. But normally, we do not cross-question in this way or ask questions to which we already know the answers, unless we wish to catch people out by way of jokes or riddles. The very way in which a teacher talks to his pupils imposes on them his definition of the situation and the form of social relationship he considers appropriate. Many pupils learn to participate in a form of interaction in which authority and knowledge are linked. Because of the nature of the teacher's authority, in terms of his control of both knowledge and behaviour, the interaction is inevitably unbalanced to the advantage of the teacher, whose status is indicated by the kind of language he uses. Thus, to demonstrate intelligence or ability pupils have to learn to answer his questions in a fitting manner. By learning to give the teacher what he wants in terms of answers, they are being socialized into a world where knowledge is possessed by those in authority. Holt (1969), Barnes (1971, 1976), and Rosen (1967) are among the most vociferous in their criticism of teachers' use of questions to determine what counts as valid knowledge in school.

We have already noted that a substantial proportion of teacher talk is directed towards classroom control. Direct instructions or commands more obviously show the teacher's authority position. But although these can be veiled when they are couched in indirect terms, it is still clear what the role relationship between teacher and pupil is intended to be. Any pupil who is told that it is not a good idea for him to sit at the back knows quite well that he has to move or else he's in trouble. There is no question of his disagreeing. There are very few situations outside school where the nature of social interaction is indicated so clearly as it is when pupils have to ask permission to speak or when what they say can be corrected. The assumption that such intervention in the language a pupil uses is permissible indicates very clearly who is in control.

In addition to these more direct ways in which control is exerted by a specific use of language, there are more indirect means which warrant attention. Pupils are easily humiliated into obedience by the use of sarcasm or wit directed against them. Woods (1975) suggested that teachers sometimes deliberately set out to embarrass their pupils in order to establish and maintain power, to punish them, or even to take revenge on them. Showing pupils up by sarcastic remarks in front of others, especially younger children, can arouse resentment which often smoulders for a long time because of the personal smart, until the object of ridicule can retaliate.

Humour and jokes in the classroom, as opposed to wit or sarcasm, are more usually shared by teachers and pupils and can often serve to enhance a sense of comradeship and well-being. Walker and Adelman (1976) and Walker and Goodson (1977) show how hidden jokes and bizarre meanings, accessible only to those who have shared common experiences, can reveal important aspects of classroom life. Humour may indicate social solidarity within a group and can also help teachers to put pupils at their ease. Walker and Goodson draw a distinction between the kind of humour used in formal and informal classrooms. In the latter, when joking relationships between pupils are generated, the humour is that of equals, whereas in formal classrooms it is easy for teachers to joke at the expense of pupils and for these to use jokes to challenge a teacher's authority. The use of language in this way proves interesting and informative to an experienced observer, provided he is well enough acquainted with the participants to recognize its subtleties.

· Any kind of social intercourse involves some sort of give-and-take arrangement where everyone's needs and wishes are satisfied as far as is comfortable. In school, where the interaction is inevitably unbalanced because of the nature of the relations between pupils and teacher, teachers will often admit to certain survival strategies to help them cope with classes of reluctant pupils. Negotiation, for example, involves not only coming to a tacit agreement about what is acceptable behaviour in class, but also deliberate appeals, promises, or even threats and bribes. Teachers who arrange activities so that the more obviously academic part, such as writing, recording, working of examples, comes early in the day, hope that the promise of something more relaxing later will serve to keep pupils down to work with the minium of disruption. Woods (1976) suggests that apologies and praise also play a part in classroom negotiation. A teacher will apologize perhaps for talking too long, explaining that it had to be done in order to progress to something more interesting. Or he will praise pupils, perhaps even flattering them a little, for having worked hard at a difficult task.

Reliance on rules, ritual, and routine is also part of a teacher's survival kit, since most pupils come to accept what occurs regularly as part of the school day. A teacher who has to struggle hard to maintain control in class can relax rather more on routine occasions such as assembly or registration.

During his participant observation study, lasting a year in a mixed rural secondary school, Woods noticed that in addition to negotiating with pupils and relying on routine, some teachers indulged in various forms of fraternization with pupils, as a means of surviving and maintaining some measure of control. Younger teachers attempted to identify with pupils in their dress, manner, and speech, often joking with them to show general bonhomie. Even flirtatious behaviour was not unknown. Others became friendly with pupils outside the classroom by genuine shared interests in television, sport, and various aspects of popular culture.

But whatever techniques the teacher may adopt to maintain control and ease personal relationships in the classroom, most pupils tend to have a similar model of the ideal teacher, as Furlong's study of a group of West Indian fifteen-year-old girls clearly showed. These girls, all reluctant pupils but by no means devoid of ability, wanted their teachers to offer them a rigidly defined and structured syllabus so that they knew exactly what had to be mastered. They preferred material to be given to them, rejecting enquiry methods, and welcomed constant feedback from the teacher about their progress. In their eyes, the teacher who could supply all this was acceptable, even if he had to be strict. Werthman too (1963) had shown how a teacher could survive even with delinquent adolescents if he were prepared to make them work hard and could demonstrate that he was fair in dealing with them.

Classroom interaction and curriculum development

Since pupils over the whole age range, as far as the studies available suggest, seem to prefer teachers who provide them with a firm, structured framework, and who adopt didactic methods, it will be interesting to see how pupils respond to more open styles of teaching. Many recent curriculum developments require a change in the role of both pupil and teacher, placing more responsibility on pupils for their own participation and learning. An obvious example illustrating the different demands upon pupils and teachers is the Humanities Curriculum Project, where the teacher is required to act as neutral chairman. Enquiry and discussion methods replace direct teaching, so that pupils can no longer rely on their teacher to provide them with information or help them to arrive at a solution in their discussion of controversial issues. Instead, he provides them with materials relevant to a particular issue, but his main responsibility lies in creating conditions and opportunities which encourage pupils to develop their own understanding of values relating to human behaviour and experience. Using the evidence supplied by the materials in the learning pack, pupils must learn to judge, appraise, and assess critically what is relevant to the topic in hand. Furthermore, they must learn to tolerate an outcome that probably does not produce consensus. All this is difficult for pupils to learn, especially if they have been used to being fed with teacher-selected information. The kind of interaction in this situation is essentially that of equals, in the sense that everyone has a right to contribute and to criticize other people's views. There is no appeal to authority, nor must the teacher intervene to assert his own viewpoint. Subsequent evaluation of the project (Walker and Adelman, 1975) reveals that both pupils and teachers found their new roles difficult to accept. Pupils found the procedure unnerving in that they were expected to put forward their own views, yet received no teacher guidance or approval to tell them whether they were right or not. The monitoring procedures developed in the Ford Teaching Project showed that when a speaker, teacher or pupil, intended an action or remark to have a particular meaning, that meaning was frequently misinterpreted. The triangulation technique, which will be discussed further in a later chapter, is intended to help those engaged in enquiry/discovery methods to understand other people's behaviour and to help teachers in particular to see themselves through their pupil's eyes. SAFARI, 'Success and Failure and Recent Innovation', a three-year project, was set up in order to investigate the impact of curriculum projects on teacher-pupil interaction, precisely because some developments had run into difficulties on account of changing role relationships. In fact some teachers, because of the difficulties encountered in the nature of their new role, had been found to adapt materials to suit their original didactic methods. Galton (1976), for example, showed that up to 25% of his sample of a hundred teachers using Nuffield Science schemes never asked pupils to plan and work out their own experiments, but rather resorted to instructing them.

Curriculum innovation presents many new demands for teachers and pupils alike, in forcing many of them to change their traditional roles and to come to grips with new kinds of content that have no traditional subject barriers. Discussion of these issues will be resumed in a later chapter.

Summary and conclusions

In this first chapter we have attempted to explain the nature of classroom interaction, and have shown how methods of examining social intercourse in school have developed with changing views of education. Studies of teacher-pupil interaction as revealed by the physical layout of the classroom, interpersonal judgements, nonverbal communication, and general rules and rituals have been discussed. We have seen how teaching styles are both influenced by pupil behaviour and themselves evoke particular kinds of behaviour among pupils.

We have shown how groups of pupils contribute towards the general give-and-take of classroom life by examining methods of grouping adopted by teachers and ways in which pupils band together in specific situations.

Use of language in the classroom, as we shall see again later on, is an important indicator of the type of role relationships developed between teacher and pupils. The discussion of the function of language in social control is particularly interesting when more subtle linguistic techniques such as jokes and humour are considered.

Finally, we have briefly commented on the relationship between curriculum innovation and classroom interaction, an issue to be developed further in a later chapter.

2 Judgements of Children

The nature of judgements

In recent years the importance of social influences on children's learning and development, in fact upon their total educational experience, has, as we saw in Chapter 1, been recognized. If their school experience is to be a worthwhile one, they must be regarded as persons in their own right, with their own individual interests, abilities, and personal characteristics, as people who are capable of making choices and decisions. Yet all too often children are labelled and categorized by their teachers as if they were not unique individuals worthy of respect and consideration.

One aim of this chapter is to promote further thought about the nature and effects of judgements that teachers make. We shall examine the implications of such judgements within the social and institutional context of the school and shall suggest how pupils' motivation, achievement, and self-image might be affected by such judgements. The personality make-up of those making judgements is explored and some practical issues such as recordkeeping and report writing are discussed.

Judging others or forming impressions of them is an integral part of all social interaction; forming judgements of children is an inevitable part of any teacher's task. And whereas in everyday life the judgements we make of others help us to get along with them, to communicate with and to understand them, they do not necessarily have long-lasting effects. However, what a teacher says about a pupil, either in informal staff-room conversation or on a more formal written record, may shape that pupil's future more than a teacher can ever imagine. It is particularly urgent then that teachers be aware of the effects their judgements may have on pupils and gain some understanding of how their opinions might be influenced by external factors as well as by their own personality make-up. They can then try to ensure that the judgements they make are as fair, unbiased, and objective as possible. But as soon as we begin to talk of objectivity, we run into difficulties, because the human being making the judgement is not a measuring instrument to be calibrated and read with any degree of accuracy. Hamlyn (1972) contrasts the objective statement with the subjective, the idiosyncratic, or the prejudiced, implying that judgements made about others purely on grounds of personal whim or preference are inevitably distorted. However,the impressions teachers form of their pupils as individuals and the judgements they make of their abilities and progress are inescapably subjective up to a point. The view a teacher has of a pupil is *his* view, since he can only see people through his own eyes. The important thing, therefore, is that teachers learn to make their judgements as fair and as just as they can, by making only those inferences about a child's behaviour for which there is direct evidence.

In addition to being fair, objective, helpful, and educationally relevant, the judgements teachers make of others must also be morally acceptable. Teachers must, in other words, not confuse judgements of performance and achievement with those about the pupil's worth as a person. A child is not better or worse as a person because he can read well or fails to learn to read, because he gains a higher or a lower intelligence test score, or because he is deemed capable or otherwise of obtaining O levels. Yet because our society is achievement oriented, intelligence, often equated with academic success, is highly valued, and, although as a concept it is morally neutral, it might mistakenly become associated with moral acceptability.

If, in making judgements of children, teachers are to avoid this confusion, it is highly important for them to remember that respect for persons is an essential part of education, part of the teacher-pupil relationship. The notion of respect for persons involves treating children as individuals, recognizing and valuing their personal characteristics. It follows then that to see them simply as members of a category could result in overlooking these individual characteristics. For a child to develop and function as a person, he needs to be treated as one. He needs to be able to develop the kind of self-concept that allows him to regard himself as of value. To treat children as persons in their own right, who are able to develop this kind of self-image, involves regarding them as responsible for their own actions and therefore having some control over what they do. To see children as passive entities whose destiny is shaped by influences beyond their control is to lose sight of their power to be autonomous. Children who are regarded as doomed failures because of their lower working-class background, for instance, are not being accorded due respect because, firstly, they are being placed in a category where all members supposedly share common characteristics and, secondly, they are not considered to have any control over their own future. If many of them are not *seen* to be able to determine their own career and in the school context are given less encouragement to do so, many will inevitably fail, thus conforming to the working-class pattern, reinforcing the stereotype and confirming the self-fulfilling prophecy.

Included in the concept of developing personal autonomy is the notion of coming to terms with constraints imposed upon one's freedom, including one's own limitations. To be allowed to try, but then to fail, helps children to learn what their strengths and weaknesses are. It would be foolish to assume that all children could be equally successful at all things; part of developing as a person is to realize where one can succeed, but also, to acknowledge that there are standards of excellence one might not reach and nevertheless to value others' achievements. For a teacher to prevent a child from attempting something in which he thinks the child will fail is to omit to treat him as an autonomous being or to show him respect as an individual. However, children do need some guidance from adults as to what they might be able to achieve; they need to know what the tasks involve that they hope to tackle, and need to be encouraged to estimate their own abilities realistically. It would surely be just as misguided to let children think they could achieve what for them would be impossible as to prevent them from ever trying because of some preconceived notion of their abilities held by the teacher. The sad cases of children who for many years aspire to be doctors or teachers when they cannot cope very adequately even with the basis skills of literacy and numeracy act as a reminder that one of the most important reasons for assessment and judgement by teachers is to help children to gain a realistic picture of their own capabilities and to make the most of them, while at the same time accepting their limitations. Recognizing and accepting one's own limitations is not incompatible with acknowledging standards of excellence in areas where one is not highly competent; if comparison between individuals is avoided, especially where it implies differential worth of persons, then it should be possible to achieve this idea in practice.

However, since children have to learn to develop as persons and to recognize their own weaknesses as well as strengths, uninformed or uncritical respect is insufficient and misguided, as it would involve regarding everything a child did as acceptable and would offer them no standards on which to base their own developing moral principles or standards of excellence in any area of achievement.

With this proviso, treating children as individuals is essential to help them develop as persons or to develop a consciousness of self. G. H. Mead's concept of the self (1934) offers a view of personality development which is essentially active, reflexive, and dynamic. In Mead's view, the individual ceases to be at the mercy of other people or external circumstances which cause him merely to *respond*. Because of an ability to reflect upon, interpret, and judge his own actions he becomes independent. However, he does not learn to do this in a vacuum. He learns to reflect upon himself by living in a social world with other people who have significance and meaning for him. The views of others, especially 'significant others' (specific people who are close to him and whose views and actions matter to him) help to influence the development of the self by a process of interaction. It follows that if such significant others, such as parents, teachers, peers, hold a view of a human being as a typical occupant of a role or status rather than a unique individual, he will fail to develop individual qualities as he too will see himself as a mere typification. Berger and Luckman (1967) in their discussion of how we experience others in everyday life talk of 'typificatory schemes' which affect our interaction with other people and which help us to make judgements of them. A *typificatory scheme* is based on our past experience of others in certain situations where specific cues lead us to interpret their behaviour in a certain way. For instance, we perceive someone who approaches us with a stern look, an unsmiling expression, who remains impassive to our first approach, as unfriendly. This is our typification of him. But in face-to-face situations, the interaction can advance so that his change of facial expression, the tone of his voice, even his posture can present us with contradictory evidence that forces us to modify our initial typification and to begin to see him as a person rather than an anonymous type. If typifications are not modified, then anonymity and type casting are inevitable, implying that we perceive others merely as members of a category, occupying a particular status. They are seen not to have an individuality but share the same characteristics as everybody else in the same category. To see our pupils in this way ('working-class pupils', 'Negroes', 'redheads' and so on) is to fail to respect them as persons and to

make judgements of them which cannot fail to be so general
unfair, rigid, and possibly damaging to their self-respect.

Categorization of pupils by teachers

A brief review of some of the recent literature on educability will enable us
to examine some of the assumptions that teachers make about the relationship between educability and social class, ability, race, and even sex.
We can then consider the implications of some of these assumptions for
pupils' school achievement and behaviour in class and ask why teachers'
assumptions or typifications have the effects that they do.

From the early 1950s onwards, extensive research has been carried out
both in this country and in the U.S.A. to show how working-class children
are at a disadvantage compared with middle-class children in school
achievement and educational opportunity. Much of this early work set out
to show the extent of these differential opportunities. In fact, there is
substantial evidence of working-class failure and this was attributed to
poor home backgrounds, lack of parental interest, and insufficient encouragement at home. Preschool programmes were set up in the U.S.A. in the
early 1960s to compensate for inferior home backgrounds, in the hope that
'disadvantaged' children would catch up before they came to school.

In this country, following the recommendations of the Plowden Committee (1967) for a policy of positive discrimination, certain areas were
designated as Educational Priority Areas. Primary schools within them
were granted a more favourable allocation of finance and resources and
teachers offered additional salary allowances, in order to reduce the high
proportion of staff changes suffered by such schools at the time. Educators
were already beginning to ask whether schools themselves had contributed towards the failure of the children who were now being offered
special help. And if part of the responsibility did rest with the schools, how
in fact had they helped children to fail? Holt (1964) had already produced
his highly personal account of why children fail, and from the late 1960s
on we find a series of investigations both in this country and in the USA
which aim to answer this question. Fuchs, for example (1968), in the USA
carried out a small-scale study of probationary teachers in New York slum
schools, in an attempt to show how teachers (perhaps inadvertently) help
children to fail. A detailed account of one young teacher's experiences in a
slum school illustrates the point. The teacher began her work in the school
by trying to examine her own methods critically, and attributed children's
failure to her own lack of experience and expertise. But very soon she was
persuaded (reluctantly) by more experienced teachers that the cause of

failure lay not with her, but in the inferior home backgrounds from which the children came. Children were thus being typified as failures right at the beginning of their school career because of their home background. As Fuchs says: 'the slum school system's tacit belief that social conditions outside the school make such failures inevitable *does* make such failures inevitable'. Furthermore, children are tracked (or streamed, in our terminology) right from the beginning, thus receiving labels which will follow them right through their school career and will result in differential teaching which serves only to widen the gap even more between those judged as able, indifferent, or poor at the age of six.

Rist (1970), aware of the dearth of studies,attempting to explain exactly how the school helps to reinforce the class structure of society, reports results of an observational study of one class of ghetto children from the time they entered kindergarten to halfway through their third year of schooling. As soon as they entered school, they were placed by their teacher in reading groups which reflected the social class composition within the whole group. These groups remained stable over the two and a half years of study and the teacher's differential behaviour towards each group was noticeable. Thus she had made initial presuppositions about the children on the basis of how she perceived their social background. These typifications were to have clear consequences for their socialization into the school system. Rist suggests the following stages in this process of differentiation and its consequences. First of all, the teacher has an ideal type of pupil in mind who possesses those characteristics necessary for success. Since the criteria could not be based on any kind of school attainment (as the children had only just entered school) the characteristics were related to social class. Thus early in their school career a subjective evaluation was being made as to the presence or absence of these desired characteristics and children were grouped accordingly. From then on, groups were treated differently according to whether they were seen as fast or slow learners. Markedly less attention and encouragement were offered to the slow group who in any case were not expected to succeed. Patterns of interaction between the teacher and children thus became rigid; later on in their school career the whole process would repeat itself but this time based on supposed evidence of success or failure – actual performance in reading.

British studies reveal a similar tendency on the part of teachers to correlate educability with social class. Part of the NFER project initiated in 1958 to study children's reading progress was concerned with teacher's attitudes towards children's home background, their expectations of children, and their assessments of children's reading ability and their actual performance on a standardized reading test (Goodacre, 1968). Teacher's subjective assessments, based on their records of book level reached by each child, suggested that children from middle- and upper working-class areas had a noticeably higher reading ability than those in lower working-class areas. Middle-class pupils were rated highest. However, when tested on a standardized reading test (NFER's *National Survey 7+ Reading Attainment Test*) this marked difference was not apparent. Lower working-class children were still inferior to the other two groups but there was no marked difference between middle-class and upper working-class children. It is possible then that teachers' assessments reflect the standards they themselves apply to pupils from different social environments. All working-class children are expected to perform less well than middle-class children and so they do, it seems. Are they held back because they are expected to be slow? Or because teachers simply do not give them more advanced reading material?

The studies referred to so far show how teachers categorize children according to what they know (or think they know) about their social background. Yet another important basis upon which teachers form their typifications of pupils is the school stream in which they are placed. In fact, stream and social class are often confounded or even taken to be parallel. Keddie (1971) shows how the 'knowledge' teachers have of children, or the way in which they judge their ability, is based on the stream in which they are placed as well as the social class from which they come. The ideal pupil is one who is seen to be easiest to teach, who is like the teacher, and who accepts what the teacher offers unquestioningly. He presents no problems in class, works quietly and independently, doing what the teacher wants. He belongs to an A stream and stems from a middle-class background. The less than ideal or problematic pupil is the one who questions what the teacher offers, demands to know the point of the activity, and in fact is generally seen as unlike the teacher. As a participant observer in a large comprehensive school, Keddie studied the progress of a Humanities Course designed to be taught as an undifferentiated programme across the whole ability range to a fourth-year group, and eventually to be examined by mode 3 of the CSE and O level. She tries to show how, in fact, although the avowed aims of the course are to develop autonomy and independence, to allow children to work at their own speed and to learn to think for themselves, in practice it seems to be designed for an ideal pupil who already exists – the A stream pupil, who because of his middle-class background already possesses the desired characteristics. Thus these docile pupils accept a new subject with a different label (Humanities, Socialization) which they readily take over from the teachers. The problem pupils are the C streamers who accept it less readily and want to recognize the content as History, Biology, and so on, with which they are more familiar.

One of the points of particular interest in the study is the way context affects teachers' typifications. Keddie sees teachers at the planning stage as acting within an *educationist context*, basing their ideas on what they deem theoretically desirable. In this context they hold ability and social class separate, condemning streaming and differentiation by ability because they are socially divisive. But in the other context in which they work, with a practical orientation, the *teacher context*, these ideals tend to be forgotten. Ability and social class are confused. Treatment of pupils is different according to their stream. For example, teachers admit to preparing different material according to the stream they are going to teach even though the programme was designed to be taught right across the ability range. They even admit to insufficient preparation for the C streamers on the assumption that these pupils won't notice and won't ask questions. They are prepared to answer questions asked by A stream pupils which they would gloss over with C streamers as trivial, irrelevant, or disruptive. Different kinds of behaviour and application are accepted and even expected, according to stream.

Further evidence showing how teachers typify pupils according to stream is found in the work of Hargreaves (1967) and Lacey (1970), both of whom based their observations on secondary schools in which they worked. In studying social relationships between teachers and boys in four fourth-year streams in a secondary modern school, Hargreaves shows the gradual deterioration of relationships and segregation which seems to follow upon streaming. Pupils are judged as different in ability at the beginning of their secondary school career and are streamed accordingly. Interestingly enough, although teachers perceive the separate streams as homogeneous in ability, they are in fact, according to IQ scores, less homogeneous than when they were first grouped in this way (for example, in the second year the D stream contained no boys with IQs above the median, whereas by the fourth year there were six). But this differentiation, now embedded in the organization of the school, has repercussions for other aspects of the pupils' behaviour. Because they come to see themselves as different (this self-image is obviously reinforced by teachers' attitudes towards different streams), their relationships deteriorate so that there is marked hostility between the A and D stream pupils. As Hargreaves comments, academic and delinquescent subcultures develop, one subculture perceiving the other as a negative reference group, so that hostility and lack of communication between the two groups becomes marked. Teachers too have grown to expect little of their D stream pupils who adapt to these lower expectations with lowered aspirations and diminished interest in the school. Not only do teachers expect less of the D stream pupils academically, but they also expect them to behave badly and accordingly discriminate against them, for example, even where school holiday trips are concerned. Little wonder then that their hostile attitude grows. Hargreaves is at pains to point out that it would be dangerous to generalize these findings to other secondary schools and this caution must be respected. But certainly the possible implications must not be overlooked.

Lacey's study takes place within a selective school where boys are segregated on the basis of first-year examination results into four streams before the beginning of their second year. Just as in Hargreaves' study, we see how the initial process of differentiation on the part of the teachers has repercussions for the boys' behaviour. Pupils in separate streams see themselves as progressively different, as is seen from a study of changing friendship patterns. Their interest in and attitudes towards school, their acceptance of school values, as well as participation in extra-curricular activities, takes on a different character according to whether they have been placed in a high or low stream. Lacey refers to this differentiation among pupils as polarization. He describes it as 'a process of subculture formation in which the school-dominated normative culture is opposed by an alternative culture ... the antigroup culture' whose members reject school values, indulge in antisocial activities, and so on.

Again it would be unwise to assume that streaming in all secondary schools would have similar repercussions as at Hightown Grammar described by Lacey. However, these two field studies serve to draw our attention to some of the undesirable repercussions that can follow where teachers are tempted to typify children and when the ensuing categories become part of the structure of the school. Progressive retardation of those placed in lower streams leads to the following sequence of processes. Firstly, we find reduced teacher expectations of low stream pupils, with less demanding academic tasks set for them. Then pupils' own level of aspiration is lowered because of lack of academic challenge and adequate or appropriate incentives and, finally, a sense of present and future failure follows, leading to an even more reduced level of aspiration, motivation, and performance.

If differentiation in the form of streaming were removed, would these undesired consequences also be alleviated? Would the removal of formal institutionalized categories that are established within the school also result in the absence or reduction of unfair typifications made by teachers?

There is in fact some evidence to suggest that where mixed-ability classes have been in operation in the lower part of the secondary school, pupils who might otherwise have been placed in a lower stream and never given the chance have been allowed to join a 'top set' and to follow a C.S.E. or G.C.E. course in their fourth and fifth years (Kelly, 1978). Such pupils do not seem to have suffered from the disadvantage of low teacher expectations as they might have done in a rigidly streamed school.

However, such evidence so far is slender and, as we have already seen, where streaming does not take place, even in classes of younger children (Goodacre, 1968) there is a tendency to typify according to perceived social class and consequently to assume a correlation between social class and ability, even where it does not manifestly exist. Some of Barker-Lunn's findings (1970) show that teachers can in effect stream within their classes, very often with an assumed social class relationship, even when the school is formally unstreamed. Even in the reception class, it is not unknown for five-year-olds to be grouped by ability, under the guise of being in different teams, or designated by different colours or names, and so on. The fact that children's progress can be affected by teachers' initial categorizations of them and assumptions about their ability and future chances of success, regardless of the way in which segregation is formally organized, still poses the all-important question to which an answer will be sought later, how exactly *do* typifications have the effect they do?

But before we come to this crucial question, it would be interesting to consider race as a further basis on which typifications are formed. It has long been recognized that immigrant children, new to British schools from their countries of origin, unfamiliar with the English language, the organization of British schools and methods of teaching, as well as the way of British life in general, are likely to be at a disadvantage in school achievement in comparison with native children. This disadvantage should in fact apply only to first-generation immigrants whose difficulties might be predominantly linguistic. Yet should second- and third-generation children of immigrant parents experience similar problems when they have grown up in the same neighbourhood as their British peers, learning the same language, be it a Cockney or a Liverpool dialect? Coard's study (1971) suggests that their educational disadvantage lies not so much in their actual ability or the actual language they use as in their *perceived* ability.

Teachers, Coard suggests, in his highly impassioned monograph, typify them as being low in ability, speaking a language inappropriate for school learning, and it is thus the teachers themselves who help them to fail. Coard quotes figures obtained from the ILEA in that year, showing that a disproportionate number of West Indian children are placed in ESN schools: 28 percent of all pupils in their ESN schools were immigrants, compared with only 15 percent in ordinary ILEA schools. Further analysis of these figures is indeed alarming, since it reveals that 75 percent of all immigrants in ESN schools were West Indian even though West Indians formed only half the immigrant population in ordinary schools. Since ESN schools are designed to enable less able children to cope with their low abilities and to make the best of them, Coard was forced to ask whether all these West Indian children needed to be socialized to a low scholastic achievement in this way or whether they had been wrongly placed because they were inappropriately judged by their teachers.

The West Indian child is seen to suffer under several crucial handicaps. Firstly, low teacher expectations affect the degree of help and encouragement his teacher is ready to offer. Secondly, the effect of low teacher expectations upon his own self-image and abilities in turn reduces his motivation to succeed in school, because he feels certain of failure. These effects are very reminiscent of those we found operating with lower working-class British children. The West Indian child may be at an even greater disadvantage because of the widely held belief (supported by the views and interpretations of the evidence offered by Jensen and Eysenck) that Negroes are in any case genetically inferior to whites in ability. Whereas the explanation of working-class failure is seen to lie in adverse home conditions and the rather patronizing argument that such children could have done better in more favourable conditions is permitted, the assumption that Negroes are genetically inferior leads those who make it to the smug conclusion that, whatever the school did for them, they could never succeed.

In spite of the public concern on the part of some vociferous pressure groups, it is doubtful whether there is an operative sex hierarchy in most schools today, although earlier evidence shows (Little and Westergaard, 1964) that fewer girls, particularly working-class girls, attained places in higher education than boys. Easthope (1975) suggests that girls are more likely to be given less prestigious subjects to study than boys, being offered practical, nonexaminable and general subjects. Evidence for this is difficult to find, though some schools certainly make a distinction by excluding girls from technical subjects, while not giving boys the opportunity to pursue courses in home economics or domestic skills. Boys are traditionally expected to do better at science and mathematics than girls, who are expected to achieve better results than boys on the arts side. Lack of evidence, however, to demonstrate any real intellectual difference suggests that any variation there is may be accounted for in terms of teachers' or parents' expectations.

Categorization of pupils by specialist agencies

Teachers are however not the only adults who might be responsible for labelling children by the judgements they make of them. Every school has officially sponsored links with certain members of the community whose concern it is to support the general welfare of children, even though they do not all work directly in the school. These include educational psychologists, school counsellors, and youth employment officers.

Children are generally referred to a psychologist when teachers or counsellors feel they can no longer cope with severe behaviour problems or marked difficulties in learning. One of the tasks frequently presented to the psychologist is to diagnose the learning difficulties of supposed under-achievers and of children thought to be in need of special education. There are several stages in this procedure which entail selecting and therefore labelling children as different from their peers. First of all, at the stage when a teacher makes his recommendation to the head to call in expert advice, he has to pick out the child as a special case, thus creating a category. It is not unknown for teachers to be reluctant to ask for expert help or even to avoid doing so altogether because they do not wish to label a child in such a way. Secondly, the child is likely to see himself as stigmatized in some way if so selected – supported often by the taunts of his peers. And thirdly, many parents see a referral as carrying a stigma, especially if a recommendation is made that their child be transferred to a special school. This does not imply that such services are unhelpful or unnecessary; it does however reveal the difficulties of judgement with which such selection is fraught. A child who might benefit considerably from psychological help or special educational treatment could suffer either because his parents refuse it on the grounds of being stigmatized or because of the attitudes of parents and peers towards him once he is receiving special treatment.

Similar problems are likely to arise in referring children to a school counsellor.

Counselling has long been subsumed under the general pastoral care duties of teachers, who have given advice to pupils of all ages when occasion demands. Class teachers in primary schools constantly act as counsellors to their pupils and are called upon more and more to offer advice to young mothers. But as pressures put upon older pupils by an increasingly complex and multifarious society have grown over the last decade, a need has been felt, especially in larger secondary schools, for specialists with experience in teaching to be appointed to act as counsellors. A counselling system has long been firmly established in large schools in the U.S.A. in response to the need expressed by parents and teachers. Many teachers are reluctant to see a similar counselling system introduced into schools in this country, partly because they consider themselves capable of doing the job alongside their teaching, and partly because they feel threatened by the presence of somebody who has access to more information about their pupils than they have.

Most counsellors would ideally like to work in collaboration with teachers so that information about pupils could be collected and pooled, thus minimizing the risk of drawing on partial or biased information which would lead to a stereotyped and limited view of the pupils concerned.

There are three main sources of information upon which counsellors can draw: direct observation of pupils during the counselling session; what pupils say about themselves; and objective records of their school performance. Each of these can be coloured by judgements made of the pupil. As we saw earlier, any one person perceives others and forms impressions of them through his own eyes. His judgement is coloured by his past experience and initially he must necessarily form typifications of those consulting him in order to have a rough idea of what kind of person he is dealing with. The very nature of direct counsellor-pupil interaction is limited, since the counsellor sees the pupil usually only during the interview session and can witness only a very small sample of behaviour under rather special conditions. Furthermore, what a child says about himself is likely to reflect the self-image built up by interaction with others. As we know from the work of Mead (1934), one's concept of self is influenced by the view of 'significant others'; and if these views have been negative or deprecatory, the pupil will have a poor self-image. Supposedly objective records of a pupil's school performance can again be coloured by a teacher's attitude towards that pupil and merely offer the counsellor labels of little use.

Gill (1967), one of the organisers of the counselling course for experienced teachers at Keele University, sees the development of a pupil's self-concept as one of the important aims of counselling. He suggests that, through counselling, individuals are helped to understand themselves, to clarify their self-image, and also to define questions they are asking of themselves about personal, educational, and vocational matters. The assumption made is that the individual is of supreme worth in and for himself. But pupils have to be convinced of this and to be shown how to use their personal qualities – a difficult task when their opinions of themselves are low. It is important to accept that counselling does not entail personality change (no counsellor is professionally equipped to do this), but involves helping pupils to find effective ways of using the aptitudes, abilities, and personal qualities they already have (Hamblin, 1974). One of the first stages in helping pupils to realize the value of their own qualities is to show them their own strengths and weaknesses and teach them to accept these as a basis for development. Thus the process of reversing any negative stereotype can begin and the shared task of counsellor, teacher, and pupil can be seen as building up self-respect in pupils who have previously learned to see themselves in a negative way through the eyes of others.

Many teachers, however, have misgivings as to the role of the counsellor, fearing that he might take over some of the responsibility that they jealously regard as their own. Further doubts about the effects of counselling are voiced by Cicourel and Kitsuse (1968), writing on counselling in high schools in the U.S.A. They are concerned with the way in which adolescents come into contact with counsellors and how pupils are selected for such contacts. They see the school system as 'an institutionalized differentiator of adolescent careers'. Included among the adolescents' problems created by the organizational structure of the school are issues related to pupils' academic work, their behaviour, especially breaches of rules, and their emotional problems. Any one pupil may of course be seen by teachers to present one or more of these problems, although the pupil himself would not necessarily be conscious of them as problems. This then is one of the crucial issues: are problems created for pupils by the presence of a counsellor whose job is to deal with them? The problems which may have been transitory can become highlighted and exacerbated when attention is drawn to them, especially with pupils who are inclined to seek attention. To be singled out for official attention on the grounds of strange or bizarre behaviour can easily reinforce the kind of behaviour under scrutiny. Furthermore, as Cicourel and Kitsuse point out, the labelling of a pupil as a troublemaker or a truant, in providing the occasion for singling him out for special treatment, may mean that he is more closely supervised and punished for minor misdemeanors which would go unnoticed in other pupils. Stebbins (1971) provides evidence to show that some teachers do in fact apply different standards of behaviour to those pupils they judge as either well-behaved or troublesome. He shows how discriminatory treatment can work the other way round: good pupils are punished whereas troublesome pupils are ignored for the same minor offence, in case the latter cause further trouble as a result of the punishment. Counsellors, officially part of the school structure, thus have the power to reinforce one kind of deviant in schools.

Although the situation in American high schools does not pertain in this country, the risks of creating academic, behavioural, or emotional deviants in school through an officially appointed counsellor does give cause for concern. The work of counsellors can and surely does make a valuable contribution to the functioning of a school. It would therefore be a pity if this were marred because the unintended and unanticipated consequences of their advice were overlooked, so that the dangers of labelling and categorizing were once more in operation on yet another front.

The ideal pupil concept

In considering ways in which teachers' judgements of their pupils are formed, it should prove interesting to ask whether teachers have a preconceived notion of an ideal pupil. If they do, then several consequences are likely. Firstly, their aims might be towards producing ideal pupils according to the model they hold. Secondly, it would follow that any pupil not conforming to the model is perceived as less than ideal in some way and therefore judged less favourably. Thirdly, teachers might see their own success reflected in the ideal pupil and conversely their failure reflected in anyone less than ideal. Several important questions can be pursued in this connection. Do all teachers have an ideal pupil in mind before they begin their teaching career? If so, what influences have helped to create this ideal? Do they set out to produce ideal pupils? Or do they claim to recognize and identify them in practice and in retrospect? Does a teacher's ideal pupil vary according to the educational aims he considers most important? Becker's concept of the ideal pupil (1952) as one who is bright and easy to teach and belongs usually to a middle-class background has already been discussed in Chapter 1. But a teacher's ideal rests not only on his view of a child's background. The ideals held by teachers vary according to their educational aims, to those of the school in which they work, and ultimately to their view of man.

A teacher who considers himself progressive and adopts child-centred ideals will have a different concept of an ideal pupil from that described by

Becker. A pupil who sits quietly, expecting to be told what to do and taking little responsibility or initiative will be less than ideal in the eyes of the progressive teacher. Instead, his model is one of a pupil who tries to be independent and initiate and direct his own learning.

And if teachers embracing different kinds of educational aim do have different notions of an ideal pupil, we need to ask how these ideals affect pupils themselves, namely their achievement, their self-concept, and their relationships with others. Neville Bennett (1976), in his highly controversial study of the relationship between teaching styles and pupil achievement, points out that teachers aim to engender different outcomes in their pupils. Formal teachers tend to lay greater emphasis on promoting a high level of academic attainment and the acquisition of skills in number and reading, whereas informal teachers value social and emotional development, stressing the importance of self-expression, creativity, and the enjoyment of school. If these are their avowed aims, how do they affect teachers' concepts of the ideal pupil? And how are children who do not conform to this ideal judged by their teachers? Although there is no hard evidence, it seems a reasonable hypothesis that pupils' self-images might be affected indirectly. One subsidiary finding that emerged in the now classic study of Getzels and Jackson (1962) of intelligence and creativity revealed that many teachers in their sample drawn from a highly selective school viewed divergent thinkers with suspicion. They preferred pupils who gave the answers they knew teachers expected to those who asked what were considered awkward, critical, or impudent questions. The unconventional behaviour and interests of divergers led teachers to regard them as disruptive in class, so that, on the whole, convergers, who are more conventional and tend not to ask unusual or awkward questions, provided the ideal pupil concept. The same teachers rated divergent thinkers as only average in ability within that school, despite the fact that their school performance compared favourably with that of convergers who were preferred in class. Similar results were obtained by Torrance (1962) and Hasan and Butcher (1966) who replicated the Getzels and Jackson study, using a sample of Scottish schoolchildren. Again teachers rated their divergent pupils as less likeable. Children who tend to see unusual problems that others might have missed or even a teacher not anticipated are likely to be disconcerting, especially to the teacher's self-image. Thus again we see that pupils who conform to a teacher's ideal tend to support his self-image. Divergent pupils may then tend to find themselves in an antiteacher or antischool position. Is it likely that they too, like the academic failures reported by Hargreaves and Lacey, will begin to form a delinquescent subculture?

The suggestion by Haddon and Lytton (1968, 1971) that divergent pupils are more popular and better liked by teachers and peers in informal schools than formal schools brings us back to the vexed issues of differences in aims, expected outcomes, and ideal pupils in two quite different educational climates.

Bennett himself (1976), as we have already seen, set out to discover whether formal and informal teaching styles affected pupils' progress and, in brief, his findings indicate that, on the whole, children taught by formal methods tend not only to achieve a higher level in the basic skills of literacy and numeracy, but are also judged superior in creative writing. What is of particular interest, however, in a discussion of the effect of a teacher's concept of the ideal pupil, is the effect of different teacher expectations upon pupils' self-concepts and self-esteem. Bennett found no evidence to suggest that there was a change in self-concept or self-esteem following a change in teaching style during the year of study. He does admit however that there is some support for the view that informal classrooms appear to have an adverse effect upon insecure or anxious pupils who are unable to cope with the responsibility of self-directed activity. Such pupils are lost without a more firmly imposed structure. We may well suppose that informal teachers hold a particular concept of the ideal pupil to which more anxious and nervous children cannot conform. Their lack of progress could then be attributed not only to lack of structure or direction in the classroom, though these seem obvious influences, but also to the discouraging effect of teachers' unfavourable judgements of them. They fail to live up to the teachers' ideals, are regarded as less than satisfactory, and their self-esteem, together with their motivation, gradually becomes depressed. Again, this supposition has to remain a hypothesis, but one well worth considering in light of other evidence.

Yet another concept of the ideal pupil must be held by teachers working in community schools in deprived areas. Halsey (1972) and Midwinter (1972) both advocate a school curriculum with an emphasis on social education, in the hope that pupils will develop the kind of social skills and competence that will enable them to take action against the environment of poverty in which they live. Halsey (1974) would like to develop in pupils a sense of 'constructive discontent' so that they are actively critical of what they find unacceptable in their community. We shall see later how similar attitudes are fostered by the Schools' Council Social Education Project (1974). An ideal pupil in this context would surely be one who does not sit waiting to absorb what knowledge his teachers think appropriate, but would welcome the right to challenge, criticize, and attempt to change his immediate community. Such a pupil would be labelled as a deviant by teachers holding Becker's ideal and most likely would be judged unfavourably by them.

Interpersonal perception

Our discussion so far has shown how typifications made of pupils become embedded in the social context of the school and are developed and confirmed by social interaction. However, a further important set of influences which affect the way an individual judges others are revealed to us by psychological studies of person perception.

Interpersonal perception can be described as the forming of judgements by people about others, especially those judgements which concern us as social beings. Such judgements are concerned with the ways in which people react and respond to others in thought, feeling, and action. Whereas people tend to form snap impressions of others, taking an immediate dislike to another on first sight, for example, in a rather intuitive manner, most of the judgements we make are by inference, both from available evidence and from general principles we hold about human behaviour. It is partly because interpersonal perception is largely inferential that such factors within an individual can have such a distorting effect on his final judgement.

But before we examine this process at work in the classroom, it is useful to look at some of the features of perception in general. The way in which we perceive other people is necessarily different from our perception of objects, in that person perception is a two-way process. Merely by perceiving another and interpreting his behaviour, we have an effect on the very behaviour we are observing which in turn affects our interpretation of it, whereas objects do not change when we perceive them. Object perception is a one-way process. Yet in spite of the fact that people change and usually have more emotional significance for us than objects, there is no fundamental difference between object and person perception since in both cases we use cues available to us and make inferences on the basis of such cues.

When we meet another person for the first time, as for instance when a teacher confronts a new class of children at the beginning of the school year, he has certain cues immediately available to him – physical cues such as physique, dress, hair colour, and style. These are static features in that they do not change under our scrutiny, and although they are of little actual value in helping to form accurate judgements, they nevertheless are used. When Secord (1958) presented subjects with still photographs of people and asked them to describe the personalities of those represented in the photographs, most subjects did so readily and without apparent difficulty, producing surprisingly uniform descriptions. There do seem to be facial stereotypes which can help produce a distorted judgement based on no further evidence. Swarthy complexions tend to be disliked and unpleasant characteristics attributed to their owners. The kind of stereotype liked or disliked will of course depend on the context and even on fashion and current approval. It is sad to note in this connection Coard's observation that his black pupils drew themselves as white. Both Negro and white pupils refused to see their teacher as black (although he was) because black skin apparently in the social context in which he was working was disliked and had unpleasant connotations. Stereotypes exist about physique, suggesting that fat people are conceived as happy, fun-loving, and thin people as anxious (Strongman and Hart, 1968). Further stereotypes are held about voice, accent and dialect, and about clothes and hairstyle (Gibbins, 1969). If teachers are equally susceptible to such stereotypes as the subjects tested in the laboratory, inferences they make about their pupils are likely to be wildly inaccurate and unfair. Dynamic cues such as facial expression, posture, movement, gestures, rate of speech and intonation offer a similar array available to the teacher on first meeting his class. But although these offer some kind of information helping to create a first impression, they are highly unreliable if further evidence is not available.

Luchins (1959) confirms that first impressions tend to be long lasting but are not the most accurate. Experiments showed that the first of two conflicting descriptions of a boy determined the final impression but that the second description tended to be ignored. It is to some extent reassuring that the rigidity of first impressions can be reduced by warning the person making the judgement of its dangers. If teachers are made aware of the misleading nature of first impressions, they can be on their guard and ready to accept further evidence. However, first impressions can easily be created by others' prior judgements. In a now classic experiment Kelley (1950) informed one group of students that a speaker was a cold person, another group that he was a warm person, thus creating prior expectations (or a mental set) for them. This mental set duly had its effects in that those expecting the speaker to be cold and distant saw him as such and participated less in discussion than did the other group. Moreover their impression of him was rigidly held and was not altered by subsequent evidence. There are clearly many occasions when teachers are exposed to a mental set of this kind created by others, such as in staff-room gossip where teachers prepare a new colleague for troublemakers (Hargreaves, 1972) or from reports and record cards made available to him. Impressions offered by others are particularly undesirable when we remember that children do in fact behave differently according to the way in which teachers treat them (Nash, 1973). To be influenced by another teacher's impressions would mean that the newcomer picked out and interpreted cues from a child's behaviour that conformed to a prior judgement with the result that similar teacher-pupil interaction would be perpetuated.

Kelly's study suggested that within a cluster of characteristics detected in a person there is a central feature which is likely to affect one's whole picture of him; a person described as warm was seen as generally acceptable and likeable, for example. Asch (1946) had already identified such a central dimension and found in fact that whereas terms like warm and cold do seem to colour one's whole picture of a person being judged, others like polite or blunt are less central in that they have little effect on other dimensions. This halo effect, as it has been called, seems to be a consistent feature of the way in which most people make judgements of others. Since most people expect their ideas about others to be consistent, they expect those they rate highly on a valued trait to possess other positive traits to a similar degree.

If this is a general feature of person perception, then its implications for teachers are obvious. A teacher who sets high store by neatness, tidiness, well-spokenness, politeness might well perceive a child possessing these characteristics as more assiduous, interested, and highly motivated than one devoid of them. Such children tend to be found on the top table in the infant classroom long before streaming is admitted to be happening. Jackson (1964) suggested that well-spoken, neatly dressed children tended to be found in A streams of junior schools. Is this because they conform to the teacher's image of an A stream stereotype or because more intelligent children *are* neatly dressed and so on? Related to the halo effect is the tendency to base one's judgements on a logical error, that is, to suppose that the possession of one characteristic automatically implies another. Such traditional beliefs as 'all redheads are hot tempered' probably originated in this way. This kind of error can be perpetuated by accidental reinforcement. The case of one redhead who is in fact hot-tempered confirms the view previously held, so that from then on one notices redheads who have this characteristic, but not those devoid of it. Such impressions can also be confirmed by particular authority sources. Many falsely held assumptions surely stem from one's parents whose word in early childhood is not doubted.

Just as in object perception, the way we judge other people can be affected by our needs and values. Several laboratory experiments have shown that where subjects value high status, they see those holding positions of high status as more powerful, more influential than those of lower status, even in the absence of any objective evidence (Thibaut and Riecken, 1955). Similarly we tend to judge favourably those who fulfil our needs. Could it be that a teacher who feels a particular need for success and fear of failure will tend to judge more favourably on all characteristics those children who do well and thus satisfy the teacher's need for success? The likelihood of this is certainly strong enough for teachers to be aware of its possible dangers.

One question arising from this discussion of person perception is whether there are certain types of people who are more susceptible to such influences and less aware of them than others. It seems that everyone is *likely* to be affected by mental set, first impressions, halo effect, but that some people are more ready to recognize further evidence than others and to alter their judgements accordingly. Adorno *et al.* (1950), in a large-scale study of personality along an authoritarian-democratic continuum, identified the authoritarian type as one who, among other characteristics, tends to hold stereotyped views of other people, failing to recognize individual characteristics, once he has labelled a person and slotted him into a preexisting category. If a teacher uses such categories as 'working-class children', 'the culturally deprived', 'West Indian immigrants' and attributes certain characteristics to all those he sees as belonging to any of these groups, his judgements are bound to be biased. Stereotypes are in fact wrong much of the time because they are over-inclusive. People holding them will not recognize contrary evidence. Frenkel-Brunswik (1948) describes such people as being 'intolerant of ambiguity', meaning that they are not ready to accept new evidence if it is inconsistent with ideas they already hold and are slow even to perceive change. A further unfortunate attribute of the authoritarian type is that he is not self-reflective. He tends to shy away from analysing his own feelings, motives, reasons for action and so is less likely to question the validity of the views he holds.

Implications of teachers' judgements for pupils' school careers

At the beginning of this chapter it was argued that some sort of categorization or typification was necessary and inevitable in any kind of social interaction. Several empirical studies were then examined to illustrate some of the bases on which teachers tend to typify children. However the consequences of such categorizations were found to be undesirable in that they had adverse repercussions for pupils' school careers.

Does this mean then that for some children typification is bound to have adverse effects which cannot be avoided? It would be useful to summarize the particular effects which typification by social class, stream, and race can have upon pupils in order to see how undesirable consequences might be avoided. One highly useful concept to draw upon is Becker's notion of the ideal pupil. But by implication any pupil who does not conform to this ideal is automatically a deviant in some way. He deviates from the ideal in terms of behaviour, being judged as unruly and disruptive in class. He is not expected to behave as well as the ideal pupil and in fact fulfils these expectations. Hargreaves' D stream boys are in fact unpopular with their peers if they conform to the teachers' standards of acceptable behaviour. Attitudes towards school of those pupils labelled as failures or belonging to an antischool group tend to deteriorate so that they refuse to participate even in those activities which they enjoy and excel at. Because their status in school is low, they seek recognition elsewhere, often prematurely adopting adult roles, as did Lacey's pupils who drank and smoked on the school premises and refused to wear school uniform. With their rejection of school values and norms goes their rejection of anything the school might offer in terms of achievement and qualification. Teachers expect them to work slowly, to find difficulty in understanding material that is accepted by the ideal pupil, thus they are presented with less demanding tasks, their aspirations and motivation are reduced, and eventually their performance is lowered. The self-fulfilling prophecy has indeed taken effect. Pupils have conformed to the picture of themselves presented to them by their teachers. Naturally the same effect works positively. Children of whom high expectations are made live up to these and A stream children succeed. Does this means that teachers were justified in placing them in an A group or that teachers' expectations raised their aspirations, resulting in superior performance? To talk of the effects of a self-fulfilling prophecy must involve some discussion of a pupil's self-image. If he sees himself as a failure, he becomes one. But what helps to create this self-image?

If we accept Mead's notion of the self as a process rather than a structure, that is, something constantly changing and developing during the course of the individual's interaction with other people, particularly with those who are important to him, we can see that the way in which he learns to see himself is influenced partly by the way in which others see him and act towards him. Because this concept of the self is essentially an active process, the individual is seen as acting towards the world and others in it, interpreting what confronts him and organizing his action accordingly.

If we consider this notion of the self in relation to pupils' self-concepts in the classroom it follows that a child can only construct his self-concept by reference to the behaviour of other people towards him, both teachers and peers. Interactionist theory (the framework within which Mead writes) predicts that children perceived unfavourably by teachers and peers will develop unfavourable self-concepts, since through interaction they learn to see themselves as others see them – unfavourably.

Nash (1973), working within this framework, put this hypothesis to the test in his study of teacher expectations. On the basis of preliminary observations made in a small primary school over a period of a year, he set out to discover whether pupils' self-concepts, as illustrated by their behaviour in class, would vary according to the way in which they were judged by teachers. His hypothesis was that the behaviour of children in classes where they are perceived favourably by the teacher would be different from where they are perceived unfavourably. An investigation of how pupils behaved towards teachers they encountered in their first year of secondary schooling confirmed the hypothesis. Children who admitted to 'playing up' in class with those teachers they did not get on with and judged to be too soft or boring, behaved well and were said to behave well by teachers who judged them more favourably. Nash suggests that teachers' expectations will also affect pupils' academic behaviour in a similar way in so far as the teacher's interaction with any pupil will contribute towards his self-concept. A further empirical investigation supported this view. Children were asked to rate themselves and others according to their relative position in class. With very few exceptions their own estimate of their relative position in class corresponded to the teacher's view of them. It is interesting to note that when Nash examined friendship groupings, he found that cliques were made up predominantly of children either unfavourably or favourably perceived by their teacher. It seems then that teachers' views of children also affect their friends' views and expectations of them, so that an unfavourable self-image derived from teachers' views is even more reinforced by peers' views. Hargreaves too noted in his study of fourth-year boys that those perceived unfavourably by teachers tended to form friendships with one another and not with those judged favourably by teachers and vice versa. Very few friendship bonds were found between A and D stream boys.

Pidgeon (1970) has indicated two ways in which a teacher's attitudes and perceptions might influence pupils' behaviour. Firstly, if he regards certain parts of his curriculum content to be above a pupil, he simply will not attempt to teach it, but will select something less demanding (*cf.* Keddie, 1971). Secondly, if a pupil is led to believe that he is capable of little, he will have low expectations of himself, low motivation and consequently will achieve little. Nash's study lends support to these views. Through their interaction with teachers, pupils discover the teachers' views of them by the way in which teachers treat them.

Bearing this in mind, we might argue that it is simply not feasible to say that lower working-class children or West Indian immigrants perform poorly in school *because* they come from poor backgrounds unless we can confirm that they *still* perform poorly even when teachers behave towards them in exactly the same way as they behave towards children from higher social classes born of British parents. This clearly is an assumption that has never been tested, and in fact would be difficult to test, since subtle cues teachers might give to indicate a different judgement of their pupils are difficult to observe and record. But until such an investigation has been made it is dangerous to make such a judgement in good faith.

One very serious consequence of judging, labelling, and categorizing pupils lies in its implications for curriculum organization. When pupils are categorized and treated differently, even though often in the interest of apparent justice, it often follows that they are given access to different kinds of knowledge from a very early age. In other words, not only can a hierarchy of pupils be distinguished but a hierarchy of knowledge as well.

Young (1971) suggests that school knowledge can be seen as socially organized or constructed. At the risk of oversimplification, this implies that different kinds of knowledge acquire a different status. In our education system high-status knowledge has the following main characteristics: it is highly abstract, unrelated to everyday life, and ranks higher than practical activities. It is based on literary rather than on practical skills or oral communication; it emphasizes individual effort rather than group work or collaborative learning; it tends to be the kind of knowledge that lends itself readily to formal assessment. The assumption that some kinds of knowledge are more worthwhile than others has dominated the curriculum in schools in this country – certainly in secondary schools – until very recently. A stream pupils have been offered high-status knowledge characterized as above whereas lower stream pupils tended to be denied access to this kind of knowledge and to be served a diet of practical skills and topic work to be carried out on a group basis. Curriculum projects such as those suggested in the Schools Council Working Paper No. 11,

'Shops and Shopping', 'The 97 Bus', 'The Press', for example, were pr
sented to them because they were supposed to be relevant to everyday life.
Such projects have been very stringently criticized by J. P. White (1968)
and others.

In fact Bantock (1971) goes so far as to suggest that we should develop a
cognitive-intellectual curriculum for able pupils and an affective-artistic
one for the less able. He claims that an academic curriculum, based on
literacy, is inappropriate for the large majority of working-class pupils
who come from a background with a strong oral tradition. He accepts
Jensen's (1969) distinction between two different levels of mental functioning – the conceptual level and the level of associative learning. Children
who can cope only with the latter will be unlikely to manage the increasing
level of abstraction characterizing curriculum content at secondary
school, and therefore he suggests providing for them an alternative curriculum based on easily attainable aspects of everyday life – television,
film, popular press, dance, and other practical skills. But how could
teachers decide who, at a later stage, would be capable of these different
levels of thought, even if a case can be made for them? Are the judgements
made by teachers early in a pupil's school career going to commit pupils to
or exclude them from kinds of knowledge which, it could be argued, are
worthwhile for all?

Shipman (1969) argues vehemently against any kind of differentiated
curriculum on the grounds that it produces inequality. He stringently
criticizes a number of recent curriculum innovations involving topic-
centred approaches, interdisciplinary enquiry, taking children outside the
school, claiming that they can deteriorate into nothing more than a pot-
pourri of trivia selected because they are believed to be of interest to pupils
– but only to pupils categorized as less able. There is a real danger in
separating the education of such pupils and denying them access to any
contact with real academic discipline and moreover in bringing home to
them the reality of their own lower status. Certainly credit is due to
innovators for attempting to make the curriculum more relevant to everyday life and thus more interesting to pupils. But there is a two-fold risk:
firstly, sacrificing academic rigour of any kind, and secondly, maintaining
the existing divisions between children of different abilities and different
social classes.

Merson and Campbell (1974) also voice a particular concern about the
effects of such differentiation, called for by some community education
projects, in terms of the curriculum. They fear that the move towards a
socially relevant curriculum which places little emphasis upon the univer-

sals of rationality or upon rigorous intellectual procedures and language style, far from preparing pupils for greater social and political autonomy, will serve rather to debar them from it. Community-educated pupils, they warn, are likely to be limited by their preoccupation with their own local needs, and will still need others who have had a more rational, universalistic education to be spoksmen for them in any public arena.

Practical implications

We have argued so far about the effects of judgements made by teachers on their pupils during the normal course of a day's teaching. Although such impressions may have long-lasting effects, they are not usually formally recorded. They are undoubtedly open to various kinds of bias, but since they form part of an interaction process, they can constantly be modified according to the way in which pupils react, develop, and change.

On a rather different level are those judgements which are formally documented for specific purposes and are usually on permanent written record for others to consult and use. Once they are written down, they are not open to modification unless further material is added at a later stage. The process now ceases to be a two-way form of communication since what is committed to writing intervenes between the teacher making the judgement and the pupils being judged. The main types of formal judgement with which most teachers are concerned are recordkeeping and report writing, though secondary school heads and sometimes careers teachers will frequently be asked to provide employers with references or testimonials for school leavers.

The main aims of recordkeeping are to assess what a child has achieved in the past and to show his general rate of progress. His achievement in specific curriculum areas is noted so that any serious academic flaw requiring remedial treatment can be spotted and dealt with before it is too late and the child perceives himself as a failure. Curriculum development involving changes in objectives, organization of subject content, and teaching method suggests an increased demand for cumulative records of a pupil's progress at school. Such statements of achievement in the cognitive field must also contain qualitative judgements about children's asethetic, emotional, or moral development. As such, however, they are open to all the biases that we have already discussed.

Teachers' perceptions of individuals can be affected by their own previous experience, the context in which their judgements are made, their own personality make-up, and, of course, by unfavourable comparisons with other pupils. In view of the importance of detailed recordkeeping in a teaching situation that is flexible and allows for individual initiative, it is imperative that due attention be given to the way in which comments are collected, formulated, and recorded. Statements about specific areas of work covered and particular difficulties encountered are more helpful to other people using the records than general comments such as 'works well', 'has not made much effort'. In fact, attempts to assess the degree of effort a pupil has made or statements about his attitude to his work are notoriously difficult. It is impossible to say with any degree of accuracy whether a child is doing his best or not. What can be observed and recorded is whether he persists in the face of difficulties or what to him appear to be boring tasks or whether he becomes so easily frustrated when faced with a taxing problem that he soon gives up. To note such details in the record of a child's progress not only helps the teacher to remember which of his pupils needs a greater degree of encouragement on specific tasks, but also conveys more precisely to others something about a child's approach, without running the risk of labelling him in an overgeneralized or stereotyped manner.

To most teachers, annual or termly report writing is an onerous, time-consuming, and unpopular task, even though the traditional school report form leaves teachers little space to be expansive. Most standard report forms, especially those used in secondary schools, still consist of a list of subjects with columns for examination results, sessional grades, and even perhaps position in class, with only enough room for each subject special-ist to write a brief comment on a pupil's progress in his area. No wonder that stereotyped comments abound. The language of school reports is telegraphic in nature, using clichés like 'works hard', or 'could do better' or even 'only average'. Because these remarks are not specific, they convey very little information to those reading the final document. Teachers' judgements and impressions of pupils which may already have been sub-ject to distortion and bias are necessarily made even more stereotyped by the format in which they are normally required. Because of the dissatisfac-tion expressed by some teachers, alternative methods of reporting on pupils' progress are being explored. S. Jackson (1971) sees the school report as having a three-fold aim: to assess, to diagnose, and to plan for the future. Most traditional reports stop short at the assessment stage, but even so, as we have seen, assessments consisting of an examination result, a grade, and a stereotyped comment are not very informative, open as they are to misunderstandings and misinterpretations on the part of par-ents. One modification of the present system which would reduce the risk of stereotyping pupils and of leaving parents to make what they will of report clichés would be, as Green (1965) and Jackson (1971) both suggest, to convert the report into a two-way communication system between parents and teachers. Parents would be invited to make a written reply on the report form and thus would have the opportunity to help to explain a pupil's lack of progress or to ask for more specific information on how to help pupils overcome difficulties. Such a report might be sent home well in advance of parents' evenings so that consultations with teachers could be based on issues which had already received thought and consideration by all those concerned. A few schools have already adopted a system of two-way reports of this kind and it is to be hoped that freer and more informed discussion of pupils' progress and personal development will in time help to eliminate or reduce the number of biased judgements made by teachers of pupils or by parents of teachers. A further possibility mentioned by Jackson (1971) and by Hargreaves (1972) is to include a space on the report form for pupils' comments. This would extend the possibilities of communication even further into a three-way network where parents, teachers, and pupils could participate and exchange information and explanations. It would surely contribute to a pupil's educational experience as well as promoting home-school relationships which are now recognized as of vital importance if pupils are to be judged fairly.

An alternative to the traditional school report, adopted by a few schools (Roussel 1973, Jackson, 1971), is to send a detailed and personal letter to parents, commenting on their child's progress. Letters, by their very nature, invite a reply. The writer is free or should feel free to use the kind of language he judges most appropriate, rather than being restricted to stereotyped phrases or clichés, as space in a letter is not limited.

Most of these alternative methods would probably prove more time-consuming than compiling a more limited report form, but should be infinitely more rewarding and worthwhile to teachers, parents, and particularly pupils. After all, any innovations or modifications which are designed to improve a system which has come to be regarded as unsatisfactory do need time spent on them. If teachers, parents, and pupils are concerned about unfair judgements made in an educational context, time and effort in attempting to improve them cannot be spared (Downey, 1977).

Summary and conclusions
In this chapter we have first of all outlined briefly the nature of interpersonal judgements and have then shown with reference to empirical studies some of the ways in which pupils are categorized. The relationship be-

tween supposed educability and social class is explored, with some discussion of differentiation according to measured ability, race, and sex.

We have considered some of the factors that influence teachers' judgements of pupils, including their concept of the ideal pupil together with their educational aims and objectives and also their own personality make-up.

The implications of biases or distortions in judgement for pupils' school careers have been pointed out and finally some practical issues relating to report writing and recordkeeping have been examined.

3 Concepts of Intelligence

The nature of intelligence

We saw in the last chapter some of the ways in which teachers judge children and some of the dimensions on which they judge them. Although not the sole aim of education, and, some might argue, not even the main aim, nevertheless, the development of children's intellectual abilities is something that most teachers hope to promote. If this is the case, judgements have to be made about children's abilities, so that an understanding of what these involve is essential if children are to be fairly assessed.

For most teachers the term 'intelligence' is associated primarily with notions of testing or measuring intellectual ability by some kind of standardized test. Few pause to consider that measurement itself assumes one particular concept of intelligence, but it is not the only one and perhaps not even the most important one. The same teachers would not feel, however, that they had to know a child's IQ (test score) in order to say whether he usually acted intelligently in the playground or laboratory for instance. A still further issue is at stake when teachers are planning appropriate work for their pupils, where one of their aims is usually to promote intellectual development. Furthering intellectual development does not mean helping them to gain a higher test score, but to develop the ability to grasp relationships, to think logically, and to deal effectively with their environment to the best of their ability. These everyday issues with which teachers are faced indicate at least two different perspectives from which mental growth or intelligence can be viewed: the psychometric view, concerned with the measurement of abilities, and the developmental view, concerned with the structure of abilities. Which approach to mental growth is adopted by investigators depends on the purposes of the investigation, but if teachers are to use theories of mental growth to guide practice they must see the two perspectives as essentially complementary, not contradictory. Both approaches provide useful starting points for the assessment and interpretation of human mental abilities on the one hand and afford practical guidance in planning of work, assessing children's progress on the other, provided that teachers understand the basis of the theoretical framework.

But before we go on to look at these two broad theoretical perspectives, it will be useful to look at the very general concept of intelligence, which is both evaluative and descriptive. It is used evaluatively in that it is considered a prized ability. It is generally thought better and more valuable to be intelligent than unintelligent for obvious reasons. It must be stressed however that the term 'intelligence' is a *morally* neutral one. There is nothing inherently moral in being highly intelligent. Such misuse or misunderstandings of the term can have unfortunate repercussions for those about whom judgements are being made. In a school system that values intelligence and achievement above all else, teachers might easily be misled into judging an intelligent pupil as a better person all round.

If, on the other hand, we use the term 'intelligence' purely descriptively, we need to know what characteristics are being picked out, and how to recognize intelligent behaviour.

Ryle (1960) suggests that to act intelligently is to think about what one is doing. Thus it would not be possible to act intelligently by accident or by chance. A young child for example might accidentally do something that for his age would appear exceptionally intelligent, but if it were not incorporated into his learning patterns and were not repeatable, in other words, if he could not yet learn from his own experience, this would not count as intelligent behaviour, but only a chance happening. Thinking about what one is doing is clearly seen in the performance of motor skills which very often give the appearance of being performed automatically, as if by habit. Yet it is only because the performer has thought about what he was doing in learning the skill that he can cope with disruptions, even serious ones, without a subsequent breakdown in performance. A skilled driver is usually able to cope with an unexpected hazard on the road because he is thinking about his actions, even though performance under normal conditions appears so smooth as to be deceptive.

It is important not to confuse the ability to carry out a complex skill which has been learned with *any* kind of complex routine. MacIntyre (1960) suggests that this would be a mark of intelligent behaviour. But if it is, then the statement must certainly be qualified. Sticklebacks carry out highly complex routines as in courting and mating behaviour, yet this is instinctive and unadaptable rather than intelligent. Similarly, obsessives perform such complex routines that one minor false step causes them to go back to the beginning of the whole ritual again – hardly intelligent behaviour since it is both maladaptive and unadaptable. This kind of complex routine fails to be intelligent because it betrays no intentionality or purpose. It is merely fixed and rigid and could not be adapted to suit any particular purpose.

It seems then that intelligent behaviour must be intentional and that it must be adaptable to a specific purpose in the mind of the person himself. A machine could be programmed to carry out apparently purposeful activities but could not be called intelligent on these grounds. Behaviour judged as intelligent must of course be related to the age of the person concerned or to any special problems that he has. Thus it would not be particularly intelligent of a normal adult to climb on to a stool to get an object out of reach, but it would be considered intelligent for a two-year-old to do so.

It is a sad fact that all too often physically handicapped children are considered to belong to a different species, when judgements of intelligence are being made. One eleven-year-old blind pupil was praised as highly intelligent because she showed she could count the number of studs on an upholstered armchair – an ability we should not consider remarkable in a normal six-year-old.

If intelligent behaviour is marked by intentionality, adaptability, the ability to profit from experiences, and the ability to think about what one is doing, these criteria might provide teachers with a useful frame of reference within which to observe children in situations other than classroom ones, for instance, watching them around the school, on their way to and from school, in the playground, and on the playing fields. But not all the information needed to assess children's behaviour is observable. What must also be discovered is why children act as they do and whether they have their own reasons for action. These issues necessarily lead to a discussion of motivation and reasons for action.

The criteria suggested however do emphasize the active nature of learning. It is not enough for children to develop intelligence, but also to *use* it to help them to think for themselves in every kind of situation not only in school. If children are taught to think for themselves in school, that is, are taught to develop independence in this respect, then there is every hope that regardless of ability differences they will continue to use their intelligence and to act as rational human beings after they have left school.

Two theoretical perspectives
The two theoretical perspectives on the nature of intelligence can now be discussed in detail, together with some of their implications for education.

Psychometry is concerned with mental measurement. The main interests of psychologists such as Galton, Spearman, and Burt lay in examining individual differences in measured intelligence and in attempting to discover what kinds of abilities go to make up what we call intelligence. Around the turn of the century there arose a pressing educational need to detect those children who, because of apparent dullness, were not able to profit from normal schooling. When Binet was asked in 1904 by the Paris Education Authorities to assist in discovering such children, he began to develop individual tests of ability, designed specifically to rank children of the same age according to their relative brightness. Without going into detail on the history of mental testing, suffice it to note that many more individual and later group tests were developed for similar purposes. The Army 'Alpha and Beta' tests in 1916 were constructed to test and place recruits to the US Army. After the war and in the 1920s such tests were used to help to select bright children for secondary schools and able adults for civil service positions and for similar selective entrance purposes. They were designed then to measure certain cognitive abilities which were thought to be largely independent of direct teaching and, although it was never claimed that purely innate capacity could be measured, the tests were assumed to give some indication of a child's innate ability to reason.

Some definitions of intelligence reveal the kinds of ability intended to be tapped by such tests. Burt's definition of intelligence (1955) as an 'innate, all-round cognitive ability' suggests firstly an emphasis on abilities a child is born with, although in a later article (1966) Burt reminds his critics that he never denied the importance of environment. Secondly, it implies that these abilities are of a general, nonspecific nature (*cf.* Spearman's 'g' factor) and thirdly that they are cognitive only, excluding by definition motivational elements.

Vernon (1969) sees intelligence as referring mainly to the ability to grasp relationships and to think symbolically, again with an emphasis on the cognitive side. But we must remember that a person's inclinations and

motivation are probably just as important in determining his achievements, including achievement on an intelligence test, as his abilities. Stott
(1966), for example, suggests that a child's ability to solve any problems,
including those in an intelligence test, depends partly on the 'effectiveness
motivation' he has developed in the past. Stott and Sharp (1968) compiled
an 'effectiveness motivation scale' designed to tap manifestations of effectiveness in preschool children over a wide range of activities. Since however it is far easier to observe and measure what a person can do than to
assess his willingness to do it, the effort he puts into it or his reasons for
doing it, psychologists have tended to concentrate on the cognitive aspects
and to neglect the motivational components of intelligence. It is therefore
interesting to come across an early definition of intelligence by Wechsler
(1944) who includes 'acting purposefully' in his definition. Indeed differences in motivation may well account for some of the discrepancy between
IQ scores gained by Negro and white children where Negro scores are
usually lower. Watson (1970) administered tests to groups of West Indian
children of seven and eight in East London. Children's scores were
significantly higher when they were tested by a member of their own race
rather than by Watson himself. He suggests that a white tester reminds
them of their socially induced inferiority in a white world where they
expect to do less well than their native counterparts. This serves to lower
their level in a test and they therefore perform less well in terms of scores
obtained.

This kind of situation indicates clearly how difficult it is to separate
ability from motivation, and it is salutary to remember how much motivation affects the way in which we use our abilities.

In order later to discover how the concept of intelligence a teacher holds
might affect his educational practice, it will be useful here to pursue some
further issues raised by a psychometric approach to intelligence and, in
particular, the debate over the relative overriding importance of innate or
environmental influences on the development of intelligence, which
became known as the nature-nurture controversy. Experimental data,
adduced to support each side of the argument, was gathered largely from
twin studies. If test scores of identical twins correlate highly, whether the
children were brought up in the same family or in a totally different
environment, then it could be argued that environment must have little if
any influence on measured intelligence. Burt's results (1966) showed that
despite wide differences in the environmental conditions of the identical
twins in his sample, who were brought up separately, the correlations for
intelligence test scores were notably high: Rho = 0.874 as compared with

0.925 for those brought up together. His conclusion was that intelligence, when adequately assessed, is largely though not entirely dependent on genetic constitution. Newman *et al.* (1937) in the USA found far lower correlations for the scores of identical twins brought up separately. For twins brought up together Rho = 0.91 and for pairs brought up apart, Rho = 0.67.*

Much research was devoted to the exploration of the determinants of correlations between test scores. Burt's critical summary of twin studies (1966) shows the kind of argument presented, although recently doubts have been expressed about the validity of these findings. More recently the nature-nurture debate has been reopened in a different context, that of racial differences. Jensen's outspoken article (1969) on racial differences in measured intelligence, with its implications of Negro inferiority, was followed by a series of attacks on his assumptions, methodology, and conclusions. What originated in the 1930s as a theoretical discussion on the relative importance of genetic and environmental determinants of intelligence seems to have been revived as an ideological and even political debate over the supposed intellectual inferiority of some races. The point of it is difficult to see, since it offers no help to teachers who have to deal with particular children rather than generalities.

Of more significance to teachers is the probability that the level of performance of many nonwhite children in British schools tends to be low in comparison with their white peers because of low aspirations and depressed motivation. The risks involved in a limited interpretation by teachers of this kind of finding cannot be overemphasized. If it is assumed that intelligence is largely innately determined, then it could easily follow that these innate differences can be accurately measured at a given age. On the basis of measured intelligence children might then be offered a different kind of education according to what was supposed to be their innate fixed intellectual capacities, as indeed was suggested by the Norwood Committee in 1943. Yet further implications for a differential educational programme would arise in our now multiracial society.

When the intellectual status of various first-generation immigrant groups is assessed by psychometric tests, differences usually are observed. But to offer different kinds of education or even a different kind of curriculum according to measured ability would be totally misguided, since test scores, as has been shown (Vernon, 1969; Watson, 1970), are so easily influenced by cultural and motivational factors (Stott, 1975).

*The values of Rho range from +1 to −1; for general purposes, a value greater than 0.5 in either direction suggests a high degree of correspondence.

It is in fact Bernard Coard's contention (1971) that West Indian children are made ESN in English schools because, as indicated by their measured ability, they are capable only of limited educational achievement. Yet since no psychologist denies the effect of environmental interaction, however small, on the development of intelligence, surely the task of teachers is to understand the nature of environmental influences since the school's job is to create an educational environment even though it can do nothing about innate capacities.

Hebb's view of intelligence A and B suggests the importance of early stimulation for future growth. He conceives of intelligence A as the innate potential for development. This is a genetic component and, since it can never be observed or measured, is purely a hypothetical construct. Intelligence B is seen as 'the functioning of a brain where development has gone on'. Intelligence A then gives the potential for growth, but is manifested only if and when growth takes place. Since growth is not the same as maturation, it depends on some sort of nurture in the form of environmental stimulation. Hebb's own work on brain-damaged patients suggested that early stimulation was most important. Those suffering from later brain damage were far less impaired in terms of thought processes and problem solving than those who suffered similar damage early in life.

This hypothesis received confirmation from two further sources, again by work stemming from Hebb's laboratory. Experimental groups of rats were reared in a 'stimulating' environment, that is, one where the animals had freedom to roam and explore, where plenty of interesting objects were provided to arouse curiosity. Control groups were reared in a restricted environment, that is, in cages where they had little freedom and no new objects to explore. On subsequent tests, the experimental groups were found to be superior in maze learning (a kind of rodent intelligence test). The wide variety of stimulus variation experienced by the experimental animals early in life had given them a head start over the impoverished controls.

The second source of positive evidence supporting the early stimulation hypothesis was the vast amount of work on sensory deprivation, or reduced sensory input, to use the later and more accurate term. Subjects, both human and animal, deprived of sensory stimulation (visual, auditory, or tactile) in early life were found to remain permanently retarded while even adult subjects (as in the well-known coffin experiments) showed impaired vision, with impaired problem-solving ability, for some time after they emerged from the restricted and monotonous environment to which they had agreed to be subjected.

It may not be very helpful to extrapolate from animal or laboratory studies in an attempt to find evidence to support a hypothesis about human growth in natural conditions. Nevertheless such evidence does suggest the overriding importance of early experience for development.

If, then, early stimulation is required for the functioning brain to grow, as it seems certainly is the case, this suggests that however small the effect of the environment might be on the development of innate potential as compared with an inborn component, it is the quality and nature of the environmental influences that are important. And for teachers concerned with practice, no less than psychologists concerned with providing a theoretical explanation, the important question is: what exactly is it that makes an environment stimulating for a particular child at a particular stage of development?

This sort of question which arises from Hebb's work seems to provide a useful link with our other broad perspective on intelligence – the developmental approach of Piaget. It is partly because of the influence of Piaget's work that educators have begun to think of intelligence as more than a mental faculty which simply matures as children grow up. Piaget (1950; 1952) has conceived intelligence in terms of a cumulative building up of complex schemata through the impact of the growing organism and the environment on one another. It is important to consider the origins of the Piagetian approach to intelligence and to remember that whereas intelligence tests were practical tools used to obtain data for educational purposes, Piaget's tasks were designed to test his hypothesis about the child's thinking and concept development. They were intended to explore and reveal differences which became apparent at various stages in any one child's development and were concerned therefore with intra-individual rather than inter-individual differences.

The Piagetian conception of intelligence is then essentially developmental and structural in nature. In his system, intelligence is broadly conceived as an adaptation to the physical and social environment. Since it is developmental, it shows the acquisition of knowledge in terms of adaptation to the environment along certain stage sequences. As children develop and interact with their environment, the structures built at an earlier stage evolve gradually into an integral part of the structure of a later stage. An infant first learns very slowly about the permanence of objects, for example, that a ball he has been playing with does not cease to exist when he cannot see it. This notion of permanence, his first step towards invariance of objects, is necessary to the notion of conservation of quantity which is learned during the stage of concrete operations. If the learning of one concept (in our example, permanence) is essential to the understanding of more complex concepts at a later stage of development, then it follows that the sequence of development must remain constant. The permanence of objects could not be learned *after* conservation of quantity since the understanding of permanence is a necessary condition of conservation. Similarly concrete operations form a basis upon which formal operations can later be learnt. To understand the notion of ratio, for instance, the child has to be able to compare different quantities and consider them in relation to one another rather than an absolute.

In Piaget's detailed description of the stages through which children pass from birth onwards, it emerges that what is of particular interest to him is not so much the products of thought, such as the answer a child gives to a conservation problem, but the processes of thought, namely the methods children use to respond to their environment or the kinds of attempts they make to solve problems set them. This suggests a qualitative approach to the development of intelligence characteristic of the interest in developmental sequences within any one child, rather than a quantitative approach concerned with comparing measured differences between children.

The period of sensory motor or practical intelligence is characterized by a gradual moving away from a world in which the self is undifferentiated from the environment, to one which the child can experience and begin to understand through his actions. He comes to this understanding by first of all making purely perceptual and motor adjustments to objects about him. During this period (lasting for roughly the first two years of the child's life) he is seen to develop from an organism governed purely by his reflexes to a human being whose behaviour is beginning to show intentionality. A young infant will, for example, first look at his own hands when he drops an object he is playing with, and only gradually after much experience in handling objects will he begin to search for it when it is no longer in sight. But he is so far able only to perform actions, not represent them. His understanding of the world is limited to his own physical interaction with it. When he begins to go beyond the purely motor stage, the beginnings of some symbolic representation are apparent.

The child now enters the stage of preoperational thought in which he no longer has to reply on action alone, but can cope with representation. One example of representation is pretending. A child who pretends that a newspaper is a pillow will lie down with his head on it and 'go to sleep'. The preoperational period is characterized still by egocentrism. A child cannot imagine what an object would look like from a different angle; he would draw it as it looks to him if asked to imagine himself in another position. He still tends to centre on only one aspect of a situation, such as the height of a column of water, disregarding its breadth. Thought at this stage tends to be static, because the child cannot understand the link between successive conditions and see them as a coherent whole. It is not unnaturally very similar to sensory motor intelligence upon which it is based.

But as the child begins to decentre, i.e., to be able to focus upon more than one aspect of a situation simultaneously and to see things from other points of view, he gradually develops the notion of invariance, without which more mature logical thought cannot proceed. During this period he shows the first signs of being able to deal with the potential as well as the actual, in that he can predict what *will* be the case even if he has not yet experienced it. If confronted with, say, a series of straws of different lengths placed in order from short to long, he will be able to predict accurately that to continue the series he will need a longer one. But he still cannot say what *might* be the case; he cannot yet deal with the hypothetical which probably belongs to the stage of formal operations. Indeed this is probably the most important general characteristic of formal operational thought. Only as a result of being able to deal logically with reality, the concrete, the here and now, can the adolescent, as he now is, conceive of reality as a part of what might be.

He is now able to deal not only with what is, with the here and now, but also to imagine what might have happened in the past or to conjecture about what could occur in the future. This implies that he must set up a series of hypotheses which in turn he confirms or rejects. This process clearly rests on the notion of invariance which he has already learned and on the ability to perform combinatorial operations. Similarly classification, seriation and correspondence which he learned at the concrete stage now enable him to develop propositional thinking. He is able to spot the logical flaw in the following, by being able to form sets and subsets, that is, to classify.

All Xs are Ys

Here is a Y

Therefore it is an X

According to Piaget's scheme, then, a child is seen as developing through several stages of thinking, each more complex than the last and each one built upon and incorporating the previous one. Piaget postulates no fixed age limits for this development, but maintains that the sequence is constant. The ages he suggests give only very rough guidance. Nor does he imply that everyone goes through all the stages and finally achieves formal operations. Many adults stop short of this. Development does not come about by maturation alone, although it is a maturational process. A child of four could not cope with propositional logic, for example. It has been stressed all along that it is through interaction with the environment that the child develops his ability to think, or his intelligence. Environment clearly plays an important part, but Piaget insists that creating a richer environmental experience for the child will not of itself accelerate his intellectual growth.

A comparison of two perspectives

We are now in a position to be able to compare and contrast the Piagetian and psychometric approaches to the theoretical study of intelligence and then consider their applications to education. Certain conceptual similarities become apparent when the origins of intelligence are considered. The controversy over the contribution of genetic factors to intelligence for instance has already been highlighted in studies taking a psychometric approach. Attempts have even been made to assess the proportion of intelligence attributable to genetic factors. Piaget too, although he does not lay the same kind of emphasis on the problem, acknowledges the importance of genetic factors for the development of intelligence. It follows from an acceptance of genetic factors as part of intelligence that maturation also plays an important part. Piaget as we have seen puts more emphasis on this than do the psychometricians.

In both approaches rationality stands out as the most central characteristic of intelligence. The ability to reason is tested by such problems as CAT:KITTEN as DOG: ? which shows whether the child can perceive relationships. In items such as the odd-man-out type the child is required to recognize which items belong to one class and which is excluded, showing whether he can classify. Or again he is required to continue a number series to show whether he can perceive relationships between numbers, for example, 1, 4, 13, 40, 121 .... For Piaget, reasoning or logical thinking is the essence of mature intelligence. He is concerned not only to find out whether children can give a rational solution to a problem but also and mainly to investigate the thought processes children adopt in trying to reach that solution.

The two approaches also show a methodological similarity in that their means of investigation are not strictly experimental. Experimental treatment would be inappropriate for a psychometric approach, since setting up control and experimental groups of human beings and contriving conditions to influence the development of intelligence would clearly raise ethical issues. The nearest approximation to this is seen in the purely experimental techniques adopted by Hebb in his animal studies and in the work he prompted in the field of sensory deprivation, both of which have a bearing on studies of intelligence. Investigations of intelligence test scores are, as with twin studies, correlational. For Piaget's work traditional experimental methods as such would be quite inappropriate since he is concerned with individuals, not broad differences between groups of individuals. Thus a clinical or natural history approach where the adult talks to one or very few children lends itself most appropriately to his aims.

Although the two approaches do not suggest fundamental differences in the nature of intelligence, they do nevertheless examine intelligence from two different perspectives. Such differences can be found in the nature of the genetic component, the course of mental growth, the relative parts played by nature and nurture, and the nature of the environment in early mental development. Both acknowledge some genetic determinant and yet the function of this is seen differently. For Piaget this genetic determinant refers to the stage sequence notion. The individual is constitutionally programmed to pass through the stages in an invariant order, though neither the rate nor the age at which he does so is fixed. In the psychometric approach the genetic determinant is taken to result from the chance combination of genes at conception – chance, because each parent contributes only half his genetic components to the infant. As mentioned earlier, a major part of measured intelligence in later life is attributed to this genetic factor (*cf.* Hebb's intelligence A).

Furthermore, the approaches differ in what they observe about mental growth. Piaget is interested in the nature of mental structures and examines how new abilities arise out of earlier ones. He is concerned with the quality of mental growth and the processes of thought. Mental growth is seen quite differently from a psychometric perspective, which lays more emphasis on the rate of growth than on its nature. Using correlational methods and data, it is claimed to be possible to predict at the age of four with 50 percent accuracy the level of measured intelligence at the age of seventeen; and at eight with 80 percent accuracy. This kind of statistical calculation led to the assumption that measured intelligence at the age of eleven would predict with almost complete accuracy the level of intelligence at seventeen – which may well be statistically correct. What does not follow, as practice has shown, is that the level of intelligence at sixteen or seventeen will correlate highly with school achievement. Tests are of course constructed using scaled items which tap different levels or quality of thought. But differences are concealed in the final numerical score, since points are given for the correct answer rather than for the type of answer or process of reasoning.

The nature-nurture controversy has already been discussed in relation to the psychometric approach where the proportion of variance in intellectual ability has been attributed separately to heredity or environment. In contrast to this rather static view, Piaget sees the contributions of nature and nurture as active in the way they control various mental activities. In his view we inherit the processes of assimilation and accommodation. Assimilation processes are prompted from within (nature), whereby the individual takes in new experiences from the outside and adapts or accommodates to them, thus building new schemata by revising or restructuring his former knowledge. Accommodation processes are thus affected by the environment. The two are constantly interacting (the process of equilibration) and, depending on the particular mental activity, their relative contribution will fluctuate. Symbolic play such as pretending is largely assimilative whereas imitation by its very nature is largely a matter of accommodation.

A fourth important difference is seen between the two approaches in the emphasis placed on the role of the environment in early mental development. Hebb, as we have seen, lays enormous stress on an environment rich in variation of experience in the early years. Yet further research has shown the importance of health factors for mental growth even before birth, for example the diet of the mother during pregnancy and of the infant from three to six months after birth (Harrell et al., 1955; Stoch, 1967); or of oxygen availability at birth. It is established too that certain diseases and drugs during pregnancy can have a serious retarding effect on the mental development of the baby. Young infants have been shown to need a rich variety of visual, tactile, and motor experiences. A child needs to explore his environment in order to become familiar with different sizes, shapes, weights. He needs to gain different tactile experiences and to recognize by touch what is hard, soft, or furry in texture. To profit from a stimulating environment he needs a background of security as a base and the freedom to explore, unencumbered, what is around him, in order to find out what his world is like and how it works. The emphasis on early experience as will be seen later led indirectly to the introduction of pre-school enrichment programmes for so-called deprived children. If evidence suggests that certain factors retard mental growth and certain others tend to accelerate it, it follows that this information could be useful in guiding favourable child-rearing techniques and planning early school programmes.

Piaget's view of the role of the environment in development is rather different, in that it is built into his whole conception of intelligence. By stressing the biological nature of the development of intelligence, with its emphasis on maturation, he does not reduce the importance of environmental interaction. On the contrary, his theory is based on the notion that intellectual development cannot take place without interaction with the environment. Intelligence for him *means* constructing one's knowledge of the world. Therefore environmental factors are the medium through which intelligence can develop at all. It must therefore be influenced by the constraints of this medium. But although environmental interaction forms an integral part of the growth of intelligence, Piaget does not acknowledge that an increased concentration of specific environmental experiences, as in training techniques, can accelerate mental growth since it is constrained by biological and maturational factors. Experimental attempts have been made to contradict this view (Churchill, 1958), but results remain equivocal, although Sigel *et al.* (1966) found that special experience helped children who were at a transitional stage. Cross-cultural evidence supports the invariance of the stage sequence notion. Yet different kinds of experience seem to suggest a retarding effect in some areas (Greenfield, 1966).

Educational implications

Now that the characteristics of the two perspectives have been outlined, together with their similarities and differences, it is appropriate to examine their educational implications. It is a pity that in most introductory textbooks of educational psychology under the chapter heading 'Intelligence' we find only a discussion on intelligence testing with an outline of the psychometric conception of intelligence. It is not surprising if teachers come to hold this as the only approach, since work on Piaget is almost always discussed in a quite different section of the book, under the heading of 'Development of thinking' or 'Concept development in young children' or simply 'The work of Jean Piaget'. However, changes that have been taking place in schools over recent years, particularly in the education of young children, bear evidence to the impact of Piaget's work on educational practice.

First however, let us explore the implications of the psychometric view for selection and grouping, teaching method, the curriculum, and motivation. If intelligence is thought to be determined largely by innate factors, then it follows that children of different abilities can be sorted out by some kind of test and, if it is deemed appropriate, the same 'kinds' of children can be grouped together in a homogeneous class for educational purposes. This would be possible, however, only if tests could predict fairly reliably what a child's ability would be like some years in the future. Evidence to support the reliability of prediction is found, for example, in the work of Bloom (1960) though contrary evidence is quoted by Vernon (1969).

It was this interpretation of intelligence that influenced the Norwood Committee when they made their recommendations for the future of secondary education in 1943.

Tripartism thus became the dominant pattern of secondary education after 1944, although it was not built into the Education Act of that year. And indeed it seemed at the time a logical argument to say that if children differ in ability then it was only fair to treat them differently. On this kind of argument equality of educational opportunity seemed to be based, as we shall see later. Unfortunately many other factors were overlooked, not least the effects of environmental influences on test performance and measured intelligence. Not only were children selected for different kinds of education, but once in the supposedly appropriate secondary school, they were again grouped by ability into streams designed to create classes of a fairly narrow ability range in the hope that the teacher's job would be easier in that all children would learn at the same pace. Junior schools too were affected by the new system of secondary selection. Streaming was even more widely practised than before, so that children in A streams could race ahead to secure coveted selective places in grammar schools.

Grouping children like this, both within the school and within the system, led not surprisingly to the attachment of ability labels to children. The A streams were the intelligent who could do well and who needed stimulating work and experienced teachers. The lowest streams were those who by nature were low on the intelligence scale and could never be expected to achieve very much in school. Teachers' judgements tended to be influenced by such expectations, as later research has shown (Goodacre, 1968; Rist, 1970; Downey, 1977) so that even without their awareness possibly they tended to underestimate those labelled as 'dull', to provide less interesting and stimulating work for them in the firm belief that whatever they did for the children, they would never be able to achieve very much.

Ability differences soon came to be associated with social class. Teachers expected children from middle-class families to be bright. As Jackson (1964) and Douglas (1964) showed, a preponderance of middle-class children, yet very few lower-class children, found themselves in A streams.

Intelligence tests as so far developed seem to test mainly those abilities, for example, certain kinds of verbal ability, which middle-class children develop apparently more easily than those from the lower working class. Such test results tend to confirm the link between class origin and measured ability. Measured intelligence was now no longer a statistical construct. It was fast becoming a social construct, with all the overtones of labelling and typification which have recently been brought into the limelight (Downey, 1977).

During the 1950s attention turned from the innate roots of intelligence to the importance of environmental factors during the early years. One of the consequences of this recognition was the interpretation of the failure of working-class children who did not develop as their early potential had predicted in terms of lack of stimulation in the home. As a result children who failed in school, especially lower working-class children, came to be known as deprived or even culturally deprived (Riessman, 1962). Intellectual stimulation was thought to be so meagre in some families that even those innate abilities with which a child was endowed could not develop sufficiently for him to profit very much from the education provided for him. Ample research, as we shall see later, showing how working-class pupils failed to gain places in an A stream or a grammar school, left school early, failed to seek opportunities offered by further education, all lent support to the deprivation hypothesis. The picture was a very pessimistic one. If a child, especially a girl, happened to be born into a large lower working-class family as a middle child she would stand little chance of developing her intelligence and profiting from education (Little and Westergaard, 1964).

In the USA research of a different kind was sparked off by this same deprivation hypothesis. If early environment is so important for the development of intelligence, the argument ran, and there are many families who do not or cannot provide their younger children with appropriate stimulation in the early years, then the school must intervene and do it for them. In this way were launched intervention or compensatory programmes such as Headstart, High Horizons, and so on, where children were given special preschool experience intended to rouse them intellectually and compensate for the deficiencies of the home, thus preparing them for school proper. This practical approach showed a more optimistic attitude than did some of the research being done in Britain at the same time. Yet early intervention programmes failed because they were founded on a mistaken view of cultural deprivation. Children may well have come from an intellectually stultifying environment, but the way to salvation was not to be via a different culture, the mainstream culture of white Americans imposed upon all children. Bernstein (1968) came near a solution when he suggested that what was needed was not compensatory education but education itself.

To consider now the effects of a psychometric view of intelligence within the classroom. Since in this view it is not intellectual development that is stressed but rather the accumulation of knowledge and skills to be assessed quantitatively, teaching tends to be largely instructional. Knowledge is selected by the teacher and directly imparted to pupils who are docile learners, absorbing what is offered to them and reproducing what the teacher knows, if they are successful. Or, if they are failures, they are passive nonparticipants in what goes on in the classroom. This model of teaching sees the teacher as the one who does most of the talking, as Flanders' analysis confirms (1971). He it is who takes the opportunity of using, practising, and extending his language skills, rather than his pupils who are required to give one-word answers to specific questions.

Curriculum content is selected for children according to their ability. The former sentiments of the Norwood Committee still seem to be followed in many secondary schools where the A stream or band is offered an 'academic' curriculum including one or more foreign languages, perhaps also Latin; specialized courses in Physics, Chemistry, Biology in addition to the basic traditional curriculum subjects such as Mathematics, English, History, Geography. Little opportunity is given to these pupils to pursue practical subjects such as Handicraft, Art, Home Economics, Child Welfare, etc., which are reserved for the less able who are not expected to be able to cope with the supposedly more theoretical disciplines. Thus develops a hierarchical view of the curriculum with a stratification of knowledge of the kind criticized by Young (1971).

Motivation on this model is usually extrinsic. If ability is innate and little can be done to change it, then children need to be motivated to use what ability they have to its fullest. To arouse this motivation we find a series of incentives in the form of good marks, prizes, class positions, and so on. Those gaining most honours tend to be most highly thought of in this system, thus the risk of producing a generation that over-values recognizable rewards is great. If children under this system become interested in what they learn rather than in the reward they get for it, it is surely largely a matter of chance.

Assessment usually takes the form of formal tests and examinations.

Results are expressed numerically, making it a quantitative rather than a qualitative issue. A bright pupil who has done little all the year can suddenly put on a spurt and attain high marks in formal examinations, thus getting more public credit than a slow one who has put in much effort throughout the year but whose performance at the end does not match his constant application.

Piaget's developmental view of intelligence implies a very different model of education. It is one whose function is to guide the developing child through the stages of intellectual growth, providing him with an appropriately structured curriculum in terms of learning sequences, yet allowing him freedom to discover and structure knowledge for himself. This naturally has implications also for teaching method, motivation, and assessment. Unlike the psychometric approach which allows children to be grouped and taught as a group according to measured ability, what follows from the developmental approach is essentially individualized teaching and learning. Not all children of a given age level have reached the same stage of cognitive development, nor indeed does an individual child show the same cognitive structures or develop at the same rate across all fronts. He may be at one stage in one conceptual area and at a different one in another. To try to teach a whole class of children as if they were all at one stage in everything is to deny the importance of individual rates of growth as revealed by Piagetian research. For those children who are not yet ready to cope with the concepts involved, the content will mean little and they will make little or no progress. For those who have already mastered those concepts, it will mean nothing but repetition of what they already know, with little or no novelty to activate their minds. Learning on this model of intelligence must by its very nature then be individualized. And since the classroom is the environment in school with which the child interacts to structure his intelligence, teaching methods must allow for this interaction. Discovery and enquiry methods are best suited to this, and to offer optimum opportunities for intellectual growth, the material must be geared to the child's own stage of development. Again, the appropriate dimension of discovery is important. As Richards (1973) reminds us, discovery learning need not always be at a concrete level as it is for younger children. Adolescents discover too, but symbolically through the use of language, by exploring hypotheses either alone or in cooperation with their peers.

We saw that on our other model it was the teacher who did most of the talking in the classroom, in imparting knowledge to children and questioning them on specific points of fact. Since children's language conveys their thought, although it is not synonymous with thought, to listen and to get to understand children's language is one of the first priorities of a teacher. Children's modes of thinking make them in a way cognitive aliens to adults so, in order to diagnose the stage of thinking they have reached, teachers clearly must learn to communicate with children and from what they say will infer what their conceptual world is like – the method Piaget himself used. The younger the child, the more tortuous his thinking and the more bizarre his world may appear to adults. In a child's world for example the sun and moon follow him as he is walking along; dreams fly in through the window; everything that moves is alive. Unless the teacher is able to talk to the child seriously at his own level, no appropriate discourse will develop during which he can confront a child, when he is ready, with the illogicalities of his own thought, thus creating cognitive conflict and preparing the way for the child to pass on to the next stage. Questioning is thus at a premium since this can reveal to a child an inherent conflict in his *own* argument. Judicious questioning serves to orient the child towards inconsistencies in his own thinking or phenomena that might otherwise be overlooked or even taken for granted. This kind of questioning is very different from that employed by teachers who merely want to find out whether a child has learned what he, the teacher, has just said. The contrast between the two kinds of questioning reveals the difference between the child as an active learner and as a passive automaton parroting the right answers. The language children use can however sometimes conceal lack of understanding of the underlying concepts. Sigel (1961) has shown how a child's understanding of the concept 'brother' is far from complete until he has acquired the notion of reciprocity and realizes that he can also be a brother. Similarly Jahoda (1963) has revealed children's partial understanding of concepts of nationality.

Teaching methods must however be geared not only to the stage of conceptual development of the learner, but also to the nature of the subject matter. Once a teacher has diagnosed the child's level of conceptual functioning, he has to be able to select appropriate content to build into the learning situation. This means having a clear understanding of the structure and organization of the areas of knowledge that lend themselves to this kind of analysis. Piaget's work offers most useful guidance in the field of science, especially physical sciences, and mathematics. His own use of material in these areas to explore the children's thinking can offer some direct guidance (Lovell, 1961). But principles of the stage sequence concept can be applied also to other curriculum areas such as geography (Prior, 1959; Peel, 1972), religion (Goldman, 1964), history (Hallam,

1969). Possibly the idea of sequential structure can also be applied to areas hitherto unexplored in this way, such as children's understanding of the tragic and of some social phenomena. Certainly Piaget's own work in the sphere of moral development is of enormous help to teachers generally and might form the basis of any programme of moral education designed for schools.

In Piaget's view, learning is a continuous process. If teachers acknowledge that children are learning something all the time, even if apparently not what they had planned for them to learn, then the question of motivation is of particular interest. Children inevitably learn by being in contact with an environment with which they interact. Motivation then comes to be built into the very process of living in a physical or social environment and coming to terms with it. Provided a child is made aware of discrepancies and inconsistencies in his growing consciousness of his world, the cognitive dissonance thus created spurs him on to make sense of his experiences and attain a more complex stage of thought. Cognitive conflict can be seen as a kind of intrinsic motivation, provided that children recognize the existence of such ambiguities.

In assessing what children have learned it would be quite inappropriate to use a right/wrong answer technique. On a Piagetian view children's answers are rarely completely wrong, but may show only partial understanding. Before he learns that left and right are relative terms, for example, a child will use them as absolutes, as they are in fact in the context of right hand/left hand. But such reasoning is not wrong, only limited. On the other hand, a right answer might score a point if a child's knowledge were being assessed quantitatively, but as we have seen, right answers frequently conceal misunderstandings. So rather than evaluating children's answers as right or wrong it is more appropriate to perceive them as an expression of the child's current stage of mental reasoning, since it is only in this way that the next step can be gauged. Evaluation itself seems to play a different function here. On the Piagetian model it serves as a guide for the teacher in planning and structuring future learning sequences for the individual child, whereas from a psychometric perspective, evaluation serves, because of its quantitative nature, to compare an individual with others.

Creativity and intelligence

So far this discussion of intelligence has centred round the ability to think rationally, to learn from experience, and to perform concrete or formal operations. The investigation of individual differences in abilities has been one of the main concerns of psychologists working within the psychometric framework, yet they have pursued an interest in the quantitative rather than qualitative differences, attempting to measure and compare individuals in a scalar fashion. Examination of the content of intelligence tests however has revealed little of qualitative difference between individuals' modes of thinking and little that is of an obviously creative nature.

Before the 1950s little interest had been shown by psychologists, or in general by teachers, in creative performance. If an outstanding individual was generally acknowledged as a genius in his own field, he was thought to be endowed with certain qualities that ordinary people did not have. In the 1950s however there was a surge of interest in creativity, especially on the part of psychologists, some of whom, such as Guilford, saw creativity as a national investment in various spheres of scientific enquiry, the space race in particular. He describes creative behaviour as including 'such activities as inventing, designing, contriving, composing and planning. People who exhibit these types of behaviour to a marked degree are recognized as being creative' (1950). Creativity and creative productivity were thought to extend far beyond the domain of measured intelligence and consequently attempts were made to trace the relationship between intelligence and creativity. Those making this attempt (for example, Guilford, 1950, 1959; Getzels and Jackson, 1962) were so influenced by the psychometric framework, within which they were working, that their efforts were concentrated on attempts to demonstrate that performance on tests requiring unusual, original, or remote responses was independent to a certain extent of performance on conventional tests of intelligence. This quest for easily objectifiable testing and scoring procedures directed attention towards measurement of something for which oddly enough no appropriate criteria has been established. Open-ended tests were thus designed to assess creativity, yet how to recognize creativity had been given very little attention.

One of the best-known studies of creativity and intelligence is that of Getzels and Jackson (1962) who attempted to differentiate two groups of adolescents on the basis of (1) their scores on conventional intelligence tests such as the Binet or WISC and (2) their scores on open-ended tests, constructed specially for the study and based on the work of Guilford. These tests, including problems of word association, unusual uses, hidden shapes, fables, and making up problems were designed to reveal the creativeness of the adolescents. Creative thinking, observed from the performance of the subjects, was characterized by the ability to 'produce new forms, to risk conjoining elements that are customarily thought of as independent and dissimilar, to go off in new directions ... the ability to free (oneself) from the usual, to diverge from the customary ... to enjoy the risk and uncertainty of the unknown'. Getzels and Jackson compare these tendencies with those of the noncreative performers, who tended to focus on the usual, to shy away from the risk and uncertainty of the unknown, and to seek out the safety and security of the known, with Guilford's factors of convergent and divergent thinking.

On the basis of the data produced by the test scores, Getzels and Jackson were able to distinguish two groups: a high creativity group (subjects in the top 20 percent on creativity measures but below the top 20 percent on intelligence measures) and a high intelligence group (top 20 percent in intelligence, below the top 20 in creativity measures) though, as might be expected, the scores were not completely independent. The experimenters then proceeded to look for further differences between the two groups, such as differences in school achievement, popularity, and personality traits. The interesting feature of this study in the present context is that the characteristics of creative behaviour were deduced from the students' performance on certain tests rather than tests being compiled to assess creative performance for which criteria had previously been set up. Guilford (1959) had suggested criteria by which to recognize creative or divergent thinking which could then be expressed in a quantifiable form. These were fluency (including word-associational-, expressional-, and ideational- fluency), spontaneous flexibility, and originality. In commenting on appropriate testing procedures Guilford says, for example, of ideational fluency that 'sheer quantity is the important consideration; quality need not be considered so long as responses are appropriate'.

Interesting as this kind of work may be, it does not help to answer some questions of real importance for education. Teachers need to know whether creative promise can be discovered in children and whether creative talents can be promoted in school. But the ability to attain high scores on open-ended tests has not been shown to bear any relationship to a child's ability to write a poem, paint a picture, invent a mechanical device, build a model, or indeed to perform any of those activities which a layman might call creative. Nor can the tests predict creative performance later in life. The ability to give an unusual answer to a test question may reveal a difference in willingness to take risks or even a desire to appear bizarre. The fact that convergent thinkers do not give unusual answers does not mean that they have no creative ability. After all, to some highly intelligent children the test may appear trivial and not worth bothering with.

To raise questions about creativity in education or even different modes of thinking requires further analysis of the concept of creativity. As we have seen, intelligence is far more than performance on a test; similarly creativity must be more than test performance. What is needed then for the understanding of the relationship between creativity and intelligence is some kind of conceptual reorientation.

Jackson and Messick (1965) attempt to construct a hierarchial model of creative responses which seems to go further than previous attempts in picking out what might be called a creative performance. Intelligent responses, they suggest, are characterized as being correct in that they satisfy objective criteria and operate within the constraints of logic and reality. Creative performances by comparison are more difficult to recognize because they have to satisfy subjective criteria and are thus open to a wide variety of judgemental standards. Jackson and Messick use the term 'good' to characterize such creative responses and attempt to analyse what constitutes the good in this sense. Their first prerequisite for a creative response or performance, whether it relates to an artistic or scientific product, is the novel, the unusual in the sense of being strikingly different from other products of the same category. A young child's painting, for example, might show features that are unusual for children of his age but would not surprise us in an adult's work. For a creative response to be merely unusual though is not enough. It might be nothing more than odd or bizarre or even totally inappropriate. Appropriateness then is a second or higher order criterion. Thus to be creative a product must be both unusual and yet appropriate to the context. But at this stage the level of creative excellence must be examined. To distinguish levels of creative excellence requires two further criteria: that of transformation of ideas or materials to overcome conventional restraints and condensation of meaning and association. These criteria are both difficult to define and to recognize. Transformation involves not just a restructuring of old ideas but a creation of new forms that generate reflection and wonder in the observer and stimulate him to further thought. Condensation is characteristic of the very highest levels of creative performance. It implies an intensity and concentration of meaning, intellectual or emotional, that can evoke constant contemplation – such as Tolstoy's *War and Peace* or a mature Haydn symphony.

We are not impressed or even awed only at the moment of contemplating a great work of art or a body of scientific theory, but we return to it again and again to discover new features, values, and relationships. For this reason it seems important to offer children aesthetic experiences. If

they have the chance to listen to music or to look at paintings and buildings, and at the same time to learn something about the traditions behind
them, they will learn to appreciate the values inherent in them.

Degenhardt's three main criteria (1976) for recognizing a creative product are interesting and useful as a complement to those set up by Jackson
and Messick. He suggests, as they do, that what is created must be novel,
at any rate to the creator. Secondly, that what is created must be of some
value and, thirdly, that it must be intentionally created. In other words,
the creator must have some idea of what counts as valuable in the field in
which he is working and must also to some extent have mastered the
appropriate skills and techniques so that he has a good idea of what he is
after.

Creativity has traditionally been associated with the notion of creating
something quite new, as if out of nothing. Such a concept of creativity,
Elliott (1971) suggests, stems from the divine myth of creation, but a
newer concept of creativeness allows far more flexibility in what can be
included as creative acts, products, or thinking. This newer concept sees
creativeness as developing novel ideas and either using them to solve
problems for which there is no adequate response in terms of existing
knowledge, methods, or techniques, or simply making them available to
others. This notion of creativity can be thought of as part of what we
understand by imagination.

It seems from this kind of analysis then that all teachers should discover
what creativity means to them and what could count as a creative
response in any particular sphere of children's activity and learning. This
kind of approach is surely far more profitable than attempting to measure
certain test responses, where one's thinking can so easily become
enmeshed in the intracacies of scoring and standardizing. As soon as a
testing approach is adopted, the notion of comparability in creativity
arises. This of all areas in education is surely not one where an element of
competitiveness is at all appropriate. It is interesting to remember, as with
intelligence, that the term creativity can be used descriptively as well as
evaluatively. If we are merely describing a child's thinking as being creative, we wish to point out certain characteristics of that style of thinking
without implying that it is better than any other style. In using the term
evaluatively, it implies that creative thinking is something worthwhile and
something that we want to promote in children. Whereas teachers would
clearly not want to promote or develop any kind of learning or skill that
they did not consider worthwhile, it would be a mistake to undervalue
those achievements which were not considered creative in favour of those

that were. After all, in order to be creative at a high level of excellence, a person must have mastered certain basic skills and have acquired a certain verifiable body of knowledge. A boy cannot be creative in the design workshop, for example, unless he knows something of the properties of the materials he is using and recognizes the constraints they impose upon his freedom to create. Similarly he cannot work upon his materials until he has mastered certain skills and techniques of handling the appropriate tools. Just as there has been a danger of associating moral values with intelligence, a morally neutral term, a similar risk can arise with creativity. Not all children are as creative as others, just as not all are equally intelligent. But those who are less creative (or less intelligent) are not worse people for that.

In recent years in nearly all statements made by teachers, psychologists, educationists about the need for flexibility in education there has been some criticism – at times very heated and at times justifiable – about the iniquities of an education system, both in this country and in the USA, which requires conformity, conventionality, and regurgitation of A level subjects. It must be remembered, in making a distinction between the two groups, that there is no clear cut-off point. Convergers are those who show a *bias* in this direction. In Hudson's study they were those who gained a higher score on an intelligence than on open-ended tests regardless of how high each score was.

However, if some pupils do show a bias towards convergence and others a bias towards divergence, it is interesting to discover whether schools can and do cater for both. A school system which is geared towards the passing of examinations and the attainment of qualifications, especially at secondary level, would seem to emphasize the ability to produce right answers or perhaps what the examiner wants. Thus convergent thinking would tend to be at a premium. Anxiety on this count, stimulated by such as Guilford and Torrance in the USA and by Hudson, Haddon, and Lytton in this country, has served to alert teachers to the dangers of undervaluing one type of thinking. If teachers are less favourably disposed towards divergent children, these children may soon learn to conceal such originality as they have by withdrawing into themselves. Thus potential creativity is stunted early in their school careers.

Schools, however, are not all the same in their social climate or aspirations. Haddon and Lytton (1968) compared two types of primary school, one using more conventional formal methods with an emphasis on achievement, rigid timetabling, and instruction, and the other a more progressive type of school, placing great emphasis upon self-initiated and creative learning. The schools were matched for socio-economic status and the children matched on verbal reasoning scores. Children in the informal schools showed higher scores on open-ended tests than those in the formal schools. Whether these are tests of true creative thinking is in doubt, but the indication that some children were more willing to venture unusual answers does perhaps reflect the freedom to learn that they had experienced in their schools where they moved freely about the classroom, had free access to the school library, and worked much of the time without supervision.

Critics of the traditional authoritarian type of education who have been writing recently within a sociological framework have contrasted two opposing paradigms in the social sciences which have formed a pattern for education (Esland, 1971). One is the psychometric paradigm which as we have seen in our discussion of different concepts of intelligence has been concerned with intelligence testing and a consequent imputation to children of specified levels of academic potential and achievement. This view diverts attention from children's thought processes and individual differences in modes of thinking and has led to a passive view of learning in which the individuality of the pupils, their interpretation of their world, and the meanings they attach to their learning experiences have been neglected to some extent. The phenomenological paradigm which Esland and others would like in its place is one which is concerned with individual ways of knowing, where an active rather than a static notion of the mind is emphasized. Processes of thought are 'seen to be part of a highly complex personal system of interpretations, intentions and recollections' (Esland, 1971). This view of development suggests that learning is a growth process, subject to an individual and personal interpretation and that the mind is capable of unlimited development in many directions.

This view of education with its interest in classroom interaction without rigid teacher control would seem to provide an important conceptual and practical framework, not only for cognitive development along Piagetian lines, but also for the growth of creative thinking. After all, one of the most unfettered and therefore least threatening occasions when creativity can begin to develop in young children is when they are at play.

Although we cannot teach children to be creative, we can provide conditions in which creative abilities can develop, by ensuring that teaching, like play, does not stifle children's imagination by its rigidity and inflexibility. In suggesting what practical action teachers might take if they wish to create a school climate favourable to the development of creative thinking and abilities, Torrance (1967) makes proposals that anticipate just those attitudes being advocated by Esland and others within a phenomenological framework in the sociology of education. Torrance's suggestions are that teachers should be respectful of children's unusual questions and ideas, showing them that these ideas have value. They should provide opportunities for self-initiated learning and for periods of nonevaluated practice, indicating that whatever children do may be of some value and is not constantly going to be assessed by some absolute criterion of correctness set up by teachers. This emphasizes not only the need to value children in their own terms, by acknowledging the worth of common sense knowledge they bring with them into the classroom, but also acknowledges the importance of freedom and flexibility to develop and grow. These seem to be not only the cornerstones of both cognitive and creative development but also part of what is meant by education.

Summary and conclusions
In this chapter we discussed first of all the nature of intelligence, then attempted to identify the ways in which teachers recognize intelligent behaviour in their pupils.

We then compared and contrasted two theoretical approaches to the study of intelligence, the psychometric and the developmental, showing the different methods adopted and the different kinds of evidence sought by supporters of each view.

This led to a consideration of the implications of each approach for educational practice, and suggestions were made about how the grouping of pupils, teaching method, motivation, curriculum, and evaluation might be affected.

Finally, we examined the relationship between creativity and intelligence and pointed to some of the problems encountered in trying to analyse the concept of creativity. We considered some of the psychological studies of creative abilities and different modes of thinking and indicated some of the classroom conditions in which creative abilities might develop.

4 Motivation and learning

The discussion of intelligence and abilities in the last chapter was concerned with one group of preconditions for learning. But to have the
ability does not mean that children will in fact learn; they have also to
wish to learn, to have some interest in what they are learning, and to have
some kind of aspirations in terms of mastery, whether of skills or a body of
knowledge. In discussing motivation we shall thus be concerned with
examining children's willingness to learn, the efforts they expend, and the
reasons they have for doing what they do.

The nature of motivation
Motivation is in many ways difficult to assess because there is no easy way
of objectifying children's actions. When a teacher writes 'Could do better
with more effort' on a child's report, what does he mean by this statement?
How does he know what effort the child is putting into his activities? What
does 'more' effort mean? Similarly, how does a teacher know that a child is
trying hard when he comments that 'X tries hard but finds the subject
difficult'?

It seems that intelligence or the use of intelligence is very closely related
to this question of motivation, so that the two must, if they are going to
make any practical sense, be considered together. It was noted in the

previous chapter that very few definitions of intelligence referred to a motivational factor. Stott (1966) criticizes Burt's view of intelligence as an 'innate, general, cognitive factor' for the very reason that it omits all reference to motivation. Stott argues that the ability a child reveals in solving problems such as those set before him in an intelligence test depends partly upon 'the strength of his intrinsic motivations during the early stages of his development'. He suggests that the ability to solve problems depends partly on the extent to which he has in the past engaged in problem solving which in turn depends upon his 'effectiveness-motivation'. A child without the confidence or desire to widen the scope of his effectiveness in this way will thus remain at a low level of cognitive development. The difficulty lies in distinguishing the influence of motivation from that of ability. It seems that neither can be effective unless developed in early childhood. Suffice it to say at this point that motivation has been a neglected factor; later in the discussion some further psychological ramifications of this will be examined.

Before pursuing further conceptual issues in this area or examining empirical evidence that could give teachers some guidance in the classroom, we must consider some of the questions that teachers would like answered when faced with problems of motivation. The questions that do concern teachers seem to be of two main kinds: those referring to what has happened in the past and those concerning what might happen in the future. Questions referring to the past are raised when children behave unexpectedly or abnormally (either compared with their own usual behaviour or with that of their peers) or when they fail to meet teachers' expectations or standards set for them. For example, a child who is normally a model of punctuality and who suddenly arrives late for school several days in succession makes a teacher ask what the cause of his lateness is. A child who interrupts others in class, perhaps disturbing them when they are absorbed in what they are doing or even destroying some piece of work, will make the teacher ask what is wrong with the deviant. What has got into him? we ask. Or again if a child is failing to learn to read, the teacher will ask what is making him fail or what is preventing him from learning. All such questions seem to require a causal explanation, as if there were some force at work making a child late, some demon inside him making him disruptive, or some barrier preventing him from learning to read. It is as if the child concerned were being made to behave in certain ways either against his will or without his awareness.

The other kinds of question are those concerning what is going to happen in the future: 'what are you doing that for?' 'what are you aiming at?' 'what have you in mind?' Questions like this are designed to find out a child's reasons for action rather than the causes of his behaviour. They show that the speaker regards the child as someone whose behaviour is intentional and who acts usually because he has some purpose or aim in mind.

The implications of these different kinds of question and explanation are various: any given view of man will affect one's view of education. Causal explanations of man's behaviour give an impression of a rather passive, machine-like creature, who is at the mercy of all sorts of forces pushing him along, just as a leaf is blown about by a gust of wind. Perhaps this is an extreme analogy and however much man's behaviour is determined by outside forces, he still retains some autonomy. But causal explanations belong really to the realm of the physical or natural sciences. When we heat a bar of metal and find that it expands, we can control the situation so carefully that we can say with confidence that the heat has caused it to expand (without here going into detail about the effects of heat on the atomic structure of the metal bar). But we cannot speak with the same confidence about human behaviour which is far more complex, since man, unlike the metal bar, has intentions and is responsible for his own actions up to a point. There are of course cases where he is not responsible and where it would be appropriate to talk of causes: if a man is pushed off the pavement in front of an oncoming car we can explain his behaviour in none other than causal terms; somebody pushed him and he could not resist, he himself had no aim or purpose in falling in front of the car. So perhaps causal explanations are appropriate for human behaviour as long as we are speaking purely within a physical framework where an external physical force is stronger than man's own.

Teachers frequently talk of causes of backwardness implying that, given a certain set of conditions, such as large family, cramped living conditions, lack of parental interest in his school progress, supposedly low intelligence, a child will inevitably be backward in school. But these family characteristics, frequently included among causes of backwardness, do not affect all children. Many coming from such homes could never be called backward. Fortunately then there is no such inevitability linking a child's background and school progress. Since many children, however, who do come from families of such a nature are retarded in school work it would be more appropriate to talk of factors associated with backwardness.

Although it would be pessimistic to try to explain all human behaviour as if it were determined by antecedent causes, it would be unwise to reject this kind of explanation altogether. The rich history of personality and motivation studies adopting this perspective must clearly not be discarded altogether, otherwise much of our behaviour would remain only partially explained.

Extrinsic motivation

Behavourist theories of personality and motivation conceived of man as a mechanical system whose actions were to be understood and explained largely in terms of various forms of external stimulation and the responses made by an individual to these. Stimulus-response theories attempted to account for personality changes and abnormalities in terms of the acquisition of new forms of behaviour that appeared as a result of experience. Since this was the frame of reference within which certain theorists, predominantly Hull, followed by Miller and Dollard, chose to study personality, the main emphasis falls not unnaturally on the learning process.

Hull, whose main theoretical assumption was the principle of reward/ reinforcement, set out to develop a general theory of human behaviour, although he relied heavily on experimental work in the laboratory with lower animals. Drawing upon Hullian theory, which itself always remained theory and never reached the stage of being applied to situations outside the laboratory, Miller and Dollard offer their view of the learning in the following terms: 'the learner must be driven to make the response and is rewarded for having responded in the presence of the cue. This may be expressed in a more homely way by saying that in order to learn one must want something, notice something, do something, get something. Stated more exactly these factors are drive, cue, response, reward.' (Miller and Dollard, 1941). Although they did not offer this model of learning specifically for learning in the classroom, it was intended to apply to learning in general. We see how highly mechanistic and devoid of any notion of choice, intention, interest, or understanding it is. If we try to apply it to a classroom situation, a picture emerges something like this: in order to learn a child must want something (drive) – teachers' approval; he must notice something (cue) – that the teacher looks pleased when he puts his hand up but displeased when he calls out; he must do something (response) – put his hand up; and get something (reward) – the teacher nods approvingly and asks him to answer her question. What has he learned then? That to get her approval he must put up his hand in class.

This may be unobjectionable so far as a way of getting children to learn to take their turn in a class teaching situation; it is a simple form of social learning. But how far does this model of learning apply? Suppose a child is learning some maths or geography. What does he want? To find out something more about what he is engaged upon or to get a good mark for his homework? What is he to notice? Is there a cue or a stimulus that can make him respond in a certain way? And how is this response to be rewarded? Is the good mark he is given by the teacher sufficient reward or would the information he discovers in the course of his work count? And what happens if the drive is not there in the fist place – if the child does not want anything, in Miller and Dollard's homely terms? S–R psychologists do not usually go as far as suggesting that we should create drives in children by depriving them of basic requirements like food (as is done with animals in the laboratory), although such practices, known as behaviour modification techniques, are used in other areas. Behaviour modification, based on rewarding good behaviour, is widely used, both for children and adults in institutions for the mentally handicapped, mentally ill, and emotionally disturbed. Not surprisingly, the methods are the cause of widespread concern, since they are open to abuse and misunderstanding. The National Association for Mental Health, according to a recent press report (*Observer*, November 1978), has expressed anxiety about the ethics of such practices in a set of recommendations shortly to be published.

To talk of a drive leading to a reward would be similar to trying to solve the problem of motivation by an appeal to needs. However, to an S–R psychologist all motivation is assumed to derive from organic drives or basic emotions which the individual can do nothing to resist. Motivation is defined as the urge to act, resulting from a stimulus; since they see all behaviour as stimulus-directed, they do not accept the notion of purpose of any kind. According to an S–R theory of motivation, a child does not have to want to learn history, say, in order to learn it (though he does have to want the reward for learning it). He does though have to be persuaded to study it and to repeat the appropriate verbal responses, which, when reinforced or rewarded in some way, become permanent – or are learned. As Bigge and Hunt point out, 'an associationist is not taught much about such things as psychological involvement or helping students to see the point of learning. Instead he engages them in activity and assumes that activity with reinforcement automatically produces learning.'

Skinner is the greatest advocate of S–R techniques in learning; he comments on the highly inefficient practices in schools that waste useful learning time, mainly because the procedures of reinforcement are clumsy. Teachers in a class of children are poor reinforcers, he claims, since they cannot supply immediate reward to each child for each correct response. In Skinner's view then, the teacher's principle task is 'to bring behaviour under many sorts of stimulus control ... teachers at the moment spend far too much time in redesigning curricula in a desperate attempt to provide a liberal education and steadfastly refuse to employ available engineering techniques which would efficiently build the interests and instil the knowledge which are the goals of education.'

It will be interesting to look at some reinforcement techniques which ·have been examined or adopted in the areas of cognitive and social learning. Skinner himself advocated the use of programmed learning in schools as a highly efficient way of ensuring that each correct response a child makes is reinforced, thus using time more economically than in a normal class teaching situation. A typical programme (which may be in textbook form or fed into a teaching machine) consists of factual content which is divided up into such small steps that in answering questions on small pieces of information given the learner can seldom make a mistake. Skinner rated the efficacy of positive reinforcement for a correct answer higher than negative reinforcement for an incorrect one. Thus the learner has no opportunity to learn from his mistakes by discovering where and why he went wrong, since on the whole he is saved from making any.

Positive reinforcement is given each time he makes a correct response; this reinforcement heightens his motivation and encourages him to continue with the task. Using operant conditioning techniques, 'learning a subject like fundamentals of electricity is largely a matter of learning a large number of correct responses to logically related sequences of questions that constitute the subject ... once a subject has been carefully divided into a series of many small bits of information (steps), a student has only to learn by repetition and reward (rapid and frequent reinforcement) the correct answer to a series of questions about the small bits of information'. (Fitzgerald, 1962).

Skinner claims certain advantages for the use of mechanical teaching devices in schools. Reinforcement for the correct answer is immediate, and since it is given by the machine or the book, the teacher can supervise the whole class, who are enabled to work at their own rate. Thus if any child falls behind either because of a slower working pace or because of absence from school, he still does not suffer by being made to keep up with the rest of the class. Similarly a child who works faster need not be held back, but can be provided with other tasks. Ideally the teacher knows exactly what each child has done and so can supplement reinforcement where necessary.

Research has shown that programmed learning, especially with the use of teaching machines, can be highly efficient in terms of retention. But how far could it encourage children to be actively involved in their own learning? Skinner (1968) claims that teaching machines encourage children to 'take an active role in the instructional process; they must develop the answers before they are reinforced.' Yet clearly this is a different interpretation of what it means to take an active role from that held by educators talking of children being active agents of their own learning in a child-centred situation. Whereas Skinner's technique forces the child to produce or develop an answer himself rather than sitting waiting for a classmate to do so, advocates of child-centred education hope that children will pursue their own interests and frame their own questions depending on what they are involved in at any one time. The content in Skinner's view is still teacher-directed, so that if all a child has to do to learn is to produce correct answers, many educators today would not call this active learning.

Furthermore, there is serious doubt whether understanding of content thus learned is achieved. Although Skinner's claim is that 'the machine insists that a given point be thoroughly understood before the student moves on', it is difficult to see how a machine can make sure something is understood when it can only do what is programmed into it. How can any programme be flexible enough to account for all possible misunderstandings, interpretations or misinterpretations a child may make? The very essence of human learning in an educative sense is that it is active, highly individual and therefore unpredictable. Certainly a machine can be programmed in such a way that the learner does not move on until he gives a correct *answer*, but there is no guarantee that a correct answer presupposes understanding. Educators concerned about the rather passive kind of learning that goes on in many secondary schools, among them Barnes *et al.* (1976) and Holt (1964), show how children can get by in class by giving correct answers to teachers' questions, by learning what cues are the important ones, whether of gesture, intonation, or verbal. Children can thus learn to give correct answers fairly easily but answers are responses to specific questions. Even if they are based on understanding, a series of correct answers would surely be a very fragmented kind of learning. The value of programmed learning is perhaps not to be challenged once an individual has decided he wants to master a body of knowledge which he has chosen for himself and has come to understand. As an efficient technique for helping a student consolidate what he has already learned, programmed methods would be unobjectionable.

In programmed learning Skinner is interpreting reinforcement as knowledge of results for each answer given and since the material is so carefully structured it is usually positive in nature. But reinforcement or reward can take many forms: teacher's approval, smiling and nodding, good marks, stars. Some evidence for the beneficial effects of rewards on classroom learning has been gathered in controlled situations. Carpenter (1954), for instance, found that in a concept learning task, different groups of children were (1) rewarded for each correct response (2) for every second response (3) for every fourth response. His results suggested that the more rewards children were given, the more efficiently they learnt. But this cannot be taken as a general rule. Questions must be asked about the relationship between the child and the teacher; about the nature of the reward; and about how informative the reward is, if at all. Page (1958) found that of three groups of schoolchildren receiving (1) grades (2) grades with general comments (3) grades with a stereotyped comment, group (2) showed most improvement on the next piece of work. Clearly the comments were more useful than simply grades or grades with a fixed comment, since they said more about individual pieces of work, rather than just placing them in a category. They conveyed more personal interest on the part of the teacher and this in turn can be motivating. If the term reward is being used in the latter sense it is far more than just a payment (just deserts) for doing something the teacher approves of.

Most S–R theorists do not seem to use the term 'reward' in this way: a few examples of how psychologists have used the term will illustrate the point. For Hull, a reward is rewarding because it reduces the drive tension in the organism; for Tolman, because it emphasizes the correct response; for Olds and Milner, because it stimulates specific areas of the brain. None of these attempts at definitions, however, is very helpful in an educational situation. Premack (1965) proposed a notion of reward that he thought useful in school situations. It is simply this: 'a reward is anything someone likes doing.' In Premack's view, the only condition is that the rewarding activity must be preferred to the activity being learned *for which it is offered as a reward*. But surely this places a very dubious value on what is to be learned; it denigrates the value of the task being performed. And suppose a child actually prefers doing some maths, designing a toy, or reading a story to any reward that could be offered for doing it? Rewarding the desired activity then becomes not only useless but nonsensical.

If we consider some of the early experimental work done, using rewards, in the field of social learning, we shall encounter some very odd situations. Homme *et al.* (1966) demonstrated the use of reward in gaining control over social behaviour of nursery school children. By first observing the normal behaviour of the children, the experimenters noted that their preferred activities were running around, shouting, and pushing furniture about (undesirable behaviour from the adults' point of view, but supposedly desirable from the children's). Using Premack's principle, the children were rewarded for sitting quietly for a period of time by being allowed to indulge in shouting, etc. At a later stage children could earn tokens for sitting quietly; they could then buy permission to indulge in shouting and screaming. The experimenters report almost perfect control of behaviour after a few days of this procedure. Certainly this is a good example of how to *control* children, if that is what adults think desirable, but what kind of learning is it?

The use of social reinforcement in the ordinary classroom through control of the teacher's praise and attention has been further developed by Becker and others (1967). Rules defining acceptable social behaviour are presented and explained to children. The teacher then rewards or praises them when they abide by the rules but ignores them when they infringe them. However, as all experienced teachers are aware, the teacher is not the only one capable of giving attention to miscreants. Unruly behaviour is most often reinforced by other pupils who naturally enough ignore their peers when they are behaving as the teacher would wish.

Barrish and others (1969) developed a so-called 'Good Behaviour Game' for teachers to use with classes of particularly troublesome children. Infringements of rules led to marks being recorded on the blackboard. The team with fewest marks was rewarded at the end of a session by being given certain privileges, such as being first in the lunch queue or having five minutes extra break.

Merrett and Wheldall (1978) carried out a study with fourth-year junior school children in an attempt to help an inexperienced teacher to control her class by the use of behaviour modification techniques. The methods used were a variation of the good behaviour game whereby acceptable behaviour was rewarded and unwanted behaviour ignored. Although the teacher experienced a measure of success as far as classroom control was concerned, the investigators noted her reluctance to comment on good behaviour. She, like many other teachers, showed far greater readiness to remark on undesired behaviour.

Successful though such techniques may be, they are, as we have already pointed out, morally dubious as well as educationally unsatisfactory. The learner is being conditioned and more easily learns to value the reward, whatever form it takes, than to understand the point of what he has 'learned' to do. However, learning clearly entails more than giving correct responses which might be sufficient for habit training.

Achievement motivation

Discussion so far has centred around rewards and incentives in the form of a tangible object or approval deliberately offered as a means of extrinsic encouragement. Other *conditions* however can also act as incentives. Lewin *et al.* developed a technique of investigating the goal-setting behaviour of adult subjects during the performance of simple tasks in experimental situations. After one performance, subjects were asked to say what they hoped or expected to achieve next time, thus setting themselves a goal or level of aspiration. Results of work on level of aspiration suggest generally that successful performance leads to the setting of higher goals and vice versa. Whether a high level of aspiration leads to a better performance is not clearly established, but what does follow is that success increases motivation and failure decreases it. This is a common sense view that perhaps does not appear to require empirical confirmation. Yet what is manifestly important is the value children learn to place on success and their reasons for learning to value it. Further research on social motives shows that some individuals are anxious to succeed mainly in order to surpass others (individuals or groups). Early work suggested a positive effect of social facilitation; individuals worked better when performing a task alongside others even when no interaction or cooperation took place.

McClelland (1958) introduced the notion of achievement motivation in which ambition is a key concept. He suggests that human beings all have some sort of ambition or aspiration either to do well enough to surpass others or to achieve a certain standard of excellence to satisfy themselves. However some kind of social motive seems always to be involved. Studies have shown a high correlation between the wish to achieve a standard for its own sake and to achieve other people's esteem by so doing. Children may thus strive to achieve mastery in a chosen field and at the same time feel greater satisfaction (leading to increased effort in future) because a teacher whose esteem they value shows pleasure in their achievement. It could be argued that the teacher's approval is rewarding, but this kind of reward effect is manifestly very different from S–R learning where the reward seems to be the main thing the child comes to value.

Not everybody has an equally high degree of achievement motivation which is usually found to be associated with independence training in early childhood. McClelland's hypothesis (1953) that children who are encouraged to be independent and self-reliant at an early age, who are treated warmly by their parents and given a high degree of freedom develop high achievement motivation later on, was confirmed by Winterbottom (1958), in his study of independence training. Children who have

rejecting or overprotective parents tend to develop low achievement motivation and instead of aiming for mastery, tend to seek social approval.
Such findings might explain different degrees of motivation in children in
school. It follows that an emphasis on teacher-directed learning where a
child is encouraged to take little initiative, will not help to encourage those
who are less ambitious initially, whereas guidance towards independence
and responsibility may well help to persuade the underconfident child that
he can succeed and that it is worth trying.

One precondition of wishing to achieve mastery is to feel some
enthusiasm; every teacher however is familiar with the sight of a child who
seems to be almost totally lacking in interest or enthusiasm, for whatever
the reason. Whether we can make a child interested is very doubtful, but
one way possibly of teaching him the interest of a topic is to show our own
enthusiasm for it. Common sense tells us that enthusiasm is very often
infectious. Children want to know what makes their teacher so excited
about a given topic and catch some of his fervour for themselves. There is
little empirical evidence so far to support this view, yet the work of Bandura and Walters (1970) suggests that modelling might be an effective
social motivator. They have succeeded in showing how powerful a model
an adult can be in evoking similar behaviour in children yet so far have
limited their studies to investigations of aggression and fear – largely the
kind of behaviour we should want to discourage in children in school.
However, from everyday observation we know that too much enthusiasm
can work in the opposite direction and become antimotivational.
Enthusiasts are sometimes regarded as cranks, (especially perhaps by
suspecting adolescents) and as such are avoided.

The concept of achievement motivation has been used not only to show
why some children have an individual urge towards mastery and others
not. It has also been drawn upon by sociologists working within the
structural-functionalist tradition, investigating school failure associated
with social class. In a commentary on family background, values, and
achievement, Banks (1968) notes that the consistent tendency of
working-class children to perform less well in school and to leave school
earlier than middle-class children, even when ability is matched, needs
explanation. Clearly this is true, but as we shall see, the kinds of explanation offered by sociologists working within this framework have been
causal in nature, because of the kinds of question that have been asked.
Kluckholn and Strodtbeck for example (1961) have attempted to trace a
relationship between value orientation and achievement orientation which
might eventually explain the link between social class and achievement in

school. For instance, Kluckholn sees the dominant (American) middle-class value-orientation as one where man can control nature, where the future is stressed rather than the past, where there is an emphasis on activity and where individual efforts are considered more important and effective than those of the group or community. Such an outlook is believed to encourage the development of ambition since it emphasizes the power of the individual and his orientation towards the future. Some studies such as the Harvard mobility project have attempted to examine how different patterns of value relate to achievements. Kahl (1965) found that from 24 boys all from a lower middle-class background chosen for an interview, two distinct groups emerged according to their expressed aspirations. The majority of the 12 boys interviewed in the college preparatory class came from families characterized by what Kluckholn might describe as future oriented. The parents looked to the future and believed in getting ahead. They were aware of their own relative lack of success and as a result encouraged their sons to regard school as a means of getting on in life – a means of getting to college and aspiring to a better occupation than that of their fathers. Parents of the other group comparable in ability and socio-economic status who were not in the college preparatory class tended to accept their own status and were oriented to the present rather than looking to the future for something better. These findings are similar to those of Swift (1966) in this country who found that more sons of working-class fathers who were dissatisfied with their own position tended to gain 11+ successes than those of fathers who accepted their lot. Although there is no confirmed or clear-cut relationship between achievement motivation and achievement values, they do, as Rosen (1956) suggests, both belong to a complex achievement syndrome. Attempts have been made to relate different patterns of child-rearing to achievement. Bronfenbrenner (1961), summarizing the findings of several of these studies, comments that high achievement motivation appears to flourish in a family atmosphere of 'cold democracy' where initial high levels of maternal involvement are followed by pressures towards independence and accomplishment.

There is, however, no clearly defined causal relationship between parental attitudes, social class, and achievement. Banks (1968) comments that this is possibly to be attributed either to methodological weaknesses in the studies or to insufficient empirical evidence. But to expect to find a causal relationship in human behaviour surely is to adopt an inappropriate model. However refined the survey design or analysis of data become, man's behaviour can never be measured or controlled as finely as this kind of model requires, because by its very nature it omits reference to man's personal interpretations of the situation in which he finds himself, the meanings he attaches to it, and his own intentions. Human beings, as we saw earlier, do not just let things happen to them as if they had no power to control their own environment or their own actions. Just because a child happens to be born into a certain kind of family, to have parents with certain kinds of attitude and aspiration, it does not mean that he will be so influenced by them that his future is predictable. This in fact would be a highly pessimistic view of man, a sort of social determinism, whereby a child's birth circumstances determined or dictated what he achieved at school and what kind of occupation he was likely to enjoy. The model is very similar to the behaviourist one considered earlier in the discussion of S–R learning. It strips the child of his very characteristics as a human being, that is, of his own understanding, interpretation, and intentions. Perhaps this has been the dominant paradigm in the sociology of education until recently, but with the change of perspective developing in the theory and practice of education generally we shall see a new paradigm emerging.

The argument pursued so far has attempted to show how the kinds of question we ask about human behaviour can determine our view of the child in school, the kinds of motivational control that can be adopted to get him to learn, and the sort of explanation we offer for his success and failure. Questions about causes of behaviour lead us to take a view of children as passive beings whose behaviour or learning can be modified by reinforcement or reward and whose life chances are patterned by social factors beyond their control. Rewards, incentives, and social motivators are generally referred to as types of extrinsic motivation. But the concept of achievement motivation, seen from the individual's point of view, with its emphasis on standards of excellence as well as other kinds of social stimulus that may be caught from a lively teacher, acts as a bridge from the view of the child as one whose behaviour can be moulded or controlled to one who can develop goals, intentions, aims for himself, an active agent rather than a puppet. Most current views of education held by teachers and educators in this country lay emphasis on children as active agents of their own learning. This of course implies that we need to consider not only causes of behaviour but also reasons for action and to ask why children choose to act as they do, learn what they learn, and how they interpret their experience.

The child as an active learner

If we view children as beings capable of purpose and intention, we imply that they are able to choose their own course of action instead of having it determined for them. But real choice implies understanding what there is to choose from; and to do this children have to learn for themselves the significance of their past and present experiences. Since one of the main purposes of this chapter is to raise questions about motivation in school, we must consider the way children interpret their experience in school, since although they may share common experiences there, they do not necessarily see the same meaning in them because of the variety of different latent cultures they bring with them from outside. Nor is their interpretation of school experience the same as that of their teacher. Unless the teacher understands, at any rate to some degree, how a child experiences his world, he will not understand how to help him to choose what interests to pursue (the content of his education) or how to help him to pursue them (his method of learning).

From a theoretical point of view then we need a different model of human behaviour from the behaviouristic one considered earlier in this chapter. Drawing upon the work of Berger and Luckman (1967) who attempt to establish a different perspective within sociology, one which regards the individual as an 'active agent making sense of and coming to terms with the world in which he lives', Esland uses this perspective against which to view children's learning in school. Thus learning is according to this view not simply repeating what the teacher has just been saying but consists of trying to make sense of it, in terms of one's own previous experience, by engaging in conversation or discussion with the teacher and other pupils. Esland refers to this process of trying to make sense of what is being said as an example of negotiation in a learning situation. Pupils attempt to question, comment, and try to find similarities with their previous knowledge, thus in some sense directing the nature of classroom interaction. Barnes (1976) gives some interesting examples of such discussions recorded in secondary school classrooms, where pupils are attempting to work out meanings for themselves, yet where the teacher is anxious to keep his own control over the pace and content of the lesson, as he has prepared it. It is interesting to note how the situation could be differently interpreted: one teacher might interpret the children's behaviour as disruptive, a deliberate intention to 'play up', while another might see it from the child's point of view – an active attempt to understand what the teacher is trying to convey. Both explanations may be appropriate, but in any case, the kind of verbal interaction that goes on in school suggests that learning is inevitably a social process where each individual concerned is striving to incorporate new meanings into his own frame of reference. One of the teacher's tasks then is to create appropriate opportunities for children to do this. By providing situations where an exchange of experience is possible through language and other kinds of activity, he is facilitating the process of interaction which is all-important in a real learning situation. This is far from the mechanistic view discussed earlier, one where learning is seen as an individual matter and where the stamping in of a correct response by reward is seen to count as learning. In the view currently under discussion learning is seen not as a change of response but as a development of understanding and meaning. Children are motivated to learn not by rewards offered for correct responses. Their learning is not teacher-controlled but instead they learn through social interaction in a situation which they can control to some extent themselves.

A similar view of man as an active agent striving after meaning is found in George Kelly's work on the psychology of personal constructs. Kelly sees man trying to make sense of his world as a scientist does: that is, in order to explain his experience he sets up hypotheses which he then revises and reformulates according to his interpretation of his experience. Although Kelly (1955) attempted to apply this theory to many fields of human experience – personality development, abnormal behaviour, psychotherapy – education was not one of them, so in practical terms he has nothing directly to contribute to a discussion of school learning. Nevertheless, his view of man is worthy of mention, since it adds support to a perspective in which man is seen as an active interpreter of his own experiences – a view which deserves attention as a theoretical framework within which to view the school context.

If in trying to show how the individual child is helped to pursue learning, to develop concepts, and to structure his own world, we first of all look at some important psychological processes involved, we shall discern interesting connections with the structural/developmental view of intelligence discussed in the previous chapter. When the child becomes aware of illogicalities in his own thinking he is prompted to go on to the next stage in logical thought, by a process of cognitive conflict, as we shall see later.

But to use cognitive conflict in the classroom as a practical procedure for getting children to solve problems for themselves involves careful planning and structuring of appropriate problem situations. It is not easy for children to recognize conflicting evidence until they know enough about the content involved. They cannot recognize what is irregular or incongruous until they know what is regularly the case. Attention towards cognitive conflict may be aroused by novelty which in turn stimulates curiosity. Curiosity impels the child to find out more about what he is doing and thus to discover how, for example, a toy is fixed together, whether all objects float, what will happen to seeds grown under different conditions. Just as intelligence does not merely develop by maturation but is a result of interaction with the environment, so children do not interact with their environment unless they are given some guidance. But before we consider what part the teacher can play, let us examine the concepts of curiosity, novelty, incongruity, and cognitive conflict in relation to their importance in motivation.

Intrinsic motivation may be distinguished from extrinsic motivation in that the latter depends upon reward extraneous to the learning process, a reward often satisfying some need condition. The former, on the other hand, depends upon factors hinging on unharmonious or dissonant relations within the learning process, for example the notion of perceptual conflict or cognitive imbalance. Reward in this system is closely related to the thought processes involved. Satisfaction in solving a problem or resolving a conflict is rewarding to the learner. Berlyne (1960, 1963) in a discussion of intrinsic motivation introduces the term 'epistemic curiosity' to refer to knowledge-seeking behaviour including questioning, observation, problem solving. Epistemic curiosity then is concerned with pursuing knowledge for its own sake rather than for any reward extraneous to it. Closely associated with this notion, in Berlyne's schema, is conceptual conflict including perplexity, doubt, contradiction, and conceptual incongruity. He suggests that conflict in this sense is related to the notion of uncertainty which is aroused by novel, surprising, or puzzling situations. Epistemic or exploratory behaviour consists in collecting information to reduce uncertainty and to make sense of a situation – thus the learner is motivated to discover new information for himself.

This is an interesting and plausible concept of motivation which sees the child as an active, exploring agent who purposefully seeks knowledge for its own sake. What he learns is not devalued by the extraneous reward offered on the S–R pattern. Moreover he is not learning responses to somebody else's (the teacher's) questions or problems, but is recognizing problems for himself and solving them for the satisfaction of getting to know more and making more sense out of his accumulated experiences.

Various sources of evidence, some experimental, some from general educational experience, suggest that this kind of intrinsic motivation is not only a plausible concept but is also effective in school learning and can help children to understand and remember new material, and encourage them to search actively for new information, to attempt to solve problems for themselves as well as to recognize problems when they occur. But since children need constant help and guidance, teachers employ various devices to stimulate and maintain curiosity. The introduction of what is surprising or novel is, for example, frequently used in the teaching and learning of science. Thus children have to accommodate to and explain the surprising fact that although whales live and swim in water they are not fish but mammals. Before this is surprising to them however they have to have some familiarity with the biological concepts of fish and mammal, since at any stage of development knowledge of the familiar must precede recognition of the unfamiliar or novel. Once a child, even a very young one, begins to show an interest in the novel, he ventures into areas of greater complexity both in terms of perception and action. McV. Hunt (1971), in a discussion of intrinsic motivation in young children, attaches great importance to complexity in relation to children's interest and curiosity. In his view, a bored child is one for whom there is too little complexity in his environment. Just as a young baby will cease to pay attention to a very familiar pattern and become habituated to it, so an older child will cease to show interest in a skill he has learned unless it increases in complexity. For instance, a beginner learning to play the piano will gain more pleasure and interest and will thus persist more if the music he is given to cope with is more complex than that which he has already mastered. Children will feel more challenged by greater complexity in dealing with number concepts than being required to practise the same skills repeatedly in which they are already competent. In planning work for children it follows that what is surprising or complex for one child will not necessarily evoke the same response in another. If surprise is to work as a motivational device, each individual child's stage of conceptual development must be considered. The planning of work must be largely on an individual or small group basis. It is interesting to note as McV. Hunt suggests that some children in the class may act as 'complexity models' for others. The fact that children see and take an interest in others performing tasks which are more complex than those they themselves can do adds support to the case for vertical grouping. In this type of grouping younger children may be motivated to imitate the complexity model of an older peer. The same advantage may be derived from a system of mixed-ability grouping in the junior and secondary school where any child may act as a complexity model in the particular skills in which he excels. It does not always follow, however, that only a child who is intellectually able will be the one to inspire others.

Conceptual incongruity or ambiguity – or to use Mc.V Hunt's term, mismatch – are further devices the teacher may use to stimulate curiosity. Faced with information that does not tally or match, as we saw in our earlier example, the child is invited to resolve the resulting conflict. Indeed this is the very situation that children find themselves confronted with in some of the Piagetian-type situations, designed to show how they are helped to pass on to the next conceptual stage. In Piaget's original experiment on the conservation of liquids children were asked to say whether the amount of liquid was the same when it was poured from a short wide beaker into a tall thin one. Many of the younger children who had not yet grasped the concept of conservation – that is, that the amount of liquid must remain the same, regardless of what it *looks* like – said that there was more water in the tall thin beaker because it reached higher up the vessel. Frank (1964) used a screening device in the usual conservation experiment to show that when children are confronted with an illogicality or ambiguity in their own thinking, they readily adopt a new thinking strategy provided that the ambiguity does not create such a large gap as to be nonsensical. Frank carried out the experiment in the way just described, noting the nonconservers. She then repeated it, this time placing a card across the front of the second beaker, so that children seeing the water being poured in could not see how high it came. Several of those who had previously thought the tall thin beaker contained more water now gave a different answer. They judged it to be the same 'because it was the same water'. They had not been influenced by the appearance of the water and were now confronted with their own contradictory replies which they had to make sense of. Programmes of science education currently used in schools, such as the various Nuffield projects, aim at providing children with practical experience in science, giving them the opportunity to spot apparent incongruities or contradictions in what they observe. They are, it is hoped, thus challenged to pursue more information to create a total schema in which these apparent ambiguities are resolved. But such learning by discovery cannot be efficient without guidance and help in checking discoveries on the part of the teacher. A child frustrated by ambiguities he cannot explain without help is not likely to be stimulated to further curiosity, but will simply give up. Thus the advice that 'we (teachers) need to get out of their way while they go about the business of learning' (McV. Hunt, 1971) is really a vain hope. Teachers certainly need to structure the environment where all children can be guided towards the learning opportunities appropriate for each one; but they cannot then step aside. Their task is one of constant vigilance if the initial interest they have helped to create is to be maintained.

Implicit in the argument for intrinsic motivation is the assumption that there is greater value in seeking knowledge or pursuing interests for their own sake rather than for any extraneous reward, whether it be an immediate one like teacher approval or good marks or a more distant one such as examination success leading to wider occupational choice. But we must not overlook the fact that children may pursue interests and activities for their own sake which are regarded as trivial, valueless, or even harmful. Interest as such does not solve all motivational problems, since to pursue interests which are not educative is not what teachers would want to motivate children to do. Some selection of those interests which are worthwhile and of value must be made. There is no easy way of setting up criteria for what counts as worthwhile, since this must be a question of personal values and priorities. As such the problem will be discussed in Chapter 8. What concerns us here, once teacher and pupils have decided what is educationally worthwhile, is how to help children to care enough about what they are doing for them to be sufficiently curious to continue without extrinsic reward. Psychological insight into intrinsic motivational processes has offered some help but it must be emphasized that an attitude of caring about what one is doing is nurtured in an atmosphere where adults, particularly teachers, show the same kind of involvement themselves. For a teacher to remark to a class in a secondary school that he's just as bored with the topic as the pupils, but since it is on the syllabus, they must get it over, is not only to devalue what they are supposed to be learning, but it is also bound to destroy an interest and kill any motivation the class may have had. It betrays an attitude of noncommitment on the part of the teacher which will never engender enthusiasm in his pupils. Enthusiasm in the sense of being deeply committed to an interest, frequently an unusual one, is often discouraged and condemned as crankiness as we suggested earlier. We must all be familiar with examples of children who have accumulated masses of information and have really come to understand a topic they personally are concerned with: windmills, rare fungi, trains or even, like Priestley, in Lacey's study, stocks and shares. Knowledgeable enthusiasts, whether children or adults, are those who have become committed to an interest for its own sake and, once committed, there is an even stronger tendency to remain involved. One problem frequently facing teachers of older children in secondary schools is pupils' lack of interest in school work or indeed in school at all. Many teachers would in fact claim that it is easier to motivate young

T.P.E.—H

children by arousing their curiosity than it is to motivate adolescents whose curiosity is often difficult to arouse and impossible to maintain. It is appropriate here to consider the relative merits of extrinsic and intrinsic motivation before going on to discuss social factors which affect children in school. To use extraneous rewards as a means of getting children to learn is, as we have said, morally dubious. Rewards can control a person's behaviour just as if he had no choice or autonomy of his own. If we are educating children and not just training them then a total reliance on extrinsic motivation is highly questionable, since we do not want to turn children into passive automata producing correct responses. Offering children rewards can both devalue what they are supposed to be learning and act merely as a bribe. This is not to deny completely the value of rewards in learning. From one point of view the rewards are just as essential to the moral aspects of education as is punishment. They serve to point out to the learner where he is on the right path; they provide encouragement and they show that the teacher is interested in what children are doing and approves of it. But to make extraneous rewards the main attraction in a learning situation is to draw attention from what is being learned on to something irrelevant to the content. Intrinsic motivation does not deny the notion of reward, but by definition it lies in the learning process itself. Epistemic curiosity is satisfied by discovering something – the reward comes from the activity rather than being offered by another person.

Learning solely in terms of correct responses being stamped in by a process of reinforcement is, as we have seen, also doubtful from the point of view of efficacy. Is this kind of learning long lasting or is it forgotten when rewards are no longer given? Does the motivation cease with the withdrawal of reward, as the S–R paradigm suggests? And this leads us to ask what we mean by learning. If we mean no more than producing correct responses (right answers to the teacher's questions) then reinforcement is a highly efficient process. However, learning in an educative sense is much more than this. It involves understanding the point of what is being learned as well as the reasons for learning it. It includes accommodating new experience to what has previously been assimilated, thus extending existing concepts and forming new ones. In order to do this the learner needs to be in a far less restricted situation than response learning allows him to be, since he needs to question, interpret, or even reject what he has learned. There are times however when extrinsic rewards can be useful and are acceptable, but if relied upon all the time they lead to highly mechanistic learning. Perhaps extrinsic motivation – attracting children to learning by some outside incentive – is a way of leading them into an interest in learning for its own sake, if this has not already begun.

The social context of learning

As we saw earlier, learning is never a purely individual matter, nor is becoming involved or motivated in an activity. Becker (1953), writing within a sociological framework, offers us several useful conceptual tools with which to analyse the problem of motivation in a social situation which may be particularly useful for those dealing with adolescents. In his investigation of the way in which marijuana users come to derive pleasure from smoking he sets out to show how the motive to learn or to involve oneself does not always have to be present before the activity is begun. He suggests that people develop a disposition or motivation by engaging in an activity, rather than having the motive to do so at the outset. The argument runs then that it is possible to learn to enjoy certain kinds of activity by doing them and that it is only through doing them that one can learn the interest of them. School learning is a far cry from learning to smoke pot, but it is nevertheless interesting and possibly helpful to ask whether there is a case for persuading pupils to engage in activities towards which they initially have no inclination in the hope that they will gradually see the point and come to understand what the activities hold for them. It is a common experience that interest grows with increasing knowledge. The more we know about a topic, the more our attention is drawn to features we either already recognize or others we wish to know more about. It is worth remembering Bruner's advice that we do not discover nearly so much as when we are already fairly well informed. 'Discovery, like surprise, favours the well prepared mind'. Becker's notion of learning motives by engaging in an activity is reminiscent of Allport's concept of functional autonomy where an individual begins an activity for purely instrumental purposes but then persists in the activity for its own sake. He argues that while many activities may originally have served some other motive, their persistence suggests that they have gained drive value of their own – that is, they are now independent of the original motives. Thus is seems plausible that if a pupil works hard at his history, say, in order to pass his examinations, he will gain an interest in historical knowledge and investigation for its own sake.

However, one problem in secondary schools, especially with the older age group is that they do not get as far as being interested in specific subject areas because they are totally uncommitted to the school. School values and all that the school offers seem alien to them so that they do not give themselves the chance of involvement. It is important to realize how the school structure itself can create alternative careers in school which are disapproved of and discouraged by the teachers. Schools that are rigidly streamed create academic opportunities for the able children who can succeed in this area and thus follow a path through school that is officially encouraged. At the same time pupils in lower streams are automatically debarred from following an academic career. By being labelled 'nonacademic' or D streamers they have been designated as academic failures. It is not surprising then that many pupils in this situation create other kinds of school careers for themselves; they form antischool or delinquescent subcultures, to use Hargreaves' term. Hargreaves' study (1967), as we saw earlier, examines the effect of streaming on fourth-year boys in a secondary modern school in which he worked both as teacher and researcher. He describes the constant hostility between the A stream boys who accept school values and the D stream pupils who reject all the school has to offer. Their growing dissatisfaction with school has led them to seek status and satisfaction elsewhere. Their rejection of the pupil role is manifested in the premature adult roles they adopt – flagrantly smoking and drinking on school premises for example. Similarly, as we discussed earlier, Lacey's study (1966) of a streamed grammar school shows how pupils become differentiated very early on, at the beginning of their second year, when they are streamed by ability. Early in their second year, the bottom stream pupils are considered difficult to teach and lacking interest in school learning and other school activities. These studies both suggest that pupils in low streams lack motivation, but we clearly need to ask how this lack of motivation originated. Lacey's findings give a clear indication that it can be created by the school. Thus motivation becomes an organizational matter rather than purely an individual one. Once pupils see themselves failing in what the school approves of they are apt to form antischool groups and by a process of situational adjustment their attitudes become even more consistently hostile to school values. Becker (1964) uses the notion of situational adjustment to explain how individuals easily turn themselves into the sort of person a given situation requires if they wish to become and remain part of it. Thus, for example, if an academically unsuccessful pupil finds satisfaction in being a member of an antischool group he adopts the habits and attitudes of members of that group so that he is accepted by them and is part of that situation, no longer an outsider. Similarly a pupil who wishes to be successful in school and to adopt its values adjusts to the situation by behaving well in class, doing his homework on time, wearing correct uniform, and participating in extra-curricular activities. But the school structure makes it very difficult for him to do this, if, in streaming its pupils, it places those who want to adopt school values in streams where the situation is hostile. Thus such pupils very often find themselves adjusting to a situation they originally found unsympathetic.

Once this process of adjustment (and therefore attitude change) has taken place, it can be difficult to escape because the individual finds himself committed by other social factors. Again we use Becker's concept of commitment to explain this. He considers that a person is committed when we observe him pursuing a consistent line of activity in varied situations, for example, consistently rejecting school values. Commitment is maintained by fruitful rewards acquired in the situation, by relationships formed with others, by high status within the group and so on, all of which Becker refers to as side-bets. Although, however, as we have seen, the structure of the school can lead to little but failure for those pupils who are placed in low streams, we cannot feel assured that in an unstreamed situation these pupils would be any more committed to school. Adolescents' commitments outside it are likely to be strong in any case. The attractions offered by pop-cultures, presented to them most successfully via the mass media, require them to make less effort than the intellectual challenges provided by the school.

Motivation and the self-concept

The organization of the school, however, can have a further though indirect effect on pupils' motivation. As we have already seen, in a streamed school teachers frequently judge their pupils according to the ability group in which they are placed. Low stream pupils who are judged unfavourably are expected by their teachers to achieve little, and very often this is the case. Teacher expectations thus affect pupils' motivation negatively by failing to encourage them, so that frequently secondary school pupils in particular in the end give up the struggle (Downey, 1977).

More long-lasting effects of teachers' judgements and expectations upon pupils' motivation can be detected if we consider the powerful influence they can have on the pupils' self-concept. The self, according to G. H. Mead (1934) is a social product, arising from the child's interaction with others of importance or significance to him, such as parents, peers, or teachers. The self is not merely a product of the environment in a passive sense, but results from the interpretations a child makes of how others perceive, judge, or evaluate him. Kagan (1967) points to the importance of a favourable self-concept for a young child's all-round development.

Children who have developed a negative self-concept before they even come to school show a high level of anxiety, have difficulty in making friends, adjust less easily to school, and are frequently hampered in general achievement. Teachers can reinforce the poor opinion a child has of himself, but fortunately they can also help to reverse this opinion and to create in the child a more positive view of himself and his capacities (Downey, 1977). Palfrey (1973) gives an interesting account of the way in which the expectations and judgements of head teachers can affect their pupils' self-concept, with a subsequent influence on their motivation and aspirations. Material for study was drawn from two small secondary schools in the same area. While the head of the boys' school considered his pupils unlikely to be favourably disposed towards school or to have any high scholastic or occupational aspirations, the head of the girls' school took a completely different view. Both head teachers made their expectations clear to their pupils, the headmaster implicitly, by offering little encouragement and showing little interest in his pupils, but the headmistress explicitly, by insisting on higher standards of behaviour and application to work and taking a committed interest in the girls' progress and job choices. An investigation of the self-concepts of fourth-year pupils in both schools suggested that their heads' expectations had had an influence on their motivation in school and their aspirations for when they left.

The task of changing a child's negative self-image and low self-esteem with a view to increasing his interest in school work and achievement motivation is regarded by some counsellors as one of the most important aspects of their job. Gill (1967) suggests that counselling can help a young person to clarify his self-image, so that he is able to accept his weaknesses but is also aware of his strengths. Counselling clearly does not entail personality change but, instead, involves helping pupils to find effective ways of using the aptitudes and abilities that they already have (Hamblin, 1974). The shared task of counsellor, teacher, and pupil is to build up self-respect in those who have previously learned to see themselves in a negative way through the eyes of others. Thus, it is hoped, motivation will be enhanced and the pupil can begin to make the best of his opportunities.

So far we have discussed the ways in which children's motivation is stifled and how teachers can help to arouse and maintain it. But we have said little about what pupils are motivated to do, that is, about the nature of curriculum content itself. Much has been written in the past few decades about using young children's interests as a basis for curriculum planning (Wilson, 1971) and about creating a more outgoing or relevant curriculum for secondary school pupils (Newsom, 1963; Schools' Council,

1968; Kelly, 1978). It will be sufficient here to draw attention to such crucial issues which will be discussed further in a later chapter.

Summary and conclusions

This chapter has set out to explain the nature of motivation and to look briefly at the kinds of question teachers ask about children's behaviour when they are concerned with motivational issues.

We have discussed questions of rewards and incentives, referring to theories of extrinsic motivation and showing how these have been applied to human learning by illustrating from classroom practice. Intrinsic motivation, which operates when children's interest and curiosity are aroused so that they wish to pursue an activity for its own sake, is compared and contrasted with a system of reinforcement and reward.

Motivation is, however, not only an individual process, but is also influenced by social and organizational factors within the school. Both school and classroom management can create structures where pupils are labelled and come to see themselves as successes or failures, sometimes very early in their school experience. The judgements and expectations which teachers hold can indirectly affect pupils' motivation and aspirations by having a long-lasting effect on their self-concept or self-image. We hope to have shown how teachers can discourage a child or, more positively, how they can bolster his self-esteem by helping him to see himself in a more favourable light.

Finally, we suggest that the nature of the curriculum itself is inextricably bound up with pupils' interests and level of involvement.

5 Language and Learning

To write an introductory book on language learning would be a highly difficult task because of the very wide range of issues that arise and the vast quantities of empirical work that are available. To write one chapter on language in an introduction to the theory and practice of education is almost an impossible undertaking. In order, therefore, to make any sense such a chapter must inevitably be limited and can only outline to its readers some of the main problems that they will want to pursue in their teaching.

This chapter sets out to deal with the nature and functions of language, early language acquisition, and the relationship between language, thinking, and concept development. Issues relating to the social context of language will include social class variations and problems of linguistic deprivation. Finally, we shall attempt to examine the ways in which the classroom can provide a context for language learning.

The nature and functions of language
Because we all use language we tend to take its nature and functions for granted. But without going into the highly complex philosophical problems raised by the nature of language, it must be recognized that there are difficulties in talking about its nature without reference to its functions.

Sapir (1949), for example, tried to define language as 'a purely human, noninstinctive method of communicating ideas, emotions and desires by means of a system of voluntarily produced symbols'; similarly Wittgenstein, writing of meaning, says 'the meaning of a word is its use in the language'. It is however useful from a practical point of view to bear in mind the distinction between *language* as a public system of symbols, agreed upon by common usage, and *speech* which refers to individual utterances, that is an individual's use of language. In the classroom context it will be mainly the latter which is our concern though the distinction in terminology will not always be observed. The language an individual uses has many functions and any one utterance may have more than one. For example, a child may be seeking to establish his relationship with his teacher or peers, while at the same time conveying information. It would be a mistake to think of language in the classroom merely as a means of presenting information as perhaps many teachers in the past tended to do, influenced by the emphasis upon propositional knowledge or curriculum content. The communication of knowledge or information is only one of the important functions of language. Others include the learning and precise use of concepts where language is initially used as a recognizing device, and the expression of thought. Language also serves as a means of exploring, understanding, and gaining control of one's world, establishing relationships with others, developing, and exploring aesthetic and moral sensibility.

Early language acquisition

Before these functions can be discussed in the light of their importance for learning in school it is essential to have some understanding of how children learn language. A cursory glance at some of the psychological literature dealing with language learning suggests that investigators until recently have been predominantly concerned with the acquisition of language in the preschool years. This emphasis has to a certain degree been misleading for teachers, many of whom tend to make assumptions about language learning that can set considerable limitations upon their own teaching, many assume that language acquisition is the concern mainly of teachers of your children and secondly, that by the time children reach junior and certainly secondary school they should already have acquired sufficient linguistic competence to cope with the demands of school. If they have not, then the fault is thought to lie in the home and there is little that they, the teachers, can do about it. In addition language is often assumed to be merely the medium for learning a certain body of knowledge. These assumptions ignore the fact that language learning is a continuous process, one that never ceases since we all constantly extend our use and understanding of language as our experience widens. They allow teachers to overlook the fact that children need to be helped to learn language at every stage and that language learning is important in its own right and is not just a subsidiary to learning something else.

Rather than take early language learning for granted it is salutary to remember how rapidly a young child learns such a complex rule system in so short a time. By the age of about four most children have acquired all the basic rules of syntax inherent in their native language. It is with this period of early language learning that much recent research is concerned, partly because of different theoretical viewpoints adopted to attempt to explain how children learn, and partly because the very rapidity of the learning makes it such a baffling process to explain and understand.

One theoretical explanation of language which is readily adopted by the layman because it appears to be common sense is in terms of reinforcement and imitation. Within this framework learning is explained in terms of rewarding the child when he makes a correct or desired utterance and either ignoring him when he is wrong or correcting him in the hope that he will be able to imitate the right utterance. For instance, if a young child says 'I goed' instead of 'I went', he is corrected. When he eventually does get it right, he is praised. This kind of explanation, of which Skinner and Mowrer are proponents, belongs to a behaviourist tradition which sees the major part of any learning process in terms of rewarding correct responses. But while reward and imitation are useful explanations of some kind of language learning, such as the learning of vocabulary or learning how to name objects, they fail to explain the far more active nature of language learning. If reward and imitation were the sole mechanisms at work, how could we explain how children come to utter sentences they have never heard before?

McNeill's study of language acquisition in a two-year-old shows how the child's language is creative and innovative. He uses phrases that convey meaning, but because they are syntactically unique he could not have imitated them from anybody else. McNeill (1966) shows how a young child builds up a limited store of words which he then uses to create novel utterances within his own simple but already structured linguistic system. From original phrases like 'the chocolate's all gone' or 'more milk' the child creates his own simple meaningful units by using the same pivot words in a different context. 'All gone outside' was his phrase to indicate that the door was closed, while 'more page' meant that his mother was to go on reading to him. Such phrases are quite unlikely to have been imitated from others and suggest the child's ability at an early age to generate his own patterns of speech rather than merely imitating other people's.

The point of this example is not merely to illustrate the limitations of one theoretical explanation (since our context does not allow us to go into this kind of detail) but to show the force of the child's active learning where language is concerned. Early utterances of this kind suggest that the child is not only imitating some of what he hears but is formulating his own rules and incorporating what he has learned from others into his own speech structure.

Further evidence to support this hypothesis stems from work on early syntactic structures. By the age of four most children have acquired the basic rules of morphology, such as the formation of plurals, past tenses and so on. (See for example Berko, 1958; Fraser, Bellugi, and Brown 1963.) Because of the surprising accuracy and rapidity with which children learn syntax, Chomsky (1959) has suggested that there must be some innate mechanism which is exclusively a human characteristic, enabling human beings to learn language. McNeill calls this a 'language acqusition device' (LAD). It enables us not only to learn the syntax of our own language quickly but also helps us to recognize sentences as grammatically correct independently of their meaning. Chomsky's example of a nonsense sentence 'Colourless green ideas sleep furiously' is nevertheless recognizable as an English sentence and illustrates this point. Such a LAD would explain why adults' attempts to accelerate children's learning of syntax by expanding their utterances from a telegraphic form to a grammatically complete one do not meet with success until the child is capable of using such structures spontaneously. Brown and Bellugi (1964) showed that a three-year-old will repeat the essential content of what an adult asks him to imitate but will contract it to his own type of reduced syntactic pattern, for example, 'He's going out', is reduced to 'He go out.' It seems that there is a strong development factor at work here, reminiscent of some kind of readiness device. Students concerned with young children will find it rewarding to pursue some of the current experimental work in this area for themselves, but since all teachers, whatever the age of their pupils, should recognize the importance of the active use and generation of language, the early stages should not be ignored.

If there is in fact some kind of LAD guiding children's ability to learn language (Cazden, 1968), we may well ask why such emphasis is laid on the nature of the home environment by those concerned about children whose language learning seems to have been deficient. The explanation is partly a motivational one. Children will cease to talk unless someone not only talks to them but also listens to them. For a child to increase his use of language and to expand his vocabulary, he needs to have something to talk about and somebody to talk to. In this way early experience is important, particularly sensory experience. Joan Tough (1973) gives lively contrasting accounts of how children in different home and school environments have a good or limited opportunity to learn to expand their use of language, depending on the skill and interest of the mother or teacher. Some of Tough's classroom examples suggest the urgent need for teachers to learn to listen to what children have to say far more than many of them do at the moment. Children are frequently misunderstood, and valuable teaching opportunities are overlooked because teachers consider their pupils deficient in language learning, and as we have seen in our discussion of judgements of children, regard them as less able and possibly already doomed to failure at an early stage. Such teachers despair of children who cannot understand them, when clearly it would be more appropriate (and much easier) for teachers, with their far greater experience, to learn to understand children even if they do speak some kind of nonstandard English, syntactically unique and lexically rich in a different way from that familiar to the teacher.

Language and thought

For most practical purposes we are concerned with thought as it is conveyed to others rather than thought which is never communicated. Teachers can only know what and how children are thinking if they can express their thoughts and, although some thought may operate at a level of signs rather than symbols, intelligible thought must involve symbols of some kind, usually language. If teachers wish to know how to develop children's understanding and thinking they must begin with what children offer them, with the words and speech structures that children use. This means that they must analyse what children do with words, that is, analyse their *function*. It is only when they understand what kind of language games children are already playing that they can go on to initiate them into further language games appropriate to other forms of thought and understanding. More will be said on this issue later but first we shall consider some of the work on the origins of thought and language.

Language is so obviously and inextricably linked with thought that in order to be able to appreciate their interdependence teachers should have some understanding of the theoretical background within which observations of their relationship have been made. To consider the origins of thought and language, we turn to the work of Vigotsky and Piaget to examine two different theoretical explanations of the interrelationship. In Vigotsky's view 'thought development is determined by language ... the child's intellectual growth is contingent on his mastering the social means of thought, that is, language'. Drawing on comparative data (the sounds produced by animals and human infants, together with their attempts at problem solving), Vigotsky recognized that speech and thought initially develop along different lines, independently of each other. Speech at this stage is preintellectual and is largely emotional in nature, for example babbling, calling, or crying. Similarly there is a prelinguistic phase in the development of thought when the infant will perform simple actions, solve simple problems, and clearly has some simple concept based mainly on recognition of the familiar, but has to accomplish all this without any attempt at speech.

In the human infant these two lines cross, according to Vigotsky, during the child's second year when he begins to learn to speak and to use his rudimentary language to help his problem-solving activities. Speech is beginning to become rational rather than just emotional and 'thought' becomes verbal. This stage is marked by a sudden increase in the child's vocabulary and attempts to use language and also a certain curiosity about words. The child's activities are now almost invariably accompanied by speech. His actions appear to be guided by his own autonomous speech which at first is overt but later on appears to die away. Everyone familiar with young children at play knows how they talk to themselves, giving a running commentary on what they are doing, regardless of whether there is anybody present. Vigotsky suggests that even when children cease to talk aloud when playing, this now inner or silent speech still plays an important function in regulating and directing activities. If the child's activities are frustrated or he encounters problems he cannot surmount in play, speech reappears at a remarkable rate, apparently to help him solve the problem.

The notion of language acting as a regulatory mechanism receives support from Luria's work. In his clinical study (1956) of five-year-old twins, retarded in all aspects of intellectual growth, he showed that when better opportunities were provided to promote language development, their behaviour generally showed signs of catching up with that of their age group. Play, which previously had been random, nonproductive, and nondirective became far more advanced with the use of language, in that the boys could now plan activities and follow them through without abandoning whatever they had been doing after only a few minutes. Further experimental work conducted by Luria (1959, 1961) supported the view that one important function of language is to guide and regulate behaviour which otherwise becomes random and inconsequential. On this view then language is seen to be a necessary condition of thought and of the development of intelligence.

Piaget's emphasis is rather different. Although ready to admit that language is necessary for thought to develop, he does not regard it as a sufficient condition (1959). Rational or intelligent activities he sees as rooted in action, which is considered important at three stages of development: the sensory-motor stage, the level of concrete operations, and that of formal operations. At the sensory motor stage, the infant learns about his world through direct sensory experience, mainly by touching, tasting, and smelling. At the early stage of concrete operations, he begins to be able to classify and to form categories, which he can best do manually before working out the problem symbolically, that is, in words. Finally, at the stage of formal operations, he begins to think logically and hypothetically. Action however, according to Piaget, is at the roots of even propositional logic.

In these three areas Piaget suggests that language alone is not enough to explain thought because operations that characterize it nevertheless must be rooted in action. Without language, however, operations would necessarily remain at the stage of successive actions which could be performed only one after the other and not simultaneously. This in fact is what language allows us to do, namely to be released from the here and now world of action to a level where future, past, and present can be combined and where the purely hypothetical is possible.

The views of Piaget and Vigotsky differ in emphasis rather than in nature. But for our practical purposes two conclusions are of utmost importance: that children's intellectual development will be impeded without the use of language and that language development itself will be impeded without opportunities for activity. Although empirical evidence has cast doubt on the hypothesis that language development can be accelerated by adult expansion (Bellugi and Brown, 1964), or that concept development can be accelerated by practice in using specific linguistic structures (Sinclair de Zwart, 1969 and Inhelder and Piaget, 1958) or by practice at specific activities before the child has reached an appropriate stage in development, we are still fairly sure that once this stage has been reached, constant use of language in an active environment is a necessary condition for continued development. Children do not talk, as we remarked earlier, unless they have something to talk about, hence the importance of a varied environment in the classroom, a rich programme of experiences outside it, and opportunities provided to talk about activities and experiences. A child's environment may be rich in opportunities, but he has to learn to recognize them and to learn the interest of his surroundings. Thus a vague idea of letting children loose to discover what is interesting for themselves usually makes nonsense. For most children, if not most adults, learning to find the interesting features of one's surroundings or experiences is a social activity, which has to be shared by a teacher who knows how to further the interest and by peers who participate in it. Barnes (1976) illustrates how small groups of twelve- to thirteen-year-olds learn to clarify their concepts in exploratory dialogue. They often ask questions of one another to establish what they already know, by putting it into a different context. Language used for exploration allows what Barnes refers to as a rearticulation of thought, which is part of a child's cognitive development.

Language and concepts
Having considered the origins and interrelationship of language and thought in a general way, we now turn to a consideration of the part played by language in concept learning. Basically, to learn a concept means to recognize an object or event as belonging to a category or to recognize something already familiar. Early concepts then clearly do not depend upon the use of language. A baby learns to recognize his mother as the one who feeds and protects him long before the concept 'mother' is learned. Animals too can be said to have acquired a concept when they distinguish between different objects. In food-seeking experiments, for example, rats can learn to distinguish between different shapes; chicks have been shown to learn a relationship concept when they seek food from the brighter of two squares (black or grey; dark or light grey; grey or white). But clearly an adult human being develops far more sophisticated concepts than these and it is useful for us to examine what kinds of concept adults do use, in order to understand how they are developed in children.

Dearden offers a useful but simple account of the main kinds of concept we use. He distinguishes three important categories, though, as noted, this is a simplified scheme and not all concepts fit neatly into one of the categories, while some categories can be further subdivided. *Perceptual* concepts include physical objects such as cat, flower, earth, blue, straight, that is, concepts which share certain manifest characteristics with other members of the same category. Young infants begin to acquire this kind of concept before they have a grasp of language, during the normal course of their random exploration of the environment. *Practical* concepts in Dearden's classification are those which are best understood by reference to their function, such as chair, post office, book, door. *Theoretical* concepts include the far more abstract ones such as wisdom, truth, freedom, mass, weight. When we come to examine how these various types of concept are learned, we shall see the rather different function of language and the implications for the ways in which teachers might help children to learn concepts of different kinds.

Children explore practical concepts by direct experience, by looking at objects, tasting them, touching and feeling them. There is no doubt that some sort of recognition goes on, but it is difficult to know whether the concept they 'discover' is the same as the one an adult has when he uses the publicly accepted symbol, its name, to denote it. If an adult points to an animal, telling the child it is a cat, how can the child know what is being pointed to unless he already has a concept of what a cat is and already understands the social convention of pointing? As far as he is concerned pointing could mean the finger used, the animal's fur, its colour, its tail, and so on. This explanation of how children learn the names of objects is clearly not very satisfactory any more than is the abstractionist model whereby a child is supposed to abstract the attributes common to the class of objects denoted by a specific label (attributes such as fur, four legs, tail) and to understand that the label denotes a cat. Simple though it may seem, the early stages of language which involve no more than learning the names of objects are highly complex to explain theoretically. Wittgenstein (1953) suggests that children learn to use language by participating in 'language games' and that they learn these rules by playing games. And before a child starts using words himself, he has had plenty of language preparation. He has handled objects, heard an adult refer to them by name, and can recognize them. It is only when a child uses language to denote objects in the same way as adults that we can even suspect that he shares the same concepts. Yet to use words correctly as labels does not necessarily mean that the child fully understands the underlying concepts. Jahoda (1963) shows how six-year-olds use geographical terms like 'town', 'city', 'capital' correctly in some contexts (for example 'London is the capital of England'), but in other contexts reveal incomplete understanding.

Learning to play language games is then a continuous process, and indeed a social process. To make themselves intelligible children must learn the public rules governing the use of words. Without these rules, which are of course not explicitly taught, there would be no common understanding and no language as we know it. This notion of public rules governing the use of language is clearly applicable to the learning of practical concepts. Children learn the uses and functions of concepts not only by observing adults using them, but by talking about them themselves. Language has gone beyond the mere labelling stage. They might learn the use of a spoon by observation, but it would be difficult to learn the use of a post office or a bank merely by observing what people are doing in them. Without language none of the activities that go on in these places would make any sense at all, so that the concepts could never evolve.

Theoretical concepts, those we aim to introduce children to in school in various forms of knowledge and understanding, would be quite impossible without using language in its widest sense. Labelling would be far too limited. How could the label 'truth' tell us anything about the concept behind it Even when specific theoretical concepts are labelled by the same word – fish, mammal, bird – (Natadze, 1963), real understanding develops only by reference to theoretical insight gained by symbolic means, that is, the use of publicly shared language.

What has been said here about the learning of concepts through language should serve to cast doubt on the validity of pure discovery learning in school. Children cannot possibly discover for themselves what they have no inkling of. They would not even recognize what they had discovered without constant checking, discussion, and guidance from their teachers. This is absolutely essential as concepts are learned, differentiated, and extended. Continuous reference to examples and dialogue between teacher and pupil are needed if pupils are to learn concepts precisely enough to make real sense of them. Group work is helpful especially when children have grasped certain concepts, but unguided group discussion can be just as fruitless as the unguided discovery a child might pursue on his own.

Since language is manifestly important in acquiring any but the simplest of perceptual concepts, how do those children come to understand their world who cannot use language? Work up to the early 1960s had suggested that deaf children, because of poor linguistic powers, are likely to be retarded in concept information. Oléron (1953) reports a study of deaf five- to seven-year-olds showing that even though deaf children achieved increasing success with age on a transposition task, they are unlikely to reach the standard of hearing children. Chulliat and Oléron (1955) had similarly found that the deaf were impeded in their ability to transpose experience to new tasks by the paucity of their language which prevented them from organizing schemes of past experience satisfactorily. Vincent (1957) found that deaf children, when required to classify things by more than one criterion, were unable to do so because of the rigidity of their mental structure. Ewing (1957), summarizing the literature to date on concept learning in deaf children, comments that 'there are indications that subnormal linguistic experience causes a lack of intellectual flexibility' and hence an inability to form concepts at the level reached by normal children.

This in fact seems a very plausible explanation of the retardation of the deaf, in view of the important function of language that we have been discussing. But Furth more recently (1966) has questioned this long-held assumption. Observing that mature deaf adults seem to differ only minimally from similar hearing adults, although they do show certain differences in thinking, he posed certain questions. Are these differences in thinking to be attributed to deafness itself and thus to reduced linguistic competence or might they be due to the fact that deaf people are ill-informed on many things that a hearing person picks up casually in the course of ordinary social intercourse? Are deaf people socially restricted because of their handicap? To what extent are their personality and thinking shaped by the emotional effects of their handicap and the years spent in the restricted environment of a boarding school for the deaf?

Such considerations prompted Furth to launch a highly ambitious programme of experiments to attempt to discover the precise nature of deaf children's thinking in order to establish whether they need necessarily remain retarded throughout life. His finding led him to the tentative conclusion that although the deaf are retarded in certain areas of concept learning (for example, in the discovery of a concept but not in its use and in shifting from one principle to another in categorization, because of rigidity of thought) this is a result of their limited social experience rather than a direct or necessary consequence of linguistic deficiency. He suggests that we should look for a relationship between *social* environment and intellectual development rather than between linguistic deficiency and intellectual deficiency. The restricted nature of a deaf child's early environment does not motivate him to ask questions, to pick up information casually, or to be offered random information in a variety of situations in the same way as a normal child does. The fact that deaf people seem unable to look for reasons or principles but are not unable to reason is to be attributed to the nature of their early training and education, Furth suggests. Parents of deaf children are not encouraged to convey information to them by pointing, gesture, or pictures. Their children therefore not only grow up ill-informed, but are not encouraged to examine facts or display any intellectual curiosity. Once they have grasped a principle it seems that they are taught to use it repetitively and therefore rigidly. The kind of thinking considered retarded, then, seems to be actively encouraged by their early upbringing, possibly because those caring for them are relieved to find some kind of thinking going on, but certainly because they lack the skills and techniques to use nonlinguistic means of stimulating curiosity. Furth makes suggestions for some kind of enrichment programme employing nonverbal techniques.

An interesting suggestion for experimentation, but one fraught with difficulties, as we shall see later, is to compare normal deaf subjects with hearing people whose experience has been restricted. Furth says 'It would simply consist of obtaining a sample of persons who could be assumed to be culturally deprived and comparing the performance of these persons with that of the deaf on some critical tasks.' It is certainly of interest and value to question the assumption that the thinking difficulties of the deaf are always due to linguistic incompetence but to regard it as a simple matter to assume that others are culturally deprived is dangerous and bound to create more problems than it would hope to solve.

The social context of language

Language, by its very nature, is a social process. Although it seems highly plausible that humans have an inbuilt ability to learn language rapidly, as Chomsky and others suggest, nothing resembling human speech would be developed if children were not brought up in a social world where people communicate with others by linguistic means. A consideration of the social context of language gives rise to two interesting aspects that warrant exploration. We shall examine first of all how language may be affected by the context or culture in which it develops, in order to discover ways in which children's experience of the world is shaped by the kind of language they learn. We shall then go on to consider how language varies according to the social situation in which it is used.

An interesting theoretical viewpoint to consider is that of the cultural anthropologists, Whorf and Sapir, who, unlike Chomsky and McNeill, deny that man possesses a biological predisposition for language acquisition. Sapir believed that our perception of the world is largely shaped by language and that therefore 'the worlds in which different societies live are distinct worlds' (1949). Similarly, Whorf, who formulated the hypothesis of linguistic relativity (1956), believed that our world, initially nothing more than a flux of impressions, has to be organized largely by the linguistic system of the culture in which we happen to be born. He comments that 'no individual is free to describe nature with absolute impartiality but is constrained to certain modes of communication even while he thinks himself free'.

Whorf was particularly interested in vocabulary constraints and suggested that the words available in our native language determine the concepts we can acquire. One of the most frequently quoted instances of this is the vast range of specific words in the Eskimo language to denote various kinds of snow and ice. Similarly the language spoken in the Brazilian jungle is abundantly rich in words for palm trees and parrots, all instances where English, by comparison, has only one or two specific words, and where differences, where required, have to be expressed in phrases, for example, 'tightly packed snow'. Whorf's hypothesis was that we perceive what we have words for, implying that the language available to us serves to shape our world. Similar claims were made for the influence of structural differences in language upon human experience. A Hopi (Red Indian) language has no verb system as we know it, but expresses duration of time by a complex series of nouns.

It would appear from these hypotheses that language is causally related to cognitive structure and, of course, if this were so it would have important implications for subcultural differences in relation to language and learning in school. But the direction of causality cannot be determined. It is not possible to be sure whether we form only those concepts for which there is appropriate language already available or whether we develop language because we need to express those concepts we have. Probably the availability or frequency of usage of concepts is in question. In English, for example, we have no specific words for certain kinship relationships, probably because we do not single them out for separate considerations. We have to talk of a paternal or maternal grandfather rather than having separate terms. Similarly, aunts and uncles are so labelled regardless of whether they stem from our mother's or father's side of the family or whether they belong by marriage or by blood. These differences are not important to our kinship structure, whereas certain cultures where such differences are important have an abundance of terms to make the necessary distinctions.

Apart from the interest of such speculations, the cultural relativist position has been briefly introduced here because it was on this view that Bernstein based his early work on language codes which he considered to vary according to subculture or class. The implications of this view will be examined later in the context of school learning.

Language and social convention

But let us first consider a rather different effect of context upon language. The cultural relativity hypothesis suggests that the language an individual has at his disposal is one shaped by a broad context, the culture into which he is born, and that he therefore contributes little to his own linguistic and perceptual development. Even if this view has been disputed, it does highlight the importance of context for language and here we shall consider context in a narrower sense and ask how the situation an individual finds himself in helps to influence the language he chooses to use. The speaker is by no means completely constrained but it will become clear that a child learns to distinguish between language deemed appropriate or inappropriate by adults according to the nature of the child's relationship towards those with whom he is speaking.

Like other areas of human action discussed in this book, language is not something static but is a dynamic process. Language can control an individual by helping to share his perception, concept learning, and thought processes, yet in the social sphere it can also be used by him to control others. The study of language can in fact reveal much about the nature and network of social relationships in any community. Language can serve as an index of social interaction, since it both unifies and divides in the sense that people sharing a common language or dialect regard themselves as belonging together. Newcomers to a group have to learn to use the appropriate language before they are fully accepted, yet if they venture to use it before members are prepared to accept them, their behaviour may be regarded as offensive. For example, for an outsider to use familiar or pet names for members of a group is usually unacceptable. It follows then that to use a different language from the majority marks one out as being different. Language can be said to be a symbol of group and individual identity. An individual's right to use language in certain ways and in particular contexts is usually controlled by what is socially acceptable, permitted, or prohibited. Just as dress, eating habits, and other social conventions are regulated by the rules established in a given community, so language and speech are to some extent governed by similar rules. For example, children in most schools are not permitted to address their teachers by their first names, though this is a rule which may be relaxed in institutions which regard themselves as particularly progressive. It is still considered inappropriate for teachers to use anything but surnames in addressing boys in some grammar and public schools and a teacher who flaunts this rule is regarded as somewhat odd. In fact a deliberate breach of such speech rules and conventions often represents a rejection of the role others expect him to play, thus disrupting the social order in his immediate community and causing a way of life hitherto taken for granted to be questioned. An unintentional breach of such rules on the other hand is regarded as social ineptitude.

Values are attached to different kinds of language whereby some kinds are regarded as of higher status than others. Standard or BBC English tends in this country to have a higher status than a Liverpool or Glasgow dialect. High-status language is deliberately chosen by those who have the choice to give some indication of their own status. Certain groups of individuals can exercise power over others socially by means of the language they use. It is fairly common, for example, for members of the medical or legal profession to be seen by their patients or clients as more powerful than themselves, partly because of the specialist, manifestly learned terminology they employ. Furthermore, accent too can be regarded as an indication of social power or high status. Giles (1971) showed that speakers of received pronunciation (RP), that is, BBC English, were rated as more prestigious, competent, intelligent than speakers with South Welsh or Somerset accents, but less favourably on social traits. Regional speakers, in this survey, were considered to have greater personal integrity, social attractiveness, and sense of humour. We saw in our discussion of making judgements of children how easily first impressions can be formed on the basis of appearance, dress, and so on. The language a child uses or the accent he has acquired may equally serve as a cue for forming a judgement. If Giles' finding is general then the 'well-spoken' child with a standard southern English accent is going to be at an unfair advantage when judgements are made.

The school is clearly one of the contexts where such rules and conventions about the use of speech and language operate. When children come to school they have to learn rules governing forms of address to the teacher, appropriate vocabulary, grammatical structure, and pronunciation that are acceptable. By subtle means they learn the role expected of them as pupils, one of its important characteristics being a greater social distance between pupil and teacher than the young child has previously experienced in his relationships with adults. He frequently has to learn to respond to verbal cues he has never yet encountered, but which his teacher expects him to act upon. Joan Tough (1973) shows how a four-year-old boy fails to respond to an indirect request such as 'Would you pick the towel up for me before someone treads on it?' 'What do we do with a towel Jimmy?', 'Would you like to hang it up?' and only does as requested when a direct instruction is given. Such phrases as 'would you like to ... '. 'would you mind ... ' are indirect ways used by adults to make a request or command seem more polite, but their implication is lost with young children who have always been ordered to do things in direct command form at home. A child used to a different set of verbal cues may easily assume that if he is not being told directly what to do, he need pay no attention to what his teacher says. He therefore appears to be deliberately disobedient, but in fact has failed to understand what is required of him.

Adolescents are more likely deliberately to flaunt rules of linguistic convention in an attempt to reject the pupil role imposed upon them. Countless examples come to mind of fourteen- and fifteen-year-olds failing to use what the teacher considers an appropriate mode of address, suitable choice of vocabulary, and so on. Social differentiation in school is recognized by pupils using nonstandard English who receive their teachers' disapproval. As we saw earlier, children's everyday language is frequently rejected by teachers who want to force pupils to use standard English. However, this can become colourless and lose vitality if the pupils regard it as something not their own. Barnes' observations (1971) show how teachers exert subtle control in the classroom by the use of an arid language of secondary education, to use his term.

We have already seen in our discussion of classroom interaction how control is exerted over children by a particular kind of discourse structure (Stubbs, 1975). This three-part sequence, consisting of the teacher's question, the pupil's reply, then the teacher's evaluation of the reply, is typical of many classrooms and enables the teacher to keep pupils in their place, as well as to control what they learn. A change in this speech structure would force the teacher to relinquish the kind of control which it supports.

Social class variations in the use of language
Poor linguistic competence, including the use of nonstandard English, has, at least since the 1950s when differences in educability caught everybody's attention, been put forward to explain the apparent disadvantage of lower working-class children over their middle-class peers. After the 1944 Education Act when equality of opportunity was interpreted as the right of all children, regardless of family circumstances, to have the chance to obtain a place in a selective school, it was found that still a far greater proportion of middle-class children succeeded in gaining grammar school places, mainly on the basis of intelligence tests used for selection purposes.

Subsequent research revealed that lower working-class children were less successful than middle-class ones not only at the stage of the 11+ transfer, but right from the time they entered school up to the sixth-form level. Fewer working-class children were placed in higher streams within the school or higher groups within the class. More were labelled as incipient failures by their teachers at the infant stage (Fuchs, 1968; Goodacre, 1968). Once at secondary school more were placed in lower streams and left early, and subsequently failed to take advantage of further education (Little and Westergaard, 1964). We have already seen how teachers help to shape these disadvantages, but little has been said so far about basic differences in learning which might depend on the ability to understand and use language. Joan Tough (1973) showed how nursery school children may fail to understand a teacher's linguistic cues if her style of speaking differs from that which a child has learned to interpret at home. Even at this very early stage, then, differences in language ability or competence lead to differences in understanding, in responding to the teacher, and in social learning.

Clearly children do come to school with different degrees of linguistic competence and it would be interesting first of all to consider various kinds of learning to see how far they depend on language and thus where the children at a linguistic disadvantage are inevitably going to be hampered in their learning. Are some of the most important types of school learning such as the acquisition of skills, the learning of concepts, the development of logical reasoning, the growth of moral understanding impeded because of a poor grasp of language? Simple skills, such as walking, climbing, running are acquired by autogenous practice before children can use or understand language, but as Luria (1956) has shown, language serves to regulate even behaviour of this kind so that it becomes better planned and more coordinated. However, more complex skills such as athletic skills, the use of tools and machinery, the use of instruments and apparatus could not simply be picked up (or if they were, would be learned clumsily and with errors) but require instruction and explanation, as well as demonstration, if they are to be fully understood. The learning of concepts has already been discussed at some length, so a reminder here will suffice. Perceptual concepts and some practical ones can be learned without language, but abstract, logical, relational concepts inevitably rely on the use of language. How for instance could a child learn the significance of 'either/or', 'neither/nor', 'although', and so on without participating in language games with others more experienced than he? Logical reasoning, although it has its roots in action, as Piaget shows, cannot develop adequately without the use of language which frees the thinker from the here and now, enabling him to deal with simultaneous mental operations and not to be confined to consecutive ones. Hypothetical thinking, which is the basis of scientific and mathematical reasoning, involving conditional propositions, would clearly suffer. Furthermore, the kind of social and moral learning that would be possible without language would be akin to training. A child, or even an animal, can be trained by conditioning techniques to adhere to certain social conventions and even to appear to behave morally. He learns to do what he knows adults want for fear of punishment and disapproval or to obtain reward or favour. But moral understanding to a point where one is able to work out one's own values must, as we shall see, develop as a result of understanding reasons for actions and being able to justify one's moral stance. Such understanding relies heavily on linguistic means. If all these basic kinds of learning, let alone the learning of different forms of understanding embodied in different areas of the curriculum, rely on language, then it is of major concern to teachers if some children begin with an initial linguistic disadvantage. Since so much formal school learning depends on the use of language, the problem for teachers is to identify the source of linguistic disadvantage.

Bernstein (1958) was one of the first to tackle the problem of differences in spoken language. Set within a sociological framework, his theory attempted to explain speech differences in terms of early social relationships the young child forms within the family. In his early papers he tried to trace the relationship between social class, language, and learning.

Social class, always a problematic term, was seen for his purposes as two broad subgroups; the working class, where neither parent has had a selective secondary education or any skilled training, and the middle class where both parents have had a selective secondary education and hold nonmanual jobs. There is too a transitional or upwardly mobile working-class group, some of whom have had some experience of selective secondary education or have been trained in a specific skill. The marked differences in language, social relationships, and control that Bernstein discusses refer mainly to the two extremes of these subgroups – *lower* working class and middle class. Scant justice can be done here to the evolution of Bernstein's theory. It is essential that those concerned with such linguistic differences should certainly pursue some of the summaries of his theory to help them to tackle his original papers, if his ideas are not to be misinterpreted, as sadly they have been, by those who are only superficially familiar with them. Working on the hypothesis that lower working-class children will be less linguistically competent than their middle-class peers because of the greater stress laid by the middle-class parents on language, he established that on a verbal test of intelligence (Mill Hill Vocabulary Test), working-class adolescent boys scored significantly lower than a comparable middle-class sample. On a nonverbal test (Raven's Progressive Matrices) the discrepancy in performance was not significant. He went on to argue from these findings, albeit from a very small sample of subjects, that a great deal of potential ability is being lost in that working-class pupils may have failed to reach grammar school because of their poor performance on the selection tests which are mainly verbal.

Differences in the kind of speech system or language code that children develop are part of the process of socialization. Bernstein suggests families from different social backgrounds have different attitudes towards child rearing and thus different kinds of relationship are formed between parents and children; these relationships in turn affect the use of language. Several general conclusions emerge from empirical studies carried out by Bernstein and his coworkers, indicating where these early differences originate. From an analysis of replies given by 50 working-class and 50 middle-class mothers, all randomly selected, Bernstein and Henderson (1969) drew conclusions about the ways in which the different types of social interaction that develop duly affect the child's dependence on and use of language to express his needs. Clearly there will be exceptions. Not all apparently working-class or middle-class mothers will conform to a general stereotype, so it is important to remember that what follows indicates only a general tendency. Middle-class mothers are less likely to use coercive means of controlling their children (including smacking or unelaborated commands) but will tend to explain to their children why they regard their behaviour as undesirable. They are more likely to enter into and encourage conversation with their children and will attempt to answer difficult questions rather than evade them as many working-class mothers do. Jean Jones (1966), again using a questionnaire technique and drawing from a sample of 360 mothers, found that middle-class mothers tend to prepare their five-year-olds for a more active role in school than do working-class mothers. They read to them, encouraging them to join a library, talk to them about school and show their children similarities between home and school, recognizing the educational significance of toys and play. In terms of language development, this active role adopted early by middle-class infants will make them more ready to talk to their teacher. Bernstein and Henderson's evidence supports this view. They suggest that middle-class children are encouraged to learn the principles of skills, whereas working-class children assume a passive learning role in that they are told by their mothers how things work and not expected to work it out for themselves, thus failing to gain autonomy or to engage actively in their own learning. Robinson and Rackstraw (1967), dealing with the way mothers cope with children's questions, found that working-class mothers are less likely to reply accurately to children's questions or even to answer them at all. They are less likely to explain or give elaborate answers and more likely to appeal to tradition in getting children to conform or obey. What emerges then from these various studies is that children are socialized differently according to the family subculture and that the emphasis put upon speech and language during the socialization process differs according to social class.

What then are the educational implications of such differences in early socialization and its effect on the use of language? Bernstein suggests the possibility of two different language codes. The restricted code is characterized by short sentences, frequently unfinished and with poor syntactical structure; by frequent use of short commands and questions; by limited use of adjectives and adverbs; by avoidance of impersonal and passive forms; and by use of clichés and idiomatic phrases without variation according to context. The restricted code speaker does not make himself explicit through language but relies heavily on gesture and intonation, and appeals to the listener in terms of 'You know what I mean?', 'See?' and so on. The elaborated code, because of its greater structural complexity, is one in which the speaker does make himself explicit, without having to rely on nonverbal cues or the shared sympathy of the listener. Because of fewer clichés and well-worn phrases, the speech used by elaborated code speakers is at once more personal and less predictable. From this brief description of the codes it can be seen that a restricted code is more likely to be used when people share common experiences and are well enough acquainted with one another for meanings and intentions not to have to be made explicit. It would normally be used by any speaker within his own family or with close friends for example.

Bernstein suggested in his early work that most working-class speakers, as a result of the way in which they have experienced socialization in the early years, are confined to a restricted code, while middle-class speakers have access to both. Since formal school learning requires children to make themselves explicit through language, those who can do so are at an educational advantage. One way in which working-class children fail to make themselves explicit in words is that meaning for them tends to be implicit, context bound, or particularistic, whereas the middle-class child can operate in a context independent situation.

The work of Hawkins (1969) with five-year-olds who were asked to tell the story depicted in a series of pictures shows these differences. Working-class children in this study tend to use pronouns instead of nouns so that unless the listener knows the context in which they are operating (in this case, unless he himself is looking at the pictures) he will not be at all clear about what the children are describing. The middle-class five-year-olds are able to make clear to a listener what the pictures contain. Their speech is universalistic or context independent. If such linguistic differences are apparent so early and in the case of working-class children do limit their opportunity to benefit from school experiences, then it is quite possible that by the time they reach secondary school the gulf between middle- and working-class children is considerable. We shall see in another context that there are gross social class differences in educational performance. Differences in the use of language may well be one important contributory factor.

Bernstein's work has been stringently criticized on methodological grounds (see especially Coulthard, 1969). No doubt much of this criticism is justified, but anybody who pursues the *development* of such a theory as Bernstein's (amply documented over the past two decades) must acknowledge that the investigator is bound to stumble and make modifications in groping his way towards further understanding. Research methods indeed would not develop at all if errors did not give rise to modification and eventually to improvement. But of greater concern here in the context of language in education are the implications Bernstein's work has had for educational practice, many of them unfortunately based on a misunderstanding of his basic tenets. His early papers, published towards the end of the 1950s, came at a time when teachers had been made aware of gross inequalities in educational opportunity in this country. The idea that working-class children were failing because of their linguistic disadvantage was seized upon eagerly by teachers, to explain why such children, in spite of the teachers' efforts, were not succeeding in school.

Linguistic deprivation

However, it was unfortunate that Bernstein's notion of a restricted code gradually came to be regarded as an inferior kind of speech, as some sort of nonstandard, second-rate language which made school learning difficult and impeded logical thinking. In spite of Bernstein's comments (though perhaps not pointed or forceful enough in the early papers) that a restricted code was not to be regarded as second-rate, and that one code is not *better* than another, since 'each possesses its own aesthetic, its own possibilities' (Bernstein, 1964), the implication seen by his critics, and by teachers, many of whom became half-familiar with his theories, was one of linguistic disadvantage or even deprivation. And the idea of linguistic deprivation as one aspect of cultural deprivation was not without support in educational circles, particularly in the USA where compensatory educational programmes have been in operation from 1960 onwards. One of the assumptions upon which compensatory programmes were based was that certain disadvantaged children have difficulty in school because of poor language development and that remedial methods can help overcome these difficulties. The hampering effects of children's early impoverished home environment were thought to be reversible by the use of certain training or enrichment techniques.

The emphasis placed on language in American compensatory programmes must be attributed partly to the assumed interdependence between thought and language though, as we saw earlier, the nature of this relationship is by no means clear. Nevertheless, great emphasis was placed upon language in the American preschool intervention programmes, such as the Bereiter and Engelmann language development programme. The basic aims of this programme are to develop in preschool children sufficient understanding of language for them to grasp 'identity statements' and their negative counterparts ('this is a cat'; 'this is not a dog'), to accelerate their concept learning and to enable them to understand from their teacher when they are right or wrong. Four-year-old children work with one teacher in groups of five for twenty-minute periods a day. Effort is concentrated on helping them to classify objects by showing them pictures and bombarding them with questions, to which they are taught to respond in chorus. It is thus a programme based on drill in sentence structure and use of words and as such has been used to teach standard English to Negro children and other nonstandard English speakers. Other programmes, such as that of Blank and Solomon (1968), giving individual language tuition to children, where the teacher works upon the child's responses and draws him into conversation about his activities while he is playing are in some ways reminiscent of the methods used by Joan Tough (1973) in the ordinary classroom. These programmes have had varying degrees of success but naturally enough have not escaped criticism, particularly because of the teaching methods employed.

Parry and Archer (1975) in this country express concern about the U.S.A. language programmes because of the heavy emphasis on language tests and of repetition and drill of linguistic patterns. The 'Talk Reform' programme (Gahagan and Gahagan, 1972) was begun in 1964 in infant classrooms in East London and was carried out under normal classroom conditions. The schools selected had large numbers of immigrant children in need of help in language development. This programme was based on peer interaction and aimed to extend children's vocabulary, encourage a variety of speech structures, and improve auditory discrimination.

The first Schools' Council Pre-School Education Project (Parry and Archer, 1975; Parry, 1975) was set up to identify the needs of preschool children who were likely to suffer from language difficulties. This was followed by a second project, directed by Joan Tough (1976), to help teachers cope with the needs identified in the earlier study. The main purpose of this programme was to help teachers make an appraisal of young children's skill in using language, as they listened to them talking, talked with them, and helped them to explore their ideas and experiences. The programme includes teachers' guides designed to help them in the classroom and for use as a basis for group discussion and workshop sessions. The next stage, namely to help teachers develop the skills involved in fostering language development, was followed up in a third project (Tough, 1977).

There are many children who come to school less linguistically competent than others and who therefore need help in this area. Joan Tough's study (1977) shows that even at the age of three there are noticeable differences between the ways in which children use language. Her comparative study indicated that, although children from disadvantaged backgrounds used language *as much as* others, they used it in a different way. In comparison with the advantaged group, they used words less frequently for reasoning about present experiences, for recalling the past, or for projecting into the future. Similar differences were observed with groups of children at the age of 5½ and 7½. The crucial question raised is not whether the language of one group is superior to that of the other, but whether the observed differences are likely to affect the ways in which children benefit from school experiences. The evidence showed that the disadvantaged group had greater linguistic resources than their typical performance revealed, suggesting that, if these resources could be stimulated and promoted, the children would be able to develop a similar degree of linguistic flexibility to that displayed by the advantaged group in Tough's study.

Of interest at this point is the distinction made by Chomsky between linguistic competence and performance. Competence refers to our understanding of language, while performance is reflected in the way in which we use it. As everyone who has tried to converse with a foreigner in his own language knows, we understand far more than we actually put into words ourselves. The same holds good for the learning of the mother tongue, in Chomsky's view. To infer that children's understanding of language is necessarily impeded because their performance is limited is probably misguided. This distinction is a useful one for teachers to remember when they express concern about the way in which their pupils use language. Perhaps the distinction might help to demolish the notion that some children whose performance is limited are necessarily linguistically deprived or even nonverbal.

One of the most virulent critics of the notion of linguistic deprivation was Labov who, working within a linguistic rather than a sociological or psychological framework, wrote an impassioned argument declaiming verbal deprivation as a myth (1970). He defends the nonstandard English spoken by Negro ghetto children, but some of his comments might well be applied to other nonstandard English speakers. The myth in Labov's view has arisen partly because speech data gathered from different social groups have been collected in very artificial situations. It is not surprising if a child, sitting in a strange room with an unfamiliar adult at the other side of a desk, fails to reply to his questions, thus appearing to be nonverbal. Labov's methods instead were to use Negro investigators who entered into conversation with Negro children in a relaxed situation. He describes the interviewer sitting on the floor, sharing a packet of crisps with an eight-year-old boy who has brought a friend along with him. This more natural context is conducive to conversation in a way that a more conventional interview technique fails to be. Labov's article is based on studies carried out with Negro boys of ten to seventeen during the period 1965-1967. Apart from suggested improvements in methodology, he examines the grammatical structure of Negro nonstandard English to see whether it does in fact have rules of its own or is merely randomly inaccurate as is frequently claimed, and to consider whether it does impede logical thinking. His findings were that Negro nonstandard English does not differ basically in syntax from standard English, having its own consistent rules, and that it does not prevent logical thinking. Samples of speech such as that of Larry, a fifteen-year-old school failure, talking about the nature of God, do show logical clarity but are clothed in a speech form which many teachers would reject and which most would have difficulty in understanding. In Labov's view then, no child is nonverbal or verbally deprived. His vernacular may be different from standard English but this in itself would not impede logical thinking or retard him in school learning. It is rather teachers' refusal to accept this vernacular and reluctance to learn to understand it that does make school learning problematic and unpalatable and eventually leads to school rejection.

Although the concept of linguistic deprivation has not met such stringent criticism in this country, probably because the term itself never became so powerful as in the USA, Rosen (1972) writes strongly against the idea of working-class speech being second-rate and inappropriate for school learning. He too questions the methods used in attempts to elicit speech from children in artificial situations, and hotly criticizes Bernstein's attempts to defend the value of working-class speech. Such remarks as 'A restricted code gives access to a vast potential of meanings of delicacy, subtlety, and diversity of cultural forms, to a unique aesthetic', are considered purely parenthetic and therefore of limited conviction, since Bernstein never goes on to examine working-class speech in detail or to investigate what a restricted code cannot do. This in Rosen's view is one of the large gaps in our knowledge of language. No one has hitherto examined in detail the strengths, richness, and potential of working-class language. Indeed only recently have attempts been made to investigate how language is actually used in school.

The classroom as a context for language learning

The importance of language learning at all levels of development is being recognized more today than ever before, especially since the publication of the Bullock Report in 1975. Language, quite rightly, is now being seen no longer merely as a means of passing on information to pupils, but is being recognized as of crucial significance in its own right. The assumption, held by many teachers earlier on, that children should already have mastered language before they come to school, or that language learning is the concern mainly of teachers of young children, is fast dying. This change of attitude is embodied in the emphasis placed on the classroom as a context for language learning by some of the major studies of language in school published during the past decade (Bullock, 1975; Barnes, 1969, 1976; Tough, 1973, 1976, 1977; Marland, 1977).

Any context for language learning must provide children with an interested and sympathetic audience, with something to talk about and with a permissive, accepting atmosphere, where children can explore and experiment with language without fear of censure. Children need opportunities for discussion with room for genuine conversation and dialogue, rather than a closed question-and-answer situation. They do not learn language by listening to the teacher, but rather by practising it themselves. As Rosen (1967) and Barnes (1969) both point out, in a teacher-dominated classroom it is mainly the teacher who has the chance of practising language and, as we saw earlier, he has on average a two-thirds share of the talking time (Flanders, 1971).

Children come to school using an everyday language of their own and much of their spontaneous talk at the early stages is devoted to telling the teacher about their families, their possessions, and their activities. A skilful teacher is one who is a good listener and who has developed the technique of knowing when to intervene in children's conversation to promote further use of language. As Joan Tough showed (1973, 1977), the teacher must become sensitive to a child's readiness to be drawn into further conversation. If he is not secure enough to be drawn further, questioning will merely deter him from spontaneous speech. Barnes too (1976) shows how teachers working with older children can inhibit their exploratory talk by intervening in group discussion. He cites an example of twelve- to thirteen-year-olds discussing in small groups some of the problems that the Saxon settlers must have had to face. One group of girls, who were beginning to use language in an exploratory way, changed abruptly to what Barnes calls a performance style when the teacher came along, because they expected the teacher to ask questions to which he already knew the answers. In other words, because they were used to having their replies evaluated and assessed, they spoke as if they were anticipating cross-questioning from the teacher.

It is easy for a teacher, perhaps inadvertently, to inhibit children's speech by insisting either on correct syntax or pronunciation, or on the precise use of specialist terms. To correct a child's syntax when he is eager to say something of importance to him is often interpreted by him as a rebuff, with the result that he does not take the risk again. Barnes (1969), drawing on observations of specialist teachers working with eleven-year-olds, shows how it is possible to overlook or devalue what a child has to say by insisting on the kind of language deemed appropriate to a specific subject. His extract from a chemistry lesson illustrates this well, showing how a teacher abruptly terminates the discussion about the suspension of solids in a liquid when pupils' contributions become anecdotal and they start talking in everyday terms of milk turning to cheese. This argument does not suggest that it is wrong for teachers ever to correct speech or to insist on the precise use of specialist terms, but points out the inhibiting effects upon children's willingness to talk when they feel that most of what they have to say is being assessed.

Conversation, dialogue, and discussion are now recognized as being important means of promoting language development (Tough, 1977; Bullock, 1975; Barnes, 1976; Stubbs, 1976). By conversing with others, a young child learns to be a listener, to see a situation from other people's points of view, and to reflect on how best to communicate what he wants to say. Through exploratory dialogue children can put what they already know into a new context, thus learning to frame ideas clearly so that others can understand them. Exchange of ideas in discussion has also been recognized as an important medium for developing and debating moral concepts. Discussion plays a significant part in moral education projects such as those of Wilson and McPhail and also in the Humanities Curriculum Project (Downey and Kelly, 1978).

Barnes (1976) makes an interesting distinction between exploratory talk and final draft language. Pupils using the former are using language creatively and experimentally to explore new concepts and clarify familiar ones. They do not expect to be criticized, corrected, or censured for what they say or the way the express themselves. Final draft language, on the other hand, does not reveal detours or processes of thought, but presents only a finished product for assessment. The kind of style used will depend on the audience. If children know that the teacher is asking questions to which he clearly knows the answers and is interrogating or cross-questioning them, they will use a final draft or performance style. Exploratory talk is used in a collaborative relationship, whether it is with peers or adults. This distinction is paralleled by the one Bruner (1961) makes between expository and hypothetical modes of teaching. A move away from the expository mode, to meet the needs of some recent curriculum projects relying largely on discussion techniques, requires a change in relationship between teacher and taught, accompanied by a change in the style of language used by both.

Language across the curriculum

It is now accepted by many, whatever their specialism and whatever age range of children they teach, that language, like moral education, is everybody's responsibility. The main sentiment behind the recommendations of the Bullock Report (1975) is that schools should develop a unified language policy to promote and extend pupils' use of language in a wide range of different situations. Many primary schools have given one teacher with a particular interest and expertise special responsibility for constructing a language policy in the school, although the teacher himself usually remains a class teacher. Marland and others (1977) have taken the main challenge of Bullock and tried to help secondary teachers implement such a policy. Marland's central tenet is that learning is not merely through language but with language. He comments that, with so much emphasis on visual communication in everyday life, many teachers have felt obliged to help children to by-pass language rather than to grapple with its problems. The belief that children from certain social class backgrounds are at a disadvantage in school because of language deficiencies has lent support to this move to help those children who might be linguistically hampered to avoid using language, either in spoken or written form. Rather than this, he claims, teachers must ensure that they use a language that all children can cope with. He offers some guidance to secondary teachers to help them lead pupils '*into* language rather than *round* it'.

It cannot be denied that specialist areas have their own particular concepts and terminology that eventually have to be mastered for a full understanding. But if a teacher becomes overconcerned with the terminology of his own subject, pupils will be baffled because the whole thing becomes too arid, distant, and difficult. Their learning is likely to deteriorate into meaningless note taking and rote learning. However, any specialist language, whether it is that of science, of aesthetics, or of moral discourse, is the language of an educated adult and, as such, can have a certain attraction and excitement for children, provided they learn to use it gradually and with understanding. To do this they need considerable linguistic preparation – just as Wittgenstein suggests in the initial learning of simple concepts in one's mother tongue. If teachers emphasize the content of their subject and assume either that language will come of its own accord for the more able pupils, or that some of the others will never be able to learn it, then they are doing an injustice not only to their pupils but also to their own subject. The teacher's own use of language in class is clearly of prime importance. If he devotes most of his teaching time to posing closed questions or formulating notes for his pupils, they will probably never gain a glimpse of the real excitement and interest his specialist subject holds.

Summary and conclusions
In this chapter we have discussed briefly the nature and functions of language, then have examined two different theoretical approaches to early language acquisition, that of S–R psychology and that of Chomsky and McNeill. No one theoretical viewpoint offers a complete explanation of how language is acquired, so it seems that an eclectic approach is more appropriate. The learning of basic syntactic rules seems to be due to an

inborn mechanism (LAD), while an S–R approach accounts for much vocabulary learning.

We have then examined the relationship between language, thought, and concept learning and have tried to show how language promotes or impedes the kind of thinking required by school learning.

In the sections on social aspects of language, we have discussed how language reflects social distance, and how teachers use language to control both knowledge and behaviour. The nature of language is shown to differ according to the demands of any particular social context. Social class variations in the use of language have been explored, with reference to the theories of Bernstein and to the empirical studies of some of his coworkers.

The concept of linguistic deprivation has been critically analysed with illustrations from some preschool language programmes.

Finally, we have examined the classroom as a context for language learning, in order to support our firm belief that language continues to develop throughout formal schooling and even beyond. Our contention that children learn language by using it reflects the recommendations of the Bullock committee and of those who have attempted to put them into practice.

6 Authority

The progress that children make at school will not depend only on the views that teachers hold about such things as intelligence, motivation, and language, and the judgements that they are thus led to make of their pupils. That progress, and indeed those judgements themselves, will depend equally, if not more conclusively, on the kinds of relationship the teacher develops with his pupils, the approach he takes to classroom control, and the kind of atmosphere that is generated by the view he takes of the competing demands of freedom and authority. It is to this question of the teacher's authority, therefore, that we must next turn our attention.

Questions about authority cause teachers concern at the levels of both theory and practice. Whether they will in fact have the authority to control their pupils is a question that worries all trainee teachers and new entrants to the profession and it is a question that continues to concern most teachers throughout their careers. Nowadays, however, many teachers are also uncertain about whether they should be exercising authority over their pupils at all or at least to what extent such control can be justified. There is a feeling abroad, strengthened by developments such as the 'free school' and increased demands for participation by pupils in decision making of all kinds, that any exercise of authority is an infringement of the freedom and rights of the child, so that a certain uneasiness results for those teachers who regard these things as important yet find themselves required by the exigencies of the school situation to place restraints on children's behaviour in many different contexts. Nor again are the practical and theoretical aspects of the problem readily separable, since to a large degree the extent to which one is able to exercise authority will depend on how clear one is about the justification of it, since confidence is needed here perhaps more than anywhere else in education and confidence can only come from a conviction that what one is doing is right. Conversely, much that can only be described as arrant nonsense has been said and written about the freedom of children by those whose view of the issues involved has not been tempered by experience of the realities of the teaching situation. Again, therefore, theory and practice need to be interwoven if we are to achieve a view of the place of authority in education that is both clear and constructive. Again, too, we must begin by attempting to sort out the different issues that are involved.

In doing this we must consider two main kinds of question, firstly, that concerning the justification of the exercise of any kind of authority by teachers and, secondly, a number of related questions concerning the nature of authority, the ways in which teachers can and do come to exercise it, and the repercussions that different approaches to control in the school and in the classroom may have on the development of pupils. These two kinds of question are not, of course, entirely independent of each other, since any discussion of the ways in which a teacher can acquire authority, and especially of the kind of authority that is appropriate to education, must presuppose and, indeed, depend for its substance on some view about its justification, but it will be in the interests of clarity to discuss the two issues separately and most useful to begin with the problem of justification.

Freedom and authority

We must begin our discussion in this field once again by attempting to clarify the concepts we are concerned with and, in particular, by trying to achieve some clarity over the notion of 'freedom' and the use of the adjective 'free'.

In its purely descriptive uses, the word 'free' denotes the absence of some hindrance or restraint. Thus to describe a piece of mechanism as 'free' is to suggest that it has been jammed or blocked in some way, while to describe a man as 'free' is to imply that he has been under some kind of restraint, in prison, for example, or with a full engagement book, or even merely married (Benn and Peters, 1959). In its most common use too, the word indicates the absence of a fee or charge that might act as a hindrance to the acquisition or possession of some object, commodity, or service. Furthermore, in all of these uses of 'free' there seems to be the added implication that the hindrance or restraint that is absent is an undesirable hindrance or restraint. As evidence of this, it is interesting to note and compare the use of the suffixes '-free' and '-less'. In most, if not all, cases the use of '-free' suggests 'good riddance' and the use of '-less' expresses regret at what is missing. What is meat-free to the vegetarian is meat-less to the carnivore and the same can be seen in the contrasting notions of carefree and careless driving (Ryan, 1965). Even in its largely descriptive sense, therefore, and in contexts that might be felt to be largely neutral, politically speaking, freedom is generally regarded as something worth having.

However, all of this does point to the need for some qualification to be made, for some specification of the hindrance that has been removed or that might have been there. In many contexts it is, of course, possible to understand or to supply the appropriate qualification. If an AA patrolman tells me the engine of my car is now free, I can assume that he has found it to be clogged up with some kind of foreign substance which he has been able to remove, but if he tells me that he himself is now free, I will need to know something of his history to be able to find some clues on the basis of which I can supply the necessary qualification to understand what he is talking about. It is this consideration that has given rise to a distinction that has been made between the two kinds of freedom, between the negative and positive views of freedom, between 'freedom from' and 'freedom to', but it is surely the case that in all contexts both of these elements are present and we emphasize that aspect that seems the more significant. It is only meaningful to speak of the freedom to do something if we are conscious that we are free from a restraint that has or might have denied us that freedom or to speak of freedom from something if we are conscious of that thing as having prevented us from being free to achieve some desirable goal or activity (Ryan, 1965).

Freedom, therefore, implies the absence of a restraint that has acted or might have acted as a hindrance to action of some kind.

Often, however, the emotive implications of the term come to the fore and we find it is being used prescriptively, not to describe a state of freedom so much as to demand that such a state be created. This is the kind of meaning the term usually has in social contexts. When Rousseau began *The Social Contract* with the words, 'Man is born free; but everywhere he is in chains', he was not describing men as he might have been if he had said, 'Man is born naked; but everywhere he is in clothes'; he was in fact prescribing or demanding that men should be treated in certain ways and similar demands have been made in much the same form in many other contexts. It is not always entirely clear, however, what such demands amount to. Again some kind of qualification brings clarification so that discussion of freedom of speech or freedom of opinion or freedom of association or freedom of worship will be more meaningful than discussion of freedom in an unqualified sense. To speak of freedom in this kind of unqualified way cannot be to demand the removal of all restraints. To demand this would be to demand licence rather than freedom, a distinction which is very important since it suggests that the existence of some restraints is not incompatible with the notion of social freedom. It is, therefore, a demand not that all restraints be removed but that their existence in all cases be justified.

If this is a correct analysis of the notion of freedom, then it provides us with a negative point that will contribute towards the justification of the exercise of authority, namely that the idea of an authority used to apply justifiable restraints is not incompatible with the notion of freedom. Furthermore, we must note that every human society must have rules and those rules must be enforced by someone if they are to have any meaning at all. As Thomas Hobbes said, 'covenants, without the sword, are but words, and of no strength to secure a man at all' (Leviathan, Ch. XVII). And so we have a further, if again negative, point that authority is a necessary part of any rule-governed society. Neither of these points, of course, offers us any positive clues as to what particular restraints can be justified. It is, however, no small thing to have established that some justification is possible in view of the doubts about this that often exist in people's minds. We must, however, turn to a consideration of more positive arguments for the exercise of authority and in particular those that may indicate the kinds of situation in which it might be argued to be appropriate.

The classical argument for social freedom is undoubtedly that set out in J. S. Mill's essay, 'On Liberty'. The position Mill takes here is uncompromising. 'All restraint *qua* restraint is an evil.' But he suggests one fundamental justification, 'one very simple principle', for the existence of restraints. 'That principle is, that the sole end for which mankind are warranted, individually or collectively, in interfering with the liberty of action of any of their number, is self-protection'. A man may be restrained from interfering with or causing harm to others. Authority exercised to apply restraint in such situations is justified. It is not justified if it is used to restrain him from doing those things which affect him only, those actions that can be called 'self-regarding' actions.

The argument here, then, is that freedom can only be reasonably demanded by anyone up to the point at which the behaviour of one individual or group in a society begins to act as a limitation on the freedom of other individuals or groups. As a judge once said to an Irishman before him on a charge of assault and battery, 'Everyone's freedom is bounded by the position of the other man's nose.' Too much freedom for some people will lead to too little for others, and it is at the point where this begins to happen that the exercise of authority can be justified to ensure that freedom can be enjoyed by all rather than licence by some.

If we apply this to education, we will find that there is beginning to emerge a case at least for one type of school rule, for the exercise of authority by the teacher in the context of general behaviour and the maintenance of order. Where the enjoyment of 'freedom' by one pupil or group of pupils is resulting in a limitation of the freedom of others, through overuse of some facility, for example, the making of excessive noise, running in the corridors, or any other behaviour which is likely to endanger the safety of others or to create an atmosphere in which the ability of others to profit from the educational opportunities offered by the school is impaired, then the teacher must exercise his or her authority to apply restraints in order to promote a proper level of freedom for all. In the sphere of behaviour, then, a good case can be made for the teacher's authority. Schools, like all other rule-governed societies, must have rules that are framed for the protection of all members from each other's excesses and, provided that these rules do not go beyond what that consideration seems to justify, a good case can be made out for them.

No argument that we have adduced so far, however, justifies the use of authority to compel children to join this rule-governed society in the first place. For the law to require that children attend school between the ages of five and sixteen and for us as teachers to demand of them not only certain kinds of behaviour but also certain kinds of learning while they are there requires a different and more positive justification than we have given so far. This proved a difficult problem for Mill too since it goes well beyond what can be justified in the name of self-protection, yet Mill was strongly committed to the value of education and the qualitative superiority of certain kinds of intellectual activity of the kind that he felt schools ought to promote (West 1965). The justification of the exercise of authority by teachers in the area of the curriculum, then, is a much more difficult problem than that in the sphere of behaviour, although we must not lose sight of the fact that even in the realm of rules of conduct, learning of a moral and social kind will go on, so that the distinction between behavioural and curricular problems cannot be pressed too far.

A more positive justification for the use of authority to require children's attendance at school and to direct their activities while they are there must be sought in the notion of education itself or ideas one has about the purposes of the school and the educational enterprise generally. However, we will see in the chapter on the curriculum how difficult it is to define education in terms that will be generally acceptable or to reach agreement on what the purposes of the schools should be or what kinds of learning we should be using our authority to require pupils to engage in. Many different views are held and, although they all need some kind of justification in themselves, each will give rise to a justification for the use of authority in the school in different areas. The view that schools should be concerned primarily to promote the development of the rational mind will result in different demands to be made of pupils, for example, from those that will be justified by the view that they should be more concerned with the social welfare of their pupils. Indeed, some views of education, such as those that have advocated non-interference and the current views of some sociologists about the dangers of imposing values on children, are such as to provide no justification for any exercise of authority at all in this area.

Once some kind of overall justification for education itself seems to have been established, however, we will have a basis for the exercise of authority in particular situations. Once we are committed to the value of a particular subject, for example, the 'discipline' of that subject will take over and provide us with our cues as to when authority can be justifiably exercised. The absence of any kind of consensus in this area, however, makes this kind of justification highly subjective and, as a result, less satisfactory a basis than perhaps we would wish to have for requiring a great deal of children and applying real and extensive restraints to their behaviour.

There is, however, one kind of argument that may reveal to us something like a lowest common denominator here, something that will offer some justification at a fundamental level for the exercise of authority in education. Whatever view one takes of the kind or selection of knowledge that should be presented to or even imposed upon children, it would be difficult to maintain that that knowledge should not be characterized by being true. In short, whether one believes that children should be introduced to physics or French, Byron or the 'Beano', Beethoven or the Beatles, the one common feature of the 'knowledge' to be presented to them that all would agree to would be that it should manifest a respect for truth. We can say, then, that there is a conceptual connection between the notion of 'education' and that of 'truth'. Some justification for the exercise of authority by teachers may be found, therefore, in an appeal to this connection and a demonstration that in particular cases authority is being exercised in the cause of promoting truth, by insisting, for example, that children explore all sides of an argument before reaching an opinion, rather than adhering to a prejudice acquired from their parents or elsewhere. If education is connected in this way, then, with the pursuit of truth, the exercise of authority by educators can be shown to be justified if it has the purpose of assisting this process.

Paradoxically, however, this argument constitutes an equally strong if not a more compelling case for the promotion of freedom. This concern with truth necessitates academic freedom and academic autonomy, 'freedom of opinion' as it is more usually called. The classic arguments in support of this are again those of J. S. Mill's essay 'On Liberty' and we must briefly note them here.

Mill argues that truth cannot be pursued nor can human knowledge develop without freedom of opinion for those who seek after it. He gives several cogent reasons for this claim. Firstly, we cannot assume infallibility so that we must concede that any opinion may be true and, therefore, ought not to be suppressed. If anything, this is an argument that has more force today when it is perhaps clearer than it was in the nineteenth century just how hypothetical and consequently open to modification all our knowledge is. Secondly, Mill argues, even if a silenced opinion is wrong, it may contain some truth and, since the prevailing opinion on any issue is rarely wholly true, we need the clash of contrary opinions to help us towards the whole truth, a point supported by many philosophers who have seen the development of knowledge as an unending triadic dialectical process of thesis, antithesis, and synthesis. Thirdly, even if the opinion that is accepted and allowed is the whole truth and nothing but the truth, it can only be held as such by those who have been able to weigh it against contrary opinion. Without that it will be 'held in the manner of prejudice, with little comprehension or feeling of its rational grounds'. It will be dogma rather than real conviction and, as a result of this, truth will lose its essence.

This, then, for Mill is one aspect of that liberty which is essential to human progress. Liberty is necessary for 'the free development of individuality' and also without liberty 'there is wanting one of the principle ingredients of human happiness, and quite the chief ingredient of individual and social progress.' Unless there is freedom of opinion, unless people are free to disagree, human knowledge will not develop. These are the classic arguments for academic freedom and they lead us to recognize not only the hypothetical and evolving nature of human knowledge, which we have had reason to note elsewhere, but also that if there are conceptual connections between education and knowledge and education and truth, there must also be such a connection between education and autonomy.

However, they would seem equally to constitute an argument for the exercise of authority in the interests of the promotion of knowledge, truth, and autonomy, or, to put it differently and somewhat paradoxically, the exercise of authority to promote freedom, either by enhancing the range and scope of the choices open to the individual or by developing in him the ability to make choices by means other than either 'plumping' for something or acting according to prejudices, wherever and however acquired. We have noted elsewhere in this book (see Chapters 4 and 8) how working from children's interests requires us also to give them opportunities to acquire interests and how 'discovery methods' are only effective if linked to careful preparatory work, if employed, as Bruner (1961) suggests, by the well-prepared mind. We now have a theoretical justification for this apparent infringement of freedom in so far as its main purpose can be to enhance freedom and to promote autonomy since, as Bruner also tells us, the freedom of the child is increased by approaches such as discovery learning. In this connection, it is also interesting to note that those psychologists, such as Piaget (1932) and Kohlberg (1966), who in considering the stages of the child's moral development have posited the existence of an autonomous stage at the end of the process, have not wanted to suggest that this stage is automatically reached by all children as a result of a purely developmental or maturational process; they believe, as we shall see in Chapter 7, that the attainment of autonomy can only be the result of education. This, then, is a task for the teacher which he can only accomplish by the exercise of authority.

If there is any substance to these arguments we have tried to set out, certain implications follow for the practice of education. In the first place, it becomes clear that the teacher must take whatever action he judges necessary to promote the progress of his pupils towards autonomy, to enhance their freedom and their opportunities to use it, to create the conditions necessary for these developments to take place and, more controversially, as we will see when we consider the problems of curriculum content in Chapter 8, to introduce and extend those studies that he feels are justified on other grounds, whether for vocational reasons, because of the choices of the pupils themselves, or because of a conviction that they are 'intrinsically worthwhile activities'. There are no hard and fast answers to be given in practice to questions about when the exercise of authority by the teacher is justified in these areas, but these are the kinds of justification to be sought.

Secondly, some negative conclusions at least emerge from these arguments. For they imply that the exercise of authority by teachers cannot be justified in areas that cannot be shown to be connected in some way with the promotion of those qualities we have just discussed. It is difficult, for example, to justify its being exercised to ensure that all pupils travel to and from school with caps on their heads, unless it can be shown that a warm head will mean a warm brain and that a warm brain will reach its educational goals faster. Nor can we, without stretching our notion of education to breaking point, find a justification in it for any requirement that relates more to fashion than to education. Fashions are too ephemeral to constitute a basis for any learning of a permanent kind. One has only to look at those headmasters of today whose hair is of a length that they would not have permitted on their pupils a few years ago to realize how shifting this ground is. The spectacle of one headteacher forbidding entry to school to a child who insists on wearing blue rather than white socks and another sending a child home for precisely the opposite reason merely trivializes in the public eye the work of the schools and retards rather than advances the progress towards anything that can really be called education.

Thirdly, we must note that if the justification of the teacher's authority is to be found in his obligation to promote the freedom and ultimately the autonomy of his pupils, it must follow that his authority is merely provisional, since if he is successful it will be progressively eroded until it disappears altogether. Certainly, university teachers have to get used to seeing their pupils draw level with and sometimes forge ahead of them, and, to some extent, this should be the experience of all successful teachers. If we are right, then the oddest thing about the teacher's authority is that it must contain within it the seeds of its own destruction, what the soap operas call a self-destruct mechanism.

This, then, is the kind of justification that can be found for the teacher's authority. In general, it leads us to the conclusion that the important question for the teacher is not that of authority and freedom, but of authority and authoritarianism, the use and the abuse of authority. The teacher's central concern in planning the work of his pupils should be not the rather naive question of whether he should direct their work or leave them to their own devices, but the rather more subtle issue of the kinds of authoritative action he is justified in taking. It is the abuse of authority not the attempt to exercise it properly that leads to resentment and progressive indiscipline in schools. Teachers often comment on the 'sense of fairness' of their pupils, especially in secondary schools; this phenomenon is no more and no less than their ability to recognize, intuitively and therefore sometimes more quickly than the theoreticians, when authority is being exercised properly over them and when it is being abused.

As every teacher knows only too well, however, it is one thing to be able to demonstrate the differences between the uses and the abuses of authority; it is quite another matter to ensure that in practice one has any kind of authority in the classroom. An understanding of its justification will be of some help, of course, but in addition to this it is necessary to have some understanding of its nature and its origins, of how we come to be able to exercise it, as this will indicate to us some of the ways in which we can work to improve it. It is to this aspect of authority that we must now turn.

Patterns of authority

There have been many discussions of the question of what authority is, whether, for example, it is the same as power or force, and it would not be appropriate or helpful for us to get ourselves too caught up in such debate here. It must be stressed, however, that authority is very difficult to define precisely. It is an ability that some people seem to have to get other people to obey them without recourse to the use of force or even sometimes to the giving of reasons. It is the quality of the well-known centurion of the New Testament who described his authority by saying, 'I say to this man "Go!" and he goeth.' At a more mundane level, it is that which makes us accept, often quite unquestioningly, the advice of anyone we regard as an authority on something, like, say, second-hand cars or coastal navigation. We do what such people instruct or advise without compulsion or compunction. If this is what authority is or if this is what it means for someone to have authority, then it is certainly not force, even though the threat of force may sometimes be there in the background. In fact, we tend to say, when we see people, teachers or parents, for example, having to use force, that they have lost their authority or that their authority has broken down. Authority, then, is this kind of ability to get things done without recourse to force or other methods of persuasion.

It is important to understand this, because it has crucial implications for the way in which we must tackle what is probably the most vital question in this area for the teacher, namely that of where he can get authority from or how he can be sure that he will have authority in the classroom. If we realize what a nebulous quality it is, we will immediately appreciate that it is not something 'given' and, therefore, not something we can look to someone else to provide. Many people in any society have authority besides teachers – policemen, referees, umpires, mayors, kings and so on – but it clearly does not make sense to ask where they get their authority from in the way in which one might ask where they get their helmets, whistles or blackboards from, even though in some cases visible trappings such as badges, white coats, academic gowns, chains of office, orbs, sceptres and the like may be worn to symbolize the possession of authority (Weldon, 1953). Nor does it even make sense to claim that authority, at least as we have defined it, has been conferred on them by the MCC, the FA, the DES, the Archbishop of Canterbury, or any other person or body. Such persons or bodies cannot confer authority on any-one, since they cannot ensure that people will do what such a person tells them to do without question. It is not as simple as that, as many teachers and football referees know to their cost. The most that a body of this kind can do is to promise to step in when one's authority has been challenged, questioned, or even defied, in other words when it is lost. Furthermore, if we ask where these bodies get their authority from, we see that we have only pushed the question back a stage. The real question, therefore, is not 'Where does authority come from?' but 'How do people come to exercise authority?'. Once we put it that way, we begin to see both how to set about seeking an answer to it and that there may be several kinds of answer to be found. We can also see that from the teacher's point of view this kind of approach is likely to be more helpful because it should indicate some of the ways in which he can himself work at developing his authority.

A number of different categories have been used in attempts to delineate the possible sources of authority and it will be worthwhile to look at these briefly. One major distinction that has been drawn is that between author-ity exercised *de jure* and that exercised *de facto*. If a man has authority *de jure*, that authority derives from a right to issue commands that goes with a position that he holds and stems from certain rules, a legal system of some kind, which authorizes him to issue commands and will back him or step in if those commands are challenged. Such a man is our referee and in the same way teachers may have some authority conferred upon them by the position they hold. On the other hand, to say that a man exercises author-ity *de facto* is not to say he holds any position or has any backing for his authority; it is to say merely that people do in fact obey him. The classic example of this is the ordinary member of the audience who takes charge when there is a fire at a theatre or a cinema and organizes an orderly exit. He is able to exercise authority perhaps because of certain personal qualities he has or a superior knowledge and experience that he is thought to process, but not from any position or status that he holds.

This latter point brings us to a second distinction that has been emphasized, that between being *in* authority and being *an* authority, between positional and expert authority. Sometimes, as we have just seen, *de facto* authority will derive from the fact that someone is regarded as *an* authority in a particular area, that he has a relevant expertise. His injunctions are accepted because of this expertise, even though he does not hold a position that confers on him the right to issue commands. We have already referred to those people whose word on certain matters, the internal mysteries of the motor-car for example, are regarded as 'law'. It will be clear that if a man who is *in* authority is also accepted as *an* authority, his position will be considerably strengthened by the possession of such expertise.

A further distinction was made by Max Weber (1947) when he suggested that there might be three possible answers to the question of how people come to exercise authority, three different sources from which their ability to issue commands and have them accepted as legitimate might derive. Firstly, he suggests that the authority of some people may derive in part from *traditional* sources. Some people are obeyed because they are seen as representatives of a traditional and accepted system. A father or mother in a family, when he or she exercises authority, does so largely for this kind of reason. In some situations too, perhaps especially in schools for younger children, the authority of the teacher will derive in part from this source. A second source of authority that Weber posits is what he calls the *legal/rational* source. An increasing number of people in modern societies exercise authority because they have been elevated to it under a system of rules, the legality and rationality of which are accepted by those over whom the authority is being wielded. They have *de jure* authority within an accepted rule-governed situation like that of the football field, the cricket pitch, or the classroom, but that *de jure* authority derives from expert as well as positional sources, since they hold their position by virtue of proven expertise. Thirdly, Weber draws our attention to the *charismatic* type of authority exercised by some people because of their personal characteristics and outstanding qualities. He himself had in mind here outstanding historical figures like Christ and Napoleon, but the notion has relevance at less elevated levels too. We might perhaps, in the case of teachers in particular, distinguish two aspects of this concept, that of

being *an* authority which we have already considered and that of the kind
of personal flair or brilliance which can lead us to obey certain individuals
without evidence of either their expertise or their legal right to issue
commands (Peters, 1966). In other words, this concept offers us a distinction between two kinds of *de facto* authority.

The authority of the teacher
With these categories in mind, let us now turn to a more detailed examination of the authority of the teacher and the factors that will affect both its
nature and its extent. The most important thing to be stressed at the
outset of this discussion is that our analysis so far indicates that it is
something which can and should be worked at by teachers. The following
discussion may indicate some of the ways in which teachers can work at
the development of their authority but it will also reveal some of the
external factors that will come into play and which must be taken into
account by them. There are two main kinds of factor that we must note,
those deriving from the school itself, its organizational structure, its goals,
and the kinds of pupil it contains, and those deriving from the personal
characteristics and qualities of the individual teacher. The kind of authority each teacher can exercise and the kind of authority he will in practice
exercise will be a result of the interaction of these two forces.

One important factor here is the age of the pupils. It is dangerous to be
too dogmatic about age differences in education since this has led to wide
variations in our practices that are difficult to justify. However, it is worth
noting that younger children are less likely to question the teacher's right
to obedience than older ones and are more likely to need a firm authority
and control to support them, so that teachers of younger children will find
that they can place greater reliance on tradition, on position, and on their
personal qualities than can those whose pupils are older and more sophisticated. Bright pupils too will more readily challenge or at least question
the authority of their teachers. Thus patterns of authority will differ quite
widely between types of educational institution.

We saw earlier that authority is an essential part of any rule-governed
society. The kind of authority that is appropriate or possible will depend
also on the nature of the rule-governed society in question. Clearly a
society that is tightly structured, highly cohesive, and has a clear view of
its goals and purposes will require and will give rise to a different kind of
authority structure from one which is much looser, more diffuse, and less
clear-cut in its view of its essential purposes. No society of course is
completely bureaucratic, but obviously there are different levels of

T.P.E.— L

bureaucracy and each will give rise to a different pattern of authority. Schools must inevitably be less clear-cut in their goals and purposes than many other institutions, and there will be great variations between schools themselves.

At one extreme we might picture a school which is based on a relatively ·fixed view of child nature and of knowledge, which regards children's abilities as readily measurable, and consequently streams its pupils according to their ability, which has a view of knowledge as something external to be acquired by pupils and as a result places its emphasis on class-teaching methods, on subject boundaries, on encouraging the kinds of stock response to questions we discussed in Chapter 5, and perhaps on regular examinations and tests, seeing its role in terms purely of the intellectual advancement of its pupils. In such a school, the relationships between teacher and pupil will tend to be distant and impersonal and the authority structure will tend to be relatively clear-cut, hierarchical, and for the most part positional, the emphasis being on the teacher as set in authority; where his expertise is relevant, it will be an expertise in a particular subject area. Tradition will also be of significance to the teacher in his attempts to establish his own individual authority in such a school (Hargreaves, 1972).

At the other end of the spectrum, we may imagine a school which sees children as having many facets to their development and their abilities as too diffuse to be readily measurable, which as a consquence does not stream them by general ability, which has a broader view of knowledge and perhaps not too much regard for the sanctity of subject boundaries, and which as a result will often abandon class teaching in favour of other methods of the kind we discuss in Chapter 8 designed in one way or another to involve the children themselves more fully in their own education; in short, a school which takes a looser view of its own role and of the nature and purposes of education. In such a school the authority patterns will be very different. Teachers will be less distant from their pupils so that the relationships will be more interpersonal. The extent of their authority will depend far more on their expertise not only in a subject area or areas but in a wide range of pedagogical abilities. Position and tradition will be of relatively little help to teachers in such a school, the onus will be much more on personal qualities of a number of kinds.

Clearly, no real situation is quite as clear-cut as these we have described, but perhaps the caricatures we have drawn will serve to indicate the extent to which the type of authority a teacher can exercise will be affected by the kind of school he is in, by both the content of what he is teaching and the method or pedagogy he is using (Bernstein, 1971). Any occupational role is governed to some extent by the institutional structure within which it is practised and this structure in turn will be subject to pressures from the headteacher, the local authority, the governing body and all other outside agencies that wield authority over the teacher himself. But this is only one kind of factor that will determine the kind of authority the teacher will be able to exercise.

The nearer a school comes to the second of the types we have just pictured, the more onus there will be on the personal qualities of the individual teacher. We must remember too that while the organization of the school will determine to a large extent the kind of authority a teacher may exercise and will make it easy or difficult for him to achieve a proper control of his classes, no kind of school can confer authority on him or ensure that his authority is accepted by his pupils. In all situations, this will depend on his own qualities and abilities.

What sorts of quality are important here? Obviously, the most important single factor is the individual teacher's expertise. Where a teacher cannot rely on tradition or position, on being *in* authority, to ensure that he is obeyed, he must depend on his skill and knowledge, on being *an* authority. It is important to remember, as we hinted just now, that there are two aspects to this. One of these is clearly his expertise in his subject, his ability to answer children's questions and provide them with knowledge in a given area of the curriculum. The other important aspect of this expertise, and one that becomes crucial as we move towards a looser and more open view of schools, of the curriculum, and of education, is his pedagogical skill, his ability to organize pupils work, to advise them on many aspects of it, to help them to frame their questions rather than merely to provide answers, to ensure that they are stretched while steering them away from work of a level that would be likely to defeat them, to develop the kinds of interpersonal relationship that will both forward their learning and establish his right to direct it. The more interpersonal these relationships become, the more onus will fall on the teacher's ability to develop them.

This ability will in turn depend on a number of factors, such as the age and the sex of both teacher and pupils, the view he takes of knowledge and of the purposes of education, and the extent to which he is in sympathy with the ethos of the school. It will also depend on those wider personal qualities sometimes subsumed under the single title, 'personality'. There is no doubt that the personality of the teacher will affect his ability to develop relationships and, therefore, to establish his authority with his pupils. The significance of this should not be overstated, however. Many teachers are too ready to exaggerate the importance of personality and to take the view that you have either got it or you have not. There are two dangers in this. The first is that it leads to a defeatism on the part of those teachers who feel, rightly or wrongly, that their personal qualities are not ·strong and a resultant failure to appreciate that there are ways, such as those we have tried to show, in which one's authority can be developed. Secondly, it can lead to too great a dependence by some teachers on a charismatic type of authority, which, while it may have certain short-term advantages, cannot in the long term lead to effective education, since it is based not on reason but on emotion and largely blind admiration. We all know what Napoleon did. As John Wilson once remarked in a similar context (1964), it is when the individual loves Big Brother that he really loses his freedom. 'Personality' is important in the development of relationships and of one's authority in the classroom, but it is not crucial and it can even be inimical to education if one comes to depend upon it to the exclusion of other, more important aspects of one's teaching.

We must finally note the changes that are taking place in the nature of the authority wielded in many areas of society and no less in our schools. These changes are due to changing attitudes in society as a whole, a growing unwillingness to be 'dictated to', and increasing demands that reasons should be given for any infringement of our liberties, a justification and a demonstration that what is being required is 'fair' and 'equal'. In this respect, it is worth remembering that Weber's main point was to stress the trend in society towards an increased bureaucratization and away from the traditional, unquestioned sources of authority towards those with some legal/rational basis. The development of the 'open society' is paralleled by that of the 'open school' (Bernstein, 1967), that school which has the looser organizational structure we were discussing just now.

We should also add that these developments are to be welcomed rather than deplored. There is no doubt that they make the teacher's task more difficult but they do so by requiring him to take a wider view of that task. We saw earlier that the only kind of justification that can be found for the exercise of authority in education is that derived from the central concern of the educative process with the development of individual autonomy. If this is what education is essentially concerned with, the only kind of authority that will forward this process is one that is rationally based on the expertise of the teacher. To expect or require pupils to obey their teachers merely because they are teachers, to rely on tradition, on status, or on personal qualities for one's authority is at root to deny the child the right to think for himself.

We mentioned earlier that these are sources of authority that are more readily available to the teacher of younger children and so it might be claimed that this makes her task easier. It is also true, however, that it makes her task a more complex and responsible one. For, while she can rely on these sources for her authority more effectively than the teacher of older pupils, she must also be aware of the threat that this may pose to the long-term educational interests of her pupils. She must, therefore, attempt the very difficult task of achieving the kind of authority that will lay the right foundations for the development of the ability to make rational appraisals of subsequent educational relationships. The more schools move towards unstreaming, integrated curricula, greater pupil involvement, freedom, and even participation in management, the more, as we have seen, the teacher's role becomes 'achieved' rather than 'ascribed' and the basis of his authority moves from the positional to the expert. Tradition and status are bent reeds now, as the current experience of many teachers and schools reveals, and increasingly the onus is on the teacher to establish his authority rather than to expect it to be conferred on him in some way by the job itself. The developments we have been considering make increasing demands on that authority that stems from the teacher's understanding of and skill in handling the many facets of present-day educational practices. These are the ways in which teachers can and should work at improving the nature and the extent of the authority they wield and these are the ways in which the trainers of teachers must help them.

However, while few teachers will want to quarrel with the desirability of the kind of rational basis for authority we have been recommending, all will know that in practice such an ideal is seldom to be attained. In fact, although we have singled out for the purposes of our discussion these different types of authority, the authority any individual teacher wields will be an amalgam of all of them and will vary from age group to age group, from class to class, even from day to day. All teachers will find it necessary to rely on sources of authority other than their own expertise quite frequently. How far they can do this will depend on many factors but particularly on the age of their pupils since, for example, as we have just suggested, the older the pupils, the less ready they are to accept authority that is not backed by expertise. However, all teachers will find themselves from time to time relying, or attempting to rely, on tradition, on position or, perhaps especially often, on charisma, on the force of their own personalities, on what might more honestly and realistically be described as sheer bluff. All will find too that from time to time they must recognize the important distinction between authority and control and the need to achieve or maintain control by the use of other devices such as punishment or the threat of punishment when their authority proves inadequate.

In this connection it is perhaps worth noting another useful distinction that sociologists have made between different bases of social control. They have suggested that our methods of getting people to obey us must be normative, calculative, or coercive (Etzioni, 1961). In other words, we can get people to do as we tell them either by persuading them that it is worth doing, that our norms are to be accepted, or by offering them incentives or inducements, or by resorting to force, whether overt or otherwise. In practice, teachers will find themselves using all of these measures or some mixture of all three, but all teachers and schools should be aiming at some kind of normative order and endeavouring to avoid as far as possible the need for coercion or even for the dangling of carrots.

There are at least three good reasons for this. The first and most straightforward of these is that based on the relative ease with which this kind of order once achieved can be maintained. There is no doubt that life is easier and far more pleasant when one is working with pupils who want to learn than with those who have to be driven and threatened or cajoled, if they are even to remain in the room and behave themselves. In fact, it is sometimes suggested that some of the changes currently taking place in schools are prompted by an awareness that it is increasingly difficult to coerce pupils, especially older pupils, that calculative methods will not work with pupils who can see nothing of value for them in school work, and that if the establishment of a normative order necessitates changing the norms in a way that will make them more acceptable to such pupils, then this must be done. If you cannot beat them your only solution lies in joining them.

The second reason for preferring a normative order is more complex but absolutely crucial. A system of control that has this kind of basis is the only kind of system that is conducive to education in the full sense. We have seen often enough that to be educated is to have come to value what one has been engaged in for its own sake. If this is not achieved, education has not taken place. Thus to force knowledge into unwilling pupils or to offer it to them purely as a means to some extrinsic reward will be positively counter-productive to truly educational ends. Furthermore, in discussing the relation of authority to freedom at the beginning of this chapter, we noted the arguments for freedom and autonomy in education and saw that the concept of education itself requires that our authority be progressively eroded in favour of the autonomy of the pupil. Again the only basis for this is a normative social order.

The third reason for preferring this kind of order derives from a consideration of the possible effects on pupils of different kinds of authority and methods of control. There are a number of facets to this and we must now turn to a detailed examination of them.

The effects of authority and freedom

We might first note how little is known about the effects on teachers of different patterns of authority and freedom in the classroom. Little research has been done in this area but it would seem to be a fruitful one since there are many things that one would like to know here. There is evidence that teachers achieve more success when they are in tune with or enthusiastic about the particular schemes they are engaged in. Teachers who believe in unstreaming, for example, have more success in teaching mixed-ability classes than those who are opposed to it (Barker-Lunn, 1970) and it also emerged in a study of the teaching of French in primary schools that more success was achieved by teachers who were enthusiastic about the experiment and pleased to be involved in it (Burstall, 1967). One would, of course, expect the teacher who is thus in harmony with what he is doing to be more successful and, indeed, to gain more satisfaction from his work. This would suggest in turn that teachers should be given the kind of flexibility that will enable each of them to develop his own pattern of working and of authority. As we have seen, however, there are factors which set limits on the extent of the variety that is possible. What does seem a more reasonable conclusion is that teachers should choose their schools and schools their teachers with the need for this kind of 'match' in mind. It is not clear how important this factor is, as against considerations of such things as salary, location and general convenience when teachers are looking for a post. It is also apparent that a greater level of job satisfaction and success is achieved in schools where there is freedom for teachers to experiment with new curricula and new methods and where they are involved in planning and policy making, but again this is probably true only in the case of those teachers who want such freedom and involvement. Those who do not want it will not only fail to take advantage of it and will thus be less efficient; they have also been known to sabotage the efforts of more enthusiastic colleagues. We need to know a lot more than we do about the effects of different kinds of structure on different teacher personality types and the effects of the teachers on the structures. There is more evidence, however, of the effects of different patterns of organization on the pupils and to this we must turn.

The first thing we must note here is the difficulties that can arise for all children, although for some more than others, from an excess of freedom given to them too soon. The work of Erich Fromm (1942) has indicated the dangers that can arise from man's 'fear of freedom' and this is an important consideration for teachers. Fromm was appalled at the limitations to the freedom of the individual that were part of the régime of Nazi Germany from which he had fled to the USA, but he was also struck by the inability of people to cope with freedom and their readiness to accept even extreme forms of authoritarianism. In looking at children in the USA, he draws our attention to the fact that they are gaining more and more freedom but that this entails emancipation from a world that offered them security, so that they experience a conflict between the freedom that they want and the fear of losing the security that reliance on authoritarian figures can provide. The same phenomenon forms a major feature of the existentialist philosophy of Jean Paul Sartre, who sees it as obligatory for every human being to choose for himself and to make his own decisions, but recognizes the constant temptation that besets everyone to abrogate this responsibility and to slip into a role which will make decisions for him.

Others have noticed the same tendencies in children. Some children reveal a real reluctance to take responsibility for their own work, for example (Musgrave and Taylor, 1969), and this has been noted also in higher education students who have asked for lectures to be made compulsory rather than attendance at them left to their own discretion (Dunham, 1965). In the realm of moral education, too, it is apparent that many children prefer to be told 'what is right and what is wrong' rather than being left to reach their own conclusions on these matters (McPhail et al., 1972).

An awareness of this is vital to the teacher. For if he does not take charge in such cases, often a leader will emerge from among the pupils themselves. Some guidance from him is needed and he must realize that the development of autonomy and the ability to cope with freedom is a gradual process; children must have time to learn to welcome and to use their freedom. They are only potentially free and, as we saw earlier, it is the teacher's job to lead them to freedom rather than to hand it to them straightaway.

It must also be kept in mind that children will react in different ways to the demands of freedom. The most influential factor in deciding how they will react will be their own backgrounds, the ways in which they have themselves been handled both at home and at school. In this connection, it is particularly important to note what psychologists have told us about the 'authoritarian personality' (Adorno, 1960). Such a person tends to value obedience highly; he obeys rules for their own sake or from fear of punishment rather than from a concern with the reasons behind them; he may resent authority but he will readily succumb to it and he himself likes to wield power over others he regards as his inferiors; he tends to be conformist rather than original and is consequently suspicious of change or of anything new; in his relationships with others he is concerned more with status than with personality characteristics and tends, as we saw in Chapter 2, to hold stereotyped views of them; as a parent his affection for his children will be conditional on their good behaviour and obedience.

Children brought up against this kind of background by parents who reveal such traits or, to a lesser extent, by teachers of this kind, tend to acquire the same characteristics themselves quite early in their development. They will as a result prefer a fairly rigid system both at home and at school; they will prefer direction and control to any freer, more suggestive or cooperative approach to education; they will have more respect for the *de jure* or legal authority of the teacher than for that based on any expertise or personality characteristics he might show. This kind of background and the resultant personality development, therefore, will be crucial in determining the reaction of pupils to the authority patterns of the school and the degree of freedom they allow. However, it will equally be a product of certain kinds of authority pattern and we must now turn to a consideration of the effects on pupils of different kinds of school and classroom organization.

Quite the best known and most quoted research in this area is that of Lewin, Lippitt and White (1939) in examining the effects of three types of leadership style which they dubbed as autocratic, democratic, and *laissez-faire*. The results of this experiment have been questioned on the grounds that it took place in a voluntary youth club rather than a school and we must also remember that the reaction of the children was not uniform in each situation, as one would expect in view of their differing backgrounds, but most people have nevertheless seen some significance in these findings.

A number of tasks was set to each group and the role of the leader in each was clearly defined. The autocratic leader was to initiate and guide all the activities of his group; he was not to reveal to them the overall programme but rather to dictate each stage of the work for each individual member. In the *laissez-faire* group, members were to have complete freedom to decide what to do and how to do it; the leader was involved only when asked for information, advice, or materials by the group. The leader of the democratic group was to generate group discussion for the formulation of policy, to ensure that all members had an overview of the programme and that each shared responsibility for the work and the final achievement.

The main results of this experiment were that in the autocratic situation children worked well while the leader was present but when he was absent this stopped and was often replaced by misbehaviour of all kinds; little initiative was shown by individuals and no pleasure or satisfaction in what the group produced – in fact, in one case a mask they had made was destroyed. On the social plain, two kinds of reaction were detected: aggression between members of the group or a submissive reaction, involving little hostility between members but a good deal towards outsiders. There was little evidence of friendliness either between the children or towards the leader.

The *laissez-faire* climate resulted in haphazard work from the children which seemed little affected by the absence or presence of the leader. Less consistent application to the work was shown and there was a good deal of time wasting. No interest at all was shown in the products of their work.

In the democratic group, the work done did not reveal the same level of industry as that displayed by the autocratic group but it went on consistently even when the leader was absent. The children were more personally involved in what they were doing, wanting to discuss it with each other and with the leader, and far more friendly behaviour was shown between individual members of the group and towards the leader.

Further evidence of a similar kind comes from the work of Anderson and Brewer (1946) who studied two types of teacher behaviour among younger children. These types of behaviour they described as 'dominative' or 'authoritarian', where the teacher tended to dominate by issuing orders and instructions, and 'integrative', where the teacher tended to accept children's suggestions and offer suggestions in return rather than giving orders. The effect seemed to be that the dominative behaviour was met with aggression on the part of the children, who showed rebellious and dominative behaviour themselves, while the integrative teachers gained the children's attention more often and the children showed more cooperation with one another and with the teacher and more spontaneity in what they were doing.

This latter point raises the question of the possible effects of different approaches on the kind of thinking that children learn to engage in. A rigid and authoritarian approach would seem to be unlikely to promote original or individual thought. Children who reveal this kind of divergent thinking are those who tend to challenge authority, to question traditional knowledge and the norms of the school, and such children are rated fairly low on behaviour and regarded as troublesome by their teachers (Getzels and Jackson, 1962). Convergent thinkers tend to express more authoritarian views than divergent thinkers, to value conformity, to respect rules and to think that obedience is important (Hudson, 1966). There are two aspects of this that seem relevant to teachers. Firstly, one of the problems of promoting 'creativity' in schools, as we saw in Chapter 3, is that 'creative' children tend to be less comfortable to work with than those who are more conformist and teachers must learn to live with this if such potential is to be developed. Secondly, it is pertinent to ask how far these characteristics of convergent thinkers are the product of the kind of approach to education and particularly the pattern of authority favoured by the teacher.

The kind of approach adopted by the individual teacher, then, will have considerable implications for the child's attitude to work, the kind of thinking he comes to favour, and his attitudes to other people, his social education. Similar effects can be discerned in the organizational structure of the school as a whole. We saw earlier that this will be a major factor in determining the kind of authority that the teacher can and must wield within it. It is clear now that it will also have its effect on the development of the pupils and the effects of the different patterns of authority generated by different kinds of organizational structure are clear, especially from studies of streaming (Barker-Lunn, 1970; Hargreaves, 1972).

It is important, therefore, that all teachers should be aware of the impact that the methods they adopt in organizing their schools and their classes and in handling their pupils will have on many aspects of the development of these pupils. It is also important that they recognize that their central concern throughout as educators is to set about these tasks in such a way as to develop the kind of authority and the kinds of relationship that will lead their pupils at a proper pace towards the point where they can exercise self-control and self-discipline and take responsibility for their own behaviour and learning. Again, what is required is that teachers be sensitive to the changing balance of freedom and authority in the upbringing of each child at each stage and in every context. Education as we defined it in our earlier discussion requires a gradual movement towards the total erosion of authority in the interests of the freedom and autonomy of the individual and all that we have said subsequently would seem to confirm this. It also suggests that where authority is necessary, it should be a rational authority, that our methods of control should be normative as far as possible, and our relationships based on mutual trust and confidence. Only a climate of this kind is likely to be conducive to the attainment of freedom by our pupils.

Such an ideal is not easy to achieve and it is impossible even for the most highly skilled and gifted teacher to maintain this kind of authority all the time. Often, as we have said before, he will be reduced to other measures and sometimes, when authority of any kind deserts him, he will have to have recourse to punishment. We must conclude our discussions of authority in education, then, with an examination of what is involved in the use of punishment by teachers and of the place of punishment in education.

Punishment

We said earlier that rules must be backed by sanctions and it would be a mistake to imagine that we can forever avoid a situation in which these rules will be broken and the sanctions will need to be brought into play. Punishment becomes necessary, then, when a rule is broken and our authority is lost, when we say to this boy 'Go!' and he saith, 'Drop dead!', when the normative and even the calculative orders have broken down, the mere threat of coercion is not enough and the coercive measures themselves become necessary. The point of punishment, then, is to re-establish authority and respect for both the rule and whoever issued it. The aim is to re-establish control.

The first thing we need to get clear about in any discussion of punishment is what precisely it is; for we need to be able to distinguish it from other related notions like vengeance, deterrence, discipline, and so on. We need to know, if we are beating or beheading someone, how we can be sure we are punishing him rather than working out our spite or indulging our sadistic propensities. It has been suggested that there are five criteria that must be satisfied if we are to use the word punishment appropriately of any act (Flew, 1954). The act must involve an unpleasantness for the victim; it must be related to a supposed offence; it must be the supposed offender who is being punished; it must be the work of personal agencies; and it must be imposed by virtue of some special authority conferred by the system of rules against which the offence has been committed.

It is one thing to say what punishment is; it is a very different matter to justify its use; yet it is to the question of its justification that we must next turn. Two kinds of answer have been offered here. Some philosophers have offered a justification of punishment based entirely on retributive grounds. They look back to the offence and answer the question, 'Why ought we to punish?' with a reason, telling us that it is because an offence has been committed. Others have offered a utilitarian justification, looking to the results, the consequences of the act of punishment, and answering the question by reference to the purposes, telling us that we must punish in order to achieve certain goals.

The retributive argument can really be summed up in the words of the Old Testament 'an eye for an eye and a tooth for a tooth' and there is a strange ring to many of the arguments produced in support of it. We are told, for example, that there is a deep-rooted retributive feeling in all of us and that this is a justification for acting retributively towards offenders, but the presence of a feeling, however deep-rooted, can never in itself constitute a justification for giving full rein to the expression of that feeling. Secondly, they claim that a moral imbalance has been created by the offence and that this must be corrected. Apart from the problem of making the punishment fit the crime, the difficulties of which have been well expounded by Gilbert and Sullivan, there is a problem here that derives from the fact that not all rules are moral rules and not all moral rules are backed by sanctions. In other words, punishment is not always a matter of a moral imbalance nor does every such moral imbalance bring punishment on our heads. This does suggest, however, the need to distinguish the use of punishment in moral contexts from other uses of it. Thirdly, retributivists often speak of the offender's right to punishment and, although this is indeed 'an odd sort of right whose holders would strenuously resist its recognition' (Quinton, 1963), it does draw our attention to the difficulties of any view that suggests that we should regard the commission of an offence as an excuse to manipulate someone, to try to turn him into a different person. These arguments are not entirely convincing, although they are certainly worthy of more elaborate discussion than we have been able to give them here. A number of interesting features do emerge, however, which we will take up in a moment when we come to consider the place of punishment in education.

The utilitarian view of punishment regards it not as retributive, but as preventive, deterrent or reformative. The view is well summed up in the words of Jeremy Bentham, 'All punishment is mischief, all punishment in itself is evil. Upon the principle of utility, if it ought at all to be admitted, it ought only to be admitted in so far as it promises to exclude some greater evil.' In other words, punishment involves pain and pain for the utilitarian is always bad and can only be justified if it can be shown to lead to pleasure, happiness or the avoidance of greater pain in the future. Only the consequences, therefore, can justify punishment.

Again this is a view that merits more detailed consideration than it can be given here. Its main difficulties, however, stem from the fact that, while it may offer us useful suggestions as to the most efficient methods of social control, it is not strictly a theory of punishment as we have defined it. For if the only criterion we are to take account of in dealing with offenders is a consideration of the likely consequences of our action, then there will be occasions when we will be led to take action that will involve no unpleasantness for the offender at all, or even action which is taken not against the offender himself but against some other person. Action taken against the mother of a juvenile offender, for example, may be more effective in curbing his behaviour than action taken against the offender himself. If a calculation of likely consequences is all that need concern us then punishment as such will not always necessarily be the best solution.

It is this feature of the utilitarian view that has made it attractive to some educationists, who have felt that deliberate acts of nastiness should be no part of education and that it is better to have the freedom in which to decide what is best for the individual child in each situation. It has been noted that there are similarities between the notion of education and that of 'reform' (Peters, 1966) and that teachers should be concerned to make their pupils 'better' rather than to act as agents of retribution. It is suggested, therefore, that they should 'treat' offenders rather than punish them. When one puts it in these terms, however, the difficulty with this line of reasoning becomes apparent. There is an equally cogent counterargument which says that the notion of education requires us to respect every individual as a person, as a moral being, to regard him as responsible for his actions and as entitled to punishment if he commits an offence; that we cannot, without doing violence to the notion of education, justify reforming him, moulding him, shaping him, or in any other way treating him like a thing rather than a person; that the only way to lead him to understanding and ultimately to autonomy is to enable him to learn the moral lessons that are implicit in acts of punishment (Wilson, 1971).

Both of these points of view seem to have some merit and some reconciliation may become possible if we make certain distinctions within the kinds of situation in which questions of the rights and wrongs of punishment arise. A distinction might be made, for example, between those offences which are committed against moral rules, where we must be aware of the morally educative dimensions of any action we take, and those where the rule broken has no real moral import, if there are such rules, and where it might as a result be possible to take appropriate action without the same kind of moral compunction. It might be important too to take account of the ages of the pupils concerned. For an act of punishment to have the kind of morally educative effect that is wanted, the child must be capable of understanding the reasons for it and appreciating its point; otherwise, it will be in his eyes an act of naked aggression.

This latter point draws our attention to the need to keep in mind the evidence of the possible psychological effects of punishment on children. There seem to be two main aspects of this. Firstly, it seems that in terms of getting pupils to learn effectively what you want them to learn, positive factors, such as encouragement, interest on the part of the adults, and rewards for successes seem to have more effect than 'negative reinforcements' such as punishment. It seems likely to be better, therefore, to reward good behaviour and success and thus to try to prevent bad behaviour than to wait until the bad behaviour occurs and punish it. Secondly, there is little doubt that if punishment is seen by children as an example of aggressive behaviour on the part of adults, as it will be in the case of children who do not understand its moral purport, the tendency will be for them to imitate it and to meet aggression with aggression. Nor is there any doubt of the adverse effects on the climate of a class or school of the widespread use of punishment, as we saw before when discussing the effects on pupils of authoritarian methods generally. In educational terms, it is likely to be counter-productive not only in the case of those pupils who are the recipients of it, but also in the case of all the others who have to live and work in the kind of atmosphere that it engenders.

Prevention is undoubtedly better than cure here. Punishment is a last resort that no teacher should welcome having recourse to. Rather than looking for a justification of it, whether moral or otherwise, we should be working at devising methods of control that will as far as possible obviate the need for it. There are several factors that should be kept in mind as we do this. We need a clearer view of how the rules of any classroom come to be agreed and of the extent to which they are the result of negotiation with the pupils, even when such negotiation is not made explicit; we need to be aware of the variations of structure and method that pupils will experience from teacher to teacher and from classroom to classroom; we need to remember that the fewer rules we have and the less explicit we are about them the more flexibility and room for manoeuvre we will have in our interpretation of them; in particular, where rules are not explicitly formulated, we can on occasion ignore breaches of them, a line that is sometimes far more effective in achieving the 'extinction' of particular forms of behaviour than the reinforcing process of recognizing the offence and punishing it, provided of course that it is not reinforced by the recognition of the other pupils. We will also find it helpful to distinguish those rules that are readily accepted and agreed by our pupils, those, for example, that relate very clearly to the agreed aims and purposes of the school or lesson, and those where their acceptance is less positive and their acquiescence less certain. Teachers and pupils will each define the goals of education differently and, clearly, where these definitions agree, the authority of the teacher will be more readily accepted.

This brings us back to a point we made early in this chapter, when we said that the exercise of authority by the teacher can only be justified when it can be shown to be conducive to the achievement of the goals of education or the agreed goals of both pupils and teachers. When this is not the case, it becomes authoritarianism, an abuse of authority, and in this day and age this is unacceptable to pupils. It is here more often than not that direct head-on clashes occur of the kind that are always to be avoided, since they act to the ultimate detriment of the pupil, the teacher, the school and education itself. These are the situations in which punishment or restorative action of some kind comes to be required. It is always better to avoid them. Since they cannot always be avoided, however, it is important to be clear about what such action is. It is action taken to restore lost authority. As such its justification is not to be sought in itself, since in itself punishment or any other such action has no merit and is at best a necessary evil. It is to be sought in the aims and purposes of the authority it is being used to support, sustain, or reestablish. Only in so far as that authority can be justified can we justify any reasonable attempts to maintain it.

Summary and conclusions

We have tried in this chapter to highlight some of the many facets of the exercise of authority in education. We began by considering the problem of its justification in relation to what appear *prima facie* to be conflicting claims for the freedom of the child. We then considered some of the different sources from which teachers might draw their authority and the ways in which they can work at developing it. We discussed some of the factors affecting the kind of authority the individual teacher can develop and some of the effects of different kinds of authority on the development of the pupil. Finally, we examined the question of the justification of the use of punishment to regain control and restore authority when it has begun to break down.

Throughout our discussion of these issues one thread has run continuously and that is the central concern of any educative process with the developing freedom of the child. This was the only basis we could find upon which to build an argument to justify the use of authority of any kind. Consequently, it was this that led us to suggest that ultimately the only acceptable kind of authority for the teacher to exercise is that based on his own expertise, that the only defensible methods of class control are normative methods, that the use of punishment in education can only be justified if it leads to greater understanding and the restoration of a rational authority, and that, although the human realities of classroom interchange will often make it necessary for us to have recourse to other methods that fall far short of these ideals, we must be aware that these are unsatisfactory in a fundamental sense and can only be justified in so far as they may help us to attain the point at which we can employ methods that are conducive to the development of pupils towards freedom and autonomy.

What we have touched upon here, therefore, is the influence of our techniques of class management and patterns of authority on the moral and social development of our pupils. It is to a fuller discussion of that aspect of education that we must now turn.

7 Moral and social education

There is an important sense in which all education is moral education, since, as we have had cause to note on several occasions, education is essentially concerned with the development within the individual of a system of values. From the very beginning of both the theory and the practice of education a distinction has been drawn between those things that children are taught because of their utilitarian value and those whose purpose is the improvement of the life and character of the individual. Furthermore, only the latter have been seen as the legitimate concern of education as such. Thus in all those traditions, Greek, Judaic and Christian, that have contributed to the thinking of the western world, the central concern of both the theory and the practice of education has been with moral development. This is a major feature of the work of all of those who have written about education from the time of Plato through to that of the 'great educators' of the nineteenth century, such as Pestalozzi, Herbart and Froebel, and it is the main explanation of the fact that, until the present century, the curriculum of schools and universities, especially in the United Kingdom, was dominated by subjects of a nonutilitarian kind, most notable among which was the study of the classics.

It was the advent of universal education that led to a more open approach to utilitarian aspects of schooling. Initially, the major intention was to provide every citizen with the basic skills of reading, writing, and elementary numeracy, to create a reasonably literate and numerate work force; and there is no doubt that a major justification of the expenditure of public money on the provision of schools has continued to be the purely economic consideration of the need to produce an ever more skilled body of workers to meet the demands of an ever more sophisticated and developing industry. At the same time, however, largely because this has been the kernel of traditional educational theory and practice, the concern with education for its own sake, with the moral and personal development of pupils, has continued. This has, therefore, created a conflict of aims for the educational system, a conflict that is reflected, although not recognized, in the demands that are made on schools from the outside. For many of those industrialists, politicians and others who are constantly demanding that schools cut out the 'frills' and concentrate on providing their charges with the basic skills that they believe industry needs are among the first to condemn the schools if they think they have failed in their duty to promote the development of character and to ensure what they would regard as an adequate standard of behaviour, in short, the very things that those 'frills' might be said to lead to. Thus the traditional concern of education with moral development has continued in spite of the fact that other kinds of demand have come to be made on the education system.

Recently, too, we have become more clearly aware of what this implies and have begun consciously to consider what should be done about it, as is apparent from the proliferation of curriculum projects in this area and the emergence of moral education as a subject on the timetable of many secondary schools. A major reason for this, as we shall see later, is the rapidity of social change that recent years have witnessed and the inability of traditional forms of morality or moral upbringing to meet these changes.

With this increase of interest, however, has also come a renewed awareness of some of those features of moral education that make it necessary to examine it separately from other areas of the curriculum. It is an area to which no clear body of knowledge can be assigned; it is an aspect of development in which the emotions play a particularly important role; it extends, like language learning, across every experience children have, both in school and outside it; and it is thus the concern of every teacher, not only those who would lay claim to being educators also, since, as the Newsom Report told us (1963, para. 160), 'Teachers can only escape from their influence over the moral and spiritual development of their pupils by closing their schools.'

It is thus an area of educational theory and practice that we must look at in some detail and, since the increased interest in it that we have drawn attention to has led to certain important changes in our notion of what moral education is, it will be as well for us to begin with a discussion of that question.

What is moral education?

There are three or four approaches that need to be made to this question. First of all, we need to ask what kind of moral upbringing children need if they are to be able to take their place in our society. Secondly, we must consider what is implied by the use of the term 'education' in this context, why people speak of moral education rather than of, say, moral training or moral instruction, and perhaps also examine the related question of what would constitute a moral education, who would be described as the morally educated person. Lastly, it will be useful if we adopt a negative stance and consider what moral education is not, since one of the major sources of difficulties in this area is that in the past we have tackled the moral upbringing of children wrongly or, rather, in a manner that would seem to be no longer suitable or acceptable, and we must be prepared to recognize this and to make appropriate changes in our provision.

The most striking feature of human societies during the last century or so is the rapidity and the extent of the change that has taken place within them. This has very great implications for all aspects of education, but especially for its central core of moral education. The most obvious features of that change, of course, are those that have affected the material circumstances of our lives, those technological developments that have transformed our styles of living – advances in communications, in facilities for rapid long-distance travel, in mechanical aids of all kinds in the home and at work, in industrial machinery, in medical and surgical devices and skills and so on.

What is less obvious and, therefore, less readily appreciated is the social and moral change that these technological developments have inevitably brought in their train. These have led to changes not only in the material but also in the social context of our lives. Ease of travel has resulted in all societies in an ever-increasing racial mix; industrial developments have led to a greater social mix; improvements in communications have led to a greater awareness of what is happening in other parts of the world, especially through the direct medium of television. These developments in turn have generated continuous changes in moral attitudes and values because of the altered circumstances not only of our social lives but also of our material lives. For, in both areas, new moral problems are posed for society as a whole and for every individual member of society by both kinds of development. No one can now side-step the moral issues presented by the greater racial mix that we find in society; equally no one can avoid making moral judgements in response to the totally new moral issues that he is faced with, often directly, as a result of technological advances which enable him, for example, to prevent birth, to abort birth, to transplant organs from one human body to another, or even, in some cases, to drop a bomb that will end the lives of hundreds of thousands of people and maim many more. Technological change, then, is constantly creating new moral problems to which new responses must be found. Traditional forms of morality cannot provide these answers because they were developed by people who were never aware of the questions.

However, we must go a good deal further than that. For it is equally clear that many different kinds of response are possible on most of these issues. There is no one, universally valid answer to any of the moral issues we have referred to nor, indeed, to any others. All shades of opinion can be observed in society on most issues and we are slowly coming to accept that it is quite right and proper that this should be so. Most advanced societies are now recognized to be pluralist, to contain within them and tolerate a wide variety of viewpoints on all questions.

It is not, then, so much the changes themselves as the very fact of change that is of crucial importance to the educator. As John Dewey was endeavouring to persuade us half a century or more ago, we must recognize the evolutionary nature of all things, including knowledge itself, and prepare our children accordingly. In the moral sphere, as in any other, this would seem to mean that we should not, indeed that we cannot, prepare children only to meet what is immediately before them but we must prepare them also to adapt to what is coming, to cope with the changes they will see in their own lifetimes. The concept of a 'general mechanical ability', which the Crowther Report (1959) suggested should be central to the preparation of pupils to meet continuous technological change, must be extended to other aspects of their upbringing and especially to those moral aspects that are our concern here.

This brings us naturally to our second area of exploration. For it is precisely that need that makes it necessary for the moral upbringing we provide to be moral education in the full sense rather than moral training or instruction. The features which distinguish education from other activities which involve teaching are such things as the development of understanding, of critical awareness, of an appreciation of the value and importance of certain areas of human experience, of a respect for knowledge and truth and, above all, of the ability to think for oneself (Peters 1965a, 1966). None of these is essential if we are training or instructing pupils; some of them, such as the ability to think for oneself, are positively to be excluded if we are indoctrinating them; all of them are vital when we are trying to offer them an education.

The significance of these general features of education for the provision of the kind of moral upbringing we have just suggested present-day society makes necessary will be clear. For it is precisely the development of understanding, of critical awareness, of the ability to think for oneself, and of those other qualities that are the concern of education that is needed in the kind of evolving social context we have briefly described. These are also among the qualities we would expect to find in a person we would describe as morally educated (Wilson, Williams and Sugarman, 1967). For what we are claiming is that people need to be morally educated, rather than morally trained or instructed, in order to be able to make their own moral choices and reach their own moral conclusions in a society that will offer them new moral problems to solve and the opportunity to respond to them in a variety of ways.

It is worth noting here that this view of moral education is supported not only by a consideration of what we mean by 'education' but also by a similar examination of what we mean by 'morality'. For we do not normally accept that a person is behaving morally if we discover that he has not thought out and deliberately chosen the course of action he has adopted. The exploration of that kind of question forms a very important part of the process of law, since we think that, like praise, blame and punishment should be meted out in accordance with the level of responsibility of the individual for his actions. There is an important distinction that Aristotle drew our attention to between acting 'willingly' and acting 'not unwillingly', between doing something because we have thought it through and doing it without such careful consideration. And so, the notion of morality itself, like that of education, also suggests that our concern should be to develop the quality of our pupils' thinking about moral issues.

Another way of looking at this is to recognize that it involves taking a different view or model of man from that that has hitherto held sway. It involves seeing man not as a passive creature, an object acted upon by external forces, but as an active creature, an agent responsible at least in part for his own destiny and able to control some of those external forces for his own ends. It is only when we see man in this light that we can regard him as capable of moral action in the full sense. If we regard him as a passive object at the mercy of forces beyond his control, then he can be no more subjected to moral appraisal, to praise or blame, than a rock or a piece of wood.

One point needs to be stressed here, however, so that we can avoid falling for too simplistic a notion of moral autonomy. The juxtaposition of notions like understanding, critical awareness, and respect for truth with the notion of autonomy suggests that we must take a rather different view of moral autonomy than one that assumes that every moral opinion is equally acceptable and every moral position equally tenable. There is a sense in which we all have autonomy regardless of any educational provision we may or may not have enjoyed; we can certainly think and hold whatever opinions we like, even if in some circumstances we are justifiably restrained from acting on them. However, once we link the idea of autonomy with notions like understanding, critical awareness, and so on, we begin to see what the role of education is. For there is a difference between producing opinions on moral matters, as much as on any other, 'out of the top of one's head' and reaching informed, considered views as a result of having acquired a sound basis of knowledge and understanding upon which these views are built. It is the essence of moral education to help people to reach this qualitatively superior level in their thinking on moral issues, just as it is the goal of, say, scientific education to improve the quality of their thinking on scientific matters. The morally educated person, then, is, at least in part, the person who is well on his way to this kind of autonomous thinking on moral issues.

This analysis leads us in turn to a recognition of what moral education is not. It is not a matter of being instructed in the moral beliefs of someone else; it is not a matter of being trained to respond to moral issues in the way that someone else, whoever that may be, thinks we ought to respond to them. There are a number of implications of this point that we must note.

First of all, this suggests that we should not be concerned only with the content of moral education, with what children come to believe. For to concentrate on this, as many people do, is to offer them moral instruction or moral training rather than moral education. Such instruction and training do have their place in moral upbringing and we must not be interpreted as advocating that it be rejected entirely, but it is only a beginning and the essential point to grasp about moral education is that it must go far beyond this.

One most important way in which it must go beyond this kind of concentration on content is that it must concern itself with the manner in which such instruction is both offered and received and with the manner in which moral beliefs are reached and held. Its concern is with how we reach our moral positions rather than with what those moral positions are. In short, its concern is to ensure that our beliefs satisfy those criteria we have suggested are endemic to the notion of education itself and should thus be informed opinions of a superior quality to those that are reached by other means. They should, as we have just said, evince understanding, they should be the result of careful and critical appraisal, they should reveal a recognition of the importance of moral behaviour, they should display a respect for knowledge and truth, and they should be reached by personal choice, decision, and commitment. Moral opinions are not to be plucked from the air; they are not prejudices inherited from our parents or caught from our teachers or our peers; they must be the result of thinking as careful as that which supports views in any other field. If a man declares a dislike for the works of Shakespeare without ever having studied them, we do not take his opinion seriously. There is no reason why we should seriously entertain moral opinions that are similarly unfounded. Yet we constantly do so, as most so-called 'discussion' programmes on television and radio amply demonstrate.

It is important also to note that, if we are to ensure that children come to hold their moral opinions in the right way, their moral education must be offered them in the right way. In particular, we must recognize that an authoritarian approach will be counter-productive to our goals and intentions. We shall note soon in our discussion of moral development the problems this creates for the teacher of young children, who may not yet be able to engage in the kind of moral thinking we have described (although it might be safer to expect this to be true of most children of school age), but we must remember that at any age, if we offer moral precepts in an authoritarian manner, as beliefs or attitudes not to be questioned, they are likely to come to be held in a similar manner and to remain unquestioned for ever. It is also worth noting in passing that at all ages moral attitudes are likely to be offered in this form by teachers who themselves hold them in this manner. As in all aspects of education, a moral education in the full sense cannot be provided by a teacher who is not himself morally educated.

Lastly, in considering what moral education is not, we must note one practical result of our discussion. If moral education is what we have claimed it to be and is not what we have claimed it is not, then it cannot be linked and must not be linked to religious education (O'Connor, 1957;

Downey and Kelly, 1978). For a moral code that is based on any set of religious beliefs must of its very nature be authoritarian, centrally concerned with content, with what adherents of that religion believe, discouraging, and even intolerant of, questioning that might lead to rejection and respecting the autonomy of the individual only up to the point at which he makes his choice of the religious and moral 'package'. In short, the moral upbringing it offers is a moral training rather than a moral education. It is because we now recognize the need to encourage a questioning approach to morals, as well as because there is no longer any one religion that can be said to dominate our multi-ethnic society and, indeed, because many people have rejected institutionalized religion entirely, that religious education cannot be regarded any longer as a satisfactory basis for moral education so that something completely different is needed. This is another reason why moral education urgently requires the attention of teachers and educationists and why projects in this field are being spawned at both national and local level. Too many schools and teachers, however, still feel that they can leave it to the RE teacher and the RE lesson. For all the reasons we have set out here, we must get away from that approach before it is too late.

So far we have been painting an ideal picture, setting out what in principle moral education ought to be. The reality, of course, will fall far short of this, although that of itself is no reason for not being clear about our goals and principles. The reality will fall short for two reasons. First, as in all aspects of education, our practice will not be perfect and we must later in this chapter consider in some detail the practice of moral education and its place on the curriculum. But, secondly, there are a number of constraints within which the teacher must work as a moral educator, not all of which are equally significant in other areas of education.

Constraints are imposed by the process of moral development, since it would seem clear that children must pass through several preliminary stages of development before they can attain that level which Laurence Kohlberg has called 'the autonomous level of self-accepted moral principles' (1966). Secondly, this is an area of human experience in which the emotions play a more significant part than they do in most areas. Thirdly, this is an aspect of education to which no pupil comes absolutely fresh and ignorant, as he might be assumed to do to the learning of, say, French. A good deal of moral learning has gone on before the child comes to school and its goes on continually outside the school as well as within it. Furthermore, such learning is necessary because the making of moral choices cannot be delayed until the process of moral education is complete; such choices have to be made all the time. All of these factors place peculiar constraints on the teacher as a moral educator. All of them, therefore, we must now consider in turn.

Moral development

The process of moral development, like that of cognitive development generally, consists of a number of stages through which children must pass if they are to reach moral maturity and this presents teachers with problems comparable to those they must face in all areas of education.

These stages have been identified and elaborated by the major workers in this field, such as Jean Piaget and Laurence Kohlberg, as well as by others who have followed the line of thinking that they have opened up. Briefly, there is general agreement that children begin at a stage of heteronomy, at which they take their principles and moral beliefs in a largely unquestioning way from others, especially their parents and teachers. Thus at the outset their approach to moral issues and their response to them is of an authoritarian kind. This stage Kohlberg calls the 'pre-moral' stage, a term that suggests that in his view too this kind of moral response is hardly worthy of being called morality at all. The second main stage is that of socionomy, a stage at which they have come to regard rules as emanating not from individuals in an arbitrary manner but from society. They have come to recognize that moral rules are concerned in some way with social cohesion and thus to realize that there are reasons for them. This stage Kohlberg described as the stage of 'conventional morality' when children conform not out of blind unquestioning obedience, but in order to gain approval and because they have begun to see the point and purpose of the rules. The last main stage is that of autonomy which, as we noted above, Kohlberg calls the stage of 'self-accepted moral principles'. At this stage the individual has learned to think moral questions through for himself and to adopt his own moral stances as a result of that thinking. It is this stage, therefore, that is the goal of moral education as we have defined it.

If this is an accurate description of the process towards moral maturity, there are several important things that teachers must learn from it. To begin with, we must note that, as in all aspects of learning, we will be wasting our time if we offer material to our pupils that requires of them a level of response too far beyond the stage that they have reached at that time. For if we do, they will not understand or absorb it. Our offerings and our approach must be suited to their particular stage of development. This, of course, has a special relevance to the teacher of young children, although, for reasons that should become apparent later, it is a mistake to assume that it does not also have significance for teachers of older pupils. However, it does create problems for us in that we may have to be largely authoritarian in our approach to the moral upbringing of young children precisely because they are unlikely to be able to think for themselves on moral matters. However, while in broad terms that might be true, there are at least two important factors that can or should take some of the sting out of it.

In the first place, if we are constantly aware of the nature of the process we are contributing to, we will appreciate that any offering or approach we make to the moral education of young children must be such as to help them on to the next stage of the route towards moral autonomy. For this reason, even when we are telling them how to behave, we do not need to be, and indeed we must not be, completely authoritarian. We can and should give reasons for our precepts, since, even if those reasons are not in themselves understood, the children will begin in this way to learn that reasons are relevant (Hare, 1964). In this connection, it is worth noting what Kohlberg has told us of how individuals pass from one stage to the next. He draws on the notion of cognitive conflict and offers us the 'one stage above' principle. Its thesis is that if the child is offered arguments at the level of the stage immediately above the stage he is at, the conflict or mismatch of those arguments will require him to resolve the problem and in doing so he will begin to move towards the next stage. Conversely, if he is only offered material suited to the stage he is at, there will be nothing to stimulate him or lead him beyond it. Thus moral education must be approached in such a way that at all points our main concern is to help children forward.

Secondly, we must note a related and perhaps even more important point. Moral development is like intellectual development in general and quite unlike physical development in that it is not a process that happens simply as a result of our living long enough to let it happen. We do not become morally autonomous just by living long enough, any more than we become brilliant intellectuals just by living long enough. As we have just suggested, we have to be helped if we are to pass through the preliminary stages and reach the stage of autonomous moral thinking. However, the converse is equally true. Just as progress through these stages will depend on our getting the right kind of experience, so the wrong kind of experience will cause us to become struck or fixated at any one of these stages or perhaps in relation to one or several interconnected areas of experience. This is the important message of the psychoanalytical approach to the study of moral development. The wrong kinds of experience, especially in early childhood, can result in our being fixated at an early stage of development and can thus cut us off entirely from the final goal of moral autonomy. Here, as elsewhere, therefore, it may be more important for the teacher to 'be aware of the harm he can do than of the positive contributions he might make.

Thirdly, for this reason as much as for any other, we must not be too ready to link these stages to chronological ages and to assume either, on the one hand, that young children are all necessarily incapable of thinking coherently and constructively about moral questions or, on the other hand, that older pupils will all be capable of doing so. These are mistakes we are inclined to make in viewing intellectual development generally and they are particularly to be avoided here. We must not link the notion of stages too closely to ages. We must avoid the dangers of seeing this scheme merely in developmental or sequential or chronological terms. Piaget was a philosopher and an epistemologist rather than a psychologist. What he is concerned with is not just a matter of stages of intellectual development; it is also a matter of qualitatively different levels of response to moral choices or dilemmas, different definitions of moral behaviour, all of which can be observed at all ages and in all people. It is thus similar to Bruner's notion of the different modes of thinking that we all employ. People, no matter how well educated they are morally nor how skilled in moral debate, will hold some of their moral principles in an uncritical manner, having accepted them without serious reflection from those who have exercised authority over them or from the society in which they live.

If we recognize the truth of this, we will cease to adopt the rather simplistic view of this kind of theory as being concerned with stages through which children pass and will realize that at all stages these different kinds of response can be expected and observed. Thus, at all stages and with pupils of all ages, teachers need to be concerned to promote an autonomous response to moral issues and to avoid reinforcing an authoritarian or a conventional response. Equally at all stages and ages they need to be aware that an autonomous response may not be functioning or even possible.

There are thus two main reasons why children can become stuck at an early stage of moral development or allowed to continue to respond to moral issues at a low level. First, they may not be provided with the right kind of help to get them on or to raise their level of understanding and of thinking on these issues. That, of course, is a problem that moral education shares with all kinds of education. Secondly, however, they can become stuck at a low level because they have wrong experiences, experiences that are painful and, therefore, positively harmful to their moral education. One reason why this factor looms especially large in moral education is that the emotions play a larger part here than in most areas of education and it is to a consideration of the role of the emotions in moral education that we must now turn.

Moral education and the emotions

A moment's reflection will reveal the central role played by the emotions in the making of moral choices. In fact, it may well be the case that most of us respond to moral issues rather more often according to how we feel about them than as a result of a carefully thought-out intellectual appraisal. It might even be argued that such a response may in the long run be more satisfactory since, although philosophers throughout the ages have been inclined to see reason as paramount in morality and to regard the presence of human feelings as an unfortunate obstacle to the free exercise of reason, few of us are really happy to contemplate an action performed coldly and without feeling, no matter how closely it conforms to what appear to be the requirements of rationality. In short, there are those who would argue that this very capacity for feeling is one of the things that makes human beings human and that, rather than deploring it, we should welcome and embrace it (Downey and Kelly, 1978).

For this reason, it has been argued that we should take greater account of the role of feeling in all aspects of education (Jones, 1972), since in all fields our concern should be with the promotion of feelings of caring and valuing for the activities we offer as part of education in the full sense of the word (Peters, 1966) and with learning to understand and cope with our emotional reactions to experiences. The experience of the more sensitive of those teachers who have been involved in the project Man – A Course of Study (MACOS) has revealed the kinds of occasion on which such an approach by teachers appears to be desirable and possible (Jones, 1972) and this is an area that teachers would do well to explore.

Whatever our opinion of the role of feeling in education generally, however, there is no doubt of its centrality to moral education and one reason for the failure to achieve an adequate view either of moral education or of morality itself is that both educationists and philosophers over the years have failed to make or even to attempt a positive appraisal of the role of the emotions. For the most part they have taken the view, first expressed by the Greeks, that, while it may be true that the presence of feeling is one of the features that characterizes human beings, the aim is to transcend one's humanity and attain the god-like level of pure intellect (in spite of the fact that the behaviour of the gods in Greek mythology was far from free of emotional complications). Thus feelings are seen as obstacles to the achievement of this state so that they are to be 'tamed', brought under control, suppressed, in the interests of the full burgeoning of the intellect.

This view offers a caricature of moral education, since it suggests that this is the only approach one can adopt to the emotions in the moral upbringing of the young. As a result, the main thrust of what has passed for moral education in the schools has been this drive towards the suppression of those feelings that are felt to be undesirable, this being one of the reasons why the task has been gladly left to religion and the teaching of religion.

The most serious effect of this approach has been that it has led and must lead to those forms of repression the dangers of which have been amply demonstrated by many psychologists. Repression is the result of the introjection of the taboos of others, especially in our early and formative years. This is, of course, part of the development of conscience, of what Freud called the superego or ego-ideal, and of the growth of a self-image, and we must not be interpreted as asserting that this process is to be totally deplored. Everyone must develop some kind of ego-ideal or self-image and this must be recognized as part of the process of moral education.

However, the dangers of a wrong approach or of regarding this as the whole of moral education must be stressed. These dangers derive particularly from the fact that repression is an unconscious process; what is internalized affects our attitudes in ways that we are not conscious of and the emotions and feelings that are repressed continue to affect our attitudes and behaviour in one way or another without our being conscious of or recognizing that this is happening. It is thus a process that is opposed to moral education in the full sense we earlier tried to give it, since it militates against understanding, critical appraisal and autonomy rather than promoting them. In fact it is this that can lead to an individual's becoming fixated at an early stage of development – if only in relation to certain kinds of issue – and thus prevented from attaining in those areas the goal of moral autonomy. It can also lead to an odd, unreasonable and distorted sense of values and behaviour, of a kind best illustrated by the research of those whose questioning of young children on moral issues revealed that they thought that the worst crime one could commit was to kill someone and the second worst to run in the school corridors (Kellmer-Pringle, and Edwards, 1964). In other words, it can lead to the overdevelopment of conscience in certain areas.

The converse is equally true and rather more serious. For it can lead to that absence of any kind of conscience that is a major characteristic of psychopathic behaviour. The behaviour of the psychopath is not so much immoral and antisocial as amoral and asocial, since he is completely indifferent to the effects of his behaviour on other people or on society (Williams, 1967).

If we choose this road to moral education, then we will find ditches on both sides into which it will scarcely be possible not to fall. We will also find that if our concern is only to suppress emotions, it will be impossible to find a set of criteria by which we can distinguish between feelings, so that we will be unable to promote and encourage those that most would agree should be developed. In short, we will have cut ourselves off from a positive theory of the role of the emotions in moral education (Downey and Kelly, 1978).

Such a theory must begin by acknowledging that feelings are not always in conflict with the intellect. It is not the case that a moral dilemma always consists of a battle between reason on the one hand and feeling on the other, between rationality and irrationality. Sometimes our inclinations and reason are in agreement and this should not be a cause for worry as it has been for some of those philosophers who have clung very tightly to a conflict model. Secondly, often reason and feeling are to be found together on both sides of a dilemma. The essence of most moral dilemmas is that there are good reasons for all of the choices open to us and, often too, feelings that pull us in all directions.

This suggests that the real mistake is to regard the emotions as irrational and not susceptible to any kind of reasoning. It is possible to speak of the 'rational passions' and this alerts us to the fact that the emotions should be seen as being responsive to some kind of education (Peters, 1973).

The first step towards a positive theory of the role of the emotions in moral education, then, is to recognize that they can be educated. The next step is to try to identify some of the ways in which this can be done.

First of all, we must recognize that some emotions are responsive to reason at what we might call a simple informational or factual level. Some feelings that we have are a result of what reason tells us about the world in which we live. When faced by a poisonous snake, I feel a fear that is the product of my knowledge of the capabilities of such a creature. Conversely, ignorance can have the opposite result, so that it can lead a child, for example, to have no fear of the same snake. It is also the case that fear is often the result of ignorance and can be dispelled if we are provided with the relevant knowledge. Thus our fear of snakes might not appear if we know that the snake we are confronted by is of a nonpoisonous variety or has had its fangs effectively removed.

Secondly, not only may reason influence the kinds of feeling we have; it often also can affect the way in which we give expression to those feelings. It can help us to resolve conflicts between feelings; it can advise us on the most sensible way to give expression to our feeling, by steering us, for example, into socially acceptable ways of doing so. In short, it can provide us with a degree of understanding of our feelings and this is a more suitable starting point for moral education than mere repression. For it recognizes that the relation of feeling and reason in human experience is one of reciprocity rather than conflict (Downey and Kelly, 1978).

This in turn will lead to a proper kind of control of the emotions. We stressed earlier that our objection to the notion of suppression of the emotions was prompted not by a desire to remove all control but by a wish to see the development of a proper kind of control. We can perhaps now see how the control of the feelings that would come from a developed understanding of them would be a more suitable kind of control. For it would be a conscious form of control, thus avoiding the dangers of repression we referred to earlier, and it would be self-control and thus in keeping with the definition we have offered of moral education as a process leading to ultimate moral autonomy. Clearly, learning to control one's feelings is an important element in moral education, since it involves developing that facility for translating moral principles into action that John Wilson has called KRAT (1967) and identified as one of the main characteristics of the morally educated person. However, we must go beyond this and ensure that such control or discipline is self-control or self-discipline, since if it is a control that comes from without it cannot be a part of moral education in the full sense.

One key element of the role of the emotions in moral education, then, is the promotion of the kind of understanding of our emotional lives that will lead to this kind of self-control and self-discipline. It will not be enough, however, if we learn only to understand our own feelings. It is also an important part of moral education to help us to develop an understanding of and a sensitivity to the feelings of others. This is one function, perhaps in some cases the major function, of several areas of the curriculum, such as drama, dance and the study of literature. It leads to the development of another characteristic of the morally educated person that John Wilson draws our attention to. 'EMP refers to awareness or insight into one's own and other people's feelings, i.e. the ability to know what these feelings are and describe them correctly. A distinction might be drawn between self-awareness (AUTEMP) and awareness of others (ALLEMP)' (1967, pp. 192–193). Thus understanding of our own feelings and sensitivity to those of others must go hand-in-hand and the development of both is a vital part of what we mean by moral education.

Finally, we must note that what this amounts to is a claim that some feelings should be positively promoted as a part of moral education. We earlier criticized the conflict model of the role of the emotions in moral education on the grounds that it does not enable us to distinguish between emotions but seems to suggest that they are all to be suppressed in the interests of rationality. We are now claiming that we must be able to distinguish among the emotions in this way so that we can pick out those that are to be encouraged and promoted. For we are arguing that we must accept rather than reject our emotional life, that we must not see it as something to be deplored but as a feature of what it means to be human that we should rather welcome and embrace. We are arguing too that it is this that provides the morality, indeed the beauty, of certain human actions, since what constitutes for most people a moral act is that it is done out of love rather than from a sense of duty. It is for this reason that John Wilson draws our attention to a third component of moral education, PHIL, which 'refers to the degree to which one can identify with other people, in the sense of being such that other people's feelings and interests actually count or weigh with one, or are accepted as of equal validity to one's own' (1967, p. 192). Again, however, we must push this on a little further and take it beyond what appears to be the largely cognitive dimension he gives it. It is not only an intellectual recognition and acceptance of the feelings of others that we are arguing for here. It is the development of those affective qualities that will result in our behaving in certain ways not only because we understand the feelings of others, but because we sympathize with them, feel for them, even love them.

This is the direction in which there lies a proper, developed, human morality and our only way of achieving this as moral educators is to take a positive approach to the education of the emotions of our pupils, to help them to become people who not only recognize at the intellectual level what they ought to do but also acknowledge the importance of doing so because they understand and symphathize with the feelings of their fellow men.

Our programme of moral education, then, must be so framed as to promote this kind of development in our pupils as well as the growth of those cognitive abilities we identified earlier. As we said before, however, our efforts in both of these directions will be affected, even inhibited, by the experiences our pupils have outside the school. We must now turn to a consideration of the constraints that this factor places on the teacher as a ·moral educator and of some of the ways in which he can respond to this problem.

Moral education and moral learning
We drew attention at the beginning of this chapter to the fact that the moral educator has to work within constraints similar to those that face the teacher in his concern with language development, since not only will a good deal of learning have gone on in this area before the child comes to school, it will also continue to go on throughout his school life as a result of his experiences outside the school as much, if not more than, those he has within it. For the growing child will be susceptible to many moral influences and he will be so mainly because from the earliest age he needs to act morally, to make choices, so that we cannot expect him to wait until he has reached a level of competence we would recognize before he begins to act as a moral being. Furthermore, as Aristotle said, we become moral by behaving morally. The two must run in parallel.

There are several obvious sources of this kind of learning. Firstly, children will from the earliest age absorb the attitudes and values of their parents and other adults, especially when they see these as emanating from a source of authority and are at the stage when they feel that that is the only reason there need be for acceptance of and obedience to such moral precepts. A good deal of racial prejudice, for example, probably begins this way. Secondly, the peer group will be an important source of moral learning. At certain ages and stages this will be the most powerful and, indeed, the dominant source of moral learning. Thirdly, perhaps the most important, certainly the most insidious, of these sources of moral learning are all forms of the mass media. So much uncritical and unreflective moral learning goes on simply as children, and adults too, watch television programmes of all kinds, listen to the radio, read their comics, newspapers and magazines and absorb the values that are concealed in everything that they are offered from these sources. Advertising may be one particularly obvious source of such influence and its importance must be recognized, but we must not forget that the same kind of persuasive processes are at work elsewhere in the media, whether by design or accident.

These, then, are the three most obvious and influential sources of that moral learning that goes on all the time. There are several important features of this kind of learning that need to be stressed. Firstly, we must note that the relative strengths of these sources will vary at different ages and stages of the child's growth. The influence of parents will probably be greater in the case of young children and that of the peer group at adolescence. Secondly, we must note that this is learning of a largely unconscious, certainly unreflective, kind. The attitudes and values that we pick up in this way certainly influence the way in which we respond to the world; they do not usually influence the way in which we think about it in the full sense of that term. Thirdly, as a direct result of this, often there is confusion and a lack of coherence in the attitudes and values we thus acquire. This will reveal itself at a number of levels. At one level there is likely to be conflict between the values pupils absorb from their parents in this way and those they pick up from their peers, and this is one important point at which the sensitive help of the teacher or some other adult may be necessary. There will also often be conflict and confusion within the values that derive from any one of these sources, since usually they are no more clearly thought out by those who provide them than they are likely to be by those who receive them. And lastly, there will be enormous differences between pupils in this respect, since both the content of what they have thus learned and the manner in which they have learned it will vary very widely. Social class differences in child-rearing practices have been shown significantly to affect children's moral development (Kay, 1968; Bull, 1969) and the multi-ethnic nature of many classrooms will also contribute to the same wide variation of moral learning. The essential factor in all of this is that this kind of learning, because it is incidental, unnoticed, and to a large extent unconscious, is by definition uncritical and unreflective. It thus represents a response to moral issues at the level of heteronomy rather than autonomy. It is, therefore, to use a good old-fashioned word, prejudice, and these views are most likely to be held in this manner if they are learned from adults who themselves hold them in this manner.

Finally, we must note that this kind of learning is not confined to those experiences the child has outside the school. A good deal of similarly unreflective learning of attitudes and values goes on as a result of what happens within the school (Downey and Kelly, 1978); this is what is meant by the 'hidden curriculum'. Sometimes this will be the result of deliberate attempts on the part of teachers to ensure that pupils develop certain habits of behaviour or attitudes without concerning themselves too much with whether they develop these in a reflective or an unreflective manner. Nor must we too readily condemn this, since certain patterns of behaviour do need to be established before pupils are able to be reflective about them. More often however, such learning will be the result of those values that are implicit in the materials we use with children, the procedures we adopt, the way in which we handle those day-to-day situations that arise in every classroom and, indeed, the overall organizational structure that the school favours. All of these will both represent and display value positions and these will be absorbed, usually quite uncritically, by pupils. Thus the school will provide the same kind of moral learning as will the society outside the school.

What are the implications of this for moral education? To begin with, we must again assert that this is not a process to be deplored. It is a natural process and one that provides pupils with that content to their moral development that they need from the earliest age. It must also be seen, however, as providing a basis for their moral education, since this kind of moral learning must be the starting point for moral debate and discussion. In other words, moral education must be seen as the process of converting this uncritical, unreflective moral learning into a fully conscious and reflective response to moral issues.

Two things follow from this. In the first place, we must try to ensure that the moral learning that we are responsible for is not of such a kind as to inhibit the development of our pupils' ability to consider it thoughtfully, even if this can only be done at a later date. This is perhaps of particular importance to the teacher of young children who, as we suggested earlier, may be as yet incapable of reflecting at a proper level on moral questions. Secondly, it means that we must recognize that all of our arrangements and provision in schools should be such as not only to avoid the dangers of inhibiting moral education but also to promote those qualities that we are suggesting are part of moral education. In particular, we should be concerned to raise the values which pupils have already absorbed to a conscious level, to encourage them to be reflective about them and to promote the kind of understanding necessary for a proper critical appraisal of moral issues in order to lead them to the ultimate goal of becoming fully autonomous moral beings.

If we are able to do this, it will only be as a result of a combined effort that not only goes across the curriculum but permeates all aspects of the life of the school. It is to a consideration of what this implies for the practical provision we make that we must turn in our next section.

Moral education and the curriculum

We suggested at the beginning of this chapter that there is an essential moral dimension to all education, that in a sense all education is moral education, and this must be the major theme of any discussion of the practice of moral education. For it is probable that the moral education we offer pupils will only be fully effective if it is the result of a concerted effort to ensure that all the experiences that pupils have in school have a morally educative effect.

This means that we must begin by acknowledging that, like language education, moral education goes right across the curriculum. It would be difficult to substantiate the claim that any curriculum subject does not have a moral import. In some areas, such as literature and history, the moral dimension is easy to identify, since there can be no real examination or discussion of any historical event or literary work that ignores its moral implications. In other areas, these implications may be less readily identified but it would be difficult to argue that they do not exist. Nor must we forget the contribution of many areas of the curriculum to the emotional and affective components of morality, to the understanding and the development of feeling that we referred to earlier. A good deal of what is done in drama, in dance and in physical education, especially when this takes the form of outdoor pursuits, has a major influence on this aspect of development.

Secondly, we must recognize the role that the total organization of the school has to play in promoting moral education. We have already referred to the hidden effects that such factors can have on the moral development of pupils, and the first thing we must do is to try to organize the school in such a way as to ensure that these effects forward that purpose of moral education. In other words, we must try to create a climate in the school of such a kind as to ensure not only that it does not hinder but that it actually contributes to the moral education of the pupils (Sugarman, 1973). This means that we must look very closely at such features of the organization of the school as the ways in which pupils are grouped, the teacher-pupil relationships, the system of rules and patterns of authority within the school, the form and purposes of any school council we might set up for the discussion of problems, and many other things, and recognize that these are not just administrative devices but parts of the total programme of moral education. For the same reason, it has been suggested that counselling should be seen not just as a mechanism for dealing with individual problems but again as part of the moral education of all pupils (Schofield, 1977).

This is why a number of the projects in moral education that have emerged in recent years, such as the Lifeline project (McPhail, 1972) and that of the Farmington Trust (Wilson, 1973), have stressed the need for the introduction into the school of a structure that will support what they are endeavouring to achieve. However, many of them also stress the need for the curriculum to include specific lessons in moral education and offer advice on what such lessons might contain. There would seem to be little doubt that some such direct examination of moral issues is desirable. The kind of discussion of moral questions advocated, for example, by the Humanities Curriculum Project (Schools Council, 1970) is clearly likely, if properly carried out, to be of great value both in encouraging critical thinking and in raising the quality of such thinking.

There are two aspects of the introduction of moral education as a subject on the timetable that we need to note, however. The first of these is that, like so many curriculum innovations, this kind of lesson is usually beamed only at the 'average or below average' pupil, so that the 'above average' pupil is deprived of its advantages. In this respect, both the philosophy and the experience of the Humanities Curriculum Project is interesting. For, although given the brief to prepare materials for the use of adolescents of 'average and below average ability' (Schools Council 1970), the project team determined to make no concessions and to avoid 'talking down' to such pupils, in short, to offer them a moral education in the full sense and thus to 'unite them with the rest of mankind'. As a result, the materials produced have been quite widely used in sixth forms.

Secondly, the inclusion of moral education on the timetable may lead the other teachers in the school to assume that they have no responsibility for moral education, just as many did, and still do, when it is left to the teacher of religion. This could result in the loss of all of these advantages that we are arguing will accrue only if every teacher acknowledges his responsibility in this area. We must finally turn, therefore, to a consideration of what all of this means for the individual teacher in his own classroom.

The first problem facing the teacher is that of providing his pupils with a continuously developing moral code that will govern their day-to-day behaviour, in short, to provide a content for their moral development, since, as we said earlier, we cannot expect them not to act morally until their moral education is completed. Positive moral guidance is necessary, therefore, from the earliest age. What such guidance should consist of is probably the most intractable problem to be solved, since, as we have already stressed, on most issues there is a wide spectrum of opinion that must be allowed and there is no longer any point in seeking after some objective basis for any one particular moral position or set of values.

However, although guidance is necessary and content of some kind is needed for moral education, it is not too much of a problem to decide what that content should be if we pay proper attention to the manner in which it is presented and bear in mind throughout the goals and principles of moral education as we have defined it. Moral guidance does not have to be an imposition of our values on our pupils if it is offered in a spirit and in a manner that will ensure that in the end the pupil will be able to think for himself and reach his own moral conclusions.

There are pitfalls here, however, that we need to be familiar with. In general, we need to be quite meticulous in our efforts to ensure that the guidance we offer is offered in this way. In particular, we need to be aware of the influence our own values are likely to have on the moral development of our pupils. Moral values are as readily caught from teachers as they are from other sources, so that we must be constantly alive to the risks we run, or rather which our pupils run, in this respect. This is one reason why moral disagreement among the teachers of any school is to be applauded rather than, as some seem to think, deplored. For if teachers themselves display to their pupils a wide spectrum of opinion, it is less likely that those pupils will uncritically accept any one viewpoint on any issue.

However, again we must stress that it is the manner rather than the matter that is important. A lack of consensus on matter may be an advantage; a lack of consensus on manner will be quite the opposite. For, not only will pupils catch particular moral values from teachers, they will also catch from them the manner in which they are held. If the teacher himself holds a particular view in an authoritarian, heteronomous manner, the pupil who absorbs it from him will come to hold it in a similar manner and it is that rather than the temporary adoption of a particular value position that puts his moral education really at risk. The message here is brief but vital. If the teacher himself is not a morally educated person, not only will he never become a moral educator, he is likely to have a positively inhibiting effect on the moral education of his pupils. No one should expect to be able to contribute to the moral education of children who is not morally educated himself, just as no one can promote education in any field in which he is not himself a fully educated person.

In brief, it is more important that teachers should know what they should not do in the field of moral education than what they should do. It is important that they be fully alive to the dangers, to the harm they can do. As in all areas of education, teachers must recognize the importance and the complexities of the job they have to do and realize how much damage they can do if they do not do it properly.

Whatever formal provision we make, the first and most lasting moral education is that which grows out of the day-to-day interaction between teacher and pupil and the guidance that the individual receives in relation to those moral problems, however trivial, he finds himself faced with. The worldwide issues are important and opportunities to discuss them must be provided, but in the last analysis the real stuff of moral education is the everyday experience of the individual. In this area in particular, the only true education is that which is developed from the first-hand experience of each child, since it is here that he is sorting out his own life-style, structuring his own world, building up his self-confidence, and developing his capacity for responsibility. All of this is essentially a first-hand matter. This is why, although the other kinds of provision we have discussed must have their place, in the end the quality of the moral education any child receives will depend on the quality of the teachers with whom he finds himself working at any and every stage of his education. In this again moral education is no different from education itself.

Social education

Just as moral learning, as opposed to moral education, can and does go on all the time, so it can be argued that social learning takes place whenever children are with other people, whoever they are. Social learning can include learning how others behave in certain situations, how behaviour varies by custom according to circumstances, and also learning how to cooperate with others. In fact, since man is a social animal, learning how to live in society must inevitably be termed social learning. And since education by its very nature is a social process, we could argue that social learning, just like moral learning, is inevitably part of education and that teachers could not disclaim their responsibility of children's social learning even if they wished to. But is this the same as social education? Most teachers would probably agree that they engage in some social education, since they all expect pupils to adhere to the norms of the school, to cooperate with others and to show respect to adults, for instance. In addition, many school curricula include some kind of social studies or community activities designed to promote social education. Yet a brief glance at the literature shows that social education is interpreted in many different ways, not only by curriculum planners but also by teachers and certainly by pupils (Schools Council, 1974; Gleeson and Whitty, 1976). In order then to understand more fully what social education entails, we must explore various interpretations given to it in practice.

Current interest in social education is reflected in a proliferation of courses in schools which would not have appeared on the curriculum or been thought appropriate until fairly recently. Such courses cover a wide range. They include the various kinds of humanities programme designed in the 1960s to provide interest and relevance for pupils who were being obliged to stay at school an extra year against their will (Schools Council, 1965 and 1967); environmental studies which provide opportunities for pupils to pursue what is required of them outside school (Schools Council, 1974); community education projects such as that planned by Midwinter in Liverpool (1972); social studies courses to introduce pupils to basic sociological concepts; and broad moral education programmes such as the Humanities Curriculum Project (1971). Closer examination of even a few of these examples reveals two striking features: firstly, that with the exception of sociology-based social studies, most of these courses are designed for pupils of below average ability, and secondly, that the aims and objectives are too varied to reveal a common understanding about what social education is or should be.

Development of social studies in schools
A brief examination of the ways in which schools have attempted to provide some kind of social education over the past two decades will help to show how the concept has been interpreted and how changing aims and objectives have guided practice.

It was not until after the Second World War that the newly formed secondary modern schools began to introduce courses in environmental studies, civics, current affairs, and so on, designed mainly to show pupils how man adapts to the problems of his environment and, implicitly if not directly, teaching pupils how to conform to the society in which they live. Few such courses, if any, were provided for pupils in selective schools, who were considered capable of traditional academic subjects, or who at any rate accepted them unquestioningly, having been successfully socialized into the ethos of their school. Public attention was drawn to the importance of social studies for adolescents by the Crowther Report (1959), which recommended such courses for the fifteen to eighteen age group, to help them to find their way around the world. Four years later the Newsom Committee (1963) strongly supported the introduction of some kind of social studies for the less able, who, it was hoped, could be more easily contained in school by studies with a less academic flavour, deemed to be more practical and relevant to their needs. It was in response to demands such as these that the Schools Council published among others its Working Paper No. 11, 'Society and the Young School Leaver' (1967), setting out suggestions for humanities programmes designed to give the pupil 'a chance to learn more about himself and more about the community in which he is to live'. This working paper, in its attempt to provide some kind of social education for pupils of average and below average ability by sending them out into their own locality to explore, for example, the 97 bus, the press, shops and shopping,, has subsequently been most stringently criticized on the grounds that it teaches pupils to accept their unfortunate lot unquestioningly.

John White's pithy comment (1968) that pupils were merely being instructed in obedience by 'interest-based indoctrination' has been echoed by other writers since then. According to Gleeson and Whitty (1976) such programmes merely became 'low status subjects taught to low status pupils by low status teachers'.

In the mid-1960s, social studies and social education took on a new look, partly as a reaction to the kind of programme that we have been describing and partly because of the influx of sociology graduates into schools for the first time. This movement, supported by influential sociologists at the London Institute of Education, became concerned with the planning and teaching of sociology-based social studies courses. This was an attempt to introduce a greater degree of academic rigour and to help secondary school pupils to pursue a more structured study of society based upon an understanding of the concepts and evidence from social science. Courses were no longer to be aimed at the less able pupils, most of whom were already labelled as academic failures, but instead set out to promote the social awareness of all pupils by developing in them an understanding of the society in which they lived. Lawton (1968) called for social studies courses that were not only socially relevant and academically rigorous but also fostered discovery and problem solving rather than mere memorization of facts.

However, such ideals were in practice difficult to achieve. Academic sterility replaced academic rigour, in that brighter pupils tended to learn whatever the teacher offered, while less able ones still questioned the relevance of the material, as Keddie (1971) describes. Social awareness and social understanding were still not being developed, it seemed; still pupils continued either to take for granted what their teachers offered or to reject it out of hand. Whichever it was, it was clear that the new social studies had failed to engender a questioning, critical attitude in pupils.

More recent approaches to social education and the teaching of social studies set out specifically to help pupils to think critically about their own assumptions and about the world in which they live, so that they are no longer content to accept their lot blindly but can learn ways of contributing towards change. Such is the aim behind some of the community education programmes set within the context of compensatory education. Midwinter's Liverpool project (1972), for example, was designed to forge links between the school and the community at all age levels and thus to enable pupils to see themselves as active members of their own community. As such they need to develop the social skills that will equip them not only to look critically at their immediate environment but also to take positive action where this is needed to make changes for the good of all. Within this framework, Halsey (1974) talks of arousing 'constructive discontent' in young people.

Aims and objectives

This brief historical outline of ways in which schools have attempted to make provision for some kind of social education since 1945 enables us to make some preliminary comment about the nature of its aims and objectives. In the early years, courses seemed to be largely instrumental in nature: they helped pupils to find their way about in the world by learning about local amenities, the kinds of jobs they would be able to do, and perhaps something about the workings of the local council and the provisions of the welfare state. However, as we have already remarked, critics were quick to attack these courses for teaching pupils to accept their position in life, thus maintaining the status quo (J. P. White, 1968; C. and M. Ball, 1973; Pring, 1975). Working on a project on the police force, for example, was more likely to teach pupils the sort of attitude towards authority that adults thought they ought to have, than to help them understand the nature of authority, of personal relations, or even of working conditions within the police force. In other words many of these earlier approaches aimed implicitly to socialize pupils so that they learned to conform to the norms and conventions of society. The term 'socialization' nowadays for some people has unpleasant overtones, smacking of indoctrination and always conjuring up a picture of pupils being conditioned or trained in a machine-like manner, reminding us of Skinnerian reinforcement techniques more appropriate to the training of animals than the education of man.

The New Social Studies movement brought an ostensible change in objectives in rejecting the ideal of socializing only the less able and, instead, introduced the notion of developing social awareness in all pupils. At first, this seemed a welcome aim. However, what was understood by this concept was not made clear enough. Learning about the structure of society through sociological concepts seemed to imply that social awareness meant understanding what society is like and how it works, moreover, largely from a sociologist's point of view. Knowing what society is like can possibly mean little more to the individual than learning where his place is in it, in other words, being socialized.

A more precise but limited set of objectives are those expressed by Taylor (1970) within a context of compensatory education. The Schools Council Working Paper No. 27 advocates the development of competence, confidence, and cooperation as the main aims of social education for culturally deprived pupils. Taylor's attempt to analyse competence in terms of roles and skills suggests that it is possible to train pupils to be socially competent by equipping them with certain social skills, just as we teach them manual skills, for example, in the workshop. But what is the nature of these social skills? We could teach pupils in a fairly mechanical fashion how to get on with others by drilling into them the importance of looking at the person they are speaking to, not contradicting or interrupting, suppressing annoyance and impatience; yet what would this mean other than rigid conformity to a set of conventions? Such a limited approach might well be called social training yet might turn out to be no more than training in hypocrisy. Social skills are far more complex to analyse than the manual skills that are required in technical drawing or pottery, for example, since they almost universally require an element of moral judgement. A similar problem arises over teaching pupils how to play the social roles which might be required of them, as Taylor suggests, since there is no one right way of playing a role such as that of a mother or a good citizen. To imply that there *is* one right way is to envisage a mechanical society where we all conform to a given model with no personal variation and, even more important, no opportunity to exercise moral judgement. Thus Taylor's approach, which uses an objectives model, can do no more than present social education as socialization or social training.

Current social education projects

We have so far explored several different ways in which schools have tried to provide some sort of social education for their pupils, by examining different approaches to social studies in secondary schools over the past twenty-five years or so. Brief reference has been made to several official recommendations, to illustrate how aims and objectives, usually ill-defined and insufficiently analysed, have changed over the years. Before we attempt to analyse in more detail what we think social education should encompass, we shall look more closely at two particular projects which are currently being used in schools: Bruner's 'Man, A Course of Study' (MACOS) and the Schools Council Social Education Project.

Bruner's MACOS (1960) provides an example of a social studies programme for children in the middle years of schooling and in this country is used mainly with the ten to thirteen age range. It is in essence an enquiry-based project, drawing upon evidence from the social and behavioural sciences, particularly anthropology and ethology. The course structure is based upon Bruner's notion of a spiral curriculum, so that pupils can explore and examine basic and universal concepts of social life, such as communication, aggression, and adaptation in a variety of social contexts. These begin with the life-cycle of the salmon, the herring gull, the chimpanzee/baboon family, then proceed to the human level, taking the Netsilik Eskimo as an example of a culture very different from that of Western man. By comparing and contrasting life-styles at these various levels, using film material as the main learning resources, pupils are encouraged to pursue three basic questions: What is human about human beings? How did they get that way? How can they be made more so? Social awareness is interpreted as the ability to understand man's nature, to reflect critically upon and analyse the human condition and to understand and respect man's capacities, emotions, and shortcomings. Not only do pupils have the opportunity to observe and discuss how different species and different cultures cope with their basic needs, survival mechanisms, and emotional forces, but they also have the chance to express and reflect upon their own emotional responses to forms of behaviour that are totally alien to Western man. Thus social awareness is enhanced by understanding others and also coming to terms with oneself.

MACOS uses the concepts, evidence, and insights drawn from the social sciences to help younger pupils towards an understanding of what society is like, thus putting into practice the principles advocated by Lawton (1968). It attempts to prepare pupils for participation in social life, without trying to equip them with specific social skills or to teach them to adhere to the norms and conventions of their own society. On the contrary, it gives them insights into ways in which very different communities organize their social world. Rather than attempting, even implicitly, to inculcate certain attitudes or values into pupils, the programme leaves important social and moral questions open to pupils, thus allowing them the opportunity of forming some kind of moral judgement of their own.Thus, as a course in social education, MACOS meets many of the criticisms levelled against other projects. Clearly, however, its success depends upon the teacher's skill in handling the materials and the pupils' responses to them. It would be easy to use didactic methods and simply present children with unrelated chunks of predigested knowledge, though official attempts are made in this country to equip teachers with appropriate skills before they are permitted to use the resources. Similarly a teacher, unskilled in handling children's responses to such incidents as the killing of baby seals, the attacking of their young by gulls, or the practice of urinating on burning sand so that it might be strewn over the body to cool it, might suppress children's emotions rather than help them to understand their own feelings. And although, as we have pointed out, there is no attempt to persuade children to adopt any particular attitudes, there remains the danger that teachers and pupils might take Westerners as their ideal concept of man, by contrast with another apparently less civilized culture.

The Schools Council Working Paper No. 51 (1974) offers a very different programme of social education. It is designed for use with less able pupils in the fourteen to fifteen age range and aims to equip them to play a fuller part in the affairs of their own community, to be willing and able to engage in cooperative activity, to challenge and change their world, thus helping themselves and others towards a more satisfying mode of social living. Williams and Rennie (1972) see social education not as a variation on social and liberal studies, but as a means of equipping pupils to contribute towards much needed social change by seeing themselves in school as part of the wider community. The aims of the Schools Council Project are expressed in its definition of what social education is, namely 'an enabling process through which children will receive a sense of identification with their community, become sensitive to its shortcomings and develop methods of participation in those activities needed for the solution of its social problems'. Thus in implementing the project, the team members, led by Rennie, were attempting to involve pupils in specific activities rather than simply adding yet another subject to the curriculum. After an experimental trial period in 1968–1969, when an attempt was made to introduce social education programmes into ten schools in the Nottingham area, the main study (1969–1971) was concentrated in four schools.

To prepare pupils for the main part of the work, time was spent initially in building up communication skills by means of mime, simple group drama, group discussion of practical problems, and later of issues involving moral elements. In the fourth year pupils were ready to study in depth the structure of some of the groups that had a direct impact on them, in preparation for an examination of a specific aspect of the area in which they lived, such as play facilities, living conditions, emergency services, and so on. The aim was that eventually pupils would reach the final step in the sense of belonging to the community, by carrying out a survey to identify and possibly help to solve a problem they considered in need of attention and action.

One low-ability class, for example, who had been following a social education programme for two years and had compiled profiles of the groups they belonged to in school, embarked on a project involving problems of redevelopment in their area. They discovered during the course of their survey that about two-thirds of the population were going to be rehoused against their will and that the move would result in increased deficiencies in public services. What particularly distressed the pupils was that the adults concerned were apparently completely fatalistic about what was to happen to them and made no attempt to express their dissatisfaction publicly or to initiate any action to avert the move. The indignation of the pupils was so strong that they made plans to take action themselves, suggesting building a mobile exhibition for use in shops, launderettes, and waiting rooms; running a poster campaign to rouse adults from their resignation and apathy; and contributing articles to the local newspaper on the implications of the redevelopment scheme.

An initial evaluation of the project suggested that it had had some success in developing pupils' self-awareness and creating in them a sensitivity towards the needs of their community and a willingness to involve themselves in community problems. Clearly this kind of programme makes more demands on the social and intellectual resources of pupils than community service projects where pupils are presented with a practical task such as shopping for the elderly or looking after small children. As C. and M. Ball (1973) point out, pupils often have no idea why they are papering an old person's walls, let alone why problems of poor housing exist. Gleeson and Whitty (1976) scathingly remark that it often amounts to nothing more than 'papering over a few cracks in the welfare state'. We might add that such schemes successfully conceal the cracks in pupils' social understanding and awareness. The Schools Council type of project, on the other hand, does enable pupils to take a more active part, in that they themselves identify the problem, take action on their own initiative, and seek adult advice and guidance rather than merely accepting teacher direction.

Although this particular project was necessarily limited in scope, it clearly shows possibilities for development. Like the Humanities Curriculum Project, it involves considerable role changes on the part of pupils and teachers who are now both seeking answers together. Teachers are no longer problem-posers and answer-givers. Likewise, it necessarily entails a move away from didactic teaching methods since pupils must be involved in formulating their own problems, in decision making, and in taking responsibility and initiative.

What we need to ask now is whether a programme of this kind is appropriate and worthwhile for all pupils in all kinds of school. If such projects are restricted to pupils of lower ability in so-called deprived areas, yet again a divisive curriculum is created against which we have argued elsewhere. Moreover, if social education is important, surely it must feature on the curriculum of all pupils? The crux of the issue lies in an understanding of what social education entails. It is rather disconcerting to find within a project entitled social education several references to 'training children in school ... in the skills required to work as groups' or to children being 'trained to act as agents of change within their community' (Williams and Rennie, 1972).

Social and moral education: the common ground

In trying to unravel crucial features of social education, we shall do well to remind ourselves of what we mean by education. Richard Peters (1966) argues that education is first of all fundamentally concerned with the developing autonomy of the individual, in a way that instructing and training cannot be. To educate children socially rather than merely socializing them must therefore mean that we should try to nurture in them what we should term social autonomy, that is, the ability to think for themselves on social issues. To socialize or to train children socially will have the opposite effect, namely to stifle their autonomy. This, as we have seen, was one of the major weaknesses of some of the earlier social education programmes such as that put forward in the Schools Council Working Paper No. 11. To learn about one's environment and one's place in it is to see oneself as a member of a category rather than as an autonomous individual who can think and act on his own initiative. Similarly, an attempt to equip children with the social skills assumed to be necessary to cope with the adult world, as Taylor suggests, even if it does not directly stifle autonomy, does little to promote it. Sockett (1976) points to the crucial element that is missing if social education is regarded merely as a set of skills that can be imparted to pupils, namely that the exercise of social skills must always be accompanied by the ability to make moral judgements. And, as we have seen, moral judgements must necessarily be made autonomously. We cannot teach children in advance what judgements to make, but we must try to teach them how to arrive at an autonomous moral choice.

Secondly, it must be remembered that education is always concerned with the development of knowledge and understanding which cannot be reduced to a set of skills, since without understanding what they are doing, pupils cannot learn to use their autonomy effectively and responsibly. Making choices or decisions about what action to take in the face of a social problem, such as the rehousing problem dealt with in the Schools Council Project, must be based on informed opinions and an understanding and critical appreciation of the prevailing social conditions and their implications. This must be part of what we mean when we talk of the development of social awareness in pupils. Thus, as Elliot and Pring (1976) point out, any worthwhile social education project cannot concentrate on *doing* at the expense of reflection and understanding. Furthermore, understanding social phenomena and social meanings must involve appreciating what it means to be human, to be a person. Thus, understanding the concept of a person and respect for persons, as Bailey (1976) argues, provide an important link between social and moral education. It is this understanding that the MACOS project hopes to develop in younger pupils.

A third important characteristic of education is that it must be of intrinsic value to pupils, who should be convinced about the worthwhileness of what they are engaged in. Thus social education in the form of some kind of community service, in which pupils merely regard shopping for old people or digging their gardens as an escape from school, must fail. Social education in its real sense must teach children the value of social responsibility and the worthwhileness of the social behaviour they choose to adopt. Thus pupils need to care about what they are doing rather than take a merely instrumental view about their social behaviour and act only out of expediency. To care about one's behaviour towards other people so that one is concerned to improve their living conditions, or, on a broader scale, help to bring about social change for the good of the community, involves the affective dimension of social education. As we argued earlier, all education has its affective side, often unfortunately ignored, but all too frequently confused thinking has resulted only in vague thoughts about feeling for others, sympathizing with them, or loving one's neighbour. To avoid vagueness or false sentimentality we must again stress the importance of understanding what it means to be human and to respect others as individuals – in short, to appreciate the concept of a person. It is a pity that although much is known from the work of psychologists about children's concept development in terms of number, space, time and of moral concepts such as fairness and justice, little research about their understanding of human and social concepts has so far been carried out. Such knowledge would provide a firm basis on which to construct a programme of social education for pupils of all ages in every kind of school.

It is to be hoped that our argument has revealed a good deal of common ground between social and moral education. Any kind of education must include the development of autonomy, understanding, and critical awareness and must be of intrinsic value to those pursuing it. Furthermore, social education, if it is concerned with developing an understanding of social phenomena, must concern itself with what is essentially social, namely with human beings and respect for persons. Any social action must rest on the formation of moral judgements and choices. Teachers themselves need to be in a position to decide on the best way of introducing social or moral education into their schools, if they believe that it is to be a deliberate policy and not merely left to chance. As we have seen, both social and moral learning can and do go on via the hidden curriculum, but this does not, of itself, provide education. Some schools might decide that a programme such as the Humanities Curriculum Project is best suited to their needs, while others, especially in downtown areas, might wish to introduce a course that has active links with the community. Both Midwinter (1970) and Rennie et al., promoters of the Schools Council Project (1974), are firmly convinced of the value of an action project for schools in deprived areas, so that pupils learn to go beyond a resigned acceptance of their lot or a crude negative reaction against it, towards a clear articulation of their needs and an ability to take action, in order to improve the quality of life. But whatever kind of programme is adopted, the essential element must be educative: it must be concerned with the development of knowledge, understanding, critical awareness, and the ability to make moral and social judgements autonomously.

Summary and conclusions
We have tried in this chapter to argue that an analysis of what we mean both by 'education' and by 'morality' requires us to see moral education as the development not of particular habits of behaviour or attitudes of

mind but of the ability to think for oneself critically, sensibly and productively on moral issues. We further claimed that the same approach to moral education is indicated by an examination of the nature of the society in which we live, since the social change that we are constantly witnessing makes it necessary to help children to attain a flexibility and an adaptability in their moral outlook, while its pluralism requires that we be tolerant of many shades of opinion on most issues.

We then considered some of the major constraints that teachers must work within when endeavouring to bring about this kind of development in their pupils. First of all, they must take full account of the stages that the individual must pass through on his way to moral maturity. Secondly, they must recognize that the emotions play a major role in our moral lives and that this is a source of particular difficulties for the moral educator. Thirdly, we noted the volume of largely unconscious moral learning that goes on outside the school and, indeed, inside the school as well, that must be seen as providing the basic material with which and within which the teacher must work in this area.

Next, we considered some of the implications of this for the practice of moral education within the school. We suggested that there was a place for the moral education lesson, for the provision of opportunities for pupils to discuss, debate, and ponder on moral questions as such. We stressed, however, that such provision should not be allowed to encourage other teachers to ignore the moral dimensions of all curriculum subjects, but that they should be aware of that dimension and make proper use of it in all areas of the curriculum. We also emphasized the need for attention to be given to all aspects of the organization structure of the school, to its climate, to ensure that its total effect is as morally educative as it can be made.

This brought us to a recognition of the central role of the individual teacher in this process. We reiterated that the quality of the moral education every child receives will depend on the quality of his teachers. We noted the kind of harm that teachers can do in this sphere and stressed in particular the need for teachers themselves to be morally educated.

Finally, in considering the relationship between social and moral education, we traced briefly the development of social studies in schools and examined some of the current curriculum projects in social education. Again, we found ourselves moving inexorably towards the same conclusions, that the main thrust of the teacher's work here must also be towards helping pupils to develop their own powers of judgement, and that, in doing so, his own role is crucial.

In the last analysis, moral education and social education depend on the recognition by every teacher of his responsibility to see that his own contribution to the processes is such as to assist, or at least not to hinder, the child in his progress towards a proper social, moral and human autonomy. And that, as we said at the beginning of this chapter, is also the goal of education itself.

8 The Curriculum

One of the most dramatic features of the educational scene, particularly in the United Kingdom, in the last twenty years or so has been the increased attention that has been focussed on the curriculum. In part, this has been due to a recognition that in a rapidly changing society there is need for continuous appraisal of and adjustment to what is done in schools. It is also, however, the result of a growing awareness that questions of curriculum lie at the very heart of the educational debate and organizational changes, such as the comprehensivization of secondary education, the introduction of middle schools, or the establishment of mixed-ability classes, will achieve little if they are not accompanied by corresponding changes in the curriculum itself. The study of the curriculum, then, is central to the study of education, so that no discussion of the theory and practice of education could be complete without a detailed examination of what this involves.

We must begin such an examination by attempting to establish a definition of what the curriculum is. It is a term that is often used to denote the range of subjects on a school's programme or even sometimes the content that is taught within any one of those subjects. Our use of the term 'curriculum' makes it the focal point of all educational debate from its use to denote timetables, prospectuses, and syllabuses. For in this sense the term must be taken as referring to the totality of the provision that an educational institution tries to make for its students, so that the best definition of it that we can take is that of John Kerr who defines it as 'all the learning which is planned and guided by the school, whether it is carried on in groups or individually, inside or outside the school' (1968, p. 16).

If we accept such an all-embracing definition we can understand why the planning of the curriculum in this sense has attracted so much attention in recent years. For it has been claimed that, if we are to attain any of the educational ideals that we have set ourselves or had set for us by society, we need to look closely at the total effect that our provision is having. For this reason there has emerged the notion of rational curriculum planning. It has been argued (Hoyle, 1969) that most of the curriculum change of the past has been of a kind best described as unplanned 'drift', so that if we wish to claim that education is a rational activity, we must give more conscious and detailed attention to it than we have hitherto done. It has further been argued (Tyler, 1949; Hirst, 1969) that when we do give it this kind of conscious and detailed attention we immediately recognize how unscientific the traditional approach to curriculum planning has been, that, in particular, it has concentrated on an examination of curriculum content only and that, if it is to have any claim to being regarded as a rational activity, it must go far beyond this and consider its objectives and its procedures as well as its content and, in addition, must submit itself to a proper kind of evaluation. The mistake of the 'traditional' approach to education, it is claimed, has been to concentrate on content, that of the 'progressive' approach to concern itself almost entirely with method. Questions of curriculum must be considered from both of these angles and from that of objectives too. In this form, the notion of rational curriculum planning was introduced into discussions of education in the USA about thirty years ago and reiterated in the context of education in the United Kingdom ten or fifteen years later.

More recently there has been a reaction against this kind of analysis of the idea of rational curriculum planning and, in particular, against the claim that it can only be regarded as rational if it prespecifies its goals. We must, therefore, begin this chapter with a careful examination of the issues of both a theoretical and a practical kind that this debate raises.

Before we do so, however, it may be as well to remind ourselves that, although it is clearly important that we do give careful thought to the planning of the curriculum, it is not possible to free ourselves from the influences and constraints of other factors and that we must not lose sight of the fact that any curriculum planning we may engage in must go on in the context of many pressures from both within and without the school itself.

To begin with, the curriculum must evolve from what is already there. Curriculum innovation must not be totally revolutionary. If it attempts to be, then, for a variety of reasons, not the least among which is the inability of many teachers to adapt to completely new approaches to education, such innovation will not 'take'. Evolution is preferable to revolution and the curriculum must be seen as in part the product of its own history. It is also the product of the history of the society in which it is to be found and, in particular, its cultural history (Williams, 1958). The historical, social and cultural influences on the curriculum offer a fascinating subject for study and must not be ignored by those who plan curriculum change.

Secondly, we must recognize the economic and administrative influences on the curriculum. It is not possible for the education system not to respond to the demands made on it by the economic needs of society. Indeed, one major reason for the upsurge of interest in the curriculum that we have already referred to is that rapid technological development and resultant economic change has led to different demands being made on schools. Such demands make themselves most readily felt in schools through the exigencies of the public examination system and the constraints that these impose on curriculum change and development. They also reveal themselves in the overt demands and pressures that are increasingly generated by politicians and industrialists. They cannot be ignored by anyone who wishes to engage in any kind of curriculum planning.

Lastly, we must note that technological change leads to social change and thus to changes of ideology. Such changes will also have their impact on the curriculum. Some of the implications, for example, of the egalitarian ideology of the 1944 Education Act in the United Kingdom are only just beginning to be appreciated by those responsible for curriculum planning. More than this, however, we must acknowledge that a major feature of advanced industrial societies is the presence within them of many competing ideologies, that, in short, they are pluralist societies, containing, tolerating, even welcoming a variety of value systems. This also has implications for education, especially for the manner in which we approach it, since it will be clear that in planning the curriculum we must not only be aware of the constraints that derive from this source but also of the need to prepare children to play their full part in such a society.

This then, briefly, is the background against which we must examine what are currently regarded as the key features of curriculum planning. Such a discussion must begin by considering what is not only the most vexed of questions in this area but is also central to most of the issues currently under debate – the question of whether curriculum planners should or should not be required to prespecify their objectives.

Curriculum objectives

We have already hinted that the main source of the demand for curriculum planners to prespecify their objectives was the desire of certain people to make the practice of education respectably scientific. This was the major reason stated by those who, quite early in this century, in the USA were advising teachers to start planning their work by stating clearly their intentions (Bobbitt, 1918; Charters, 1924), and of those who, as we have seen, later reiterated these demands (Tyler, 1949; Hirst, 1969). Most of them are, on the one hand, concerned at the lack of clarity in the responses of teachers to questions about the goals of their work and, on the other, impressed by the precision and effectiveness of attempts to adopt a scientific approach to the planning of activities in industry. In short, the main tendency is towards a job-analysis method of curriculum construction, and the appearance of taxonomies of educational objectives, such as that of Benjamin Bloom and his associates (1956), is a natural development of this kind of view.

At the practical level, this approach has been slower to gain a footing, although attempts have been made from earliest times by some teachers to adopt this system in areas of the curriculum where the emphasis was on vocational training. There were also attempts by school inspectors and those responsible for the training of teachers to require teachers and student teachers to state the aims and objectives of their lessons, and in the United Kingdom all of the early Schools Council projects began their work in this way. In spite of this, however, teachers have continued to tackle their work in the same somewhat imprecise or vague manner. In part, this might be attributed to the prevalence of a 'romantic' approach to education at the level of the primary school and to the obsession with content and the demands of public examinations that we earlier suggested has characterized education at the secondary level, but it may also indicate that practitioners of education have always recognized that education is more than a simple scientific process of this kind.

However, other reasons have been offered in justification of this approach besides the demand that educational planning should be tackled scientifically. It has been claimed that it is a characteristic of any kind of rational activity that it should have goals or purposes and that teaching is an intentional activity, so that teachers must be prepared to acknowledge and state their intentions. It has been argued too from a political and economic standpoint that we cannot be certain that society is getting value for the money it invests in its education system unless there is some clear statement of what the goals of that system are to be taken to be, since without this kind of statement it is felt that we cannot measure how successful the system and the people who operate it are being in their pursuit of these goals. Such a view is implicit in the demands currently being made in the United Kingdom for the greater accountability of schools and teachers, and it was certainly a major factor in the obsession of early Schools Council projects with objectives, since it was felt that this kind of prespecification was an essential prerequisite of proper evaluation. Some have even argued that this is an important tool of educational planning and curriculum development, that there can be no evaulation without the prespecification of objectives, and that curriculum evaluation is essential not only for effective teaching but for curriculum development itself, since without the feedback of information that such evaluation procedures provide we have no data upon which to base further planning (Taba, 1962).

More recently, however, there has been a strong reaction against this approach to curriculum planning, the reasons for which may emerge if we consider in a little more detail its major characteristics.

In the first place, it might help to be clear about what the proponents of this view mean by an educational objective. An educational objective is seen as a highly specific teaching goal. A distinction has come to be drawn between objectives and aims in education, the latter being very broad goals or purposes, the former quite precise and specific intentions derived from such broad aims. Some writers in fact have suggested that there should be at least three levels of specificity for our teaching goals, 'ultimate', 'mediate' and 'proximate' goals (Wheeler 1967), and it is the last of these that are most properly described as objectives.

Secondly, these objectives are seen as being behavioural; they are 'intended learning outcomes' defined in terms of the behaviour the pupil is intended to display in his thoughts, actions or feelings (Bloom, 1956). 'The most useful form of stating objectives is to express them in terms which identify both the kind of behaviour to be developed in the students and the content or area of life in which this behaviour is to operate' (Tyler, 1949, pp. 46–47). 'A statement of an objective is useful to the extent that it specifies what the learner must be able to DO or PERFORM when he is demonstrating his mastery of the objective' (Mager, 1962, p. 13). 'A satisfactory instructional objective must describe an observable *behaviour* of the learner or a *product* which is a consequence of learner behaviour' (Popham, 1969. p. 15). And again, 'If the teacher's aims are to help to guide his practice, then they should be expressed in behavioural terms. That is to say that they should state what the child will actually be able to do when the aim is achieved' (Ashton, Kneen and Davies, 1975, p. 15).

Thirdly, systems of objectives are seen as hierarchically organized and involving close interlocking and interrelationships of objectives. Firstly, it is felt that groups of objectives can be divided into families or 'domains', as in the classification of objectives into cognitive, affective, and psychomotor domains by Benjamin Bloom (1956), and the division into those related to intellectual, physical, aesthetic, spiritual/religious, emotional/personal, and social/moral development of the Schools Council's Aims of Primary Education Project (Ashton, Kneen, and Davies, 1975). Secondly, it is also claimed that within these domains they can be arranged hierarchically according to levels of complexity. Within the cognitive domain, for example, it is suggested (Bloom, 1956) that there is a natural progression from knowledge of specifics to classification to comprehension to application to analysis to synthesis and so to the making of evaluative judgements; and, within the affective domain, from receiving to responding, valuing, organization and characterization by value and value complex. In short, the assumption is that all learning is of a linear kind. Similarly, the Aims of Primary Education Project divides its aims on a second axis into those 'to do with knowledge, skills and qualities' (Ashton, Kneen, and Davies, 1975). Thirdly, the relations of objectives to aims, or of proximate to mediate and mediate to ultimate goals, is one chiefly characterized by a logical interconnectedness, the proximate goals being derived or deduced in some way from the mediate, and so on. In general, objectives are seen as forming a network carefully structured both horizontally and vertically.

Lastly, these systems of objectives are value-neutral. There is never the intention in any of their authors' minds to suggest to teachers which objectives they *should* choose or to help them with such choices. The intention is merely to offer a blueprint, a scheme for teachers to use as they think fit. Thus this is a model of curriculum planning that recognizes that education is concerned to change behaviour but quite deliberately avoids making any pronouncement on the directions in which behaviour should be changed or on what kinds of behaviour education should be concerned to promote. These questions are left to the persons using the model (Sockett, 1976).

Once we begin to examine in more detail what this approach to curriculum planning involves, therefore, we begin also to see why it has attracted an increasing amount of adverse comment and criticism. For there are several features of it that seem to run counter to what many people believe education to be centrally concerned with.

Probably the most serious source of problems with this theory is its dependence on a model of man, a view of human nature, that many find unacceptable. For among its basic assumptions are that human beings are passive creatures whom it is legitimate to mould according to certain intentions we might have, and that human behaviour is to be explained in terms of external causes rather than the inner purposes of autonomous, thinking beings. Its premises, therefore, are essentially those of behaviourist psychology, a movement with which this approach to educational planning is closely associated, and it is no surprise to note that most of its proponents are psychologists rather than educationists. It is thus not acceptable to those who regard man as an active, dynamic creature who can and should take responsibility for his own destiny.

For this reason, among others, it is also an approach which is incompatible with the view of education that regards it as a process that differs in several important ways from other activities that involve teaching, such as training, instruction, and indoctrination (Peters, 1965; 1966). For this view of education is based on a dynamic model of man and one of its major features, as we have had cause to note several times, is the notion of individual autonomy. It is thus not only those who take a 'romantic' view of education who reject this kind of scientic approach to educational planning. Those who see education as centrally concerned to promote the autonomy of the individual recognize that this cannot be done if we begin the process by specifying 'intended learning outcomes', since to do that is to engage in a process that looks rather more like indoctrination. The point of this in relation to teaching in the area of the humanities is quickly appreciated, since the essence of the teaching of, say, literature is to elicit a personal response from the pupil (Stenhouse, 1970) and for this reason this approach was deliberately rejected by the team responsible for the Schools Council's Humanities Curriculum Project (Schools Council, 1970). It must, however, be equally true of all educational activities.

Secondly, this is in part also due to the fact that a further feature of this analysis of education is that it is seen as a process that is centrally concerned with activities that have or are felt to have intrinsic value, that are engaged in for their own sake, so that the very concept of an educational aim has been shown to be a difficult one to elucidate (Peters, 1973). The idea that certain activities should be planned with a view to attaining objectives extrinsic to them may, therefore, be seen as appropriate to a process like training but cannot be compatible with this kind of view of education. Education cannot be seen as a means to an end so that the notion of an educational objective would appear to be a contradiction in terms. In this connection it is interesting to note that most of the specific examples of objectives given by the opponents of this approach to educational planning are of a relatively simple kind and more readily seen as examples of training than of education in the wider sense that many people wish to give it.

Thirdly, such a means-end view of education leads in turn to an instrumental view of knowledge, since the content of our curriculum is to be selected as a means to the achievement of our goals. Pupils are to be required always to engage in learning for the sake of something else and never because it is worth doing for its own sake, so that all knowledge comes to be regarded as of utilitarian value only, a view whose implications for attitudes to life generally are quite sweeping and worthy of serious consideration (MacIntyre, 1964).

Fourthly, it has been argued (Pring, 1971) that this approach is based on an inadequate analysis of the nature of knowledge anyway, that its epistemological base is unsound or even nonexistent. The division of objectives into domains is unacceptable because in practice, and perhaps in theory too, educational goals cannot be separated in this way. It is not possible to envisage engaging in an educational activity with the cognitive goals of developing certain skills, for example, but with no concern at all for the simultaneous promotion of a feeling for those standards of truth and beauty which are part of what it means to have knowledge and to be educated. In fact, almost every educational activity will have indistinguishable cognitive, affective, and psychomotor goals. Furthermore, the hierarchical interconnectedness of objectives is also unsatisfactory as an analysis of any educational process. Understanding, for example, is not something that comes after we have acquired knowledge but something we aim for simultaneously with its acquisition. Thus we cannot break the educational process down into this kind of step-by-step procedure, since neither the horizontal nor the vertical division of objectives is tenable in theory or in practice.

Again, it has been argued (James, 1968) that this approach restricts the freedom of both teachers and pupils to the point where education becomes virtually impossible, since both will accept the objectives as given, much in the way that both regard examination syllabuses as immutable, and will work steadfastly towards them. In this way, it is argued, both will lose the opportunity to play an active role in the educational process. The curriculum is as much the result of the dynamic interaction of teacher and pupil as of any preplanning, however detailed and thoughtful; education goes 'beyond curriculum' (Holly, 1973); and it is this that is lost when we adopt this kind of scientific approach. We must recognize the individual context of every act of teaching (Sockett, 1976) and the need for constant adjustment in the light of continuous feedback. As we said earlier, education is an art as well as a science. In short, education is seen as essentially an ongoing, open-ended process, subject to constant reassessment and modification in the light of the immediate responses that every teacher receives from every pupil. As such it does not lend itself to precise and exact preplanning. The process of education is far too complex and sophisticated to be elucidated in terms of this simple model.

Lastly, this leads us to an awareness of some of the practical difficulties of this approach. These can be summed up briefly by saying that teaching is just not like this. Planning education is not like planning industrial processes because education is not analogous to such processes. The realities of the teacher's task are far more complex and that task cannot be successfully carried out if approached in this way. It is for this reason that where this approach has been attempted in practice it has not worked out in the manner envisaged, as has been revealed by the experience of several curriculum projects, such as the School Council's project in History, Geography and Social Science 8–13 (Blyth, 1974) and the Nuffield 'A' level Biology project (Kelly, 1973). For teachers do make the constant adjustments we are suggesting are necessary and their objectives thus are changed. If this does not happen, then the objectives of our teaching remain at a simple level, we act according to a narrow concept not only of the curriculum but of education itself and all that is educational in the full sense is put at risk. This is the most seriously threatening aspect of the current demands from outside the schools for a greater concentration on objectives framed in a necessarily oversimplified manner.

We are thus faced by a dilemma. For, on the one hand, we want to ensure that education should be a rational activity and to that end should be clear about its goals; on the other hand, those attempts that have been made to approach curriculum planning from such a perspective have raised all of the difficulties we have just listed. We must finally consider, therefore, some possible sources of a resolution of this problem.

In broad terms, it is possible to distinguish at least four kinds of solution. The first of these we have already touched upon briefly. For it amounts to a claim that, while all of the objections we have listed will apply to the use of prespecified objectives in certain areas of the curriculum, they do not have the same significance in all areas, so that a solution may be found by looking at different areas from different points of view. In particular, it is argued that, while such an approach to the planning of the curriculum might not be acceptable in those areas constituting the humanities, there are areas within the sciences where the same objections might not apply. We have already suggested, however, that such a distinction is difficult to maintain and it has been claimed with some justification that it is contrary to the essence of scientific method and enquiry to approach the study of science with a clear view of one's intended outcomes (Sockett, 1976). In short, the objections we have just considered have relevance for educational activities in all areas of the curriculum.

Another version of this argument claims not that this approach to curriculum planning is appropriate in certain areas of the curriculum but that it is appropriate to certain kinds of teaching. In particular, it is claimed that it does have application in vocational courses and we noted earlier that it is in that kind of context that it has been most often used by teachers. We must be cautious, however, in considering such claims. As an approach to vocational training it is fine, but we must not let that lead us to believe that we can too readily divide the curriculum up into areas of training and of education; we must especially avoid the temptation to separate out the teaching of certain 'basic skills' for this kind of treatment when their prime function is to support areas of the curriculum that would be justified in educational terms. For example, it is not possible to separate out the skills involved in the learning of reading from other dimensions of this process without doing violence to those other dimensions. There are serious dangers in attempting to teach the mechanics of reading in isolation from the promotion of understanding, the ability to appraise critically what is read, and, perhaps most important, the development of feelings of enjoyment in reading as an activity undertaken for its own sake. This is a further threat posed by those demands currently being made for an increased concentration on the teaching of 'basic skills', especially in primary schools.

A second line of approach to this problem has been to seek for an alternative model for educational objectives. Thus Paul Hirst (1975) has argued that most of the problems that we have discussed arise not because of the desire to prespecify curriculum objectives but because such objectives have been regarded as necessarily behavioural. Education, he claims, is not a form of engineering so that this model is inadequate. Equally, however, he argues that a 'horticultural' or 'growth' model of education is no better. We must find a more suitable model and seek for educational objectives that are concerned with more complex forms of personal and mental development than a behavioural model allows. This is an interesting quest but it is difficult to envisage how teaching objectives could be other than attempts to change behaviour and especially difficult to conceive how our achievement of such objectives could be measured other than by reference to the behaviour changes we have brought about in our pupils, and it is precisely this predetermining of these behaviour changes that causes the difficulty.

The work of Elliot Eisner (1969) might be seen as a conflation of these first two approaches to the problem. For he suggests that we should distinguish between 'instructional' and 'expressive' objectives. The former are the behavioural objectives we have been discussing. However, 'an expressive objective describes an educational encounter. It identifies a situation in which children are to work, a problem with which they are to cope, a task in which they are to engage; but its does not specify what from that encounter, situation, problem or task they are to learn.... An expressive objective is evocative rather than prescriptive' (Eisner, 1969, pp. 15–16). The question that must be asked here is whether these are objectives at all, whether it is helpful to use a term that has connotations of travelling with an end in view for a process of this kind.

This brings us naturally to the third approach to the problem, that of those who have rejected the notion of the prespecification of objectives of any kind. It has been suggested (Stenhouse, 1970; 1975) that, instead of this, we should begin our curriculum planning by defining the 'value positions embodied in the curriculum specification or specifications' (Stenhouse, 1970, p. 82) or that we should attempt to reach agreement on the principles of procedure that will inform our classroom practice rather than on prespecified goals (Pring, 1973). This is the approach that was adopted by the Humanities Curriculum Project, since it was recognized that to prespecify learning outcomes in those areas of controversy with which the project was concerned would be to risk indoctrination. It might be argued further that such an approach is in any case nearer to truly scientific method, since it is less dogmatic, more tentative and aware of the possibilities of failure and the need for constant readjustment in the light of experience. It thus does not deny the essential nature of education as a continuous lifelong process to which terminal goals cannot be attributed and it does allow for the continuous development of education and of the curriculum.

It also reflects the practical experience of many curriculum projects and this brings us to the last kind of solution to this problem, which is closely related to and, indeed, not incompatible with the one we have just discussed. Many curriculum projects, as we suggested earlier, have begun by stating their objectives, but the form in which these objectives have been stated makes them appear rather more like Eisner's 'expressive' objectives than the behavioural objectives of the psychologists. In other words, although they have stated their objectives, they have not done this in behavioural terms; they have accepted the notion of long-term goals or procedural principles and they have learned to welcome unintended learning outcomes (Hogben, 1972). They have also come to realize that any objectives they begin with must be tentative and open to modification and adjustment, so that they have recognized that such objectives must be provisional, as was the experience of the project in History, Geography and Social Science 8–13 (Blyth, 1974) or mutable, as was the experience of those concerned with the Nuffield A level biology project (Kelly, 1973). Such an approach is not only closer to what we really understand as a rational activity and rather more like genuine scientific exploration than the approach it rejects; it also reflects more closely the realities of teacher behaviour and experience. Finally, it is argued that no other approach to curriculum planning can make possible a proper curriculum development, since no other approach recognizes that in education 'objectives are developmental, representing roads to travel rather than terminal points' (Taba, 1962, p. 203).

These last two views, as we have just suggested, may perhaps be reconciled. Certainly, it would seem that the most productive approach to this question is one that eschews dogmatism, avoids the kind of tight preplanning that removes the freedom essential to any educational encounter, and allows for continued development and change in the light of experience. It is in this direction that the solution lies to the question of how we can plan our educational provision rationally without planning it out of existence.

One of the major reasons for the problem we have been discussing in this section is the conviction that schools should be concerned with education in the full sense of the term. This same conviction also creates problems for us in the selection of curriculum content and, indeed, it might be argued that it is in part because there is so much room for controversy over the selection of a content for the curriculum that many of these problems over objectives have arisen. For both of these reasons, therefore, we must now turn to an examination of the bases on which we might choose a content for the curriculum.

Curriculum content

One approach to this question has started from an analysis of the nature of knowledge itself. Traditionally, this was the approach adopted by Plato to decisions about what education is and what it should be concerned with, but similar views have appeared more recently and in more sophisticated forms. Starting from the assumption that education is centrally concerned with the development of the rational mind, Paul Hirst, for example, has tried to show what this entails for education by an analysis of knowledge which he claims reveals that there are several logically distant forms of understanding and that the development of the rational mind entails initiation into all of these forms, that what it means to be educated is to have been brought to an awareness of these distinct forms of understanding and to have acquired the ability to operate within and between them (1965, 1969; Phenix, 1964). Such areas as mathematics, the physical sciences, the human sciences and history, literature and the fine arts, morals, religion and philosophy are said to be logically distinct from one another and the central concern of education should be to initiate pupils into all of them. If our concern is with the principles of rationality, autonomy, and understanding, as we have proposed that the notion of education itself suggests it should be, then these are to be attained by involving pupils in all of these forms of knowledge or understanding.

Let us be clear about the logical considerations involved here. It is not differences of subject matter that we are to be concerned with but certain fundamental logical differences by virtue of which we can recognize these as separate *disciplines*. What are these logical differences? Firstly, we are told that each form has 'certain central concepts that are peculiar in character to the form. For example, those of gravity, acceleration, hydrogen, and photosynthesis of the sciences; number, integral and matrix in mathematics: God, sin, and predestination in religion; ought, good, and wrong in moral knowledge' (Hirst, 1965, p. 19). He does not want to say that these concepts are never used outside that particular form but that, when we are building up a rational structure of knowledge, these concepts fall naturally into their appropriate form in such a structure (1969).

Secondly, each form has its own distinctive logical structure. When we build up a systematic body of knowledge, we will find that we are building up networks of relationships through which we can understand experience and that these networks fall into the categories we referred to earlier. A network of mathematical relationships will be of a distinct logical kind from a network of scientific relationships and so on. Again this is not to say that there is never overlap, since, as Hirst tell us, 'certain areas of knowledge presuppose others, parts of the physical sciences, for instance, are ·plainly unintelligible without a good deal of mathematical knowledge' (1969, p. 153) but the logical differences stand.

Thirdly, each form has its own distinctive truth criteria, its own way of testing and establishing the validity of the assertions that it consists of. Thus the truth of a mathematical assertion is established by reference to whether certain logical requirements are satisfied in its relationship to the agreed axioms of mathematics, while a scientific assertion is verified by appeal to observable experience and empirical evidence acquired by appropriate experimental procedures.

Lastly, and following from what has already been said, each form has its own distinctive methodology. In each form it is possible to see 'particular techniques and skills for exploring experience' (Hirst, 1965, p. 129). Each has developed its own unique procedures for extending human knowledge in its own peculiar field, its own methods for extending and categorizing those aspects of human experience that fall within its purview.

This kind of analysis of human knowledge provides a very positive basis for curriculum planning in so far as it offers within its own terms a justification for a whole range of decisions we might make concerning curriculum objectives, content, and procedures. If education is concerned with the development of the rational mind and if rationality can be defined by reference to these several forms of understanding, then many of our difficulties over curriculum planning are solved. It is clear what teachers and schools should be bending their efforts towards.

It does not, of course, in itself provide a justification of all traditional school 'subjects' since some, such as geography, are *fields* of knowledge rather than forms, to be distinguished by their subject matter rather than by any distinctive logical structure, and have emerged as convenient focuses for particular areas of knowledge rather than as distinct logical networks. These will need to be justified on other grounds. On the other hand, it is claimed that it does not rule them out, any more than it rules out other interdisciplinary activities that are to be seen on school curricula (Hirst and Peters, 1970) as we shall discover later when we look at the problems of integrated studies, and it does provide a justification for large areas of curriculum planning.

A similar or related view, and one which has been explicitly combined with this notion of forms of understanding in order to provide a justification for certain kinds of curriculum content (Hirst and Peters, 1970), is that which begins from an analysis of 'education', of what it means to be educated, and suggests that to be educated is not only to have developed understanding or some kind of cognitive perspective, to have achieved a level of autonomy, and to have come to care about what one has been involved in, but also to have been initiated into certain worthwhile activities (Peters, 1965, 1966). In short, it is suggested that an analysis of the concept of education reveals that the content of education must be seen as being intrinsically valuable, that it cannot be something whose justification is to be found outside itself, that education cannot be instrumental, a means to something else, that, as Dewey said, 'the only end of education is more education', since, as we have seen, to teach or to learn something with only an extrinsic aim in view is to be engaged in a process that is more properly called 'training' than 'education'. Thus the content of education as such must consist of that which is valued for itself.

It has been further argued that one can pick out certain kinds of activity like 'science, history, literary appreciation, philosophy and other such cultural activities' (Peters, 1966, p. 160), and show that these are worthwhile in a way that other activities are not and that they are, therefore, the very stuff of education since these are the activities we find ourselves engaged in whenever we reflect upon or try to explain any form of human activity. In short, these are the forms of understanding that are essential to any attempt to take a rational view of human life and existence.

It is at this point that the connection between these views of the curriculum becomes explicit and we see that both will lead to a justification of the same kind of curriculum content, although one must not forget that this kind of argument is relevant only to the educational aspects of the curriculum and that it is quite reasonable, not to say necessary, for schools to be concerned with much that is not educative on this kind of analysis.

On the face of it, however, this general approach would appear to lead to the justification of a largely traditional form of curriculum so that, at a time when the traditional is not fashionable, it has not escaped criticism. In fact, it could be claimed that at the practical level curriculum development has been following a course which is directly the reverse of that which this approach points to, since the predominant characteristics of curriculum change in recent years have been the appearance of new subjects that fall between these disciplines and the development of such things as integrated studies, interdisciplinary enquiry, and project work of all kinds based on pupils' interests and calling for a degree of individualization of provision and self-initiation of work by pupils not usually associated with the 'traditional' approach to curriculum planning.

Critics of this approach to the curriculum have expressed their dissatisfactions with it in a number of forms. The most cogent criticisms are those that derive from some important questions that can be asked about the view of knowledge, of truth, of values, even of mind itself on which this approach is based. It can be argued, for example, that the epistemology of the division of knowledge into logically discrete forms is far from fully worked out. It is one thing to propose the hypothesis that knowledge is divided into several distinct kinds; it is quite another matter to spell out what the differences between these forms are. No satisfactory explanation of any of them other than the logical/mathematical and the empirical/scientific has been given and, while this does not necessarily imply that no such explanation could be given, it certainly does not constitute very satisfactory evidence for the existence of other separate forms. Furthermore, some philosophers have taken a different view of knowledge and have argued, as John Dewey did for example, that all knowledge does fall into one or other of these two categories, that all knowledge which is not of the logical/mathematical form is, like our knowledge of the natural sciences, hypothetical and empirical, so that the truth of an assertion in any of these fields is to be assessed not by whether it satisfies the demands of a peculiar form of logic that cannot be elucidated but by whether as a hypothesis it 'works', whether it is the best and most useful explanation we have yet been able to work out for a particular set of phenomena, whether scientific, aesthetic, moral or even religious.

A further and associated point that has been made in criticism of this approach to curriculum planning is that it leads to what many would regard as an undue emphasis on cognitive achievement. To start from the conviction that education is the development of the rational mind is to be committed to a view that must lead to this kind of emphasis and to a disregard of other aspects of the development of pupils. If it is the case, as Richard Peters has argued (1965, 1966), that the concept of education itself also requires that the educand must be brought to care about and to value the process he has been involved in, that some sort of affective development must be involved, then any view that ignores this dimension, as a view based entirely on logical and epistemological considerations must, will provide a less than adequate basis for the planning of an educational curriculum.

The attempt to base curriculum planning on an analysis of the concept of education such as that of Richard Peters does have the merit of recognizing the importance for the teacher of this affective aspect of the development of children. It also highlights, as we have seen, several other features that must be present if we are to use the term 'education' properly. It goes too far, however, in the view of many people, when it attempts to argue that, as a result of this, certain kinds of curriculum content must be chosen in preference to certain other kinds; in short, when it presses the idea of education as necessarily concerned with intrinsically worthwhile activities to the point where it asserts that these activities can be objectively identified. For to argue this is to assume a theory of knowledge similar at root to that associated with the view of education as the development of the rational mind. In other words, it assumes an objective status for human knowledge, for truth and for judgements of value, the difficulties of which become apparent as soon as we attempt to decide at the practical level what these intrinsically worthwhile activities are. When we do this, we quickly realize that worthwhileness is not something which inheres in objects, in bodies of knowledge or in activities, but that, like beauty, it is to be sought in the eye of the beholder. It is almost certainly true that the use of the term 'education' implies a conviction on the part of the person using it that the activities he is referring to are to be valued for themselves, but to say that is not to say that everyone does or must view them in the same way. The difficulty of deciding who is to be the cultural weights and measures officer is the reason why this approach cannot resolve the problem of curriculum content for us, since a variety of views are expressed, by teachers, parents, and pupils, for example, on what is intrinsically valuable. Logical considerations alone can never constitute a justification for anything.

A further criticism of this kind of approach derives from the view that is being put forward currently by a number of sociologists based on what they have called 'the stratification of knowledge' (Young, 1971). Briefly, these sociologists are concerned about the difficulties we have already identified in the view of knowledge as objective and, accepting the subjectivity of knowledge, they see it rather as 'a product of the informal understandings negotiated among members of an organized intellectual collectivity' (Blum, 1970) and the curriculum in consequence as a social system. Socially constructed knowledge is ideology, that is, it is the knowledge of an organized interest group, and the present dispute over curriculum content is seen as a result of competing ideologies, so that any attempt to impose a particular body of knowledge on children is regarded as an attempt to gain control of them by exposing them to the influence of only one such ideology. Whether this is done intentionally or is merely an

214 Theory and Practice of Education

accidental by-product of the system, the values of the school are imposed on all of its pupils and this is one reason for the demands of people like Illich, Freire, and others for a deschooling of society.

Thus a distinction is drawn between educational knowledge or theoretical thought and common sense knowledge, everything that passes for knowledge in a society (Berger and Luckmann, 1967), and it is claimed that we must explore the activities of teaching and learning from this point of view (Esland, 1971) and examine the possibilities of basing the content of the curriculum on the common sense knowledge of the pupils rather than the educational knowledge of the teacher, thus avoiding the alienation that results when pupils are presented with knowledge to which they cannot relate and which has no meaning or significance for them in the context of their own experience and existence (Keddie, 1971).

A major difficulty of this view is that it offers no help with the question of how we are to decide what 'common sense' knowledge to promote or how to promote and extend it. It also appears to polarize the issue of the status of knowledge by assuming that, if knowledge cannot be shown to be objective in any absolute sense, it must be seen as totally subjective, so that attempts to communicate any kind of knowledge to pupils are seen as indoctrination, whether sinister and deliberate or thoughtless and accidental.

It does have the merit, however, not only of drawing our attention again to the difficulties of regarding knowledge as having some kind of status independent of the knower, but also of alerting us to some of the dangers of taking such a view. It reminds us that the school is a part of society and that changes in that society must be reflected in the school curriculum. It is not enough to base our curriculum planning only on a consideration of the nature of knowledge, since it would then be subject only to very limited kinds of change. Nor is it possible to discern elements in our culture which are objectively worthwhile. Any culture is the product of the interaction of the individual members of a society and what the members of that society regard as intrinsically worthwhile will change; indeed, the pluralism of advanced industrial societies will result in there being no general agreement over this kind of issue at any time. Curriculum development must reflect this and the curriculum itself must be open to this kind of influence on its development; it must be sensitive to variations of culture within a society and to the continuous process of change (Lawton 1973). This view alerts us, therefore, to the need to give full attention to the social dimension of curriculum planning, while adding its weight to the growing argument against the idea of curriculum planning based on a concern with the nature of knowledge alone.

A final point that must be made in listing the main difficulties that some educationists have found in this approach to curriculum planning through a concern with the nature of knowledge is that it leads to no fundamental concern with the psychology of the child. The main preoccupations of the psychological research that has been associated with this kind of view have been the differences between individual pupils or groups of pupils in the rates at which they can assimilate certain bodies of knowledge and questions concerning the most effective ways of presenting material to children and the sequences in which such material can best be organized to facilitate the learning of it.

The general trend away from this view of education which we noted earlier has been a result of all of the difficulties we have listed but in particular it has derived from a concern that more attention should be given to the nature of the child than is required by that sort of approach. This was certainly the starting point for Jean Jacques Rousseau, who has as good a claim as any to be considered the initiator of a new approach to education. If the view we have been considering is sometimes described as 'traditional', it is not only because it has tended to be associated with a curriculum organized in the best traditions of English education, it is also because fundamentally the view of education as the development of rationality through the acquisition of certain kinds of objectively true knowledge goes back at least as far as Plato and it was this Platonic/Christian tradition in educational practice that Rousseau inveighed against in his *Emile*. Rousseau urged us to start from the child in making our educational provision rather than from the subject matter. 'We know nothing of childhood; and with our mistaken notions the further we advance the further we go astray. The wisest writers devote themselves to what a man ought to know, without asking what a child is capable of learning. They are always looking for the man in the child, without considering what he is before he becomes a man.' Thus did Rousseau begin a movement that was taken up by educators like Dewey and Montessori and that has culminated in many of the changes that we can see in our schools today.

This general movement is sometimes characterized as 'progressive education'; sometimes it is called 'child-centred' or 'learner-centred'. At root it is an attempt to plan the curriculum on the basis of the 'needs' or the 'interests' of the child, to seek for a justification for the content of education not in the nature of knowledge nor even in the nature of society but in the nature of the child, the one who is to be educated. We must look now at some of the forms this approach has taken and some of the ways in which this kind of argument for the content of the curriculum has been developed.

Rousseau's own proposals for the practice of education do not help us much here since basically they amount to the advice that, in the early years of childhood at least, we should try to leave the child alone to develop naturally, to grow, and thus protect him from the corrupting influences of society – a primitive version of one aspect of the view currently being put forward by certain sociologists which we looked at just now. However, this points to curriculum abolition rather than curriculum planning and this policy of non-interference cannot provide any kind of basis either for the theory or the practice of education, since it raises both practical and conceptual difficulties. Growth in itself cannot be an adequate or helpful criterion for educational decisions since education is not maturation (Dearden, 1965) and teachers, if they are to have any *raison d'être*, must have a positive role to fulfil.

Attempts have been made, however, to reconcile this view of the desirability of promoting the natural development of children with an acceptance of the fact that those who are to attend to this development must have some criteria to help them to decide on the direction of this development and on the kind of 'interference' in the growth of children that might be desirable or permissible. We have already referred to the work of John Dewey and, in particular, to his view that all our knowledge of the world is hypothetical and that learning is a matter of framing and testing hypotheses. From this basis he developed a view of education as concerned to promote the ability of children to learn in this way and to go on learning and adapting their knowledge throughout their lives. This approach, he believed, would avoid imposition by the teacher, which he regarded as indoctrination and as likely to inhibit real learning; it would also obviate the undirected and possibly useless learning that might go on if children were left entirely to themselves. The criterion by which teachers are to evaluate children's activities and direct them into certain channels is a consideration of the extent to which these activities are likely to lead to further learning, to progress along what he called 'the experiential continuum' (Dewey, 1938). Thus education is a matter of promoting continued experience for children, since it is only from experience that they will learn in the fullest sense of that term. If we were to proceed in this way, Dewey felt that we would promote not only the education of the individual child but also the continued evolution and development of mankind.

Further support for this kind of view has come more recently from the work of those psychologists such as Piaget and Bruner who have explored the process of concept development and in doing so have come forward with a new view of intelligence, as we indicated in Chapter 3, and a new view of education as the process by which cognitive growth is promoted rather than propositional knowledge acquired. This view places the emphasis on the kind of learning that takes place rather than its content, suggesting that it is the task of education to enable children to acquire a range of concepts which they can use in their continuous interaction with the environment. It suggests, furthermore, as we have seen in Chapter 5, that concepts can only be acquired by using them both in action and in speech, so that children must be given opportunities for activity, not always of a physical kind, and for experiences if they are to be able to acquire these concepts, the teacher's job being to structure these activities and experiences in such a way as to promote cognitive growth and conceptual development. This, it is claimed by Piaget, is particularly important in the early years, at the stage of concrete operations, when children learn best from concrete activities (Inhelder and Piaget, 1958). This view is reflected also in the often quoted words of the 1931 Hadow Report on Primary Education that the curriculum of the primary school should be thought of 'in terms of activity and experience rather than knowledge to be stored or facts known'. Thus it becomes the task of the educator to get to understand the child's unique ways of thinking and learning and to decide on the content of the curriculum by reference to what will stimulate and promote such thinking and learning.

To some extent, however, any approach to curriculum planning that starts from a consideration of child nature will find it difficult to give helpful and positive answers to questions about curriculum content, in the same way and for much the same reasons as the approach that begins from an examination of society. An attempt has been made by some, therefore, to set up the notion of need as the focus of this kind of curriculum planning, to suggest that all decisions as to curriculum content should be made by reference to the needs of the children. Some psychologists have tried to discover for us the needs of children in order to provide us with the basic knowledge we must have to begin to plan a curriculum along these lines. Maslow, for example, has proposed a theory of motivation in terms of need reduction (1954). He has identified three sorts of need, primary needs, those for food, air, sleep and so on; emotional needs, those for such things as love and security; and social needs, those for acceptance by a group and the confidence that comes from an awareness that one has something to offer to a group. The theory is that, if these needs are reduced, the patterns of behaviour associated with this need reduction will be reinforced and that this is how learning takes place.

Such a theory may help us in our search for effective methods of teaching; it does not help us with questions about the content of our teaching. For all such theories of need or attempts to define need must involve some kind of evaluation on the part of the person propounding the view and more so on the part of anyone attempting to implement it. Once one gets beyond the needs for food, drink, sleep, and other physical requirements of this kind, it becomes increasingly difficult to separate what a child needs from what he wants or from what someome thinks he ought to have. In other words, 'need' is a term which has a prescriptive as well as a descriptive connotation. These two aspects of the meaning of the word must be kept distinct from each other, since no description can ever give rise to a prescription and no amount of information about what children do need could ever resolve for us the question of what they ought to have. We must have other criteria by which to decide which needs should be catered for since the notion of need cannot of itself be such a criterion (Dearden, 1969; Wilson, 1971). The same argument applies with equal force to the claim that curriculum content can be decided by reference to the needs of society. There is, of course, a trivial sense in which every curriculum is based on the notion of needs, since no one would include in it anything that was not thought to be needed (Komisar, 1961), but in this context the notion is largely otiose and offers us no practical assistance with the problems of curriculum planning.

In order to bypass this difficulty with the idea of needs as the basis of curriculum planning without at the same time losing the advantages that are thought to be associated with an approach that takes full cognisance of the psychology of the child, some educationists have stressed the desirability of using children's interests as the criterion. It is argued that children learn best through interest, that they are manifestly not interested in much of what is presented to them by a 'traditional' curriculum and thus do not learn in the full sense of the word and that we might achieve more success if we were to find out what interests them and work from that.

There are at least two aspects of this argument that must be distinguished from each other. In the first place, it may be that what is being advocated here is a change of method rather than a change of content. For if we accept that children do in fact learn best when interested in something, we need do no more than improve our methodology in such a way as to make them interested in what we want them to learn. This, after all, is no more than many teachers have always tried to do.

However, there is a further, deeper sense in which the interests of children have been suggested as a basis for curriculum planning. For it has been proposed (Wilson, 1971) that education is the development of children's interests in such a way as to help them to pursue them more effectively and with more discrimination, to organize their experiences and to gain a clearer view of the intrinsic value of their activities. We have seen that the notion of education implies that its content must be intrinsically valuable, but we also saw that this assertion does not in itself help us to decide what activities have this intrinsic value. It is being suggested here that our best approach to the problem of discovering what is intrinsically valuable is to consider what is intrinsically valued, to look for what pupils do in fact value for itself rather than to engage in the essentially metaphysical exercise of attempting to discover intrinsic value inhering in certain activities independently of the way in which human beings view them. Such a view is not, of course, unrelated to the view of Dewey which we considered earlier and it will lead to similar major changes in curriculum content. It also throws up similar difficulties and we must consider some of these now.

It has been argued against this view that we must distinguish what a child is interested in from what is in his interests. In one sense, this assertion reveals more a predilection for the pithy saying than a serious criticism, since those who have argued for an interest-based curriculum have usually been very clear about this distinction; indeed it lies at the very root of their argument which is that the development of what a child is interested in is in fact what is in his interests. However, it does draw our attention yet again to the central problem of the 'child-centred' approach, whatever form it takes, namely the difficulty of choosing or deciding between competing claims. We have seen the difficulties of equating education with maturation and providing teachers with no clear indication of the role they must play in the process. This view has the merit of giving the teacher a clear directive, that it is his job to identify the interests of his pupils and to develop them by deepening them, widening them, revealing new dimensions to them and so on. However, he is still faced with the problem of deciding which interests can or should be developed and which should be discouraged, and, even if he resolves that problem, he still has to decide on the direction in which he should develop them. Again his own values will impinge on the situation so that this view is no more successful than any other in offering objective criteria by which we can make decisions of this kind.

This difficulty becomes particularly apparent when we ask questions about the origins of children's interests. It must be the case that their origins are to be found in the experience of the child and particularly in his cultural background. It has been argued with some force, therefore, that if the interests of the child are socially determined, then to base the curriculum on those interests is to risk trapping the child in his culture and, in particular, where the child's background is culturally impoverished (if such a notion is acceptable), education through interests is likely to aggravate rather than to alleviate that impoverishment (White, 1968, 1973). Indeed, it has been claimed that this is likely to result in a kind of social control that is based on not allowing individuals to escape from the cultural environment into which they have been born. The same danger is implicit in the demands we considered earlier of certain sociologists for a curriculum based on the 'common sense' knowledge of the child, the experience he brings to school with him. Furthermore, as we shall see in Chapter 9, if our curriculum is differentiated in this way, knowledge becomes hierarchically structured and those who are allowed access to high-status knowledge may come to be deemed more worthy as persons than those offered mere 'common sense' knowledge.

This criticism seems to be based on a somewhat naive and simplistic view of what it might mean to educate a child through his interests and it need not be a serious criticism of a view that stresses the need to develop and extend children's interests in the way we have just discussed. It does draw attention, however, to a serious danger of this approach if it is not allied to an awareness of the need for some adequate basis for curriculum decisions that is independent of the inclinations of the children themselves. It need not lead, as John White seems to think (1971), to the idea of a common curriculum resembling that which derives from a concern only with the nature of knowledge, but we must heed his warning of the dangers of generating one curriculum for an élite and another for the rest of the school population. The notion that there be some kind of common curriculum is an important one, as we shall see in our concluding section. If all pupils are not given access to what is deemed valuable in our culture, then those who are will continue to enjoy many social advantages over those who are not and our society will remain a divided one.

Again, therefore, we come up against the fundamental difficulty of any approach to the curriculum that begins from a rejection of the idea that certain bodies of knowledge are objectively worthwhile and can as a result be imposed upon pupils without qualms. Any such approach must appear process-bound or method-bound, to be more concerned with the 'how' of education than with the 'what', as we noted at the beginning of this chapter, and to offer little help with decisions of content. If taken to its logical conclusion, it is also likely to result in a loss, or at least a devaluation, of much that many would regard as valuable in our culture and this may be particularly to the detriment of those pupils who are not likely to meet these things if they are not introduced to them at school. It is clearly important that we should not ignore the child in planning a curriculum; equally it is true that we need some other, external criteria to appeal to. How can these two positions be reconciled?

It may be that the difficulty arises from too ready an acceptance of this polarization. Education cannot be properly conceived or planned in relation to either the child or society or the subject matter but must pay due regard to all of these (Thompson, 1972). It cannot be centred exclusively on any one of them without being distorted. Education cannot be seen as growth alone or as moulding alone; it must be seen as directed or controlled growth. If this is to be so then teachers need an understanding and a respect for the nature and the interests of the child, an awareness of the social setting in which they are working, and a concept of education in the light of which they can promote continued development. Both the means and the ends are equally important and any view that ignores either one must be inadequate as a basis for realistic curriculum planning. Knowledge continues to develop; society evolves; people change; and the curriculum must keep pace with all three. If this is to be possible, if the curriculum is to continue to develop and evolve, then it must be open-ended and not firmly tied to any rigid presuppositions. No extreme position allows for this kind of open-endedness. There is no doubt that a curriculum that is planned out of respect only for certain canons of knowledge is likely to lead to the alienation of many pupils and, therefore, to be self-defeating. There is no lack of empirical evidence to substantiate this view. Some attention must be paid, therefore, to the nature of society and to the many facets of child nature and of individual children. It is equally clear, however, that a curriculum based entirely on what pupils want to learn or what the social order of a given time or place seems to require would lead to the loss of much that seems to have value both for society and for the children themselves. Some reference must be made also to what is felt to be valuable, therefore, in planning a curriculum.

In practice, this is the sort of compromise one can see in the work of most teachers and most schools. It is only at the level of theory that it gives real trouble, for it is here that the polarity appears. It can only be solved by an acceptance of the inevitability of the same subjectivity in education that exists in all human activities and endeavours. To expect an objective justification for all educational decisions is to deny that in the last analysis education is a matter of the subjective interaction of minds. In this situation, what distinguishes education from other more sinister activities like indoctrination is not its objectivity nor even the objectivity of its content; it is the intentions of those who practise it. If their intention. are to broaden the experience of children, to enhance their freedom by increasing the range of experiences open to them, and to guide them to that autonomy of mind that characterizes being human and which we have seen to be an essential component of the notion of education itself, then any decisions that are made as to the kinds of curriculum content that are most appropriate to these goals are justified by very dint of the intentions they are serving. To say this is not to say that teachers will not make mistakes in the decisions they make, it is to say, however, that they should not be led into error by being required by educational theoreticians to make unnecessary choices between particular ideological positions. The most that any concept of education can lead us to is a respect for the freedom and autonomy of the individual child. How this is to be interpreted in practice is a matter for the professional judgement of every teacher.

A further point must be stressed here, one that we have made before. The problem that we have been discussing at such length is one that concerns only those activities that we encourage in schools on the grounds of their intrinsic value. Many of the things we teach or urge pupils to learn are justifiable by other, perhaps less controversial arguments, since they are seen not so much as valuable in themselves as instrumental in the achievement of other kinds of goal, such as certain social or vocational achievements. Most curriculum decisions are, of course, in practice made by reference to a mixture of both intrinsic and instrumental considerations. Not all decisions of curriculum content, therefore, need to be made by reference to the thorny problems we have been discussing. In many cases it is enough to be able to show reasonably convincingly that what we intend to teach is the most efficient way of achieving certain vocational outcomes, for instance, or certain skills, that have a social value, unless, of course, we want to involve ourselves in similar debate about the worthwhileness of the social ends to which these means are appropriate. Education is not socialization, but a good deal of what goes on in schools must be seen as socialization of one form or another and is to be justified in these terms. Education is only one aspect of schooling.

Nor must we allow the polarization that has characterized the discussions of educationists to lead us to believe that even the educational content of the curriculum must be justifiable entirely in terms of one kind of approach or the other. There is plenty of scope in the timetable for a number of different kinds of activity, some involving a great deal of pupil choice, others perhaps far less. If we are to include certain elements in the timetable on grounds of their social or vocational usefulness, there is no reason why we should not also have both interest-based activities and compulsory studies at other times, no reason why the timetable should not offer scope for a whole range of activities, each to be justified in quite different terms (James, 1968). We must not assume that all the purposes of the school, whether they be social, vocational, cultural or educational, will be or can be met by one kind of provision. The curriculum must include a number of quite different elements if it is to meet a variety of purposes.

This is particularly apposite to the arguments that have raged in recent years over the merits or demerits of integrated studies. Too often these arguments have suffered from the same tendency to polarization, an assumption that to favour the introduction of some form of integrated studies is necessarily to fly in the face of the logical differences that, as we have seen, some have claimed exist between disciplines and *vice versa*. In spite of this, the integrated approach to learning has spread very rapidly through our schools in the last decade and has perhaps been more significant in curriculum change than any other single form of curriculum innovation. It is also an issue that more than any other illustrates the problems of curriculum content we have just been discussing. No discussion of the curriculum would be complete, therefore, without an examination of some of the main features of this development.

Integrated studies

Most of the views we have considered that have tried to base their curriculum planning on a concern for the child and his place in society rather than the subject matter have been linked, albeit often in a rather confused way, with some form of integrated studies. There are good reasons for this. Children's experiences do not fall into neat subject areas or into single disciplines, nor do their interests nor their enquiries, nor do most of the things that seem socially or culturally important, so that, once one begins to plan a curriculum from any of these bases, some form of integration almost always follows. This is not inevitable, since it is possible to structure an enquiry or a project, even to develop an interest, within one subject area only, as many of the projects of the Schools Council have done. However, one reason why the curriculum of the primary school has been largely undifferentiated and treated as a unity has been the emphasis that has often been placed at that level of education on an enquiry or discovery approach to learning. For the same reason, it has often happened that a move towards these methods in secondary schools has been accompanied by an attempt to establish some kind of integrated studies programme.

We must devote some time, therefore, to a consideration of the different kinds of reason that teachers have had for introducing various forms of integrated studies. Not the least important reason for devoting some time to this here is that, as we have just said, it illustrates better than any other recent development in the curriculum the point we tried to make in the last section, namely the kind of development that takes place when we pay due regard in our curriculum planning to the children we are planning for and the society in which they live and not only to the nature of the knowledge we are purveying.

The first thing that must be stressed about integrated studies is that, like all other examples of curriculum innovation, it takes many different forms according to the particular requirements and characteristics of each situation in which it has been introduced (Warwick, 1973). All curriculum developments should be adapted to the peculiar conditions of the school into which they are introduced, since each situation is unique and needs its own unique programme, but this does make it as difficult to generalize about this particular development as about any other. There are schemes in which integrated studies programmes are based on very careful structuring by the teacher or teachers concerned of both the content of the programme and its methods; there are others, such as the Goldsmiths' College IDE scheme (James, 1968), in which almost complete freedom of choice in matters of content is given to each individual child, often within related areas centred on a common theme, but sometimes entirely freeranging. In some cases, this kind of development has been associated from the first with some form of team-teaching and thus with the combined working of several classes together; in others it is handled by individual teachers adopting a 'generalist' approach with one class. Sometimes the methods adopted have been largely heuristic, with pupils encouraged to explore and 'find out for themselves' or 'learn by discovery'; on the other hand, often a directly didactic or instructional approach has been used. There are also many variations in the range and type of subjects included in such schemes depending again on the purposes of the teacher or teachers involved and even on their individual preferences, since one crucial factor in all curriculum innovation is that, if it is to be successful, the teachers operating it must believe in its value. Thus there are integrated science schemes, integrated humanities projects, and other schemes which have attempted to integrate scientific and humanistic studies with each other. There are thus so many variables that generalization becomes impossible and teachers have enjoyed a great deal of freedom in planning courses to suit their own purposes within these variables.

The particular form of integrated studies that emerges in each situation, however, will depend on the purposes and views of the teachers responsible for it, so that the most helpful thing we can do here in attempting to introduce some clarity into discussion of this issue is to examine some of the purposes that teachers have had when adopting this kind of approach to teaching.

The most extreme view that has been taken here, what is sometimes called the 'strong' view of integrated studies, is that which bases itself on the belief that all knowledge is one anyway and that, far from requiring to justify integrating it, we need a better explanation than has so far been given of why it should be 'fragmented'. This is the sort of view that was taken, as we saw earlier, by John Dewey, who saw all knowledge as ultimately of a scientific kind, a result of the experience that each individual has as he solves the problems presented to him by his environment, physical, social, cultural and aesthetic, problems which are solved in all of these spheres by the application of the scientific method of framing and testing hypotheses. Thus, for Dewey, subject divisions might appear in the later stages of education when reasons emerged for dividing knowledge into convenient parcels, but there were no fundamental logical reasons, such as those that Paul Hirst puts forward, for dividing it up and certainly not for the creation of as many as six or seven discrete 'forms'. The logical positivists too have argued that once we have distinguished between the axiomatic knowledge of mathematics and logic and the empirical knowledge that we have in other spheres, we have gone as far as we can in dividing knowledge up, (Ayer, 1946), although we must remember that on this view many areas such as the moral and aesthetic are regarded as not areas of knowledge as such at all. Views about the wholeness of knowledge in fact have a long history in epistemology from the time when Plato offered us his 'dialectic' as the master science that would weld all knowledge into one supreme system to the more recent claim of A. N. Whitehead that 'you may not divide the seamless coat of learning' (1932, p. 18).

This view of knowledge is given further support by the difficulties we have already referred to as inherent in the notion of knowledge as divisible into several 'forms' and the manifest fact that knowledge has in practice

T.P.E.—Q

been organized by man not into logically discrete 'forms' but into convenient 'fields' to suit his particular interests and purposes. Thus an important and necessary field of study has long been geography, the study of man and his natural environment, a study which has drawn on mathematics, on physical science, on social science, and so on. Indeed the study of education itself has little point or relevance to human affairs if it does not include philosophical, psychological, physiological, and social dimensions. The suggestion, therefore, that irreducible logical problems are created by the attempt to integrate geography with, say, history, or comparative education studies with, say, philosophy is in any case nonsensical. If such problems are ever to arise, it will only be in relation to the integration of disciplines, not of subjects. Furthermore, it will be a problem not only for new versions of integrated studies but also for those established subjects like geography or comparative education which are and always have been forms of integrated studies in themselves.

Thus one view that some teachers and educationists have taken of integrated studies is that since all knowledge is fundamentally reducible to one, or at the most two types, children, especially in the early years of their education, should not be introduced to it in a fragmented form and that subject divisions should emerge only when they have point for the learner in the organization of his own experience and knowledge.

A second and related reason for the introduction of integrated studies has been for many teachers the awareness that many of the things that appear to be of most importance to children and crucial to their development do not fall into neat disciplinary categories anyway. Much of what seems to be important to society and of value in our culture does not fit into these tidy divisions. Live issues in most spheres of human endeavour, like the concerns of the study of education to which we have just referred, straddle the boundaries that are said to exist between the disciplines. Sex education is a good example of a topic that is clearly of importance to pupils but which cannot be adequately tackled within any one of the 'disciplines'. Indeed, much of the inadequacy of what has been done in this sphere is directly attributable to the practice of dealing with it as a part of biology, while ignoring its social, moral, and aesthetic dimensions. Similarly, the Humanities Curriculum Project, to which we have already referred, in recommending that senior pupils should be involved in open discussion of many controversial issues that are of concern in contemporary society, has inevitably been led to an integrated approach. Whether one accepts the arguments put forward in favour of regarding all knowledge as one or not, therefore, it is difficult to argue that some study of an integrated kind is not needed.

Many have, as a result, accepted the 'weaker' thesis that, even if the arguments for separate disciplines are accepted, we must also recognize the need for knowledge from different 'forms' to be grouped around particular 'topics'. Indeed, Paul Hirst himself, whose name has come to be eternally associated with the notion of 'forms of knowledge' recognizes the need for an interdisciplinary approach, for studies in the 'fields' as well as the 'forms' of knowledge and stresses the need to devise an interdisciplinary logic that will enable us to operate properly between as well as within the 'forms' (Hirst and Peters, 1970).

A second purpose behind the introduction of some programmes of integrated studies, therefore, has been the desire to offer pupils opportunities to study areas of importance and concern that cross the boundaries of the disciplines. In a sense, therefore, this has merely been an extension of a form of integrated studies that has long been with us, since, as we have seen, interdisciplinary studies such as geography have long been well established on the curriculum of schools, colleges and universities. In fact the question of which combinations of disciplines are regarded as integrated studies and therefore as constituting some kind of new development that needs justification has been more a matter of tradition than of logic at both school and university level. All that has been said so far, then, suggests no more than a concern to base the curriculum on topics rather than or as well as on subjects and to that extent it may be felt to involve little that need necessarily be characterized as new or 'progressive'.

A third consideration that has led many people to favour the introduction of integrated studies schemes into the school curriculum has been the belief that such schemes are likely to lead to a higher level of motivation in pupils and, therefore, to a better level of work satisfaction for both pupil and teacher. We have already referred to the claim that many pupils suffer feelings of alienation in relation to the curriculum. Many teachers have felt that one factor in this is the undue concern with the needs of the subject that has characterized much curriculum planning in the past and that it can, therefore, be overcome if pupils can be engaged in the study of those things that have some point or relevance for them. The difference between this and our second point is that here it is not necessarily the case that what they will be studying will be seen by the teachers as being of value; the crucial consideration is that it is seen as such by the pupils. It is argued, therefore, that if this is so then they will be motivated by what they see as the intrinsic interest or value of the subject matter and the teacher's increasing lack of adequate devices for extrinsically motivating them will not matter so much. In any case, it is argued that intrinsic motivation is more appropriate to education than extrinsic devices, as we saw in Chapter 4.

This is, of course, the argument that we have already seen being put in favour of regarding the interests of the children as the central concern of curriculum planning, although they need only be accepted as providing an initial motivating factor that the good teacher can use to lead his pupils on to those things that he wants them to learn. Others, as we have seen, would take a strong position on this issue and regard the interests of children as important not only from a motivational point of view but as the only acceptable determinant of curriculum content. Whichever position one takes, however, as we saw earlier, a commitment to some form of integrated studies becomes more or less inevitable in the practical situation of the classroom. For children's interests do not often fall exactly into recognized disciplines and the areas that are of most concern to them are more often than not of a wider kind. Thus some form of integrated approach to learning must follow if one is committed to taking the interests of children seriously in planning the curriculum.

This, then, is a third reason why some teachers have come to accept the integrated studies approach; they have been led inexorably to it from a conviction that their curriculum planning should take full account of what their pupils are interested in and of the need to try to promote an intrinsic form of motivation. This is one reason why such schemes have often been tried initially with the older and less able pupils in their last years of schooling, if only on the grounds that if you can't beat them, you would be well advised to join them, as we have noted elsewhere.

Finally, some teachers have embarked on integrated studies projects because of a desire to promote enquiry methods in their teaching. This is not unrelated, of course, to the point we have just been making, since working from pupils' interests will usually involve allowing the development of enquiries of an individual kind. The enquiry approach also usually leads to the crossing of subject boundaries since a pupil's explorations will seldom be confined within one subject field. The heuristic approach is preferred by many teachers to more didactic methods and, although it can be used within individual subject areas, as many of the Nuffield science projects have shown, it is more often associated with integrated studies. Those who favour this approach often do so, like Dewey, from a conviction not only that this is a more effective way of learning and that it leads to better retention of what has been learned, but also that it is more appropriate to what they see as being the essential nature of education. If one views education as being essentially experience, as Dewey does, or as involving a dialectical relationship between the pupil and his environment, as Charity James and Dewey both do, or as being concerned with the intentions that lie behind the conscious activity of the pupil, as Paulo Freire believes, or as being an extension of the 'common sense knowledge' that the pupil brings to the teaching situation rather than initiation into anything that can be dubbed objective knowledge, as we have seen a number of contemporary sociologists do, then one must accept that education must be a two-way activity in which the learner must be an active participant rather than a mere recipient of knowledge. If one tries, as a result of this kind of conviction, to promote this sort of active learning in which the pupils' learning consists of genuine experiences, then it will be difficult to confine these experiences within those subject boundaries that we as teachers have found useful for achieving our own purposes and organizing our experience. Some form of integration will, therefore, follow, especially in the early stages of education, and, as we saw above, it is only later that divisions will emerge. Furthermore, these will be divisions that have sense and meaning for the learner himself. They may indeed be divisions based on some notion of logically discrete forms of knowledge, but the significance of the divisions will have become apparent to the learner. In other words, he will have been led to the 'forms' from an initially undifferentiated view of knowledge, so that he can see the point and significance of them for himself.

If, for whatever reason, then, we believe that children should have some control over the direction of their education, we will find ourselves being pushed inexorably towards some kind of integrated curriculum. It is for this reason, among others, that, as we will see in Chapter 10, Basil Bernstein has posited a link between this kind of development in schools and certain developments in society at large and in particular changes towards a pluralistic, 'open' society.

There are, then, a number of quite different reasons why teachers may want to introduce integrated studies programmes or, indeed, may find themselves involved in them willy-nilly. It is possible to be led to such a step from a belief in the wholeness of knowledge, from a desire to introduce pupils to interdisciplinary topics that are felt to be important, or from a commitment to other positions in education, such as the importance of pupils' interests, enquiry methods, or any other route to the full involvement of children in their own education.

We saw also that schemes of integrated studies can take many forms and clearly the form that any particular scheme takes will depend very much on the purposes of the teacher or teachers concerned with it. Obviously, a scheme that is prompted by a desire to promote heuristic methods will involve less teacher direction and more free-ranging pupil enquiry than one which is designed to focus the attention of all pupils on a particular topic or issue. Similarly, one which is intended primarily to enhance motivation, to get the pupils interested and attentive so that their attention can then be turned to areas of knowledge the teacher wishes them to acquire will be more structured than one that sees children's interests as being more central to decisions concerning the content of the curriculum. There are many variables and, therefore, many variations. Hence, as so often in education, the important thing is to be clear about one's intentions so that one's practices can reflect this.

One further important point must be made concerning the practicalities of introducing any scheme of integrated studies. It is the practical and administrative problems this will create that are the source of most of the difficulties that arise. Any epistemological problems there might be will pale into insignificance when viewed alongside the practical difficulties of securing the cooperation of two or more subject departments, whether at school or university level, or, in many cases, two or more heads of departments. This is another reason why curriculum integration has always been fraught with particular difficulties in secondary schools and universities. For these are the difficulties that loom largest and it may be that they are the only serious difficulties that we have to face (Kelly, 1977). Certainly, they do have to be faced because, whatever the educational merits of any scheme, it will stand or fall by the attitudes towards it of the individual teachers on whose good offices its success will hinge.

Finally, we should note that it has also been claimed (Kelly, 1977) that the introduction of some kind of integrated approach to learning is the most efficient means available to us for facilitating the evolution not only of the curriculum but also of knowledge itself. Knowledge evolves by a process of constant reorganization around particular topics, themes, or focuses of interest. As, with the evolution of society, these focuses change, so the organization of knowledge must change in parallel. One obvious example of this has been the coming together of design studies with science and technical studies to form the new area of Design and Technology, but there are many other such developments that can be identified in recent curriculum change. This is a process that cannot go on if opportunities do not exist for appropriate forms of linking and collaboration between subjects. This fact alone constitutes sufficient justification for attempts to find a solution to the problem of curriculum integration.

In concluding this discussion of integrated studies, we must also repeat what we said when we began. It is not a matter of having to go all out for one approach or the other. There are many advantages in including a number of different elements, activities or approaches in our curriculum and there is nothing inconsistent in engaging pupils for part of the week in integrated studies and at other times in the 'straight' study of subjects. Indeed, this makes very good sense, since not only does it lead to much needed variety for the pupils, it also ensures that a number of competing interests can be attended to. The curriculum must be a compromise between the competing demands of society and of the individual pupil.

Methods or procedures

We have said a great deal about the problems raised by discussion of the objectives and the content of the curriculum. It should not be necessary to dwell in as great detail on questions concerning methods or procedures. In part this is because these will follow more or less automatically once we have reached agreement on our aims, our principles of procedure, and our approach to decisions concerning content, since it is inevitably bound up with these. In part it is because for the same reason we have touched on several points concerning method in what we have said already. Indeed, it becomes increasingly difficult, even at the conceptual level, to discuss any one aspect of the curriculum without reference to the others.

One general feature of educational methodology, however, does merit brief discussion, not only because it has been central to much of the debate over the curriculum that recent years have witnessed but also because we have already referred to it at some length in our discussion of integrated studies, and that is the growing commitment to heuristic methods, to encouraging children to 'find out' for themselves, to 'learn by discovery'. Increasingly, even the classrooms of the secondary schools have come to be places of activity rather than centres for instruction and more and more emphasis has been placed on project work of all kinds. The various curriculum schemes sponsored by the Schools Council, the Nuffield science schemes, and the Design and Technology projects, for example, have begun from the basic principle that the child must be an active participant in his own education.

We have also seen that learning through some form of enquiry is advocated by some educationists not only as an effective method but also as required by the notion of education itself, as an essential part of the development of understanding and autonomy or as crucial to a process of guided growth through genuine experience.

Whatever reasons one has for advocating such an approach, whether one views first-hand experience as the only source of real education and sees this as the the only way of enabling children to have that first-hand experience, or whether one sees this approach merely as an effective device for ensuring that children learn what you want them to learn, it is important to be clear about what is involved, especially as a number of criticisms have been levelled at this technique.

It has been argued, for example, that learning by discovery is not logically possible since it does not make sense to speak of people discovering what is already known. It has also been said that this kind of learning is impracticable since it is not possible for children in the short time of their sojourn in school to discover for themselves all of those many things that man has discovered over the countless centuries of his existence on earth; whereas instructional methods can condense much of this into a quickly assimilable form. Discovery learning is, therefore, dubbed as wasteful and inefficient as well as logically impossible. It has been argued too that while such an approach may be of value for certain kinds of learning, theoretical concepts cannot be acquired in this way, so that in this kind of learning discovery methods are not only slow but useless (Dearden, 1968).

Furthermore, there is the related point that theoretical concepts learned need to be built up into interconnected systems and learning, if it is to include understanding, must involve a growing awareness of and familiarity with these interconnected systems. In fact, without this growing understanding it will not be possible for children to know what there is to be discovered, to see what questions should be asked about a particular set of experiences, or to recognize the significance of what they have discovered. Learning by discovery, it is argued, therefore, is too naive and unsophisticated a notion to be of any value as a model for the complex process of conceptual development. It is logically nonsensical, impracticable, and useless.

On the other hand, we referred earlier to some powerful arguments in support of its desirability, not least those derived from the notion of the need for pupils to be active participants in their own learning and the view of education as the development of the individual's awareness and understanding of his world rather than the acquisition of ill-digested and largely propositional knowledge handed on to him by others. Furthermore, we must not lose sight of the arguments of those who, like Paulo Freire (1972), see this kind of question as having a significance for society far beyond its implications for the methodology of the classroom, who see an opportunity to attain the skills necessary for problem solving as being the only viable means of getting the poor of the world to see their own problems in a reflexive perspective and to act on them rather than be 'dopes' whose curriculum content is decided for them by others. Supporters of this method argue, therefore, that if the acquisition of theoretical concepts in a coherent form is not possible when discovery methods are employed, there is ample evidence to illustrate that it does not happen very regularly either when directly instructional methods are used.

Once again the problem seems to arise from too extreme a polarization of the two ideas. There is no doubt that discovery is logically possible for everyone, if we realize that we mean by this only that an individual finds out something that is new to him; it does not have to be taken as implying that one has discovered something new to human knowledge or else we would have very infrequent need to use the word. This is perfectly normal usage of the term. It is possible for a man to discover that his wife is having an affair with someone else, even though many others have known about it for some time: indeed, we are told that the husband is always the last to know, and, at the very least, it seems reasonable to assume that the wife and the lover have known about it from the first. There is no logical contradiction involved, then, in the notion of learning by discovery, if it is interpreted intelligently.

The arguments that it is impracticable and inefficient are also based on an extreme view of what learning by discovery is to be taken to mean. There is no doubt that if we were to leave children completely alone to find out everything for themselves this would be a long and wasteful process and one from which they would be likely to get little of value. Clearly, they would not have the prior knowledge and experience to know what questions to ask, to discriminate between the experiences they had, to see the full significance of what they discovered, or to build their growing experience and knowledge into any kind of coherent system. If learning by discovery is to have any value, there is need for a good deal of careful preparation by the teacher and of judicious interference in the process, since, as we saw when considering the notion of education as growth or natural development, there is no place for the teacher and no meaning to 'education' if he or she is not to interfere in the learning process in this way in order to ensure its efficiency and its significance for the learner. As Jerome Bruner has said and as we have quoted before, 'discovery, like surprise, favours the well prepared mind' (1961) and we must accept that the only intelligible notion is that of guided discovery.

As we saw when discussing the content of the curriculum, education must involve the interaction of a number of forces, the pupil, the teacher, society, knowledge and so on, so that to plan a curriculum from the point of view of any one of these is to create a caricature of the real thing. This is equally true of the methods we adopt. Any approach that is based on a consideration of only one or two of these elements will be distorted and, as a result, vulnerable to criticism. The process of education is far too subtle to be characterized as simply as it has often been characterized both by some of the proponents of the idea of learning by discovery and by some of its critics who have shown themselves to be equally naive.

Indeed the whole process may be too subtle for the attempts we have been making to discuss goals, content, and methods in isolation from each other ever to be really successful. As our discussion has revealed, these are interwoven in such complex ways that it is very difficult to achieve a coherent examination of any one of them in isolation from the others. The view that we take of education itself will affect the goals or the procedural principles that we adopt, the decisions we take about content, and the methods we choose. In both theory and practice all three are so closely interwoven that in trying to separate them even at the conceptual level we run the risk of forgetting the ways in which they are interrelated. It may well be that this very interconnectedness is a more important area of study than any of these three areas in themselves.

At the very least it should be clear that curriculum development must be an ongoing, open-ended process of a kind that will allow for continuous adaptation and development at all three levels. It is not curriculum innovation that should worry us; the time to start worrying is when innovation stops and the curriculum freezes up again.

Evaluation

This is the point from which we must begin our discussion of the fourth aspect of the curriculum that we identified at the beginning of this chapter, evaluation, since the need for continuous adaptation presents us with particular problems in this area.

We suggested earlier, in our discussion of the use of objectives in curriculum planning, that one reason why that approach has been advocated is that it has been thought to make the process of curriculum evaluation easier. We also noted that a major reason why the evaluation of curriculum innovation has been felt to be necessary has been the desire to ascertain that the public money invested in education is being well and sensibly used, as was the case with the early projects of the Schools Council. More recently, the demands for such evaluation have grown, at least in the United Kingdom, as a result of a conviction that teachers should be more publicly accountable for what they are doing, so that events such as those at the William Tyndale school (Auld, 1976) which attracted so much adverse public attention might be avoided. Furthermore, as we have just noted, evaluation of some kind is crucial to the development of the curriculum and this is another reason why the need for it has been increasingly felt.

In general, then, there has been a growing interest in curriculum evaluation but that interest has derived from several different kinds of consideration and has been a result of a number of diverse demands. The differences in the kinds of demand being made of curriculum evaluation allied to the fact that it is a new and largely undeveloped area of curriculum theory, make any brief discussion of it a particularly hazardous matter. We may avoid the worst dangers, however, if we confine ourselves to a discussion of four issues and consider some of the problems that arise from these very differences in the demands made on curriculum evaluation, some of the types of evaluation that have been identified or have evolved in response to these different demands and purposes, the important question of whether evaluation is or is not linked to the prespecification of curriculum objectives and, lastly, the question of who can or should be responsible for the evaluation of the curriculum.

There is no doubt that the difficulties that abound in this area of curriculum theory derive in the main from, or are at least compounded by, the variety of purposes that one can have in making any kind of evaluation and the resultant impossibility of achieving any one definition of curriculum evaluation. The great diversity of curriculum projects that recent years have seen has led to a corresponding diversity of evaluation procedures (Schools Council, 1973; Tawney, 1975; Hamilton, 1976). Furthermore, every one of these projects has offered a definition of evaluation that represents a commitment to one or more particular views of evaluation (Harris, 1963; Cronbach, 1963; Wiley, 1970; Stenhouse, 1975), and it is only quite recently that attempts have been made to look at the issue of evaluation in its own right.

When we do this, we quickly realize that the procedures we adopt for evaluation and even the definition of it that we accept must vary according to the area of the curriculum we are dealing with, the curriculum model we have chosen and, especially, the purposes we have in mind when we set up the evaluation procedures. The most important task, then, for the evaluator is to be clear about what those purposes are. For there are a number of purposes we might have in undertaking curriculum evaluation.

We might, for example, be attempting to do no more than to ascertain that the particular innovation we are concerned with is actually taking place, since there is often a wide gap between the plans of the curriculum developer and the practice of the teachers responsible for implementing those plans. We might be concerned merely to discover whether the programme is acceptable to teachers and/or pupils (Schools Council, 1974). We might, on the other hand, be engaged in a comparative study of the effectiveness of a particular programme in relation to other programmes or methods in the same area. Or again, we might be trying to establish whether our objectives are being attained or whether our chosen procedures or content are right for the attainment of them or, if we are operating without prespecified objectives, we might be concerned to discover just what has been achieved. There are, thus, many different purposes that any process of evaluation might have and it is vital that we be clear about the purpose or purposes of any particular programme of evaluation before we begin.

One especially important distinction must be noted. The questions to be asked in any process of evaluation are of at least two logically distinct kinds (White, 1971). Some of them are empirical questions which explore a project in terms of its effectiveness, its costs, its merits in comparison with other projects, and so on. Such questions are similar to those asked by organizations such as the Consumers' Association of the brands and products they investigate. These are questions about means and it is relevant empirical data that we must gather in order to answer them. Sometimes, however, we are also interested in questions about the desirability of a particular project in itself and these raise those difficult problems of value that can never be far away in any discussion of education. These are questions about ends rather than means, since they ask not whether we are achieving our aims but whether those aims themselves are the right aims, whether they are worth striving after, whether the principles underlying our practice are sound, whether the experience we are endeavouring to offer pupils is of educational value. Here we are attempting, therefore, to evaluate the fundamental principles or the goals of the curriculum itself and not only the effectiveness of its procedures. These are questions, then, that cannot be answered merely by appeal to empirical data. This is a distinction that must be kept clearly in mind.

Because processes of curriculum evaluation can have this variety of purposes, some of them displaying a difference as fundamental as the one we have just discussed, a number of different types of evaluation have evolved to meet these, several of which have been identified. In all cases too, as we suggested earlier, the type of evaluation used will be closely linked to the curriculum model that has been adopted, as has become clear from the procedures employed by a number of different Schools Council projects (Tawney, 1973).

The simple classical linear model of objectives, content, procedures and evaluation that we considered at the beginning of this chapter has generated a process of evaluation that has been desribed as 'summative', since it asks questions at the end of a project which are largely concerned with the extent to which the objectives that were prespecified have been attained. It is a form of postcourse evaluation and sums up the experience of the project after it is over; it thus provides data that can be used to modify the project only if it is to be implemented again. It may, of course, be concerned to assess the objectives of the project themselves with a view to subsequent modifications, but its main concern is likely to be with empirical questions about the effectiveness of the procedures adopted.

Contrasted to this is a form of evaluation that has been called 'formative'. This is the kind of evaluation that is necessary when we adopt a more sophisticated model of curriculum planning, recognize that all the four elements we have identified are closely interrelated, and thus regard evaluation as a continuous process that will lead to and make possible in-course modifications. This form of evaluation will involve a number of dimensions. It will be attempting both to assess the extent of the attainment of the objectives of the project and to discover and analyse barriers to the achievement of these goals (Stenhouse, 1975); but it will also be directly concerned to evaluate the goals themselves, in short, to ask those value questions we mentioned earlier.

Both of these forms of evaluation assume to a large extent that the curriculum model adopted will begin with some prespecification of objectives and many people have assumed that such prespecification is necessary if any kind of evaluation is to be possible. Recent experience, however, has demonstrated that this is not so. We do not need to state our objectives in advance in order to make a proper evaluation of the curriculum. We do need, however, to adopt a different approach to the task of evaluation if we wish to plan a curriculum without objectives. This has become clear from the experience of two particular Schools Council projects, the Keele Integrated Studies Project and the Humanities Curriculum Project.

The team associated with the former of these projects adopted a 'horizontal' curriculum model 'in which aims, learning experiences and material were developed concurrently' (Tawney, 1973, p. 9). In that kind of context, evaluation was seen not as a process of measuring the results of an experiment but as a device for continuously monitoring the project as it developed. The approach adopted in the evaluation of the Humanities Curriculum Project, which deliberately eschewed the prespecification of objectives, was 'holistic'. 'The aim was simply to describe the work of the project in a form that would make it accessible to public and professional judgement' (MacDonald, 1973, p. 83). The intention was to provide information for consumers, to describe what was happening for the benefit of those who might be concerned to make decisions about the curriculum in these particular areas.

The same kind of approach is adopted by those who have seen evaluation as 'portrayal' (Stake, 1972) and as 'illuminative' (Parlett and Hamilton, 1976). The former attempts to offer a comprehensive portrayal of a curriculum programme which views it as a whole and tries to reveal its total substance. The latter is primarily concerned 'with description and interpretation rather than measurement and prediction' (Parlett and Hamilton, 1975, p. 88).

It will be clear that these recent developments in techniques of and approaches to curriculum evaluation have begun to raise the process to a level of sophistication well above that of simple devices for the measurement of pupil progress. They have also begun to reveal more clearly the role of evaluation in curriculum research and development generally. For the data they offer usually have relevance far beyond the particular project they are concerned to evaluate, so that from attempts to approach curriculum evaluation in this way we have learned a good deal both about curriculum innovation itself and about processes of evaluation. In short, they have recognized that evaluation is part of a continuous process of curriculum research and development, that the curriculum is a dynamic and continuously evolving entity, and that, since it is such, both its ends and its means must be under constant review.

One important issue that these approaches to evaluation have also raised is that of who should undertake the task of evaluation, and we must finally turn to a brief discussion of that. Again, of course, the answer that we give to this question will depend on the particular purposes or form of evaluation we have adopted. However, it is almost certainly always the case that our procedures will be designed to meet several purposes and will be an amalgam of several forms. It will also be the case that different people will have different perceptions and conceptions of the project (Shipman, 1972), even if its objectives have been quite clearly stated, so that everyone will have different purposes and expectations and will be looking for different kinds of data.

However, in the end this issue boils down to one of whether the evaluator should be external or internal to the project. The strongest argument for external evaluation, of course, is that of objectivity. An evaluator coming fresh to a project from outside might be expected to have few preconceptions or expectations and a more open mind than a teacher or other member of the project team. On the other hand, curriculum projects are highly complex entities with an intricate interlinking of theoretical and practical elements of a kind that it is difficult for an outsider to get fully to grips with. There is thus a danger that external evaluation will lead to an oversimplification of the project and perhaps to an undesirable pressure on the curriculum developers or the teachers themselves to simplify their work, especially by a clear statement of their objectives, to the point where they feel an external evaluator can understand it or, worse, to put all their efforts into those aspects of it that are most likely to show up in an external evaluation. One way around this problem that has been used is to make the evaluator a member of the project team, sometimes from the very beginning of the project. This has many advantages but it does seem to exclude the teacher himself from the process and for many reasons, not the least among which is the fact that the involvement of teachers in and their commitment to a project is probably the essential ingredient for its success, this would seem to be undesirable.

The teacher must be involved in some way with curriculum evaluation since, in the last analysis, he is the one who possesses most of the data that is needed for a proper evaluation. However, it would also seem that he has a contribution to make beyond that of merely providing this data in an inevitably simplified form by filling in elaborate questionnaires. The relationship between the teacher and the evaluator must be a two-way relationship, since it is important not only that evaluators should have access to the insights of teachers but also that teachers should begin to understand the problems of evaluation and should be directly privy to the evaluation findings. Clearly, there are problems for teachers in attaining the level of objectivity and the capacity for self-criticism that this requires of them. The work of those associated with the Ford Teaching Project has revealed in detail what these problems are. However, their experience has also led them to be 'optimistic about the capacity of the majority of teachers for self-criticism' (Elliott and Adelman, 1974, p. 23) and to believe that these problems are merely practical difficulties which can be overcome. One method they have devised for overcoming them they have called 'triangulation', since it involves a three-way process of evaluation by teachers, pupils and independent external observers.

It would seem that this might be the most productive approach to adopt to the question of who should make an evaluation of the curriculum. For it leads to a style of evaluation that is 'democratic' rather than 'autocratic' or 'bureaucratic' (MacDonald, 1975), since its concern is not to evaluate from outside in accordance with the values of those who control the purse-strings of curriculum development but to provide information for teachers and others in the interests of forwarding curriculum development.

In this kind of evaluation the teacher himself is a key figure. Furthermore, his place here is justified not only in terms of a right he might be considered to have to be involved in curriculum evaluation, but also because of the central role he must play in curriculum development. To some extent that role has for a long time been recognized by the system of education operating in England and Wales in the autonomy given to teachers and schools in curriculum matters, a privilege which is not enjoyed by teachers elsewhere. It is now being suggested, however, that that autonomy should be taken away and that a common curriculum should be established centrally and monitored from outside. The conflict that such a proposal creates between the demands of society and the central role of the teacher in curriculum development and evaluation we must examine in our final section.

A common curriculum

The question of whether there should be a common curriculum or at least a common core to the curriculum is one that brings together all or most of the threads that have run through our previous discussion of the curriculum, since it has relevance to most aspects of curriculum theory. It is thus a topic that will lead us naturally into a summary of what we have tried to cover in this chapter.

It is also an issue that is currently of great interest in the United Kingdom both inside and outside the teaching profession. The recent, public, and so-called 'great debate' on education has concentrated on the problems associated with this issue in response to demands from politicians, industrialists, and others, and it is worth noting that there has been a similar trend towards this kind of approach to the planning of education in most countries of the world, while some of them have long regarded the need for central control of the curriculum as almost self-evident.

It is important to be clear from the outset about what is involved here, particularly since there are two different, although interrelated, dimensions to the problem. At the most obvious level, demands for a common curriculum constitute claims concerning the content of education, statements of what all pupils should be introduced to and why they should be given this particular educational diet. At a second, less readily apparent but probably more significant, level, they also represent demands for a monitoring of the standards of attainment being achieved by pupils in schools and thus for an increased measure of external control over the work of teachers in an attempt to ensure that standards in certain areas of the curriculum be maintained. And so this is an issue that is of importance at all stages of schooling, primary as well as secondary, and it is salutary to remember in this connection that it was certain public reactions to the work of one particular primary school, the William Tyndale school, that were largely responsible for sparking off these demands for greater public control of educational practice.

The arguments for the establishment of a common curriculum are of four major kinds: philosophical, sociological, ideological, and politico-economic. The first three of these we have covered already in our earlier discussions, particularly that on the content of the curriculum. For we noted there those arguments that have been mounted by philosophers throughout the ages for the intrinsic value of certain kinds of human activity and the corresponding claim that it is these activities that should form the core of any education worthy of the name (Peters, 1965; 1966). A view of knowledge as God-given, transcending the subjective opinions of individual men or even of mankind in general, must lead to this kind of view of education. We noted too that this approach is also the result of seeing knowledge as irrevocably organized into several 'forms of thought' (Hirst, 1965) or 'realms of meaning' (Phenix, 1964), since the consequence of that kind of theory of knowledge must be that pupils should be given access to all of those forms of experience.

The sociological argument for a common curriculum may well be incompatible with this kind of epistemology since its claim is not for the God-given status of certain kinds of knowledge so much as for the necessity of including in the curriculum that knowledge which is regarded as valuable within the culture of any particular society. However, inconsistent as this may be, it does attempt to draw on the same kind of belief in the intrinsic value of certain activities, suggesting that the curriculum should consist of a selection of what is valuable in that culture (Lawton, 1973; 1975) and that pupils should be initiated into the culture of their society. Such arguments are never really clear about whether they are pressing these claims for utilitarian reasons or on grounds of the intrinsic value of what society finds or deems valuable. One suspects that they would not be happy to admit the former but, if it is the latter that is their claim, their case is no different from and thus no more cogent than that of the philosophers. At all events, it is time they explained more clearly what their position is.

The ideological case for a common curriculum takes this argument a step further. For, starting from a commitment to the idea of equality of educational opportunity, it argues that, without some kind of common core to the curriculum, we cannot safeguard the right of every child to access to the best or at least to all aspects of the culture of his society, that to provide him with an education in some way tailored to his needs and his existing interests may be to trap him in the particular subculture from which he hails and thus to limit the range of choices open to him. In particular, as we have already seen, this argument has been applied to the education of pupils from lower socio-economic backgrounds and has been used to oppose the generation of two or three different forms of curricula designed to meet the needs of pupils of differing abilities.

The politico-economic arguments are the most recent additions to this discussion and they are of two unequivocal and basic forms. The first of these starts from the belief that schools exist to serve the needs of the community, that public money is invested in them for this purpose, and that the prime needs of an advanced industrial society are for citizens who have attained minimal standards of literacy and numeracy and for those who are capable of it to have attained the highest possible level of achievement in science and technological studies so that they can meet the continuing needs of an ever-developing technology. The event that sparked off the 'great debate' in the United Kingdom was a speech by the Prime Minister, James Callaghan, in which he deplored the fact that too few sixth-formers were choosing to study the sciences and, conversely, too many the arts. The second and associated aspect of this case is the demand for greater control over the activities of teachers, for a higher level of public accountability than has hitherto been required of them.

We have already examined the difficulties of those arguments that are based on the notion that certain kinds of knowledge or certain aspects of the culture have a self-evidently superior value. And we have shown that there is no general agreement about what these are nor, indeed, about the theory of knowledge upon which this kind of claim is based. There are other difficulties, however, with the arguments for a common curriculum and these we must briefly consider here.

In the first place, because of this lack of agreement over what is intrinsically valuable or worthwhile, problems arise as soon as we try to list the things that a common curriculum or its core should contain. One of two things will happen when we begin to do this. For either we offer a statement at such a level of generality that it ceases to have any significance or we immediately start up petty squabbles over what should go into such a core curriculum and what should be left out. The first of these traps is apparent in the definition of a core curriculum we are offered by such writers as Denis Lawton (1973, 1975), since the broad areas he suggests a common core curriculum should consist of are so wide as, on the one hand, to constitute no kind of help to curriculum planners and, on the other hand, to do no more than to describe what all schools are currently engaged in doing anyway. For there can be no school in the United Kingdom, nor anywhere else in the world, that does not in some way try to introduce its pupils to literacy, numeracy, some kind of social awareness, and to offer them a moral and aesthetic education. Indeed, it would be difficult to imagine what else schools and teachers could do.

However, if, in order to avoid being trivial in our claims, we try to be more detailed than this in our definition of the common elements of a core curriculum, we immediately discover the impossibility of reaching agreement at any level. For, while few would disagree with the claim that all schools should concern themselves with literacy and numeracy, there will be a complete lack of consensus over precisely what these claims imply for educational practice. Few too would oppose the need for some kind of social education but it will be difficult to find any one definition of what that should be. Some people still want the teaching of religion, currently the only compulsory element in the curriculum of schools in England and Wales, to continue to be a requirement of all schools; others would and do take quite the opposite stance, as is clear from the embargo placed on such teaching in certain other countries, notable among which is the United States of America. Thus, the question of who is to have the right to resolve these disagreements and make the final decisions on these matters also becomes crucial.

We must further recognize the difficulties that arise when we face up to the problem of deciding where such central direction should stop. For even if agreement could be reached over essential subject areas, we must ask whether all schools should be required to pursue a common content within these areas. In short, should there be common syllabuses too? For if there are not, how common will a common curriculum be? This would certainly seem to be the view of those whose demands for a common curriculum are based on the need to cater for the increased mobility of schoolchildren, to ensure that the child whose home is moved from one part of the country to another will find the same things being taught in the same way when he gets there. Furthermore, if this is to be so, every teacher will know that it is not enough for syallabuses to be common; there will need to be greater control over methods too, and even the textbooks used, in order to ensure that what each child gets from each individual teacher does not vary unduly, as is clear from the most cursory survey of the many different activities that go under the heading of religious education in our schools at present.

This leads us naturally to a discussion of the monitoring of teachers' work and of the standards attained by their pupils. This question is beset by the same kinds of problem, not least because it is equally difficult to state precisely what is meant by 'standards' or to reach agreement on what standards we should be aiming for. It is a good, emotive word for the politician to use, but it has little place in serious debate because it is a very difficult notion for anyone to explain or define. Such definitions as are offered tend to be couched in highly simplistic terms and the problems of evaluation that we have already discussed, when combined with such definitions, are likely to encourage teachers to accept the short-term goals they set, to work to simple prespecified objectives, to concentrate, for example, on the more easily recognized and measurable 'skills' aspects of reading or number work, to promote reading and computational performance rather than the wider educational aspects of these activities and thus to deprive pupils of what we have tried to argue are the essential components of an education in the full sense.

It is also argued that this kind of central control of the curriculum will lead to a loss of freedom for the child, since it will no longer be easy for teachers to base their work on children's interests or on their existing knowledge. At one level, it is felt that this will lead to pupils' being offered the kind of meaningless and irrelevant material that leads to their becoming in many cases alienated from their schools, their teachers and, ultimately, their society. At a further level, it is even argued that to adopt this approach is to use knowledge as a form of social control, since it makes certain kinds of 'educational' knowledge the key to success within the system and denies the validity of the 'common sense' knowledge that the child brings with him from his own subculture (Young, 1971). Thus an ideological argument against the establishment of a common curriculum strongly emerges from the same kind of ideological and egalitarian position we saw earlier being used to support it.

Finally, we must briefly consider those arguments against the establishment of a common curriculum that are based on the claim that it limits the freedom and autonomy of the teacher and that this militates against effective education in the full sense. There is no denying the central role that the individual teacher must play in the education of his pupils. To play that role he must be free to exercise his professional judgement. Teachers cannot be operated by remote control. It is for this reason that, as we have come to realize in recent years, it is not possible to control the curriculum from the outside with any degree of efficiency. Attempts at curriculum innovation that have employed what has come to be called the centre-periphery model of dissemination, that is, to plan a programme at some central place and then endeavour to disseminate it to schools, have generally been unsuccessful (Schon, 1971). One reason for this is that teachers need to understand and, perhaps more importantly, to be committed to what is required of them if they are to make it work (Barker-Lunn, 1970) or, worse, if they are not to sabotage it (Kelly, 1975). In other words, central planning cannot work since no amount of monitoring of standards can ensure that teachers will make it work (Kelly, 1977).

We need to go further than this, however, and recognize the implications of this for the development of the curriculum itself. One essential feature of schools in a changing society, as we have noted before, is that their curricula must also change. Such change, however, can only be successful if it is in every sense a process of development and, if it is to be so, it must be in the hands of the teacher (Stenhouse, 1975). It may be possible to change the curriculum from outside the school but, if such change is to be development in the full sense of the word, it must be school-based and it must be in the hands of the teacher. For the notion of development implies organic growth rather than the grafting on of foreign matter. The teacher is the central figure in such development and he needs a high level of freedom and autonomy to fulfil that role.

It has been suggested, therefore, that 'the process to which the term "dissemination" is conventionally applied would be more accurately described by the term "curriculum negotiation"' (MacDonald and Walker, 1976, p. 43), that teachers need to be involved in continuing discussion of the curriculum if the right kind of curriculum change is to take place, and this process would seem to be put at risk by suggestions that anything but the most general and loose directions should be imposed from the outside.

The arguments against the detailed specification of what schools should be teaching seem to be strong. On the other hand, looser and more generalized direction seems to be unnecessary, since the constraints, both hidden and overt, placed on schools by the many demands that are made on them make it impossible for them to diverge too much from what would be the content of any such broad directions. At this level of generality, we have a common curriculum already. At the more detailed level, it would seem to be not only undesirable but also impossible to introduce one. In many respects, therefore, it might be argued that, the 'great debate' notwithstanding, this is a non-issue.

Two final points might be made, however, that emerge from such a discussion if we can get beyond a superficial concern with statements of curriculum content. The first of these is that there is a strong case to be made for a commonality of educational goals or principles. Whatever debate there might be over definitions of literacy, over what we mean by 'standards' or over the place of religion on the curriculum, it is possible to argue, as we have seen on several occasions, that what is distinctive about education is that it is a process that is concerned with developing qualities of mind such as the ability to make critical judgements, to respect truth, to distinguish understanding from dogma and to think for oneself. In short, in educational terms a 'process' model of curriculum development is likely to be more productive than an 'objectives' model (Stenhouse, 1975) and it might not be difficult to define a common curriculum in these terms (Kelly, 1977).

Lastly, it need not be assumed that, if we give teachers the kind of freedom that this approach necessitates, albeit limited by many existing constraints, they must inevitably remain unaccountable. The logic of the term 'accountability', however, would seem to suggest that it should occur *post eventum*. Teachers must be permitted to exercise their professional judgement in an area in which they possess an expertise that others lack but, like all other professionals, they can and should be required to render an account of and a justification for the judgements they have made. It was this rather than the making of collective decisions in advance that was the keystone of that form of democracy that was devised by the Athenians in ancient Greece. Such accounts, however, must be rendered, at least in part, to others who understand the complexities of the teacher's task, that is, to fellow professionals. Furthermore, as we saw in our discussion of evaluation, they themselves must be, indeed have a right to be, involved in the processes of monitoring and evaluating their work. If the demand for public accountability is founded on democratic premises, the involvement of teachers in that process is required by those same premises. Only in this way, then, can we achieve a form of accountability that is both professional and democratic. If it is to be undertaken entirely from outside, its effect must be to inhibit rather than to promote education in the full sense.

Summary and conclusions

We suggested at the beginning of our discussion of the notion of a common curriculum that that discussion would in itself act as a summary to this chapter. This has in fact proved to be the case, since it has taken us back to important issues of curriculum objectives, content, procedures and evaluation. It has also, however, highlighted two points that we should note here in concluding this chapter on the curriculum.

The first of these is that difficult question of values that must constantly appear in any discussion of education. We have seen that it is this that is the source of most of the difficulties we have examined not only in this chapter but throughout the book. It is this question that we unearth when we dig deeply into the problems of objectives, of curriculum content, of evaluation, of a common curriculum or, indeed, of any other issue that is of such a kind as ultimately to hinge on what we believe to be good, valuable or worthwhile. The notion of value is fundamental to education but at the same time and for this very reason every educational dispute is in the last analysis impossible to resolve. As we saw in our discussion of the content of the curriculum, value questions cannot be answered in any hard and fast or final way. What is important, however, is for us to be able to recognize such questions when we see them. It is the failure to do that rather than the failure to come up with final answers to such questions that is at the root of so many unsatisfactory discussions of education, among teachers and educationists, let it be said, no less than among those outside the profession.

The second major theme that has emerged from our discussion in this chapter is the central role that the teacher must play in education. It is a truism, but one that cannot be repeated too often, that the quality of the education received by children depends on the quality of their teachers. If pupils are to receive an adequate education and if, as we have argued here, the teacher must carry the major responsibility for the development of the curriculum and thus of education itself, it is vital that we raise the quality of teachers to the highest possible level and maintain that level by continuous support and in-service education. If it is the case, as so many now believe, that curriculum development is essentially teacher development, we would do better to direct our attention, and indeed our financial backing, to what that requires, so as to ensure that our teachers are capable of doing the job we require of them, than to attempt to manipulate them like puppets from somewhere above and beyond the real educational stage.

9 Equality

All that we have said so far in this book and particularly what we have said about the curriculum in the last chapter illustrates how dramatically both the theory and the practice of education have changed in the last twenty or thirty years. One reason for that change has been the increase in our knowledge and understanding of many of the facets of education that we have been discussing. Another, and perhaps more cogent reason, however, has been the fundamental change in ideology that recent years have seen. The most prominent feature of the new ideology is its egalitarianism and the desire to promote educational equality has been a major theme in those changes that have been made and are being made in the content, the method, and the organization of education both in the United Kingdom and elsewhere in the world. The work of every teacher, therefore, has been affected by this development so that no discussion of the theory and practice of education in present times would be complete without a careful examination of the implications that a commitment to this kind of egalitarian philosophy holds for education practice.

Much has been done in the name of equality not only in education but also in other sectors of society. It can be argued that the entire development of state education has been prompted at every stage by the central desire to promote equality of educational opportunity and few would be prepared to admit openly that they were opposed to it. Yet very different and sometimes conflicting views are expressed on how it is to be achieved in practice and the practical provisions that have been advocated and implemented have varied enormously, from those that involve careful streaming and selection of pupils to those that would open the doors of all kinds of institution to any pupil who wished to enter them without applying any selection procedures.

The main reason for this discrepancy and confusion is that the notion of equality in education, and even the apparently more precise notion of equality of educational opportunity, are too general and vague to provide any clear directives as to how education should be organized to achieve them. A system can be said to provide equality of opportunity if all pupils have the same chance to compete for a place in a grammar school or a university; it is not necessary that they should all actually gain such places. Indeed, equality of opportunity would exist in a sense even if it amounted to no more than an equal opportunity for every child to take a test at 5+ to decide whether he should be admitted to the school system or excluded from it altogether. For this reason, a distinction has been drawn between the 'strong' or 'meritocratic' interpretation of equality, which would provide educational opportunities for all who are capable of taking advantage of them, and the 'weak', or 'democratic' interpretation, which demands suitable provision for everyone (Crosland, 1961)

The notion of equality is an imprecise one, therefore, and not one upon which any practical proposals can be based without a great deal of further clarification and definition of what is to be taken as its meaning. Until we have achieved this, it will not be possible to make a proper evaluation of those major developments that recent years have seen in the education systems of many countries, such as the comprehensivisation of educational provision at a number of levels, the abolition of selective practices such as streaming within the schools, and the introduction and extension of various programmes of what has been called 'Compensatory Education', all of which have been based on some notion of educational equality.

A historical view of equality

It is important not to start from an assumption that the notion of social equality is a relatively new one or that it is a product of the twentieth century. It may be that this century has seen man come nearer to the achievement of something like the ideals implicit in the notion, although many would want to dispute even that, but as an idea it is almost as old as man himself; certainly it dates back to the beginnings of organized thought in the Western world.

From the very beginning, however, the confusion and the tensions between different interpretations of the notion that we have already referred to are apparent. For while there is distinct evidence, particularly in the works of the Greek dramatist, Euripides, that from the beginning for some people equality implied impartial treatment of all human beings, an egalitarianism in the full sense, both Plato and Aristotle accepted the idea of equality as operative only within categories of human being. Thus Plato's 'ideal state', as he described it in the *Republic*, contained three types of citizen – the prototype for many subsequent tripartite systems – and each of these groups had a different role, different responsibilities and, therefore, different rights within the state, 'equality' and 'justice' being achieved by basing membership of each group on talent and suitability rather than on the accident of birth. Plato has also been charged with deliberately opposing egalitarianism in the fuller sense by refusing to discuss it seriously in the arguments he produces to support his view of the ideal state (Popper, 1945). Aristotle too believed that there existed quite distinct categories of being and that, as he is so often quoted as saying injustice arises as much from treating unequals equally as from treating equals unequally. Each person has his own place; the husband is superior to the wife, the father to his children, the master to his slaves (so long as these are 'barbarians' and not Greeks); to step beyond this place is unjust. 'The only stable principle of government is equality according to proportion.'

However, the other view also took hold, if at a less influential level philosophically. The stoic view of the brotherhood of all men, so well expressed in the words of Pope's *Essay on Man*, 'All are but parts of one stupendous whole, Whose body nature is and God the soul', allied to the Christian doctrine of the equality of all men in the eyes of God, ensured that the idea of human equality without regard to categories should also flourish, and so influential was the Church on man's thinking that when, at the time of the Renaissance, philosophers began for the first time almost since the time of Plato and Aristotle to examine philosophical questions independently of theology, the idea of human equality was accepted by most of them as if it were a self-evident truth and was used by them in a largely uncritical manner. John Locke tells us, for example, that the state of nature is 'a state also of equality ... there being nothing more evident than that creatures of the same species and rank, promiscuously born to all the same advantages of Nature, and the use of the same faculties, should also be equal one amongst another, without subordination or subjection' and also that 'the State of Nature has a law of Nature to govern it, which obliges everyone. And Reason, which is that law, teaches all mankind, who will but consult it, that being all Equal and Independent, no one ought to harm another in his Life, Health, Liberty or Possesions'. This is a view that is clearly reflected in the assertions of the American Declaration of Independence of 1789 that 'all men are created equal' and that 'men are born and live free and equal in their rights', not to mention the 1948 declaration that 'all human beings are born free and equal in dignity and rights'. This was the view that took hold, therefore, and was further developed in the later doctrine of Utilitarianism and in the socialist political philosophy that emerged and grew in the nineteenth and twentieth centuries.

However, we must not lose sight of the fact that, in spite of this, the continued influence of Plato and Aristotle on the thinking of the Western world has been enormous, so that the view of equality within categories has never been far away. Furthermore, the egalitarian movement has always had its opponents, particularly after it seemed to have led to the excesses of the French Revolution. For example, the anti-egalitarian view was put strongly in the second half of the last century by the German philosopher Nietzsche, whose theory that equality led to mediocrity, to the suppression of outstanding individuals who ought to be given their heads and encouraged to be 'unequal' if human evolution was not to be held back, was taken up, albeit in the context of a nationalism that Nietzsche himself would have rejected out-right, as one of the basic tenets of the Nazi version of fascism that led to the Second World War. It is a form of argument that, in a somewhat weakened and disguised form, is still put forward by certain opponents of such innovations in education as comprehensive secondary schools and mixed-ability classes.

The tension, then, is still there and its continued presence is due in part to the failure of those who advocate egalitarianism to be clear about what this means. We must now turn, therefore, to a consideration of some of the sources of this confusion in the notion of equality itself, the lack of clarity over the logical grammar of the word 'equal'.

The concept of equality

That all men are equal is clearly not true in any descriptive sense. It is not even true in a qualified sense – except perhaps at the trivial level of bodily functioning – since there are no respects in which all men can be said to be the same. Some of the confusion that bedevils discussions of equality derives from the fact that some philosophers, such as Locke, and some politicans, such as those who framed the American Declaration, have used it as if its meaning were, at least in part, descriptive. We must distinguish the use of 'equal' in mathematical contexts where it clearly signifies that certain things are descriptively 'the same' and its use in political and social contexts where it asserts an ideal, a demand for certain kinds of behaviour in our treatment of other people. In other words, in this kind of context its main force is prescriptive and moral rather than descriptive and mathematical. A confusion of these uses of the term is one source of many of the difficulties associated with it.

The confusion does not end there, however. For, once having accepted that the notion of social equality constitutes a moral demand for something, we still have the problem of discovering exactly what is being demanded. Again confusion results from a failure to answer this question with precision. Again too the mathematical and descriptive connotations of the word compound the confusion. For many people accept that all men are not in any respect the same, but seem to regard the demand for social equality as a demand that in certain respects they be made the same or be made 'equal'. There are at least two good reasons why such a view is untenable.

One difficulty with this interpretation of equality is that it involves a conflict with other social ideals that many people – even among the egalitarians themselves – hold equally dear. In particular, it has been suggested that the demand for equality, if understood in this way, leads to direct conflict with the demand for freedom (Lucas, 1965). It is clear that to try to make people equal will involve considerable interference with their personal liberties. A redistribution of wealth, for example, which many have regarded as a desirable step towards social equality, can only be effected with a great loss of freedom for individuals. This tension is very much apparent in the arguments for and against the continued existence of private schools. To say this is not to say, of course, that such a position is untenable; it is merely to draw attention to one of its implications.

A more serious objection to this view, however, and one which, if true, does render it untenable is the claim that it is not possible to make everyone equal in any sense of the term. One of the fundamental difficulties with the social philosophy of Karl Marx was that it had as a central concept the notion of the classless society and such a society is unattainable. The kind of redistribution of wealth, for example, which we have just discussed, could only result in a crude form of financial equality and would in any case be only temporary, since the differences in people's attitudes to wealth and uses of it, in part responsible for the original inequality, would very soon lead to new inequalities very like the old. One would have to redistribute wealth so regularly – at least daily as far as most punters and bookmakers are concerned – that the whole process would become meaningless.

This is one example of a more general point that must be stressed here, that inequalities are an inevitable part of any kind of society. It has been argued by Ralf Dahrendorf (1962), for example, that, since every human society is a moral society in which behaviour is regulated according to certain norms, there will always be inequalities that will result from the differing degrees to which the behaviour of each individual measures up to these norms. To use one of Dahrendorf's examples, in a society of ladies that is held together by the desire to exchange news of intrigue, scandal and general gossip, individual members will be distinguished according to the quality of the stories they produce and their manner of recounting them, so that inequalities of rank will result. It is not difficult to see how the same principle will apply in larger and perhaps more serious social groupings. 'The origin of inequality is thus to be found in the existence in all human societies of norms of behaviour to which sanctions are attached' (Dahrendorf, 1962). These sanctions will take many forms but they will all lead to inescapable inequalities of rank. The demand for social equality cannot, therefore, be a demand that all should be made equal.

It has been suggested that talk about social equality is a demand not for all to be made equal but for all to be treated equally. Again, however, the descriptive connotations of the term bring confusion. For it looks as though this is a demand that all should be given the same treatment, whereas a moment's thought will reveal that such a practice would seldom lead in any context to equality in the moral sense of justice and fairness (Benn and Peters, 1959; Peters, 1966). It is clearly not just or fair or even desirable, for example, that all patients should be given the same medical treatment or all offenders the same punishment or all children the same educational diet. Clearly there are differences between people that require differences of treatment and only confusion can result if we allow the words we use when we wish to talk about fairness and justice to obscure this important requirement. Some have suggested that social equality is a demand for equality of respect for all people but it has also been pointed out that in this phrase it is the word 'respect' that is doing all the work, the word 'equality' being entirely otiose (Lucas, 1965). Furthermore, this idea in itself gives us no help with the problem of deciding what kinds of treatment of others this equality of respect should lead to nor how we can make decisions about the appropriateness or inappropriateness of adopting different practices in relation to different individuals.

What this seems to point to is that equality is not a demand for similarity of treatment at all but for a justification for differential treatment, a justification which must take the form of demonstrating that our reasons for discriminating between people in certain contexts are relevant reasons and, therefore, arguably, fair, just and impartial reasons. Thus differential treatment of patients is justified if they are shown to ha 'e different diseases or different constitutions; differences in our treatment of offenders are to be justified by reference to differences in the nature of their offences or the circumstances under which they were committed; and differences of educational provision are to be justified by appealing to differences exhibited by pupils in their ability to profit from education or what appear to be differences in their eductional needs.

Major difficulties in attaining equality in education, however, derive from the problems of defining 'need' and of deciding what shall count as relevant differences of educational need or ability. We have already referred to Aristotle's often quoted dictum that injustice comes as much from treating unequals equally as from treating equals unequally. We are now saying that this is the only reasonable interpretation that one can give to the notion of social equality. However, we must as a consequence face the problem of how one decides on who is to count as unequal, the grounds on which such decisions can be taken and justified, and the different kinds of provision that then become appropriate. In education this means an acceptance of the necessity of making differential provision but at the same time an awareness of the difficulty of deciding what these differences of provision shall be and on what basis discriminations between pupils are to be made. Two main points must be made about this.

In the first place, a difficulty immediately arises if we interpret this as meaning that we must try to place people into a limited number of categories. We have already distinguished the notion of equality within categories from more thorough-going versions of egalitarianism. The main weakness of this approach is that it does not provide us with the subtle instrument we need to make decisions about differential treatment or provision; it offers only the rather blunt instrument of a limited number of discrete categories – masters and slaves, husbands and wives, fathers and children, bright and backward, grammar, technical, and modern, A, B and C, and so on. What is wrong with Aristotle's analysis of social equality is not his identification of the need to treat people differently but the lack of subtlety in his interpretation of the practicalities of this. It is the same lack of subtlety that has bedevilled many of our attempts to secure equality in education. We would not regard as just and, therefore, we would not countenance a judicial system which operated by meting out to all offenders one of two or three kinds of sentence, nor would we have much confidence in a doctor who presented one of three or four types of pill to every patient. The corollary of the assertion that men are not descriptively equal in any way and that justice requires treatment of them in accordance with the differences between them is that our approach to them must be always an individual approach, so that the educational provision we make for each pupil must be based on what seems to be appropriate for him as an individual and not on the allocation of him to one of two or three broad categories.

This kind of consideration also draws our attention to the irrelevance of the claims we noted in Chapters 2 and 3 of certain contemporary psychologists, such as Jensen (1969) and Eysenck (1971), concerning the general intellectual capacities of different racial groups. Even if their assertions have any justification or basis, they are meaningless in relation to any practical provision we may want to make, since in practice we will always be dealing with individuals or groups of individuals and never with one racial group as a whole. They merely reveal the fundamental weakness and illogicality of any racist position. Indeed, any comparison of groups, whether offered as a basis for an egalitarian or an elitist system, makes little sense in the context of the individual differences we know to exist between all human beings.

Once we accept this we are nearer to an understanding of what is entailed by demands for equality in education. However, we still have the problems of deciding what are to count as relevant differences between individuals and what differences of provision they should give rise to. The notion of equality itself gives us no help in establishing such criteria of relevance. This, then, is the second point that must be made about this interpretation of social equality in the context of educational provision. We need some criteria by which both of these questions can be answered if we are to be clear about the kinds of educational practice that will lead to the achievement of this kind of equality.

Unfortunately, such criteria are not easy to find. One point must be made, however, and it is a point that has at least two facets that are important to anyone undertaking a search for such criteria. If a difference that can be detected between people is to be regarded as a basis for differential treatment, it must, as we have seen, have some relevance to the context in which we are operating, there must be some connection between the factor we are taking account of and the nature of whatever it is we are trying to distribute justly. Thus in making differential provision of education the only differences we should recognize as relevant to this, if we wish to achieve a fair and just system, are those that can be shown to have a connection with education itself.

To say this is not, of course, to solve the practical problem in any way; it is, however, to point to the direction in which a solution is to be sought. For clearly there are different views of what education is and each will give rise to a different solution to this problem. This has been another source of the confusion that has surrounded the notion of equality in education. For if one sees education as largely or entirely a matter of intellectual growth, this will give rise to one kind of view as to how it should be organized, although for the reasons we gave above it will not suffice to offer only two or three broad types of provision even then. Similarly, views of education as a national investment or as the right of every child regardless of intellectual ability will result in other kinds of answer to questions about relevant differences and kinds of provision (Crowther Report, 1959). All that is entailed by the notion of equality itself is that we should be able to produce relevant reasons for differences of provision; it does not in itself provide us with the criteria on which these differences are to be based.

However, a further point can be made and a second, very important facet of this general feature of equality highlighted. Whatever view we take of education and, therefore, of what criteria shall be relevant to differential educational provision, the notion of equality itself does require those who accept it to repudiate any suggestion that irrelevant factors can be allowed to take a hand. To some extent all discussions about equality that take place in any practical context are negative pleas against what are regarded as unjustifiable inequalities. In other words, it is usually some form of inequality we are talking about and much of what has been said and written about equality in education has been concerned not so much with its promotion in a positive sense as with the need to put right certain inequalities that were felt to be acting as barriers to its achievement, to remove or to remedy certain factors seen to be giving rise to differences both of treatment and of attainment, which were felt to be unconnected with education itself and were, therefore, regarded as irrelevant, unjust, and unequal.

We must now consider in greater detail some of these factors unconnected with education in any sense of the term that have nevertheless been affecting the educational achievement of many pupils. For it is on these that recent discussions of equality have focussed and it is these considerations that have given rise to the major changes in the organization of education we referred to at the beginning of this chapter, so that no discussion of the realities of educational equality in contemporary society is possible without a full awareness of the social factors that have given rise to such impassioned demands for it and the changes in the education system that some have felt would lead to the achievement of it.

Some sources of educational inequalities

The 1944 Education Act established in England and Wales the concept of education for all 'according to age, aptitude and ability' and thus a view of equality that required adequate educational provision to be made for all children. In particular, it was intended that such provision would be achieved by making secondary education in some form available to all pupils.

Within a very short time after the implementation of the Act, however, it become alarmingly clear that the realities of a system offering education for all were very different from the ideals that had led to its institution. For it became apparent that many pupils were not finding it possible to take advantage of the opportunities thus offered. The Report on Early Leaving published in 1954 revealed some very disturbing statistics concerning the wastage from the education system of a high proportion of pupils and, most surprisingly, of those pupils whose intellectual capacities, as measured by intelligence tests, appeared to be of a very high order. Such a situation was clearly very worrying not only in the light of what the new deal of the 1944 Act had hoped to achieve but also in the context of an industrial society dependent on its human resources for economic survival. The same depressing picture emerged from the researches of the Crowther committee in 1959. Nor was Britain alone in this; a similar situation was found to exist elsewhere, not least in the USA (Riessman, 1962). Equality of educational opportunity existed apparently in name only; in practice many inequalities persisted.

In fine, many irrelevant factors were coming into play to decide what profit individuals were able to gain from the educational provision that was made and it was equally clear that these factors were irrelevant whatever view one took of the aims and purposes of education, since even if one took a very narrow view of education as primarily concerned to develop the highest intellects it was apparent that many pupils of high ability were being excluded from educational success by factors that had little or nothing to do with intellectual potential.

In general, the reasons for this wastage appeared from the first to be closely linked with the social class origins of the pupils. For the figures of the Early Leaving and Crowther Reports themselves revealed that the situation was at its most serious among those children who came from families of low socio-economic status and in the USA a similar situation was seen to exist, particularly in relation to black pupils – a problem that subsequently became significant in the United Kingdom after the large-scale immigrations of the 1950s and early 1960s.

A great deal of attention was immediately directed, therefore, towards these families in an attempt to identify the particular sources of the problem so that appropriate steps might be taken to eradicate them and this has been a source of concern and of continued attention ever since. A number of studies were undertaken from which it quickly became apparent that there were many such factors and that the situation was a highly complex one. Some of the reasons for this failure of pupils to take advantage of the educational opportunities supposedly made available to them were to be found, as one would expect, in the cultural background of the homes in which they were growing up but, more disturbingly, it soon began to emerge not only that the school system was failing to compensate for these disadvantages but that in many ways it was itself aggravating them and introducing additional factors into the situation that worked to the further disadvantage of the 'culturally deprived' child.

The elements in the home background of certain pupils that make it difficult for them to profit from the educational opportunites opened to them were not hard to find. In many cases a straightforward desire on the part of parents for an extra wage-packet to supplement the family income or on the part of the young person himself for a steady wage and the independence that goes with it have led to departure from school at the earliest date on which it was legally possible. The one real argument for the raising of the school leaving age to sixteen is the need to keep pupils of this kind at school at least until they have had a chance to take some kind of public examination for their own benefit as much as for that of society as a whole. The desire to leave school for reasons of pure economy, then, accompanied sometimes but not always by a reluctance to be 'educated out of one's class', was a prime factor in the situation we have been describing. This one would expect.

It became apparent, however, that this was not the only reason why such youngsters were leaving school early. It was also due in some cases to the fact that neither they nor their parents knew what the opportunities open to them were nor what facilities existed to enable them to take advantage of them. Many were unaware, for example, of the existence of student grants that would enable them to go on to some form of higher education. Sheer ignorance was a major factor, then, in discouraging many from continuing their education beyond the statutory leaving age. It seemed further, however, that many lacked not only a knowledge of but also any real interest in the educational opportunites that were being offered them. One study suggested that only certain identifiable kinds of family in this sector of society could be seen to be really interested in education and, therefore, prepared to support their children, their sons at least if not their daughters, and to encourage them to take full advantage of it (Jackson and Marsden, 1962). Among these families the study identified the 'sunken middle-class' family, the family which had, say, once owned a shop or other small business and had fallen on bad times or which was a branch of a largely 'middle-class' family and wished to regain that kind of status by way of the education of the children; secondly, the families of foremen or others whose work brought them into contact with the more highly educated and gave them thus some inkling of the advantages of this kind of position; and, thirdly, other families, such as those where the mother had herself been educated in a grammar school but had 'married beneath her' and where there was a frustration and a consequent excitement about the possiblities of social advancement through the education of the children. For the rest, a certain apathy was apparent as a result of which there was no encouragement for the children to do well at school and no desire for them to stay there longer than was required by law.

Furthermore, the whole ambience of this kind of home seemed to lead to a different view of education from that normally taken by teachers and others who were concerned with its provision and also, it has been claimed, to certain personality traits that made success in the system more difficult for children growing up in such homes. It has been suggested, for example (Riessman, 1962), that in many such families, if education is valued at all, it is valued only as instrumental towards vocational improvement or the avoidance of exploitation in a competitive and fast-moving world, whereas to some extent at least the ethos of most schools is based on a commitment to the idea of education for its own sake or for the development of self-expression. Such a fundamental conflict of attitudes and values must lead to difficulties. One illustration of this is the interest shown by many pupils in apprenticeships and other courses of vocational training, the point of which is more readily appreciated than the need to learn French irregular verbs or abstruse Latin grammatical constructions.

So far the reasons we have produced to explain why children from certain kinds of family do not get on at school have been those that derive from a fundamental lack of interest in or understanding of what is involved in this. Attention has also been drawn, however, to certain elements in the upbringing of these children that make it difficult for them to cope with the demands of the system even when they are motivated to do so. It has been claimed, for example, that the child-rearing practices usually associated with families of this kind lead to the development of certain character traits that are not conducive to educational success, that the granting of food to babies on demand or giving them comforters and even the quick and immediate smack for any kind of misdemeanour creates a need in children for immediate gratification in all spheres and makes it difficult, if not impossible, for them to direct their energies towards any activity the point of which is to be appreciated only by reference to certain long-term goals, such as examination successes or later career prospects. It has also been suggested that the pace of life is often slower in families of this kind, that, as a result, children from them do not reveal that quickness in their approach to learning that teachers tend to associate with potential educational success so that they come to be regarded not merely as slow learners but also as poor learners and thus do not succeed in a situation where speed of working seems so often to be at a premium. It has even been argued that the patriarchal ethos of such families makes it difficult for their offspring to accept what is felt to be the largely matriarchal ethos of most primary schools.

The most important single factor, however, that has been identified as contributing to this failure of pupils from such backgrounds to cope successfully with the demands of the school system is, as we saw in Chapter 5, the nature of the language that they have acquired through their preschool experiences. The child who has initially acquired his spoken language in a home where a 'restricted' code of language is used will have difficulty in using the formal or 'elaborated' code of the school and thus will not find it easy to learn to read, to extend his vocabulary, to acquire the conceptual understanding necessary for educational progress especially at an abstract level, in short to attain all of those skills that are fundamental to educational achievement (Bernstein, 1961). Indeed, Bernstein suggested further that this problem of language is the most important single factor in educational disadvantage, leading not only to verbal difficulties but also to a certain rigidity of thinking, a reduced span of attention, a limiting of curiosity, impulsive behaviour in which the interval between feeling and acting is short, an inability to tolerate ambiguity, a preference for the concrete and, in general, a distaste for, not to say a positive suspicion of, education as traditionally conceived. As we have seen, there has subsequently been a certain retraction from this extreme position to one which, while maintaining that the language code of such pupils is different, no longer claims that it is inferior or lacking in any way (Bernstein, 1964; Labov, 1969), but, so long as the content of education is couched in a formal 'elaborated' code of language, the pupil whose own language is of a 'restricted' or 'public' kind will be at a disadvantage.

This brief discussion of language, which was developed more fully in Chapter 5, introduces the suggestion that there are factors in the school itself, as well as in the home, that need to be looked at if we want to discover what contributes to the difficulties experienced by pupils of the kind we are here concerned with. For it has become increasingly clear not only that schools have not been doing enough to help these pupils but also that there are many ways in which they have been aggravating the problem and themselves creating further barriers to success. We must now consider some of these in more detail.

To begin with, it should be clear that most of these homes will be in poorer districts, especially in the large cities, and that the schools these children attend will also be in these poorer areas. It is almost certainly not the case now, as it once was, that these schools are badly equipped or less generously provided for than those in wealthier neighbourhoods, but in terms of human resources they are often less well endowed since they are not attractive places of work for most teachers and the turnover of staff in them has tended to be very high. Certainly most teachers will not be keen to live in such areas themselves so that they will have to be prepared to travel quite long distances to teach in them. Too frequent changes of teacher and too much time spent with supply teachers or well-meaning but inexperienced probationer teachers do not create conditions conducive to educational success.

Furthermore, the attitudes of the teachers themselves often do not help to alleviate these difficulties. Whatever their own origins, teachers by their long education and training have usually developed values very different from those of these pupils and are sometimes less than sympathetic towards those pupils who do not share these values. We have already referred to the problem of confusing slowness in learning with low ability. When this is done, teachers come to expect a low level of performance from such pupils and, as we saw in Chapter 2, the demands made by teachers of their pupils and the expectations they have of them seem to be quite crucial in determining the levels of achievement reached (Pidgeon, 1970). Teachers can also be put off, as we all can, by appearance and dress and will often not expect much from children who are not very well turned out and will not give them as much attention as they need or are entitled to. Difference of language will also lead to difficulties of communication and will thus seriously reduce the efficiency of both the teaching and the learning. Finally, even teachers who are aware of these difficulties and take positive steps to avoid them may unwittingly contribute to the disadvantage. They may quite reasonably fail to answer those important questions that remain unasked, questions like those about grants, career and other possibilities which we mentioned earlier. Furthermore, in their efforts to do what seems to be best for these pupils they may sometimes talk down to them, lower their standards or take the lack of interest for granted (Riessman, 1962). Teachers in the USA, for example, have been known to advise Negro children against aiming too high, doing this honestly in what they see as the best interests of the pupils. This kind of patronization can be in itself a form of discrimination, 'discrimination without prejudice', as Riessman calls it. The attitudes of teachers, then, constitute one major factor within the school that can aggravate the disadvantages that some pupils experience.

It has become increasingly apparent over the last twenty years or so that many elements in the organization of the school system also contribute to this wastage and the inequality of opportunity. In particular, the existence of selective procedures at various stages in the individual's school life have appeared to result in grave disadvantages for many children, but particularly for those who come to school already disadvantaged in the ways we have indicated. Streaming, the practice of grouping children according to measured ability, is one device that creates difficulties of this kind at whatever stage it is used, although clearly the earlier it is introduced the more influential it will be. There are quite clear indications too that it works particularly to the detriment of the child whose home background is not educationally supportive (Jackson, 1964). Similarly, a selective form of secondary education which necessitates some kind of allocation of pupils to different schools or different forms of education at 11+ or at some other equally early stage of a child's school career will result in inefficiencies and errors which will particularly affect such children. In part this is due to all of the factors we have mentioned above, the barriers to achievement created by the home background, teachers' attitudes and expectations, language difficulties and so on, but they all culminate in the difficulties created by the testing procedures used and especially those that involve some attempt to measure intelligence.

The difficulties of doing this have been fully discussed in Chapter 3 and attempts to base differential educational provision on tests of this kind must for a variety of reasons lead to the misallocation of large numbers of children (Yates and Pidgeon, 1957). It is particularly detrimental to the progress of the socially disadvantaged child for a number of reasons. In the case of verbal tests, language differences will clearly play an important part. In all tests the need for speed, often a crucial factor in measuring intelligence, will militate against a high score by the child who sees no particular merit in doing things quickly. A lack of interest or motivation is also unlikely to help a child to show up well in these situations and, where an interview forms part of the testing procedure, the resultant social situation, the relationship with the examiner, will be an added problem for the child who lacks some of the social graces. For all of these reasons children from underprivileged homes can be seen to do themselves less than justice in tests of this kind, so that wherever selection procedures of this type are in use they lead to inequalities of opportunity for such children. The same factors are even resulting in a large proportion of coloured pupils in the United Kingdom, particularly those of West Indian nationality, being allocated to institutions for the educationally subnormal, having been 'dubbed' or 'made' ESN (Coard, 1971).

It is perhaps worth noting at this point that many other irrelevant factors come into play when this kind of testing and allocation of pupils to different kinds of school or streamed class are employed, factors which affect the progress not only of pupils from underprivileged backgrounds but many others too. We have heard a lot about the effects of 'nerves' in test situations and interviews and also about the advantages of those who possess 'good examination technique', but these are minor factors when compared with others which are less obvious but equally, and perhaps even more, irrelevant and often far more significant. Sex is one such factor; educational advancement at all levels has always been much more difficult for girls than for boys since, in addition to the greater reluctance of parents to support girls through the system, there have been fewer places for them in all selective institutions. There may be those who would want to argue that sex difference is not an irrelevant factor in differential provision of educational opportunity. It can hardly be maintained, however, that the month of one's birth is relevant. Yet it has been shown (Jackson, 1964) that this can and does affect the allocation of pupils to streamed classes in junior schools and thus to different types of secondary school, for the very good reason that the month of one's birth governs the date at which one is admitted to the infant school and consequently the length of time one has spent in full-time education up to the time at which the selection is made. Childhood illnesses and the absences that they involve also play their part in this process. The place of one's birth or at least the part of the country in which one has one's education is another crucial factor in determining the kind of education one has, since provision varies dramatically in both quantity and type from one organizing authority to another. Yet this too would seem to be an irrelevant consideration in the decision about what kind of education an individual can best profit from.

It will be clear, then, that equality of opportunity in education is far from a reality whatever interpretation one puts on the term. Even the most confirmed elitist, committed to nothing more than the education of the intelligent, can hardly believe in the face of this kind of evidence to the contrary that even this hard-line kind of equality is being achieved by the system as it has been organized. Only an elitism based on the advancement of the privileged could leave one satisfied with the situation that the enquiries of the last twenty years or so have revealed and few would want to maintain such an extremist position as that.

It has been clear for a long time, therefore, to those with any real understanding of the situation that changes needed to be made and steps taken to rectify the position. Consequently, recent years have seen the introduction of a number of schemes aimed at putting right these deficiencies in the system and at combating the disadvantages of the underprivileged, in order to promote something that could more appropriately be called educational equality. We must now turn to a consideration of the form some of these have taken, the intentions that lie behind them, and some of the difficulties they have themselves given rise to.

Compensatory education

One major kind of solution that has been suggested to deal with some of the problems we have listed is that of what the Plowden Report (1967) called 'positive discrimination'. This amounts to a suggestion that equality does not require that we give all schools and all pupils an equal share of the educational cake but that it is more likely to be attained if we give larger, and therefore unequal, shares to those with greater needs, if we allocate a larger share of resources of all kinds to certain pupils in order to compensate for the disadvantages under which they labour. Certain children must be given unequal treatment if they are to have equal opportunities. This kind of view has led to a number of different forms of 'Compensatory Education', each designed to make good the cultural deficiencies we have referred to and to try to compensate for and to put right those factors that have been hindering the educational success of such pupils. This is an idea that had appeared earlier in the USA in answer to the problem of the education of black children.

One of the solutions offered by the Plowden Report itself, although it had other reasons also for making this particular recommendation, was an expansion of the provision of preschool, nursery education. One of the arguments adduced in favour of this recommendation was the need to provide early opportunities for children to receive some kind of formal educational provision that might make up for various forms of social deprivation. Certain children, it argued, suffer later in the system because of poverty of language and 'even amongst children below compulsory school age, the growth of measured intelligence is associated with socio-economic features' (para. 302) so that educational provision from the age of three years onwards may offset this.

The importance of nursery education in this and other respects is now recognized and the British Government affirmed its intention to expand it on a large scale. Furthermore, although this appeared likely to be one of the first casualties in educational provision that has been necessitated by the economic difficulties that have recently been encountered, public demand and the recognition of its value seems to have ensured some continued expansion of provision in this area. In the USA too, attempts have been made to introduce compensatory education programmes at the preschool stage in order to try to ensure that the child from the culturally impoverished background might start his formal school career on a par with his more fortunate colleagues. The 'Headstart' programme was just such an attempt to bring children from poorer homes, especially Negro children, up to the starting line level with their fellows.

This, then, has been one form of positive discrimination. Where it has been tried, however, it has not been entirely successful. In part this is due to the fact that when nursery schools or nursery classes are created, unless the local authority adopts a deliberate policy of establishing them in areas of social priority, they are used more by children from 'privileged' than those from 'underprivileged' homes. There is little that can be done about this. One cannot make attendance compulsory at this age nor can one exclude the 'privileged' from it, since the arguments for the provision of education at this age for all pupils are strong. One can only recommend, as the Plowden Report does, that all possible means of persuasion should be used by health visitors and other social workers to encourage mothers of children who seem to be in particular need of nursery education to make greater use of the facilities available.

The attitude that is implied towards the culture of these homes has been another factor in the lack of success of this kind of venture. To regard children from poor homes as culturally deprived is to imply that these homes are fundamentally inferior; this in turn leads to the continuation of a form of education that is linked to a different kind of culture and consequently creates a gap that is difficult to bridge and which does not make any easier the task of convincing the parents, especially the mothers, of these children of the value of what is offered in nursery education. They are unlikely to see it as more than a useful child-minding service which they will use only if they have no more convenient service, such as a resident granny.

This latter point draws our attention also to a third difficulty that is being experienced in this area, the problem of establishing nursery education in a form that has more substance to it than a mere child-minding service, the provision of suitable accommodation and resources and the training of suitable teachers for this kind of work, teachers who understand what is needed and have the expertise to provide it. The conversion of accommodation, resources, and especially teachers who were originally prepared for teaching older pupils is more important than has often been realized. It is also, at least in the case of the teachers, a long process, so that the only suitable form of preparation is the concurrent course of three or four years leading to a first degree in education itself. If nursery education is to be established properly, it will be a long and expensive task. Only if it is done properly, however, can we hope that it might contribute something towards the solution of the problems we have been discussing.

A second kind of approach that has been adopted in the attempt to provide compensatory education has been directed not at preschool children but at all of the school population. It has taken the form of putting extra resources into schools in deprived areas, providing extra payments to teachers, larger allowances for materials and other recurrent expenditure, favourable building grants and financial assistance of this kind in all relevant fields. In suggesting this remedy, the Plowden Report tells us that 'the principle, already accepted, that special need calls for special help, should be given a new cutting edge. We ask for "positive discrimination" in favour of such schools and the children in them, going well beyond an attempt to equalize resources.... The first step must be to raise the schools with low standards to the national average; the second, quite deliberately to make them better. The justification is that the homes and neighbourhoods from which many of their children come provide little support and stimulus for learning,' (para. 151).

As a result of this recommendation, many areas in Britian have been officially designated as Educational or, more recently, Social Priority Areas and the schools in them have been given the kind of preferential treatment suggested. Teachers in these schools have been paid more in an attempt to secure a stability of staffing and to halt the rapid staff turnover that we suggested earlier was a significant factor in the lack of success of the pupils in these schools. Additional money has also been made available in order to make possible the establishment of special programmes either in the schools themselves or in outside centres to remedy the deficiencies in experience, language, and other cognitive skills of the children in them. At the same time the back-up services have been strengthened both by increased provision of social services of all kinds and by the appointment of social workers or counsellors to the schools themselves.

While one would not want to deny that this kind of approach has done much to improve the educational lot of certain pupils and to put right some of the inequalities of the system, there are difficulties with it of which we ought to take note. In particular, there are two fundamental problems in this approach.

The first of these arises from the difficulty of establishing adequate criteria for designating an area as an area of priority. The Plowden Report suggested a number of criteria that should be used, the proportions of unskilled and semiskilled manual workers in the area, the size of families, the extent of the entitlement to supplementary benefits of all kinds, the amount of overcrowding and sharing of houses, the incidence of truancy, the proportions of retarded, disturbed or handicapped pupils, the number of incomplete families, and the proportion of 'children unable to speak English'. Many of these are criteria that can be measured with a high degree of exactitude; others are less easy to determine. Not all of those who are entitled to supplementary benefits actually avail themselves of them, for example, as the Report points out, so that it is not easy to apply this kind of criterion accurately. Furthermore, criteria such as the incidence of truancy is based not on objectively identifiable conditions in the home background of the pupils but on the way in which they react to their schools. Some cynics have claimed, therefore, that this and other criteria that have been used, such as that of a high staff turn-over, create a situation in which an inefficient or incompetent school is 'rewarded' by additional resources and payments to staff, while a school that successfully tackles problems of this kind as they are presented to it is, in a sense, 'penalized'. A certain amount of tension and dissatisfaction has consequently resulted among teachers from this kind of scheme.

This is one aspect of a wider problem. Whatever criteria are used, they will inevitably be rather rough and ready. A line will be drawn somewhere which must be somewhat arbitrary. This is another example of the problem of establishing categories that we referred to earlier. It will also always be the case that wherever that line is drawn there will be many pupils in these areas of priority whose home background is such that they will not need compensatory educational provision and there will always be those outside these areas whose need for it will be every bit as great as that of any of those who are within them, and for the very same reasons. The Plowden Report itself was aware of this and spoke of special groups, such as gypsies and canal boat children whose difficulties would not be met by any such scheme. The problem, however, is not only one of special groups; again we find ourselves dealing with categories, the main need is to provide for individual pupils. Attempts have, therefore, been made to identify pupils rather than areas with special needs and to use the additional resources to develop and provide special programmes for them. It is almost certainly true that a judicious combination of these approaches is the only route that is likely to lead to any kind of solution for all such pupils.

A further point that must be stressed is that, to quote the Plowden Report yet again, 'improved education alone cannot solve the problem of these children' (para. 157). Education cannot compensate for society. (Bernstein, 1970). To put extra resources only into the education of such children is to attempt to deal with the symptoms without getting at the root causes of their difficulties. The process of equalizing the life-chances of children must begin outside the school and, unless it does, there is little that the school alone can do. Again to quote from the Plowden Report, 'simultaneous action is needed by the authorities responsible for employment, industrial training, housing and planning' (para. 151). Indeed, it may well be the case that the failure to mount successful attacks simultaneously on these areas has been one factor in the lack of success achieved by some attempts to improve the educational provision of these pupils. This draws attention to the need for a total approach to this problem and this has emerged very clearly from the practical experiences of many of those who have been involved in compensatory schemes of this kind. In many areas of priority it has quickly become apparent that little can be achieved by improving the facilities within the schools if no attempt is made to integrate the schools more fully with their communities. Thus compensatory education has appeared to be possible only if the parents themselves can be brought into the picture and only if one can relate what is being provided for and required of pupils in schools to the realities of the environment of the community in which they live for the other seven-eighths of their young lives.

This brings us directly to the major problem of the concept of compensatory education. The schemes we have been discussing have all started out as attempts to make people equal and we suggested earlier that such an approach is fundamentally mistaken. The notion of compensation implies the existence of a deficiency and, while there is no doubt that on any definition of deficiency real deficiencies do exist in many familes, the considerations behind programmes of compensatory education have too often assumed that these deficiencies are always cultural ones and that they are an inevitable part of the social background of all children from certain socio-economic or racial groups. It implies that the language and culture of 'working-class' or West Indian families, for example, are inferior to the culture that the school is concerned to impart and that pupils from this kind of background must be 'cured' of their linguistic and cultural deficiencies if they are to be brought to a 'proper' standard of educational achievement. The problem with this attitude is that at root it perpetuates and reinforces a conflict which, as we have already seen, is itself a major contributory factor to the educational failure of these pupils. It attempts to do no more than to discover new and more effective ways of imposing an 'alien' culture on them and thus does nothing to overcome the alienation and the conflict of values that we suggested earlier was a major obstacle to the educational achievement of these pupils.

This view of what is needed here is, of course, based on a view of knowledge and of the intrinsic merits of certain activities, pursuits, culture and values that, as we have seen in Chapter 8, is of questionable validity. It has recently been suggested, therefore, that we should reconsider what we mean by 'education', especially in relation to such pupils. (Keddie 1973). The view that is now taken of what has been called the 'restricted' language code of children from certain kinds of home background is no longer, as we pointed out earlier, that such a code is inferior to that of the school but that it is merely different. It is no longer felt that it need necessarily hinder or limit the development of rationality, since it can be shown itself to be capable of sustaining the most abstract and abstruse relationships (Labov, 1969). If the development of rationality in such pupils is inhibited, it is because the language of teachers and of education is different and no concessions are made to them nor attempts to bridge the gap between the codes, other than to try to push them into using the different and largely 'alien' code of the school.

For this reason, as we saw when discussing the curriculum in Chapter 8, questions are being asked about the content of education. It is being asserted that human knowledge does not have the kind of objective status often claimed for it and that there is little real foundation for the claim that certain kinds of knowledge have a value that is superior to that of other kinds in such a way as to justify an insistence that all pupils acquire such knowledge and accept the values implicit in it. Views have been expressed about the 'stratification of knowledge' (Young, 1971), suggesting that decisions about the value of certain kinds of knowledge are linked to the class structure of society and that by such decisions the dominant class attempts to impose its own culture on its society.

If there is any truth in this kind of assertion, to engage in forms of compensatory education such as those we have discussed is to do no more than to attempt to ease and to make more efficient this imposition of values by the dominant class on society as a whole. As a result, it is being suggested that we look again at the content of educational provision and try to relate this to the existing knowledge and culture of the pupil, that we try to base our educational provision on the 'common sense' knowledge of the pupils themselves rather than on the 'educational' knowledge of the teacher. If we do this, some of the barriers to the education of these children will disappear – deferred gratification, for example, need create no problem if there is immediate satisfaction in the subject matter of education here and now – and there might be some hope that a relevant education might be provided for pupils from 'working-class' and Negro homes, so that they will not become alienated by their experiences at school, at a serious disadvantage in relation to their own personal development and subsequently perhaps delinquent and antisocial. In short, it is being claimed that we should not be attempting to convert such pupils to a new language or a new culture, but that rather attempts should be made to bridge the gap between the cultures if education is to cease to play the divisive role it has hitherto played in society.

The same sort of conclusion is being reached by many of those who have been engaged at a practical level in attempts to deal with the problems of the EPA areas. As we have seen, they have come to realize that the problem of the gap between the culture of the home and that of the school requires more than merely building a bridge from one to the other; the gap itself needs to be closed by a rapprochement of school and community, an integration of the school into the community. In order to achieve this, major changes must be made in what the school regards as its role and function and what it considers to be the essential content of education.

The problem, therefore, becomes one of introducing modifications to the curriculum of the school in order to achieve these purposes and we have already noted in Chapter 8 some of the difficulties of ensuring that curriculum planning achieves an adequate balance between the needs of the pupil, the needs of society and the demands of knowledge itself. In particular, we must not lose sight of the dangers of imprisoning pupils in their own culture and of failing to broaden their horizons by not offering them adequate opportunities for experiencing many things they may come to value that are beyond their immediate environment (White, 1968, 1973). On the other hand, it is clear that many of the current difficulties we are experiencing in our schools arise from a failure to question the validity of much of what we are offering and in particular to do this in the light of the background of many of the pupils we are supposed to be catering for. As we have said, a rapprochement is needed if we are to achieve a form of education that is relevant and, therefore, acceptable to pupils from all kinds of background. What is needed now, therefore, is a careful examination of the form such a rapprochement should take and in particular an awareness that here, as so often, there will be no panaceas. Again it will be necessary to answer these problems at the practical level in relation to the particular contexts of individual schools and it may be that the first-hand experience of those who have worked in Educational Priority Areas will be of more value than the ideas of the theoreticians from this point on. Certainly, one of the weaknesses of the theoretical discussions of these issues has been their failure to offer any clear advice as to how teachers might in practice set about seeking solutions to the problems they have identified.

One way of attempting to achieve educational equality through changes in the educational system, then, is to look very closely at the curriculum and to take account in our curriculum planning of factors other than traditional views about what kinds of knowledge are valuable. Changes must also be made, however, in the organizational structure of the system, since, as we saw earlier, there are factors here that militate against equality. There is little point even in the most sweeping attempts to correct any deficiencies that do exist in the backgrounds of pupils if we do nothing to rectify those features of the system itself which aggravate these problems and create further barriers to the progress of many pupils. Other innovations have been introduced, therefore, designed to meet some of these problems. In particular, attempts have been made to correct the inequalities that have arisen from the use of selective procedures of various kinds and at various points within the system. We must conclude our discussion of equality by considering the two major developments in this area, comprehensive education and the abolition of streaming.

Comprehensive education

The idea of organizing secondary education in England and Wales on a comprehensive basis had been raised and aired, particularly within the Labour movement, in the years between the two World Wars, but it received its first real impetus from the intention made explicit by the 1944 Education Act to provide secondary education for all pupils on an equal footing 'according to age, aptitude and ability'. Once this kind of egalitarianism had been given official sanction in this way, it became increasingly difficult to maintain that this idea was being realized or could be realized through the provision of two or three different types of secondary school.

The development of secondary education in England and Wales during the period between the two world wars had resulted for the most part in the emergence of a selective system which allocated pupils at age eleven to two or three types of school on the basis of a diagnostic test or series of tests of attainment and ability that came to be known as the 11+. In some areas an attempt was made to correct some of the inevitable errors of this procedure by arrangements for the further transfer of some pupils at 13+. But the number of pupils thus transferred was notional and the effects of this attempt to set up a long-stop device were negligible. Children were thus allocated to a grammar school or a modern school at the age of eleven. Sometimes provision was made for a third type of school, the technical school, but there were few of these and, where they did exist, transfer to them was usually at 13+ rather than 11+, so that effectively, although known as tripartism, in most parts of the country this resulted in a bipartite system.

This was a natural development from an earlier scheme in which all pupils went to an all-age elementary school and those who were successful in the 'scholarship' at eleven were offered free places in grammar schools until the age of leaving. It was a system that was given the official blessing of the Hadow Report of 1926, the Spens Report of 1938, albeit with a few sympathetic comments on the idea of the multi-lateral school, and the Norwood Report of 1943. The latter even went so far as to posit the existence of three types of mind for which these three types of school, conveniently enough, were ideally suited to cater.

In spite of this official view, the 1944 Education Act, which was the culmination of these discussions, did not impose this system on the country but gave the local authorities the freedom to organize secondary education in whatever way they felt appropriate to their particular situations. One would like to feel that it took this line because it accepted the implications of its own fundamental egalitarianism; it is more likely, however, that it was the result of the pressures of the Labour Party participants in an Act that was the work of the wartime coalition government.

The immediate reaction of many authorities to the requirements of the 1944 Act was to develop and extend the selective system of secondary education they had been building up before the Second World War started. Indeed, the more progress an authority had made with its plans in the thirties, the more committed it was to proceeding along similar lines now. Clearly, this made good sense in terms of the economic use of existing plant and the conservation of resources in what was a time of great economic stringency. Others, however, did begin to experiment with comprehensive schools. In particular, where new schools had to be built anyway because of the effects of bombing, as in London and Coventry, it was no extravagance to build a completely new system and, indeed, where very large schools were built there might even have been some saving. The years immediately following the Act, therefore, saw the emergence of a number of different systems, bipartism, tripartism, comprehensivism of a number of different kinds, 'all-through' and 'two-tier', and even systems which attempted to reconcile selective and non-selective methods by having grammar and 'comprehensive' schools in the same scheme.

Throughout this time, however, the pressures against selective systems were mounting, backed not only by the ideological arguments of the Labour Movement but also by the growing evidence of the hidden effects of such systems, some of which we have already referred to, so that comprehensivization slowly spread. In 1965, a Labour government issued Circular 10/65 which requested all local authorities to submit to it plans for the comprehensivization of secondary education in the areas under their jurisdiction. This requirement was withdrawn by a later Tory government but then reasserted by the next Labour government and because of this vacillation over official policy some local authorities have refused to take any steps towards meeting it. However, most have now responded to it, even if in some cases this is only because they had gone too far towards doing so when the request was withdrawn to be able to change direction again.

The most unfortunate feature of the development of comprehensive secondary education in this country has been that it has in this way been debated almost entirely at the level of political ideology and prejudice and has been implemented for political rather than educational reasons, so that emotion has tended to play a larger part than reason both in the discussion and the development of it and the educational issues at stake have thus been often lost or ignored. It is due in no small part to this feature that we have made so many mistakes in the development of the comprehensive system so that we have so few comprehensive schools that one can approve of either on political or on educational grounds. We must look now at some of the educational issues involved here and at some features of both the notion and the realities of comprehensive education itself.

The first thing we must note is the problem of any kind of selectivity in education. Selective systems have been criticized on ideological grounds as being socially devisive and as resulting in inequalities of all kinds. Parity of esteem between types of school which was stressed as a vital concomitant of any selective system was never a realistic aim, since no matter how hard anyone tries to ensure that all types of school have equality of provision, there is no way in which they can be assured equality of status and no doubt in anyone's mind that different types of school are not on a par, if only because of the different kinds of career their pupils enter, a criterion that is very commonly applied by both parents and teachers in evaluating schools (Banks, 1955). Thus inequalities result as the 'best' teachers choose to go to the 'best' schools and parents choose to send their children to these schools if they can.

However, ideological arguments of this kind have no force with those who reject the ideology itself and to say that selective procedures result in inequalities between different types of school is not to condemn the system in the eyes of those who would argue that such inequalities are acceptable, even right and proper. As we saw earlier, the notion of equality in itself requires no more than this.

The educational arguments against selection, however, are more cogent. At basis they are the same arguments we have seen as applying to any attempt to use broad and rather crude categories in planning our educational provision. It is impossible to allocate pupils to categories of this kind with any acceptable degree of accuracy or efficiency. Some of the reasons for this we have encountered elsewhere. It is worth briefly bringing them together here.

The belief that one can use tests of any kind to assess educability and thus to allocate pupils to certain kinds of educational institution was criticized at a very early stage in the development of such tests. The Hadow Report of 1931 questioned the use of intelligence tests for these purposes and earlier than that, in 1924, a report on 'Psychological Tests of Educable Capacity' described the use of such tests for transfer at 11+ as 'gravely unreliable'. Nor is the problem merely one of devising more accurate and sophisticated techniques of assessment. The difficulties are much more complex than is recognized by those whose solution to it is to abolish the 11+ test and replace it with a series of tests supported by teachers' and headteachers' assessments.

One aspect of this issue that we have already noted is the extent to which irrelevant factors such as sex, date and place of birth, socio-economic background and other such features influence the allocation of pupils. But the problem goes even deeper than this. Yates and Pidgeon (1957) suggested that even at its most efficient any system of selection must result in an error of 5 percent each way, and 10 percent of any age cohort will be wrongly placed even by the most accurate system, these being the pupils who fall on either side of the borderline wherever we draw that line. An error slightly in excess of 10 percent which the same study claimed to have discovered in the practice of local authorities at the time represented a very creditable performance and yet, in human terms, it meant that a lot of children were being placed in educational institutions that were not suitable for most of them.

The prime reason for this is that intellectual growth is a constantly changing and developing process and the rate of such growth varies greatly from one child to another. It is possible to test with reasonable accuracy the level of an individual's attainment at any given time but to use this as a basis for assertions about that individual's potential for further growth, to try to predict future performance on the evidence of present achievement, to assume that one has measured ability rather than attainment is to read far more into the results of such tests than is legitimate, as we saw in Chapter 3.

Furthermore, to do this is to make no allowance for what we know about the importance of achievement for motivation and the effects of both success and failure in raising or lowering the motivational level of pupils and therefore their standards of performance, points which we discussed in detail in Chapters 2 and 4. There is clear evidence of this in tests given to pupils shortly after 'success' or 'failure' in the 11+.

Finally, we must remember the effects of teacher expectation here. As we saw in Chapter 2, teachers will raise or lower the demands they make of their pupils according to whether they view them as 'bright' or 'average' or 'backward' and this will itself contribute to a widening of the gap between those who 'succeed' and those who 'fail' in a selective system, so that the process becomes a 'self-fulfilling prophecy', an expression that has been used to describe the comparable practice of streaming (Jackson, 1964). It was for this reason, among others, that the 'fail-safe' device of the er between schools did not work.

damental argument for comprehensive education, then, is the
ifficulty of any system of selection, its inability to select with
a... or to correct errors once they have been made.

A growing awareness of the many facets of this problem has reinforced
the increasing ideological and political pressure and has brought about a
rapid expansion of comprehensive or nonselective secondary education in
recent years. This has taken a number of different forms, which can be
broadly grouped into two main types, the 'all-through' comprehensive
school (a term that has a sad ambiguity) and the 'two-tier' system. The
'all-through' comprehensive schools are those schools, usually rather large
in size, that have been established by some authorities to take pupils of all
abilities on their transfer from junior schools at 11+ and provide for them
until they leave school at sixteen, seventeen, or eighteen. In some cases
these schools have been purpose-built or have been developed from an
existing grammar, technical or modern school, where the site offered scope
for building development. In other places, units of this kind have been
created by the amalgamation of several existing schools of different types,
even where in some instances these have been widely separated geo-
graphically. This seemed to some authorities to be the most economical
way of responding to the request of Circular 10/65 and there has resulted a
number of 'botched up' schemes that have done the concept of comprehensive education little good and in some cases much harm.

The main difficulty with any kind of 'all-through' system is that it gives
rise to educational units of a size that some people have argued is too great
to cater adequately for aspects of education other than intellectual
development. This is a view that has support too from many who have
first-hand experience of the realities of these institutions. Such large units
cannot easily provide the secure, warm, face-to-face environment that
many pupils need and attempts to break the school down into smaller
units by the creation of houses, year groups, tutor groups or some other
such device can only work where the physical structure of the school is
such as to make these subdivisions real and meaningful to the pupils. This
is possible only in a few, fortunate cases. On the other hand, it has been
argued that unless the school is of a certain minimum size it will not be
capable of producing from a fully comprehensive intake a viable sixth
form, even allowing for the new and wider concept of sixth-form studies
that has emerged since the appearance of the comprehensive school, nor
will it make possible the variety of courses that it is felt should be made
available, especially at sixth-form level. The problem of size is, then, a

very serious one and has created problems for many schools, the failure to cope with which has led to severe criticisms of the notion of comprehensive education itself.

For this reason, some authorities have introduced various forms of two-tier systems on the assumption that to break the large all-through school into two units will give all the advantages of a nonselective scheme without the attendant problems of great size, and that it will avoid both the need for expensive new buildings and the 'botched up' amalgamations that might otherwise result. Thus some authorities have introduced schemes in which transfer from the junior school at 11+ is followed by further transfer to a 'high' school or a grammar school at 14+. Others have established Sixth Form Colleges which pupils who choose to stay on at school beyond sixteen may attend for a variety of courses. In addition to removing from the secondary school the sixth form which, as we saw just now, has led to the need for very large schools, this kind of scheme has the additional advantage that it makes possible the education of early maturing teenagers in a 'college' rather than a 'school' environment, where they can be given more freedom and responsibility and may thus be encouraged to persevere with their education more willingly. The trend that seems to be developing of late, as sixteen-year-olds increasingly leave their schools for the A level classes of the technical colleges, would seem to support the need for some development of this kind. Lastly, some authorities have taken up yet another suggestion of the Plowden Report (1967) and have decided to reorganize the whole of their educational provision into three phases, first, middle and secondary, with transfer at 8+ or 9+ and at 12+ or 13+. The main advantage of this kind of scheme, again apart from the smaller units that it makes possible, would seem to lie in the opportunities it creates for allowing twelve- and thirteen-year-olds to continue to enjoy some of the best features of our primary education, although no clear philosophy of the middle school has yet emerged and some would see it as an opportunity to extend downwards the age at which children can begin some of the specialized learning associated with the secondary stage of education.

Many of these developments are still in their infancy, so that it is difficult to evaluate them in any helpful way. Some have, of course, been in operation for some time, but even here the evidence is unclear and even conflicting. One or two general points can be made, however.

In the first place, a great deal of concern has been expressed about the fact that the introduction of comprehensive education in the full sense can only be achieved at the cost of abolishing the grammar schools which have been regarded by many people as the jewel of the English system. This is put by many people with an eye for an elegant turn of phrase as being equality at the expense of quality. There is no doubt that this is a serious issue. It must, however, be put into a proper perspective. While it is true that the work of many English grammar schools has been of a very high order, no one could begin to maintain that this has been true of all of them. The reputation of the very best ones too derives more from their academic record than any ability to cater for the wide spectrum of educational need that is generally recognized today. Furthermore, if the evidence we have considered concerning the inaccuracies of the selective procedures has any weight at all, it is difficult to argue that this quality of educational provision should be the preserve not of those who in educational terms most deserve it or are most able to profit from it but of those who for a variety of irrelevant reasons have been lucky enough to be offered it. The aim of comprehensive education should be to achieve this kind of quality in both the breadth and the depth of the education it offers to all pupils. If educational equality can really only be achieved with an attendant loss of quality, then we must think again about its desirability. Before we do so, however, we must ask whether it is in fact inevitable and, indeed, we must also ask some searching questions about how we are to define quality in education.

A second major criticism of comprehensive education is that it results in the growth of neighbourhood schools and thus does not achieve the social mix that some supporters of the idea feel is important nor even, perhaps, a fully comprehensive mixture of abilities. Attempts to ensure an adequate spread of abilities have resulted in schemes for admitting to each school a fixed proportion of pupils from each of three or four ability bands. This kind of approach may in turn result also in a certain social mix, since it invariably involves bringing in pupils from outside the immediate neighbourhood of the school. More positive attempts to ensure a social mix have been made through various schemes for 'bussing' children, sometimes from long distances, as has been done in some parts of the USA in an attempt to ensure a balanced racial mixture in schools.

The advantages of such schemes are doubtful. For one thing they necessitate the continuation of selective procedures even within the comprehensive system with all the difficulties and tensions for pupils and parents that that creates. The strain on pupils who have to travel long distances to school must also not be minimized. Finally, if there are any advantages in the development of the community school, the use of the facilities of the school by pupils in the evening, the involvement of parents in the work of the school, and, in general, the integration of the school with the community to which it belongs, then the school must be a neighbourhood school; it must draw its pupils from its own community. No community school can develop if its pupils are drawn from several areas.

This seems, then, not to be as serious a problem in the context of current educational thinking as was once felt to be the case. Provided that the parent's right to choose another secondary school for its offspring is safeguarded (although, of course, if this right were extensively asserted the whole system would break down), there seems little to be lost and perhaps much to be gained, not least from the loss of the stress and strain on children and parents, by transferring pupils from their junior or middle schools directly to their neighbourhood or community comprehensive secondary school. It is perhaps enough if the schools can avoid creating social barriers; we may be asking too much if we expect them also to destroy for us those that already exist, since this may deflect them from doing their own job properly.

The last comment that must be made about comprehensive education in the context of a discussion of educational equality is one that may have some bearing on the problem we noted earlier of the inadequacy and conflicting nature of some of the evidence that has so far emerged as to its success or failure. In trying to evaluate comprehensive education, we must maintain the very important distinction between the notion of comprehensive education and the realities of comprehensive schools as they have been established. If the evidence is not conclusively in their favour, we must remember that this may reflect on the inadequacies of the schemes that have so far been tried rather than on the idea itself. We have already noted, for example, that many authorities have kept some or all of their selective schools in existence alongside what they have called 'comprehensive schools'. In such situations, it is clearly unfair and unhelpful to judge such schools on their academic achievements, unless one regards any achievement in this sphere as a success. Similarly, where comprehensive schools are the result of 'botched up' amalgamations of existing schools or where the units created have been too large or housed in buildings too badly designed for them to have any real chance of success, we must beware of condemning the idea of comprehensive education because of the inept way it has been put into practice in many places.

Finally, comprehensive education does not follow merely from joining several schools together nor even from abandoning selective procedures, particularly if the old divisions remain within the school, as they have done in so many cases. Comprehensive education, if it is to mean anything, must involve a much more fundamental rethinking of the whole of education. It cannot be discussed or planned in isolation from the kind of rethinking about the curriculum we have referred to earlier in this chapter and elsewhere in this book, nor can it be undertaken without a fundamental reappraisal of the internal organization of the school. If we adopt a system of schools that is based on an abandonment of selective procedures, we must look very hard at any such procedures it is proposed to use within the school. This is why we must now conclude our discussion of equality by considering the process of streaming, itself an 'education system in miniature' (Jackson, 1964), which may be creating within some comprehensive schools the very difficulties that those schools have been established to overcome.

Streaming

Streaming is the grouping of pupils according to both age and intellectual ability. It is a system that was first introduced in England and Wales in the 1920s. The method of grouping which it replaced was that of 'standards', grouping by attainment but not by age, a system under which pupils moved from one standard to the next only when and if they reached an appropriate level of attainment. Such a system worked satisfactorily when most pupils remained in the same all-age elementary school throughout their school careers and it was little affected by the 'creaming off' of the very bright few to the grammar schools at 11+.

Two factors led to the change to streaming. The first of these was the move towards establishing secondary education for all which began with the Hadow Report of 1926. The 'decapitation' of the all-age elementary school which this entailed resulted in the disruption of the standards system and the emergence of the dull and backward in the new junior and secondary schools. Secondly, psychologists were beginning to concern themselves with the characteristics of age groups and to suggest that it might be unwise to group children without reference to their chronological ages. Indeed, this was one of the factors that had led to the Hadow Report's recommendation for separate primary and secondary schools. At the same time, the work of other psychologists, such as Binet and Simon (1916) on intelligence and Burt (1937) on backwardness, was encouraging the view that intellectual ability was largely innate, relatively static, and readily measureable and that, as a result, it could be used as a basis for grouping pupils, not least in order to make possible the provision of special treatment for the less able. These factors together suggested that in the new schools standards should be replaced by streams and in fact a 'triple track system of organization' of pupils into A, B, and C classes was explicitly advocated by the Hadow Report on Primary Education in 1931. In 1937 this official view was reiterated in the Board of Education's 'Handbook of Suggestions for Teachers' and the same system was suggested as appropriate for the multi-lateral school by the Spens Report on Secondary Education in 1938. As a result, streaming began to appear in primary, elementary and, where they were introduced, modern schools throughout the 1930s.

The assumptions of this system are several. Firstly, it assumes that intellectual ability is relatively fixed and static; secondly, that it can be measured with a higher degree of accuracy; and thirdly, that to use this as a basis for grouping pupils will give homogeneous teaching groups. It further assumes that the central concern of the school is the intellectual development of its pupils through certain kinds of subject content and that a class-teaching approach is the most effective and suitable method of attending to this. It also assumes that such a method of grouping is best for all pupils, not only the bright but also and equally the less able. Indeed, there are many teachers who today advocate this method of grouping primarily from the conviction that more can be done for the less able if they are kept together in small groups and not exposed to the discouragement of working next to their brighter peers (Daniels, 1961).

However, the years since the Second World War have seen a reaction against streaming and a developing trend towards the introduction of mixed-ability groupings in schools. As early as 1945, the newly formed Ministry of Education questioned the desirability of streaming in a pamphlet, 'The Nation's Schools', and by 1959 its report on Primary Education, although not explicitly condemning the practice, did stress the value of the mixed-ability form of organization in the primary school, a form of organization that it claimed had begun to appear in the previous decade. Indeed, although the immediate postwar years had seen, if anything, an increase in the incidence of streaming in both primary and secondary schools, as they dealt with an enlarged school population along with a shortage of resources and increased demands for educational success both at 11+ and in public examinations at 16+, the late 1950s and early 1960s saw a move away from streaming in primary schools, particularly in those areas where the introduction of some form of comprehensive secondary education removed the pressures of the 11+, and recent years have seen this trend spreading into the lower forms of secondary schools and, in some cases, the upper forms too.

Several reasons can be adduced to explain this trend. For the most part they are the same reasons as those we saw behind the movement towards the comprehensivization of secondary education. The assumptions about the nature of intelligence upon which selection of any kind is based have been strongly questioned by psychologists and educationists and, as we saw in Chapter 3, few would now feel justified in claiming that intelligence is a faculty, let alone that it can be measured with any accuracy. Consequently, it has become increasingly apparent that selective procedures are no more possible within a school than between schools. The problem of categories again comes into play in respect of establishing both adequate theoretical criteria and efficient practical devices. The idea that it is acceptable within the school because of the supposed ease of transfer between classes has little credence in the light of the extent to which transfers do in fact take place in streamed schools. Transfer between streams happens at a rate far below that which even teachers who support streaming believe to be necessary (Daniels, 1961), and the reasons for this are those that we saw also resulted in the failure of the 'fail-safe' device of transfer between schools at 13+. The expectations teachers have of pupils labelled A, B, or C again effects the pupils's performances, a point we discussed in detail in Chapter 2, as do the effects of success or failure, achievement or non-achievement, on the motivation of pupils, as we also saw in Chapter 4. In fact, it has become apparent that streaming has the effect of creating differences where none need exist, that it is indeed a 'self-fulfilling prophecy' (Jackson, 1964).

Furthermore, many irrelevant factors of the kind we have already discussed again affect the selection of pupils (Jackson, 1964; Douglas, 1964) and the evidence that mounted from a clutch of studies undertaken during the 1950s and 1960s suggested not only that streaming did not help schools to alleviate the inequalities that we referred to earlier but that, as we also suggested, it was doing much to aggravate them and, indeed, itself creating further inequalities. In particular, it emerged as a major factor in the wastage of talent we noted earlier.

Another factor in this reassessment of the merits of streaming has been the changes we have commented on elsewhere in the view taken of education and of the purposes of the school. We saw just now that one of the underlying assumptions of streaming is that the main, even the sole, concern of the school is or should be with the intellectual development of its pupils. If one views education in wider terms than that, one will want to consider the implications of streaming for other aspects of schooling. In particular, concern has been expressed about the effects of streaming on the development of divergent thinking and creative abilities in pupils and also on their personal, moral, and social development.

There is some evidence that more divergent thinking is to be found in unstreamed than in streamed schools (Ferri, 1972) and there is also some indication, as we saw in Chapter 3, that schools which use formal, conventional methods are less successful in promoting creative abilities than schools where the learning is more self-initiated (Haddon and Lytton, 1968). This evidence is far from conclusive, not least because of the difficulties of measuring these kinds of ability; and many other factors may be involved too, such as the attitudes of the teachers, which may be even more influential than the method of grouping (Barker-Lunn, 1970). However, this is an aspect of the problem that must not be ignored if we consider the development of these kinds of ability to be an important part of the school's task. It is thus an area that is worthy of further investigation.

There is little doubt, however, about the adverse effects of streaming on the social and emotional development of pupils. The study of streaming in the primary school mounted by the NFER (Barker-Lunn, 1970) devoted a lot of attention to these aspects of streaming, starting from the assumption that they are as important a part of education as 'more formally attained skills'. The study claimed that in unstreamed schools pupils of average ability and boys of below average ability developed better relationships with their teachers, that relationships and friendship patterns between pupils correlated less highly with ability levels, that average and below average pupils revealed more positive attitudes to school and that there was generally a higher level of participation in school activities. The studies of Hargreaves (1967) and Lacey (1970) revealed similar advantages to the social and emotional development of pupils, especially the less able pupils, in unstreamed schools or corresponding disadvantages when classes were streamed. There is little evidence of friendships between A and D stream pupils in streamed schools and, as we saw in Chapter 4, streaming seems to encourage the formation of delinquescent subcultures within the school (Hargreaves, 1967). It was once argued, as we saw, that the less able pupils should be grouped separately because they would become discouraged if required to work in the shadow of their brighter colleagues. It seems in fact that discouragement comes more from the official rejection that being placed in a lower stream implies. This results in harmful effects on the self-concept of the child, a negative attitude to school and all that school stands for, and the kinds of behavioural problems that all teachers are familiar with in lower streams, especially in the secondary school (Rudd, 1958). Nor must we forget the effects of streaming on parental attitudes to the school. Little research has been done on this, but it would not be surprising to discover that the experience of many headteachers of lack of cooperation from the parents of their less able pupils was to some extent explicable in terms of the loss of interest, ambition and involvement that must follow the allocation of one's child to a lower stream.

A further and significant factor in the move away from streaming has been the lack of any positive evidence as to its efficacy in promoting even the intellectual development of pupils, its original *raison d'être*. The most interesting feature of all the attempts that have been made to assess the relative merits of streaming and unstreaming in relation to intellectual attainment has been the lack of evidence that streaming makes any real difference. Such evidence as there is suggests either that there is no real difference (Barker-Lunn, 1970), or that pupils do slightly better overall in the unstreamed school (Daniels, 1961; Newbold, 1977). There is also a suggestion that unstreaming leads to a reduction in the spread of attainment between the bright and the less able (Daniels, 1961). A survey undertaken by the UNESCO Institute of Education in Hamburg in 1962 noted the widely varying results of English schoolchildren when compared with those in eleven other countries. It suggested that this was due to the fact that English educationists expect a wide difference in performance. It has further been suggested that this wide spread of achievement is a direct result of having streamed classes within a streamed system (Jackson, 1964) and the findings of Daniels (1961) lend support to this view since he detected a significant reduction in the dispersion of attainment scores in the unstreamed primary schools which he studied. It seems fairly clear, therefore, that the less able, for whose benefit in the view of many people streaming was introduced, do better in an unstreamed situation.

It may be, however, that the gifted children do less well and it is this possibility that gives pause to many people for whom the other evidence might well be conclusive. Clearly, this is a very important consideration. Pupils should not have to pay for their intellectual education at the cost of their social education, but it is equally important that we should not be too ready to adopt on social grounds a system of grouping that is likely to be detrimental to the academic achievement of any pupil. The same problem arises here, then, that we saw when discussing the comprehensivization of secondary education. We must not purchase equality at the cost of quality of any kind nor should we accept equality if it can be achieved only by holding back the more able.

It is here that another finding of the NFER study perhaps has particular significance. One of the most interesting findings of that study was that the success of either system of grouping, at least in relation to intellectual development, depended more on the attitudes of the teachers involved than on any other single factor. Both systems worked more effectively when the teachers believed in them than when they did not. Here may lie a clue to the solution of the dilemma we are faced with. If unstreaming, with the advantages it obviously has for the social and emotional development of pupils, is to attend with equal success to the intellectual needs of all pupils, it must be in the hands of teachers who believe in it and this in turn implies that it must be in the hands of teachers who are willing to adapt their methods to the totally new situation that an unstreamed class presents them with. It may well be not only the attitudes of teachers but the resulting unsuitability of their methods that leads to lack of success. In other words, if unstreaming is not to result in holding back the very bright pupils and if it is to ensure that all pupils get full value from their education, we must make sure that we get right the methods we use in attending to the work of unstreamed classes.

This means, in the first place, that we should examine the possibilities of flexible groupings in schools, especially with older pupils, accepting that one rigid form of grouping to which we adhere unflinchingly for every purpose is no better when it is an unstreamed form than when it is a finely streamed grouping, that different purposes require differently constituted groupings and that for some purposes, again particularly with older pupils, a system of setting or grouping according to specific abilities and attainments might be desirable. The main difficulties in particular subject areas of a streamed form of organization stem from the fact that it groups pupils on the basis of a limited set of criteria for all purposes. Correspondingly, the greatest merit of an unstreamed system of grouping is that it offers opportunities for adjusting our groupings to meet the many varied purposes of the school. A mixed-ability class can be the teaching unit for a wide range of subjects throughout the school; it can also be the basis upon which other groupings can be built. For pupils can be withdrawn from their mixed-ability classes. They can be regrouped according to optional choices of subject; they can also be formed, especially in the upper forms of the secondary school, into units that make possible different levels of working in certain subjects (Kelly, 1978).

Again it is the polarization, the apparent need to choose one or the other system, that leads to difficulties, and again what seems to be required is a much more subtle and flexible scheme, if we are to provide each child with the kind of education he or she needs.

Secondly, a lot more attention needs to be given to questions about the methods appropriate to the unstreamed class. Quite clearly the class-teaching approach in which an attempt is made to take all pupils through the same material at roughly the same pace, which we saw was one of the basic desiderata that led to the introduction of streaming, although it will still have a part to play, must for most purposes give way to more subtle methods and it would seem that those methods must be individual methods (Kelly, 1974, 1975, 1978). The streamed class is intended to be homogeneous so that all of the pupils in it can be taught almost as one, although in practice, of course, such homogeneity can never be achieved. The unstreamed class by contrast is overtly heterogeneous and the logic of this is that each individual must be catered for on his own terms. If we believe that the social advantages of the unstreamed class are important and worth having, then we must try to ensure that there are no concomitant disadvantages in the academic sphere. We can only do this by a complete change of approach which will involve us in adopting more individual methods. It is because many teachers have not been prepared for this kind of teaching that some experiments with unstreamed classes have not been entirely successful.

If this is so and it can be put right, certain advantages would seem likely to accrue in relation to the achievement of equality in education. For such a system makes it unnecessary to exercise selective procedures from an early stage within the schools so that we can avoid the errors and consequent inequalities that we have seen to be an unavoidable concomitant of such procedures. Furthermore, we no longer have to devise categories, which we have seen brings inevitable difficulties in relation to both the theoretical criteria by which they are to be established and the practicalities of putting them into operation. Instead, we will have created a climate in which it becomes necessary to treat every individual strictly and fairly on his or her own merits and this, in the ultimate, would seem to be what the notion of equality demands.

Summary and conclusions

We have in this chapter considered some of the difficulties, both theoretical and practical, that attend attempts to attain equality of educational opportunity and provision. In doing so, we have suggested that failure to achieve it in practice is in part a result of the lack of a clear conception of what in essence we are seeking. We, therefore, began by attempting to attain a clearer notion of equality and immediately were made aware of some of the difficulties that process is fraught with. We were forced to conclude that educational equality is an ideal which, like all ideals, is unattainable in its pure form but that it does, nevertheless, provide us with certain criteria by which we can evaluate the practical provision we make and, in particular, by reference to which we can recognize when we are failing to attain it. Like many of those concepts that derive from political or social philosophy, equality is what some philosophers have called a 'trouser' word; it is something that is interesting and worth talking about only when it is not there. We were thus led to suggest that a more productive approach to this issue might be to identify some of the sources of inequality so that we might work to eradicate them.

For this reason, we went on to examine some possible sources of educational inequalities in the home, in the school system, and in the individual school and classroom. We then considered some of the major innovations that have been introduced into the educational systems of many countries in recent years in the attempt to combat these sources of inequality. In particular, we considered both the theory and the practice of schemes of compensatory education, the comprehensivization of secondary education, and the introduction of mixed-ability grouping. Inevitably, we discovered not only the positive contributions of these devices to the fight against inequality but also some of the problems and difficulties that they themselves in turn have presented us with.

Throughout this discussion, two themes seem to have emerged clearly and vividly, two factors that appear to lie at the heart of the issue. These are the related problems, firstly, of establishing appropriate categories for the making of differentiated educational provision and, secondly, of achieving adequate and fair selection procedures for the allocation of pupils to these categories. We suggested, therefore, that the theoretical difficulties of the former allied to the practical impossibility of the latter rendered this whole process one that must always effectively militate against the achievement of anything remotely approaching the ideal of equality of educational opportunity or provision.

This is a problem which, we have seen, dogs all attempts to achieve equality. It can only be avoided if we cease to look for categories and recognize that every individual is different and entitled to be catered for on his own merits. To say this is not to suggest, of course, that it is an easy process; it is to suggest, however, that it may be a more fruitful way of working towards equality than the provision of two or three or any number of types of curriculum or school or class or any other kind of educational offering.

For this kind of approach may make more readily possible the adapta-

288 Theory and Practice of Education

tion of the content of education to the individual's needs, interests, and requirements. We have seen some of the inequalities that can result from attempts to fit 'off-the-peg' curricula or programmes to all pupils and we have considered some of the demands that pupils should not have an 'alien' culture imposed upon them. All of this would seem to point to the desirability of individually tailored provision. The paradox of equality in education is that it is only when the educational diet of every child is different from that of every other that we can really hope that we are near to achieving it.

10 In Conclusion – The Open School

Most of the issues explored in the earlier chapters of this book have merited exploration by teachers and others concerned with the development of education because they are the result of significant changes that have occurred in recent years, not only in the climate of schools but also in the very fabric of society itself. There are two major features of this change that we must familiarize ourselves with if we are to understand the processes that we are part of and play our roles in them effectively.

The first of these features is that progressive shift towards a greater social and educational egalitarianism which we identified in the preceding chapter and whose implications for educational practice we examined in some detail. The second is the developing sense of freedom that has characterized many societies in the last few decades and which has led to an opening up of many areas of social living, of schools no less than of other social institutions. It is to a brief examination of some of the implications of this development for the practice of education that we must turn in this concluding chapter, not least because it will provide us with a unifying theme that will draw together many of the issues we have looked at in the earlier chapters.

The process we are concerned with is that progressive democratization of society that has resulted in a loosening and an opening up of many social structures. It is a process that educationists should welcome and embrace, since it might be argued, as we ourselves have from time to time argued in our earlier chapters, that education itself is essentially a democratic process which requires of us that we open up the minds of our pupils, so that freedom is an essential element in any educational process worthy of the name. Such developments within society, therefore, may be regarded as totally appropriate to true educational practice. Their precise implications, however, must be picked out.

But first we must consider what they have meant for society itself, since the change we have referred to as occurring in our schools is a reflection of a corresponding change in society. In broad terms, it is a shift from what Durkheim called 'mechanical solidarity' to what he referred to as 'organic solidarity' and its major features have been identified clearly by Basil Bernstein (1967). The concept of organic solidarity implies that the form of social integration within a society is one that emphasizes differences between individuals rather than similarities; these differences between individuals lead to their social roles being *achieved* rather than, as under mechanical solidarity, *ascribed;* and this in turn leads to the development of a differentiated or pluralist society in which not only are social roles diverse but there is a similar diversity of values, whereas 'mechanical solidarity refers to social integration at the level of shared beliefs' (Bernstein, 1967). Such societies, then, are characterized by a high level of individuality, diversity of values, and a greater sense of individual freedom, all of which lead in turn to different patterns of interpersonal relationships and authority structures. In short, this represents a shift towards a more democratic and open society.

Such a shift has implications for all social institutions and schools are no exception to this. Its impact will not, of course, be felt equally in all schools; there may even be some that for a long time will escape it altogether; but in general most will experience a similar shift in their own forms of social integration which will represent the same kind of move from mechanical to organic solidarity, from purity to diversity. This will have many facets of which we shall try to pick out here the most important and those that appear to have special relevance for and to illuminate the issues we have examined in previous chapters.

To begin with, those changes in our approach to the curriculum which we noted in Chapter 8 are examples of this general change we are discussing. The move that we noted there towards new combinations of subjects and various forms of curriculum integration, to a theme- or topic-based curriculum rather than a subject-centred one, reflects, as we suggested there, a freeing of the curriculum for continued development and is thus an especially good instance of the impact of this kind of change on the curriculum. It represents a new approach to curriculum planning in which the subject is no longer dominant but is expected to subserve the interests and the needs of the learner. It thus reflects a new concept of knowledge itself, as we also tried to explain, since it recognizes that knowledge must change and develop and that it must be allowed to change and develop. At another level, it has also led to that emphasis on the development of creative abilities that we discussed in Chapter 3 and to a reduction in the level of insulation between pure and applied studies and thus to a weakening of the boundaries between 'high-status' and 'low-status' knowledge.

The same movement is also apparent in those changes of method that we noted in our discussion of procedures and, especially, of the idea of 'learning by discovery'. 'There is a shift – from a pedagogy which, for the majority of secondary school pupils, was concerned with the learning of standard operations tied to specific contexts – to a pedagogy which emphasizes the exploration of principles; from schools which emphasize the teacher as a solution-giver to schools which emphasize the teacher as a problem-poser or creator' (Bernstein, 1967).

Such changes in the foundations of education must inevitably lead to changes in relationships of all kinds. From time to time throughout this book, but especially in our discussion of equality in the preceding chapter, we have noted how the barriers once erected between different 'types' of pupil, like those between subjects, have been slowly eroded by the introduction of such devices as comprehensive education and mixed-ability groupings. In our discussion of the latter we also noted that it has often led to a greater flexibility of groupings, in the same way as those methodological changes we have just considered. Again, this involves a greater mixing of pupils and entails new kinds of relationship between them, thus leading to that kind of unity in diversity that Basil Bernstein is claiming characterizes the organic solidarity of the open school. The unfortunate consequences of labelling pupils and of placing them in rigid categories have been highlighted in Chapter 2 in our discussion of interpersonal judgements in education.

Relationships between teachers and pupils have also changed, as we discovered when we discussed the nature of classroom interaction in Chapter 1 and also the changing patterns of authority in schools in Chapter 6. New and less formal methods of working will require new, and also less formal, forms of authority and control. There is more to it than that, however, since, as we also noted in Chapter 6, the process of increased democratization that we are describing requires that in schools, as in society, the basis of our authority should be expert rather than positional, so that the teacher must be *an* authority rather than attempt to claim that he stands *in* authority. Again, we might also note with Basil Bernstein that the shift is 'to more personalized forms of control where teachers and taught confront each other as individuals. The forms of social control appeal less to shared values, group loyalties and involvements; they are based rather upon the recognition of differences between individuals' (1967). Some of the implications of this for the moral education of pupils we examined in Chapter 7, while its implications for language in the classroom are discussed in Chapter 5.

There are also implications for relationships within the teaching profession, between teachers and others. Authority patterns there have also changed so that, for example, the headteacher is no longer the unquestioned autocrat he once was in many schools. Changes in the knowledge base of education have also led to a reduction of power for heads of subject departments in schools (Musgrove, 1973), since the subject is no longer sacrosanct and the introduction of some form of integration or new grouping of subjects will necessitate cooperation between departments and thus again will require different kinds of relationship. The change in pedagogy towards less formal methods that we mentioned earlier will require similar adjustments on the part of all teachers. Often such changes in method are accompanied by the introduction of schemes involving some kind of team-teaching; sometimes even the architecture of the school is changed to require that the learning that is to be promoted be tackled in an 'open-plan' way; but, even when this is not formally demanded, doors are opening and teachers are having to learn to work together more often and more closely than before. Lastly, we must note that what we said about the involvement of teachers in evaluation and the role that teachers must play in any system of accountability that is to provide them with a proper professional appraisal of their work will require that teachers get used to working together and accepting constructive criticism from their colleagues. This is why, as we indicated in Chapter 8, the work of the Ford Teaching Project is of such importance, and this is why the notion of school-based in-service education in support of school-based curriculum development must also be fully explored.

Mention of evaluation and accountability brings us naturally to the last aspect of these changing relationshps that are associated with this opening up of our schools. For relationships between teachers and those outside the school have been changing equally dramatically. Recent developments in the United Kingdom, as a result of the Taylor Report (1977) on school management, have brought increased representation of parents on the governing bodies of many schools. In most schools, this has been accompanied by, or even preceded and anticipated by, an opening of the school doors to parents on a scale undreamed-of in the days of the notorious white line in the playground beyond which no parent was to stray without an appointment. Parents are often to be found in the classroom either helping the teacher or merely watching and trying to understand what is going on. Accountability to parents at this personal level is well advanced. The notion of the community school is a natural extension of this, since its major premise is that the school is and should be an integral part of the whole community that it serves and should be seen and used as such by all members of that community. It is thus, incidentally, a concept that is ill-matched to ideas such as that of a centrally determined common curriculum or that of 'bussing' pupils from other neighbouring communities to ensure a complete racial or ability mix in any one school.

Lastly, the demands for the accountability of teachers to society that we examined as part of our discussion of proposals for a common curriculum in Chapter 8 must also bring teachers into new and different relationships with the community outside the school. As we suggested there, teachers can no longer expect to be free to do whatever they wish in schools without offering any explanation or account of what they are doing. To be willing, to be able, or even to be required to offer such justification of their practice will necessitate entering into quite new stances with regard to many outside agencies. But, again as we suggested in Chapter 8, this is also an important, an inevitable and even a welcome development, since again it has to be seen as part of that process of democratization that we have claimed is essential to education in the full sense and which is leading us closer to the realities of the open school.

Summary and conclusions

We have tried in this brief postscript to delineate some of the ways in which the changing face of education that has peered at us through all our earlier discussions is to be seen as the product of major social changes leading towards the emergence of an open society and, within it, open schools. We make no apology except perhaps to Basil Bernstein himself, for relying so heavily in this discussion on that article of his, published now over ten years ago, the full significance of which has become ever clearer as those years have unfolded. For it is perhaps even more important now than it was then that teachers should be aware of what is happening in society and in its schools, so that they can respond appropriately to it and use it to the advancement of education.

To say that is to be reminded of another theme that cannot have been far from the thoughts of anyone who has read this book. The processes we have described and the complex issues we have debated can leave no one in any doubt that the shift that has taken place in educational theory and practice has led to a vast increase in the demands made on the expertise of the teacher, on his professional skills but, above all, on his professional understanding. We are still a long way from establishing, or even recognizing the need for, forms of initial training and the continuing education of teachers that will ensure that they can develop and maintain both those skills and that understanding. The need for skills most people can readily recognize; the need for understanding, although equally, if not more, vital, is less commonly acknowledged. However, the open school, as we hope this chapter has revealed, will require 'open' teachers, teachers who have learned to think for themselves and have recognized the importance of doing so in many areas of education beyond the immediate concerns of their own classrooms, teachers who have come to realize that in any case their work in their own classrooms will be enhanced by the wider understanding that a familiarity with educational theory can give them.

Education theory is not something to be learned and applied in school. As we said in our introducton, we need a far more sophisticated model than this of the relationship between the theory and practice of education. If this book has led teachers and student teachers even one step towards the achievement and appreciation of such a model, its major purpose will have been attained.

BIBLIOGRAPHY

Adams, R. S. and Biddle, D. J.: *Realities of Teaching*, New York, Holt, Rinehart & Winston 1970

Adelman, C. and Walker, R.: Developing Pictures for Other Names. Action Research and Case Study in **Chanan, G. and Delamont, S.:** *Frontiers of Classroom Research*, NFER 1975

Adorno, T. W.; Frenkel-Brunswik, E.; Levinson, D. J. and Sanford, R.N.: *The Authoritarian Personality*, New York, Harper and Row 1960

Allport, G.: *Personality, a Psychological Interpretation*, New York, Holt 1937

Anderson, H. H. and Brewer, H. M.: Studies of Teachers' Classroom Personalities. *Applied Psychological Monographs of the American Association for Applied Psychology*, Stanford University Press 1946

Archambault, R. D. (ed.): *Philosophical Analysis and Education*, London, Routledge and Kegan Paul, 1965

Argyle, M.: *The Psychology of Interpersonal Behaviour*, Harmondsworth, Penguin 1967

Aristotle: *Politics*

Asch, S. E.: Forming Impressions of Personality in *Journal of Abnormal and Social Psychology* 1946

Ashton, P.; Kneen, P. and Davies, F.: *Aims into Practice in the Primary School*, London, University of London Press 1975

Ashton, P.: *The Aims of Primary Education: A Study of Teachers' Opinions*, London, Macmillan 1975

Ayer, A. J.: *Language, Truth and Logic*, 1936; 2nd edition 1946, London, Gollancz

Bailey, C.: Knowledge of Others and Concern for Others in **Elliott, J. and Pring, R.:** *Social Education and Social Understanding*, London, University of London Press 1975

Ball, C. and Ball, M.: *Education for a Change* Harmondsworth, Penguin 1973

Bandura, A. and Walters, R. H.: *Social Learning and Personality Development*, New York, Holt, Rinehart & Winston 1970

Banks, O.: *The Sociology of Education*, London, Batsford 1968

Bantock, G. H.: Towards a Theory of Popular Education in **Hooper, R.** (ed): *The Curriculum*, Oliver and Boyd with Oxford University Press 1971

Barker-Lunn, J. C.: *Streaming in the Primary School*, NFER 1970

Barnes, D. *et al.: Language, the Learner and the School*, Harmondsworth, Penguin 1971

Barnes D. *et al.:* From *Communication to Curriculum*, Harmondsworth, Penguin 1976

Barrish, H.: Saunders, M. and Wolf, M.: The Good Behaviour Game, *Journal of Applied Behaviour Analysis* 1969

Becker H. S.: Social Class Variations in the Teacher-Pupil Relationship in *School and Society* Cosin, B. (ed), London, Routledge & Kegan Paul with Oxford University Press

Becker, H. S.: Personal Change in Adult Life, *Sociometry* 1964. Reprinted in *School and Society, op. cit.*

Becker, W. C.; Madsden, C.; Arnold, C. R. and Thomas, D.: The Contingent Use of Teacher Attention and Praise in Reducing Classroom Behaviour Problems, *Journal of Special Education* 1967

Benn, S. I. and Peters, R. S.: *Social Principles and the Democratic State*, London, Allen and Unwin 1959

Bennett, S. N.: *Teaching Styles and Pupil Progress*, London, Open Books 1976

Bereiter, C. and Engelmann D.: *Teaching Disadvantaged Children in the Pre-School*, New Jersey, Prentice-Hall 1966

Berger, P. L.; and Luckman, T.: *The Social Construction of Reality*, London, Penguin 1967

Berko, J : The Child's Learning of English Morphology, *Word*, Vol. 14, 1958

Berlyne, D. E.: *Conflict, Arousal and Curiosity*, New York, McGraw-Hill 1960

Bernstein, B.: Open Schools, Open Society? *New Society*, 14 September 1967

Bernstein, B.: *Education Cannot Compensate for Society in Language and Education*, (ed) Cashdan, S., (ed.) London, Routledge & Kegan Paul with Oxford University Press 1972

Bernstein, B., and Hedenon, D.: Social Class Differences in the Relevance of Language to Socialization, *Sociology* 1969

Bernstein, B.: *Class, Codes and Control*, London, Routledge & Kegan Paul 1971

Bexton, W. H. *et al.:* Effects of Decreased Variation in the Sensory Environment, *Canadian Journal of Psychology* 1954

Bigge, M. L. and Hunt, M.P.: *Psychological Foundations of Education*, New York, Harper & Row 1962

Binet, A. & Simon, T.: *The Development of Intelligence in Children*, Baltimore, Williams & Wilkins 1916

Blank, M. and Solomon, F.: A Tutorial Language Programme to Develop Abstract Thinking in Socially Disadvantaged School Children, *Child Development* 1968

Bloom, B. S.: *Stability and Change in Human Characteristics*, New York, Wiley 1960

Bloom, B. S. (ed): *A Taxonomy of Educational Objectives*, London, Longman 1964, Vol 1 (1956), Vol 2 (1964)

Blum, A. F.: The Corpus of Knowledge as a Normative Order in **Young, M.** (ed): *Knowledge and Control*, New York, Collier MacMillan 1971

Blyth, W. A. L.: One Development Project's Awkward Thinking about Objectives, *Journal of Curriculum Studies* 1974

Bobbitt, F.: *The Curriculum*, Boston, Houghton Mifflin 1918

Britton, J.: *Language and Learning*, Harmondsworth, Penguin 1970

Bronfenbrenner, V.: The Changing American Child, *Journal of Social Issues* 1961

Brown, R. and Bellugi, V.: Three Processes in the Child's Acquisition of Syntax, *Harvard Educational Review* 1964

Bruner, J. et al.: *Studies in Cognitive Growth*, New York, Wiley 1966

Bruner, J. et al.: The Act of Discovery, *Harvard Educational Review* 1961

Bruner, J. et al.: *The Process of Education*, New York, Vintage Books 1960

Bull, N,.: *Moral Judgment from Childhood to Adolescence*, London, Routledge & Kegan Paul 1969

Burstall, C.: French in Primary Schools: Research Project, *New Research in Education* 1967

Burt, C.: *The Backward Child*, London, University of London Press 1937

Burt, C.: The Evidence for the Concept of Intelligence, *British Journal of Educational Psychology* 1975

Burt, C.: The Genetic Determination of Differences in Intelligence, *British Journal of Psychology* 1966

Cashdan, A. and Grugeon, E.: *Language in Education*, London, Routledge & Kegan Paul with Oxford University Press 1972

Cashdan, A., and Whitehead, Z.: *Personality Theory and Learning*, London, Routledge and Kegan Paul 1971

Cazden, C. B.: Environmental Assistance to the Child's Acquisition of Grammar referred to by **Slobin, D. I.** in **Endler, N. S.; Boulter, L. R. and Osser, H.** (eds): *Contemporary Issues in Developmental Psychology*, New York, Holt, Rinehart & Winston 1968

Chanan, G., and Delamont, S.: *Frontiers of Classroom Research*, F E R 1975

Charters, W. W.: *Curriculum Construction*, New York, MacMillan 1924

Chomsky, N.: Review of Skinner's Verbal Behaviour, *Language* 1959

Chulliat, R. and Oleron, P.: The Role of Language in Transposition Tasks referred to in **Lawton, D.**: *Social Class, Language and Education*, London, Routledge & Kegan Paul 1968

Churchill, E.: The Number Concepts of the Very Young Child, *Leeds University Research Studies*, Nos 17 & 18 1958

Cicourel, A. V. and Kitsuse, J..: The Social Organisation of the High School and Deviant Adolescent Careers in **Cosin, B.** *et al.* (eds) 1971, *op. cit.*

Coard, B.: *How the West Indian Child is Made Educationally Subnormal in the British School System*, New Beacon Books 1971

Coopersmith, B.: *The Antecedents of Self-Esteem*, Freemantle 1967

Cosin, B. *et al.* (eds).: *School and Society*, London, Routledge & Kegan Paul with Oxford University Press 1971

Coulthard, M.: A Discussion of Restricted and Elaborated Codes, *Educational Review* 1969

Cronbach, L.: Course Improvement Through Education, *Teachers' College Record* 1963

Crosland, A.: Some Thoughts on English Education, *Encounter* 1961

Dahrendorf, R.: On the Origin of Social Inequality in **Laslett, P. and Runciman, W. G.** (eds) *Philosophy, Politics and Society*, 2nd series, Oxford, Blackwell 1962

Daniels, J. C.: The Effects of Streaming in the Primary School: A Comparison of Streamed and Unstreamed Schools, *British Journal of Educational Psychology* 1961

Daniels, J. C.: The Effects of Streaming in the Primary School: What Teachers Believe, *British Journal of Educational Psychology* 1961

Dearden, R. F.: *Philosophy of Primary Education*, London, Routledge & Kegan Paul 1968

Dearden, R. F.: Instruction and Learning by Discovery, in **Peters, R. S.** (ed): *The Concept of Education*, London, Routledge & Kegan Paul 1967

Degenhardt, M. A.: Creativity in **Lloyd, D. I.**: *Philosophy and the Teacher*, London, Routledge & Kegan Paul 1976

Delamont, S.: *Interaction in the Classroom*, London, Methuen 1976

Delamont, S.: Beyond Flanders' Fields: The Relationship of Subject Matter and Individuality to Classroom Style in **Stubbs, M. and Delamont, S.** (eds): *Explorations in Classroom Observation*, New York, Wiley 1976

Dewey, J.: *Experience and Education*, London, Macmillan 1938

Downey, M. E.: *Interpersonal Judgments in Education*, London, Harper & Row 1977

Downey, M. E. and Kelly, A. V.: *Moral Education: Theory and Practice*, London, Harper & Row 1978

Dumont, R. V. and Wax, L. M.: Cherokee School Society and the Intercultural Classroom, 1969, in **Cosin, B.** (ed), *op. cit.*, 1971

Dunham, J.: Appropriate Leadership Patterns, *Educational Research* 1964

Easthope, G.: *Community, Hierarchy and Open Education*, London, Routledge & Kegan Paul 1975

Eisner, E. W.: Instructional and Expressive Educational Objectives: Their Formulation and Use in Curriculum in **Popham** *et al.*, 1969

Elkind, D.: *Children and Adolescents*, London, Oxford University Press 1970

Elliott, J. and Adelman, C.: Innovation in Teaching and Action-Research, Norwich Centre of Applied Research in Education 1974

Elliott, J. and Pring, R.: *Social Education and Social Understanding*, London, University of London Press 1975

Elliott, R. K.: The Concept of Creativity in *Proceedings of the Philosophy of Education Society of Great Britain* 1971

Endler, N. S.; Boulter, L. R. and Osser, H. (eds): *Contemporary Issues in Developmental Psychology*, New York, Holt, Rinehart & Winston 1968

Esland, G. M.: Teaching and Learning as the Organisation of Knowledge in **Young, M. F.**, *op. cit.*

Etzioni, A.: *A Comparative Analysis of Complex Organisations*, New York, Free Press 1961

Ewing, A. W. C. (ed).: *Educational Guidance and the Deaf Child*, Manchester, Manchester University Press 1957

Eysenck, H. J.: *Race, Intelligence and Education*, London, Temple Smith 1971

Ferri, E.: *Streaming: Two Years Later*, NFER 1972

Flanders, N. A.: *Analysing Teacher Behaviour*, New York, Addison-Wesley 1970

Flavell, J. H.: *The Developmental Psychology of Jean Piaget*, New York, Van Nostrand Reinhold 1963

Flew, A.: The Justification of Punishment, *Philosophy* 1954

Frank, R.: referred to in **Bruner, J.** *op. cit.*, 1966

Fraser, C.; Bellugi, V. and Brown, R.: Control of Grammar in Imitation, Comprehension and Production, *Journal of Verbal Learning and Verbal Behaviour* 1963 Reprinted in **Oldfield, R. C. and Marshall, J. C.** (eds): *Language*, Harmondsworth, Penguin 1968

Freire, P.: *Pedagogy of the Oppressed*, Harmondsworth, Penguin 1972

Frenkel-Brunswik, E. and Sanford, R. N.: The Anti-Semitic Personality: A Research Report in **Simmel, E.** (ed): *Anti-Semitism: A Social Disease*, New York, International Universities Press 1948

Fromm, E.: *The Fear of Freedom*, London, Routledge & Kegan Paul 1942

Fuchs, E.: How Teachers Learn to Help Children Fail, *Transactions* 1968 Reprinted in **Keddie, N.**: *Tinker tailor ... the Myth of Cultural Deprivation*, Harmondsworth, Penguin 1973

Furlong, V.: Interaction Sets in the Classroom: Towards a Study of Pupil Knowledge in **Stubbs, M. and Delamont, S.** (eds) *op. cit.* 1976

Furlong, V.: Anancy Goes to School: A Case Study of Pupils' Knowledge of Their Teachers in **Woods, P. and Hammersley, M.:** *School Experience*, London, Croom Helm 1977

Furth, H.: *Thinking Without Language*, New York, Collier-Macmillan 1966

Gahagan, D. M. and Gahagan, G. A.: *Talk Reform*, London, Routledge & Kegan Paul 1970

Galton, M. J. *et al.*: *Processes and Products of Science Teaching*, London, Macmillan 1976

Getzels, J. W. and Jackson, P. W.: *Creativity and Intelligence*, New York, Wiley 1962

Gibbins, K.: Communication Aspects of Women's Clothes and Their Relation to Fashion Ability, *British Journal of Social and Clinical Psychology* 1967

Giles, H.: Our Reactions to Accent, *New Society* 1971

Gill, C. J.: Counselling in Schools, *Trends in Education* 1967

Gleeson, D. and Whitty, G.: *Developments in Social Studies Teaching*, London, Open Books 1976

Goffman, E.: *The Presentation of Self in Everyday Life*, 1959, Harmondsworth, Penguin 1971

Goldman, R.: Researches in Religious Thinking, *Educational Research* 1964

Goodacre, E.: Teachers and Their Pupils' Home Background, NFER 1968

Green, L.: Should Parents Report Too?, *Where?* No.20, Spring 1965

Greenfield, P. M.: On Culture and Conservation in **Bruner, J.** *op. cit.*, 1966

Guilford, J. P.: Traits of Creativity in **Vernon, P. E.** (ed).: *Creativity*, Harmondsworth, Penguin 1970

Guilford, J. P.: Creativity, *American Psychologist* 1950. Reprinted in **Cashdan,** (ed): *Personality Growth and Learning*, London, Longman with Oxford University Press 1972

Haddon, F. A. and Lytton, H.: Teaching Approach and the Development of Divergent Thinking Abilities in Primary Schools, *British Journal of Educational Psychology* 1968

Haddon, F. A. and Lytton, H.: Teaching Approach and Divergent Thinking Abilities – 4 Years On, *British Journal of Educational Psychology* 1971

Hallam, R.: Piaget and the Teaching of History, *Educational Research* 1969

Hallam, R.: Piaget and Moral Judgments in History, *Educational Research* 1969

Halsey, A. H.: *Educational Priority*, D.E.S. and Social Science Research Council 1972

Halsey, A. H.: Government Against Poverty in School and Community in **Wedderburn, D.:** *Poverty, Inequality and Class Structure*, Cambridge, Cambridge University Press 1974

Hamilton, D.: *Curriculum Evaluation*, London, Open Books 1976

Hamlyn, D. W.: Objectivity in **Dearden, R. F.; Hirst, P. H. and Peters, R. S.** (eds): *Reason*, London, Routledge & Kegan Paul 1972

Hamblin, D.: *The Teacher and Counselling*, Oxford, Blackwell 1974

Hare, R. M.: Adolescents into Adults in **Hollins,** *op. cit.*, 1964

Hargreaves, D. H.: *Social Relations in a Secondary School*, London, Routledge & Kegan Paul 1967

Hargreaves, D. H.: *Interpersonal Relations in Education*, London, Routledge & Kegan Paul 1972

Harrell, R. F.: *The Effect of Mothers Diet on the Intelligence of the Offspring*, New York Teachers' College 1955

Harris, A.; Lawn, M. and Prescott, W. (eds): *Curriculum Innovation*, London Croom Helm 1975

Harris, C. N.: Some Issues in Evaluation, *The Speech Teacher* 1963

Hartshorne, H. and May, M. A.: *Studies in the Nature of Character*, London, Macmillan 1908–30

Hasan, P. and Butcher, H. J.: Creativity and Intelligence: A Partial Replication with Scottish Children of Getzels' and Jackson's Study, *British Journal of Psychology* 1966

Hawkins, P. R.: Social Class, the Nominal Group and Reference, *Language and Speech* 1969

Hebb, D. O.: *The Organisation of Behaviour*, New York, Wiley 1949

Hirst, P. H.: A Liberal Education and the Nature of Knowledge in **Archambault, R. D.** (ed): *Philosophical Analysis and Education*, London, Routledge & Kegan Paul 1965

Hirst, P. H.: The Logic of the Curriculum, *Journal of Curriculum Studies* 1969

Hirst, P. H.: and Peters, R. S.: *The Logic of Education*, London, Routledge & Kegan Paul 1970

Hirst, P. H.: The Curriculum and Its Objectives – a Defence of Piecemeal National Planning in *Studies in Education – 2*, The Curriculum – The Doris Lee Lectures, London, University of London Press 1975.

Hogben, D.: The Behavioural Objectives Approach: Some Problems and Some Dangers, *Journal of Curriculum Studies* 1972

Hollins, T. H. B. (ed).: *Aims in Education: The Philosophic Approach*, Manchester, Manchester University Press, 1964

Holly, D.: *Beyond Curriculum*, St Albans, Hart David MacGibbon 1973

Holt, J.: *How Children Fail*, Harmondsworth, Penguin 1964

Homme, L. E. and Addison, R. M.: The Reinforcing Event Menu, in *National Society of Programmed Instruction* 1966

Hooper, R. (ed): *The Curriculum: Context, Design and Development*, Edinburgh, Oliver and Boyd with Oxford University Press 1971

Hoyle, E.: How Does the Curriculum Change? a Proposal for Inquiries, *Journal of Curriculum Studies* 1969. Also in **Hooper, R.,** *op. cit.*

Hudson, L.: *Contrary Imaginations,* Harmondsworth, Penguin 1966

Hunt, J. McV.: Using Intrinsic Motivation to Teach Young Children. Reprinted in **Cashdan, A. and Whitehead, J.** (eds), *op. cit.*

Inhelder, B. & Piaget, J.: *The Growth of Logical Thinking from Childhood to Adolescence,* Basic Books 1958

Jackson, B.: *Streaming: An Education System in Miniature,* London, Routledge & Kegan Paul 1964

Jackson, B., and Manda, I.: *Education and the Working Class,* London, Routledge and Kegan Paul 1962

Jackson, P. W. and Messick, S.: The Person, the Product and the Response.: Conceptual Problems in the Assessment of Creativity, *British Journal of Educational Psychology* 1969

Jackson, S.: Those Bad School Reports, *Where?* No. 54, February, 1971

Jahoda, G.: The Development of Children's Ideas About Country and Nationality, *British Journal of Educational Psychology* 1963

James, C. M.: *Young Lives at Stake,* London, Collins 1968

Jensen, A. R.: How Much Can We Boost I.Q. and Scholastic Achievement?, *Harvard Educational Review* 1969. Reprinted in **Eysenck, H.** *op. cit.,* 1971

Jones, J.: Social Class and the Under-5's, *New Society* 1966

Jones, R. M.: *Fantasy and Feeling in Education,* Harmondsworth, Penguin 1972

Kagan, J., et al.: *Child Development and Personality,* London, Harper & Row 1967

Kahl, J.: Some Measurements of Achievement Orientation, *American Journal of Sociology* 1965

Kay, W.: *Moral Development,* London, Allen and Unwin 1968

Keddie, N.: Classroom Knowledge in **Young, M. F. D.** (ed): *Knowledge and Control,* New York, Collier Macmillan 1971

Kelley, H. H.: The Warm-Cold Variable in First Impressions of Persons, *Journal of Personality* 1950

Kellmer-Pringle, M. L. and Edwards, J. B.: Some Moral Concepts and Judgments of Junior School Children, *Journal of Social and Clinical Psychology* 1964

Kelly, A. V. (ed): *Case Studies in Mixed Ability Grouping,* London, Harper & Row 1975

Kelly, A. V.: *The Curriculum: Theory and Practice,* London, Harper & Row 1977

Kelly, A. V.: *Mixed-Ability Grouping: Theory and Practice* (2nd edition), London, Harper & Row 1978

Kelly, G. A.: *The Psychology of Personal Constructs*, New York, Norton 1955

Kelly, P. J.: Nuffield 'A' Level Biological Science Project, Schools Council 1972

Kerr, J. F. (ed): *Changing the Curriculum*, London, University of London Press 1968

Klein, S. S.: Student Influence On Teacher Behaviour, *American Education Research Journal* 1971

Kluckholn, F. R. and Strodtbeck, F. L.: *Variations in Value Orientations*, Row Peterson 1961

Kohlberg, L.: Moral Education in the Schools, *School Review* 1966

Komisar, B. P.: Need and the Needs-Curriculum in **Smith, O. B. and Ennis, R. H.:** *Language and Concepts in Education*, New York, Rand McNally 1961

Labov, W.: The Logic of Non-Standard English, 1969. Reprinted in **Cashdan, A. and Grugeon, E.,** (eds) *op. cit.* 1972

Lacey, C.: *Hightown Grammar: The School as a Social System*, Manchester, Manchester University Press 1970

Lawton, D.: Social Science in Schools, *New Society*, 25 April 1968

Lawton, D.: *Social Class, Language and Education*, London, Routledge & Kegan Paul 1968

Lawton D.: *Social Change, Educational Theory and Curriculum Planning*, London, University of London Press, 1973

Lawton, D.: *Class, Culture and the Curriculum*, London, Routledge & Kegan Paul 1975

Lewin, K.; Lippitt, R. and White, R. K.: Patterns of Aggressive Behaviour in Experimentally Cleared Social Climates, *Journal of Social Psychology* 1939

Lewin, K. *et al.*: Level of Aspiration in **Hunt, J. McV.** (ed): *Personality and Behaviour Disorders*, Ronald Press 1944

Little, A. and Westergaard, J.: The Trend of Class Differentials in Educational Opportunity in England and Wales, *British Journal of Sociology* 1964

Locke, J.: *Second Treatise on Civil Government*, paragraph 6

Lovell, K.: *The Growth of Basic Mathematical and Scientific Concepts in Children*, London, University of London Press 1961

Lucas, J. R.: Against Equality, *Philosophy* 1965

Luchins, A. S.: *Primary-recency in Impression Formation in Order of Presentation in Persuasion*, New Haven, Yale University Press 1959

Luria, A. R.: *Speech and the Development of Mental Processes in the Child* (U.S.S.R. 1956), St Albans, Crusby Luckward Staples 1959

Luria, A. R.: The Directive Function of Speech in Development and Dissolution, *Word*, 1959 Reprinted in **Cashdan, A.** (ed) *op. cit.*, 1972

Luria, A. R.: *The Role of Speech in the Regulation of Normal and Abnormal Behaviour*, Oxford, Pergamon Press 1961

MacDonald, B.: Humanities Curriculum Project (1973) in *Schools Council* 1973

MacDonald, B.: Evaluation and Control of Education in **Tawney,** 1975

MacDonald, B. and Walker, R.: *Changing the Curriculum*, London, Open Books 1976

MacIntyre, A. and Nowell-Smith, P. H.: Purpose and Intelligent Action, *Proceedings of the Aristotelian Society*, Supplement 1970

MacIntyre, A. C.: Against Utilitarianism in **Hollins** *op. cit.*, 1964

Mager, R. F.: *Preparing Instructional Objectives*, Belmont-Feason 1962

Marland, M.: *Language Across the Curriculum*, London, Heinemann 1977

Maslow, A. H.: *Motivation and Personality*, New York, Harper & Row 1954

McCelland, D. C. *et al.*: *The Achievement Motive*, Appleton-Century-Crofts, New York 1953

McIntyre, D.; Morrison, A. and Sutherland, J.: Social and Educational Variables Relating to Teachers' Assessment of Primary School Children, *British Journal of Educational Psychology* 1966

McNeill, D.: The Creation of Language, *Discovery* 1966. Reprinted in **Cashdan, A.** *op. cit.*, 1972

McPhail, P.; Ungoed-Thomas, J. R. and Chapman, H.: *Moral Education in the Secondary School*, London, Longmans 1972

Mead, G. H.: see **Blumer, H.** Sociological Implications of the Thoughts of G. H. Mead, in *American Journal of Sociology*, 1965

Merrett, F. and Wheldall, K.: Playing the Game; a Behavioural Approach to Classroom Management in the Junior School, *Educational Review* 1978

Merson, W. W. and Campbell, R. J.: Community Education: Instruction for Inequality, *Education for Teaching* 1974

Midwinter, E.: *Priority Education*, Harmondsworth, Penguin 1972

Mill, J. S.: *On Liberty*

Miller, N. E. and Dollard, J.: *Social Learning and Imitation*, New Haven, Yale University Press 1941

Moreno, J. L.: Who Shall Survive?, Washington, Nervous and Mental Disease Monograph, Series No. 58, 1934

Mowrer, O. H.: *Learning Theory and the Symbolic Process*, New York, Wiley 1970

Musgrove, F.: Power and the Integrated Curriculum, *Journal of Curriculum Studies* 1973

Musgrove, F. and Taylor, P. H.: *Society and the Teacher's Role*, London, Routledge & Kegan Paul 1969

Nash, R.: Pupils' Expectations of Their Teachers, *Research in Education* 1974

Nash, R.: *Classrooms Observed*, London, Routledge & Kegan Paul 1973

Natadze, R. G.: The Mastery of Scientific Concepts in School in **Simon, B. & J.:** *Educational Psychology in the USSR*, London, Routledge & Kegan Paul 1963

Newman, H. H.; Freeman, R. N. and Holzinger, K. J.: *Twins: A Study of Heredity and Environment*, Chicago, Chicago University Press 1937

Newbold, D.: *Ability Grouping; the Banbury Inquiry*, NFER 1977

Observer: November 5, 1978

O'Connor, D. J.: *An Introduction to the Philosophy of Education*, London, Routledge & Kegan Paul 1957

Oléron, P.: Conceptual Thinking of the Deaf, *American Annals of the Deaf* 1959. Reprinted in **Adams, P.** (ed): *Language in Thinking*, Harmondsworth, Penguin 1972

Page, E. B.: Teacher Comments and Student Performance, *Journal of Educational Psychology* 1958

Palfrey, C. F.: Headteachers' Expectations and Their Pupils' Self Concepts, *Educational Research* 1973

Parlett, M. and Hamilton, D.: Evaluation and Illumination in **Tawney,** 1973

Parry, M.: *Preschool Education*, London, Macmillan 1975

Parry, M. and Archer, H.: *Two to Five*, London, Macmillan 1975

Peel, E. A.: Understanding School Material, *Educational Review* 1972

Peters, R. S. 1965: Education as Initiation in **Archambault** *op. cit.*, 1965

Peters, R. S.: *Authority, Responsibility and Education*, London, Allen and Unwin 1959

Peters, R. S.: *Ethics and Education*, London, Allen and Unwin 1966

Peters, R. S.: *Reason and Compassion*, London, Routledge & Kegan Paul, 1973

Peters, R. S. (ed): *Aims of Education: A Conceptual Inquiry in the Philosophy of Education*, London, Oxford University Press 1973

Phenix, P. H.: *Realms of Meaning*, New York, McGraw-Hill 1964

Piaget, J.: *The Moral Judgment of the Child* (1932), London, Routledge & Kegan Paul 1960

Piaget, J.: *Language and Thought of the Child*, 2nd edition 1959, London, Routledge & Kegan Paul 1960

Piaget, J.: *The Origins of Intelligence in Children*, New York, International Universities Press 1952

Piaget, J.: *The Psychology of Intelligence*, New York, Harcourt Brace 1950

Pidgeon, D. A.: *Expectation and Pupil Performance*, NFER 1970

Plato: *Republic*

Popham, W. J.; Eisner, E. W.; Sullivan, H. J. and Tyler, L. L.: Instructional Objectives, *American Educational Research Association Monograph Series on Curriculum Evaluation*, No. 3, Chicago 1969

Popham, W. J.: Objectives and Instruction in **Popham** *et al., op. cit.*, 1969

Popper, K. R.: *The Open Society and Its Enemies*, London, Routledge & Kegan Paul 1945

Premack, D.: Reinforcement Theory in **Levine, D.:** *Nebraska Symposium on Motivation*, University of Nebraska Press 1965

Pring, R. A.: Bloom's Taxonomy: A Philosophical Critique, *Cambridge Journal of Education* 1971

Pring, R. A.: Objectives and Innovation: The Irrelevance of Theory, *London Education Review* 1973

Pring, R. A.: Socialisation as an Aim of Education in **Elliott, J. and Pring, R. A.** *op. cit.*, 1975

Prior, A.: The Place of Maps in the Junior School, Birmingham University dissertation 1959

Quinton, A. M.: On Punishment in **Laslett, P.** (ed) *Philosophy, Politics and Society* 1st Series, Oxford, Blackwell 1963

Richards, C.: Third Thoughts on Discovery, *Educational Review* 1973

Riessman, F.: *The Culturally Deprived Child*, New York, Harper & Row 1962

Rist, R. C.: Student Social Class and Teacher Expectations. The Self-Fulfilling Prophecy in Ghetto Education, *Harvard Education Review* 1970

Robinson, W. P. and Rackstraw, S. J.: Variations in Mothers' Answers to Children's Questions as a Function of Social Class, Verbal Intelligence Test Scores and Sex, *Sociology* 1967

Rosen, B. C.: The Achievement Syndrome: A Psychocultural Dimension of Social Stratification, *American Sociological Review* 1956

Rosen, H.: The Language of Text-Books in **Britton, J.** (ed): *Talking and Writing*, London, Methuen 1967

Rosen, H.: *Language and Class: A Critical Look at the Theories of Basil Bernstein*, Talking Wall Press, 1972

Rosenthal, R. and Jacobson, L.: *Pygmalion in the Classroom*, New York, Holt, Rinehart & Winston 1968

Rousseau, J. J.: *Emile*

Roussel, G. D.: The Open Report and Its History, *Comprehensive Education* No. 25, 1973

Rudd, W. G. A.: The Psychological Effects of Streaming by Attainment, *British Journal of Educational Psychology* 1958

Ryan, A.: Freedom, *Philosophy* 1965

Ryle, G.: *Concept of Mind*, London, Hutchinson 1967

Sapir, E. in **Mandelbaum, D. G.** (ed): *Selected Writings of E. Sapir*, Berkeley, University of California Press 1949

Sartre, J. P.: *Being and Nothingness*, London, Methuen 1957

Schofield, A. J.: Pastoral Care and the Curriculum of a Comprehensive School, unpublished MA dissertation, University of London 1977

Schon, D. A.: *Beyond the Stable State,* London, Temple-Smith 1971

Schools Council: Working Paper No. 2: *Raising the School Leaving Age,* HMSO 1965

Schools Council: Working Paper No. 11.: *Society and the Young School Leaver,* HMSO 1967

Schools Council: Working Paper No. 27.: *Cross'd with Adversity,* London, Evans/Methuen 1970

Schools Council: *The Humanities Project: An Introduction,* London, Heinemann 1970

Schools Council.: *Education in Curriculum Development: Twelve Case Studies, Schools Council Research Studies,* London, Macmillan 1973

Schools Council.: *Social Education: An Experiment in Four Secondary Schools:* Working Paper No. 51, London, Evans/Methuen 1974

Schutz, A.: *Collected Papers,* Vol. I, Nijhoff 1962

Secord, B.: The Role of Facial Features in Interpersonal Perception in **Tagiuri, R. and Petrullo, L.** (eds): *Person Perception and Interpersonal Behaviour,* Stanford, Stanford University Press 1958

Shipman, M.: Curriculum for Inequality? In **Hooper, R.** *op. cit.,* 1971

Shipman, M.: Contrasting Views of a Curriculum Project, *Journal of Curriculum Studies* 1972

Sigel, I. E.; Roeper, A. and Hooper, F. H.: A Training Procedure for the Acquisition of Piaget's Conservation of Quantity, *British Journal of Educational Psychology* 1966

Sinclair de Zwart, H.: Developmental Psycholinguistics in **Elkind, D. and Flavell, J.** (eds) *Studies in Cognitive Development,* London, Oxford University Press 1969

Skinner, B. F.: *Verbal Behaviour,* New York, Appleton-Century Crofts 1957

Skinner, B. F.: *The Technology of Teaching,* New York, Appleton-Century Crofts 1968

Sockett, H.: Aims and Objectives in a Social Education Curriculum in **Elliott, J. and Pring, R.** *op. cit.,* 1975

Sockett, H.: *Designing the Curriculum,* London, Open Books 1976

Stake, R.: Analysis and Portrayal. Paper originally written for AERA Annual Meeting Presentation 1972. Republished as Responsive Education in *New Trends in Education,* Institute of Education, University of Goteborg, No. 55, 1974

Stenhouse, L.: *An Introduction to Curriculum Research and Development,* London, Heinemann 1975

Stenhouse, L.: Some Limitations of the Use of Objectives in Curriculum Research and Planning, *Pedagogica Europaea* 1970

Stebbins, R. A.: The Meaning of Disorderly Behaviour: Reader Definitions of a Classroom Situation, *Sociology of Education* 1971

Stoch, M.B.: The Effect of Undernutrition During Infancy on Subsequent Brain Growth and Intellectual Development, *South African Medical Journal* 1967

Stott, D. H.: Commentary on 'The Genetic Determination of Differences in Intelligence; A Study of Monozygotic Twins Reared Together and Apart, *British Journal of Psychology* 1966

Stott, D. H. and Albin, J. B.: Confirmation of a General Factor of Effectiveness-Motivation by Individual Tests, *British Journal of Educational Psychology* 1975

Stott, D. H. and Sharp, J.: Effectiveness Motivation Scale publication pending

Strongman, K. T. and Hart, C. J.: Stereotyped Reactions to Body Build, *Psychological Reports* 1968

Stubbs, M.: Teaching and Talking in **Chanan, G. and Delamont, S.** (eds) *op. cit.*, 1975

Stubbs, M.: *Language, Schools and Classrooms*, London, Methuen 1976

Stubbs, M.: Keeping in Touch: Some Functions of Teacher Talk in **Stubbs, M. and Delamont, S.** (eds) *op. cit.*, 1976

Stubbs, M. and Delamont, S., (eds.): *Explorations in Classroom Observation*, New York, Wiley 1976

Sugarman, N.: *The School and Moral Development*, London, Croom Helm 1973

Swift, D. F.: Social Class and Achievement Motivation, *Educational Research* 1966

Taba, H.: *Curriculum Development: Theory and Practice*, New York, Harcourt Brace Jovanovich 1962

Tawney, D.: Evaluation and Curriculum Development in **Schools Council,** 1973

Tawney, D. (ed): *Curriculum Evaluation Today: Trends and Implications*, Schools Council Research Studies, London, Macmillan 1975

Taylor, P. H.: Children's Evaluations of the Characteristics of the Good Teacher, *British Journal of Educational Psychology* 1962

Taylor, P. H.: *Curriculum Planning for Compensatory Education: A Suggested Procedure*, London Schools Council 1970

Thibaut, J. W. and Riecken, A. W.: Some Determinants and Consequences of the Perception of Social Causality, *Journal of Personality* 1955

Thompson, K. B.: *Education and Philosophy*, London, Blackwell 1972

Torrance, E. P.: Education and Creativity in **Taylor, O. W.** (ed): *Creativity: Progress and Potential*, New York, McGraw-Hill 1964

Torrance, E. P.: Give the Devil His Dues in **Gowan, J. C.** *et al.* (eds): *Creativity: Its Educational Implications*, New York, Wiley 1967

Tough, J.: *Focus on Meaning*, London, Allen and Unwin 1973

Tough, J.: *The Development of Meaning*, London, Allen and Unwin 1977

Tough, J.: *Listening to Children Talking*, London, Ward Lock 1976

Tough, J.: *Talking and Learning*, London, Ward Lock 1977

Tyler, R. W.: *Basic Principles of Curriculum and Instruction*, Chicago, University of Chicago Press 1949

Vernon, P. E.: *Intelligence and Cultural Environment*, London, Methuen 1969

Vigotsky, L.: *Thought and Language*, Cambridge, Mass,. M.I.T. Press 1962

Vincent, M.: The Performance of Deaf and Hearing Children on a Classifying Task, referred to in **Lawton, D.** *op. cit.*, 1968

Walker, R. and Adelman, C.: Strawberries in **Stubbs, M. and Delamont, S.**: *Explorations in Classroom Observation, op. cit.*, 1976

Walker, R.: *A Guide to Classroom Observation*, London, Methuen 1975

Walker, R. and Goodson, I.: Humour in the Classroom in **Woods, P. and Hammersley, M.** *op. cit.*, 1977

Warwick, D. (ed): *Integrated Studies in the Secondary School* London, University of London Press 1973

Watson, P.: Can Racial Discrimination Affect I.Q.? in **Richardson, D.** *et al.* (eds) *Race, Culture and Intelligence*, Harmondsworth, Penguin 1972

Weber, M.: *Theory of Social and Economic Organisation*, London, Oxford University Press 1947

Wechsler, D.: The Measurement of Adult Intelligence Testing and the Theory of Intelligence, *British Journal of Educational Psychology* 1959

Weldon, T. D.: *The Vocabulary of Politics*, Harmondsworth, Penguin 1953

Werthman, C.: Delinquents in Schools, 1963 in **Cosin, B.** *et al. op. cit.*, 1971

West, E. G.: Liberty and Education: John Stuart Mill's Dilemma, *Philosophy* 1965

Wheeler, D. K.: *Curriculum Process*, London, University of London Press 1967

White, J. P.: Instruction in Obedience, *New Society* 1968

White, J. P.: The Curriculum Mongers: Education in Reverse in **Hooper, R.** *op. cit.*, 1971

White, J. P.: *Towards a Compulsory Curriculum*, London, Routledge & Kegan Paul 1973

White, J. P.: The Concept of Curriculum Evaluation, *Journal of Curriculum Studies* 1971

White, R. K. and Lippitt, R.: *Autocracy and Democracy: And Experimental Enquiry*, New York, Harper & Row 1960

Whitehead, A. N.: *The Aims of Education*, Williams and Norgate 1932

Whorf, B. L.: Science and Linguistics 1940. Reprinted in **Maccoby, E. E.** *et al.* (eds) *Readings in Social Psychology*, London, Methuen 1959

Wiley, D. E.: Design and Analysis of Evaluation Studies in **Wittrock and Wiley** *op. cit.*, 1970

Williams, W. and Rennie, J.: Social Education, in **Rubinstein, D. and Stone-**

man, C. (eds).: *Education for Democracy,* 2nd edition, Harmondsworth, Penguin 1972

Williams, R.: *Culture and Society 1780–1950,* London, Chatto and Windus 1958

Wilson, J.: Education and Indoctrination in **Hollins, T. H. B.** *op. cit.,* 1964

Wilson, J.: *Practical Problems in Moral Education,* London, Heinemann 1973

Wilson, J.; William, N. and Sugarman, B.: *Introduction to Moral Education,* Harmondsworth, Penguin 1967

Wilson, P. S.: *Interest and Discipline in Education,* London, Routledge & Kegan Paul 1971

Wiseman, S. (ed): *Examinations and English Education,* Manchester, Manchester University Press 1961

Winterbottom, M. R.: The Relating of the Need for Achievement to Learning Experiences in Independence and Mastery in **Atkinson, J. W.** (ed): *Motives in Fantasy, Action and Society,* New York, Van Nostrand Reinhold 1958

Wittgenstein, L.: *Philosophical Investigations,* Oxford, Blackwell 1953

Wittrock, M. C. and Wiley, D. E.: *The Evaluation of Instruction: Issues and Problems,* New York, Holt Rinehart & Winston 1970

Woods, P.: 'Showing Them Up' in Secondary School in **Chanan, G. and Delamont, S.** (eds) *op. cit.,* 1975

Woods, P.: Teaching for Survival (1976) in **Woods, P. and Hammersley, M.** *op. cit.,* 1977

Woods, P. and Hammersley, M. (eds).: *School Experience,* London, Croom Helm 1977

Wragg, E. C.: A Study of Student Teachers in the Classroom in **Chanan, G. and Delamont, S.** (eds) *op. cit.,* 1975

Yates, A. and Pidgeon, D.: *Admission to Grammar Schools,* Newnes 1957

Young, M. F. D. (ed): *Knowledge and Control,* New York, Collier Macmillan 1971

Official Reports Quoted or Referred To:

Hadow Report: The Education of the Adolescent, HMSO 1926
Hadow Report: Primary Education, HMSO 1931
Spens Report: Secondary Education with Special Reference to Grammar Schools and Technical High Schools, HMSO 1938
Norwood Report: Curriculum and Examinations in Secondary Schools, HMSO 1943
Early Leaving Report: HMSO 1954
Crowther Report: 15 to 18, HMSO 1959
Newsom Report: Half Our Future, HMSO 1963
Plowden Report: Children and Their Primary Schools, 1967
Bullock Report: A Language for Life, HMSO 1975
Taylor Report: A New Partnership for Our Schools, HMSO 1977
Primary Education in England: HMSO 1978

Index of Proper Names

Subject Index